301

An Introduction to Sociology

This reader is one part of an Open University integrated teaching system and the selection is therefore related to other material available to students. It is designed to evoke the critical understanding of students. Opinions expressed in it are not necessarily those of the course team or of the University.

An Introduction to Sociology

a Reader

edited by Robert Bocock, Peter
Hamilton, Kenneth Thompson
and Alan Waton
at the Open University

assisted by Chris Pinches

FONTANA PAPERBACKS
in association with
The Open University Press

First published by Fontana Paperbacks 1980
Fourth impression June 1989

Selection and editorial material copyright
© The Open University 1980

For further details of copyright ownership,
readers are referred to page 497

Set in Linotype Times

Printed and bound in Great Britain by
William Collins Sons & Co. Ltd, Glasgow

A hardback edition of this book is published
by Harvester Press

Contents

Contents

Editors' Introduction

Sociology repeats itself. It moves on, then seems to slide sideways and finally backwards. What looks new is often a restatement of a position articulated in the past development of the subject. Each generation of students rediscovers these old themes and revitalizes them by adapting them to the concerns of their time and place.

Sociology is not best seen, therefore, as a science which moves on and progresses, forgetting its past in the way the natural sciences do. It is an attempt to grapple in a systematic way with fundamental problems of human social life, problems such as individuality, order, tradition, inequality, power and change. We cannot assert *a priori* that social life has constant features, but nor can we assert that it does not. We cannot say societies will always be repressive or elitist, nor that the millennium is inevitable. To discuss these issues, we must examine what has happened in the course of social development, placing ideas in their historical context.

An Introduction to Sociology reflects this humanistic approach to the subject. It is not, therefore, full of the most recent articles, which may temporarily seem to be important; nor is it a collection of writings by the basic theorists in sociology.* This collection is something unique and different: it brings together pieces which have been written during this century, but which contain issues and arguments central to sociology now.

Some of the ways in which old problems constantly reappear in new guises are represented here, for example in the discussion of legitimation, from Lipset in the 1950s to Habermas in the 1970s. Old lessons may also, however, be forgotten.

* Such a collection is provided in the companion reader for the course, *Sociological Perspectives* (Thompson and Tunstall, 1971).

This book attempts to re-introduce the importance of Freud. The absence of discussion of his theory of culture, and particularly of his work on social group life, has been a curious omission from recent British sociology texts. In a small way we attempt to rectify this by including not only Freud himself but also Freudian ideas developed in the work of sociologists such as Habermas and Marcuse.

The continuing ambivalent relationship between sociology and Marxism is also reflected in this book. The tension between Marxism and so-called bourgeois social science began with Marx himself, and has gone on ever since. It cannot be easily resolved, although the tension is often stimulating, because sociology must remain an open-minded discipline in which *all* rationally grounded theoretical viewpoints are discussed. In particular, Marxist theories of class structure have been important in forming part of the current dialogue concerning issues of social stratification, so that, whilst not all sociologists would accept the Marxist emphasis on economic determinism, it has proved vital to take these ideas seriously. Similarly, a concern with Marxism inevitably raises the question of the relationship between political values, political action, and an objective analysis of a situation. Many sociologists would say that as sociologists they have no political objectives, but rather that they seek to understand and explain how societies operate and change, no matter which political direction the change is taking. Many Marxist sociologists would dispute their claim and suggest that political values were implicit in these analyses. Some would go further and claim that such political involvement is inevitable. Within this debate, it is important to remember that our knowledge of social life is obstructed if the parties to a dispute, of whatever side, blindly stick to preconceived dogma. Scientific understanding is not derived from, or formed by, a set of immutable propositions which are eternally true, or which claim a meaning outside the process of their discovery in a scientific profession.

Sociology is not Marxism. On the other hand, it finds that discussion of Marxist positions about societies is impossible to avoid, because they often lead to important debates about the nature of class structures, elites, political power and authority, and social change. The peculiar relationship continues, never quite resolved, in which sociology sometimes seems to ignore Marxism, and at other times seems to be taken over by it.

Sociology can never be finalized. It will always appear as a threat to those who do not want, or cannot cope with, open-ended but often irreverent discussion of social problems and of human societies. This now includes those who claim to know truths about human societies on the basis of either revelation from a supernatural source, such as the Bible, the Koran, papal encyclicals, or on the basis of a political ideology which excludes contributions from alternative theories. Not all societies are open enough to allow the sceptical approach inherent in sociology. Nevertheless, in order to arrive at an unprejudiced understanding of social life, such an approach is necessary.

Where does this leave sociology in general and this Reader in sociology in particular? It would seem best to see sociology as an arena into which various contending parties enter from time to time, and where they are assessed according to the criteria of rationality – logical consistency, coherence, and the sense that the different theories make of changing human societies. This 'sense' will vary from one group of assessors to another depending on their social and historical location, but it should never vary so much that there is no possibility of agreement about what seems to be a good theory for a given social situation. Sociology should remain open-minded enough to allow new perspectives, or new versions of old perspectives, but firm enough to retain a sense of what it is to be rational and reasonable about human beings' social worlds.

*

The course for which this collection of pieces was compiled – D207 – is divided into three main 'blocks', which correspond to the sections in this book. Each deals in a characteristic way with the complex interrelationships between social structure, culture and social change. Block one places most emphasis on *culture*, and deals with the problems raised in attempts to understand the internalization of moral rules and the imposition of social order. However, a central theme in the consideration of such problems is the difficulty of conceptualizing the *individual* as a sociological category. The first reading in this book, by the American sociologist Dennis Wrong, is devoted to a discussion of the ways sociologists have tried to resolve these problems, which have in some ways led to a highly deterministic view of the individual's role in social processes. Roughly speaking, then, the first block picks up this problem of the individual's relation to wider structures and cultures, and indicates that there have been two main approaches to it. The first presents culture and moral order as structural features of societies, with the individual seen as formed by the social structure. The second approach sees the self, the personality and the 'roles' which are played out as dependent upon the individual to whom they are attached, and portrays social structure and culture as consequences of the characteristics of individuals. Two theoretical traditions come together in this approach, the first associated with the psychoanalytic work of Sigmund Freud, and the second connected to the symbolic interactionism of sociologists such as Erving Goffman and Howard Becker. But as with so much of sociology, there is also a tendency for the two approaches to cross-cut each other. Thus while the two readings by Freud and the readings by Wrong and Plummer clearly derive from the second approach, and the reading from Young is a good example of the first approach, Marcuse and Sennett are not easy to categorize. Marcuse in particular has been interested in linking together the theoretical insights of Marx and Freud, and thus in showing how personality factors have a dialectical relationship with the structure of domination and control in modern society. Sennett is similarly concerned with showing how the family operates as a nexus of personal adjustment, its role produced by the social structure of late capitalism. Yet the relative independence of the family as the sphere of emotionality is ultimately a form of imprisonment, for it prevents those individuals brought up in the intensely privatized world of the bourgeois family from grasping social and political realities in anything but personal terms.

The first block exhibits a novel approach to introductory work in sociology by placing emphasis on the influence of

Freud's theories of personality formation, particularly in devoting attention to what they offer for the understanding of cultural processes.

That Freud has been neglected by British sociology is undeniable. Yet the problem for anyone brought up in the tradition of empiricism is to reconcile the speculative and almost metaphysical tone of Freud's theories of culture and civilization with more rigorous and apparently more 'scientific' conceptions of explanation. However, Freudian theory, like Marxism, is not a static entity but a *corpus* of ideas constantly subject to change, criticism and evolution. It is this dynamic element of Freudian theory which is developed so strongly in the course as a whole, and which finds its most powerful exposition in the first block.

Neurosis and mental idiosyncrasy, the starting points for Freud's theories, are frequently presented as forms of deviant behaviour. Yet there are many ways of understanding social action which violates legal and moral rules, not least in the field of criminology. At the end of the first block of the course some of the complex issues which revolve around the concepts of deviance and criminality are discussed.

At one time criminology was the only academically respectable way in which many forms of social deviance could be investigated. This field of study was dominated by a central concern with legal categories of deviance and the organizational forms adapted by the state to ameliorate, or at least restrain, its socially most disruptive consequences. In its traditional forms, criminology relied to an important extent upon a psychologistic theoretical base which did not permit any critique of the institutionalization of social processes of deviance nor of the policies which the state adopted to control and incarcerate those which its legal agencies defined as deviant.

The impact of sociology upon these aspects of social process has been significant, but as in so many other spheres, limited in its full effects by the critical role in which it has been cast. This is inevitable because the sociologist – of whatever position or persuasion – is committed to uncovering the actual basis of the social practices which he investigates. The section of the course dealing with deviance and criminology

11

presents this critical framework in a highly developed form. The reading from Walton and Young is an extended appraisal of the new sociological approach to criminology and puts forward many of the principal theories of 'critical criminology'.

The second block of the course deals at length with social structure. In practice, we are concerned here with what some would call the central problematic (or even the *raison d'être*) of sociology – social class, stratification and their political consequences. The five readings in Section II of this book thus form a complement to a major part of the course dealing with this topic. Broadly speaking, each reading arises from and, despite great internal differences, returns to a fundamental issue within modern sociology – the theoretical and methodological role of Marxism in sociology. Block two considers a range of concerns about class, stratification, race and other forms of social differentiation, together with the crucial role of the state, in covering a number of relatively distinct problems. Thus in covering such topics as the concepts of class and politics in Marxist theory, the contemporary debate over theories of class and stratification, the complex issues of race, immigration and migrant workers, the class and status systems of socialist states, and the power of state organizations within modern societies, a theoretical polarity is constantly in view. This polarity is produced by the differences between Marxist theories of class formation and those other competing sociological paradigms of class and status. Hence the over-riding theme of this block, although it may be led into brief excursions around particular empirical areas, remains the question of the validity of Marxian class theory *vis-à-vis* other types of sociological theory which portray economically defined classes as one amongst a range of bases in terms of which societies differentiate their members into recognizable groups. In one sense this problem is not resolvable: the core assumptions of most variants of Marxist theory deal with a social world which cannot be reconciled with the core assumptions of sociological theories of stratification. Thus many Marxist sociologists are led to question the status of sociology as a discipline distinguishable from Marxism.

In the third and final block of the course the emphasis shifts again, towards the consideration of social change. This is not to say that 'change' is in some mysterious way a different sort of problem or a different class of phenomena, but rather that the two previous blocks have dealt with change and development only in relation to their interests in culture and structure respectively. By block three it is appropriate to examine the dynamic aspects of culture and social structure more closely.

One important feature of sociology is that it has had perennially to grapple with the enormous diversity of human social forms, and to make sense of them in ways which are as free of the value judgments of particular cultures as is possible. A genuinely comparative sociology is not an easy thing to create and debates about the appropriate ways in which to conduct comparisons between societies are a continuing feature of the development of sociological theory. The consideration of processes of social change, of the historical development of social structures and cultures, poses the problems about comparison in a particularly acute way, and is the reason why considerable attention is devoted to the methodology of comparison in block three of the course. The reading by Jack Goody on the comparison of family forms and domestic groups provides a useful example of the difficulties of comparison. Even with what appears to be a relatively simple concept like 'family', the actual diversity of kin-related domestic groups makes it very hard to draw neat conclusions about what it is that even minimally constitutes a 'family'.

If the concept of family poses extreme difficulties to the sociologist who wants to examine the processes of change of such an 'institution' over time and space, then the term 'community' seems to be almost as replete with misleading theoretical innuendo. The reading by Gans is linked to discussion of the widely varying, and ultimately ideological, meanings given to the term *community* within sociology, which have made the job of comparing small-scale social systems and residential patterns more difficult than perhaps they need to be. The reading by Andre Gorz, by contrast deals with a more precise form of structural change – the changing nature and composition of the workforce in capitalist society, and its effects on the forms of industrial organization which may obtain in such a society.

The final readings from Habermas, Lipset and Touraine exemplify the problems of grasping complex and far-reaching processes of social-historical change, each from a different perspective but all ultimately concerned with social order, and the legitimacy upon which any stable form of social structure must depend. And here again we return to a perennial tension within sociology.

It has been said by many radical critics of sociology that it is frequently dominated by essentially conservative theories of society. Often, what is meant by these criticisms is that social theories emphasize those factors which assist the maintenance of social order, and pay relatively little attention to the dynamics of social change. A more sophisticated view, however, would be that any theory capable of explaining order must logically include a reference to factors which would disrupt it. Thus it is that the dominant ideas and concepts which mould this section of the course are those concerned with processes of legitimation, whether they be found in the student protest movement, within the family and the education system, or within the industrial system. For it is these processes of legitimation which act so as to preserve a particular system of social relations over time, in the face of disruptive forces which attempt to create new systems, by reinforcing a code of values supporting the 'rightness' of the *status quo*. To explain the legitimating process therefore requires consideration of the system which is being maintained as well as the social forces which are controlled or restrained by it.

In conclusion, then, to reiterate the point made at an earlier stage of this introduction: *An Introduction to Sociology* is the product of a group of sociologists who worked together to create a new introductory course in sociology. This book, however, can be read quite independently of the course, and it will no doubt frequently be used to complement an approach to the teaching of sociology different to the one we devised. But it still remains true that this book is part of a greater whole.

Finally, it remains only to thank those members of the Course Team who have been so helpful in compiling this reader. Especial thanks must go to Chris Pinches for her sterling editorial work. Thanks must also go to Val Byrne who helped produce the manuscript so efficiently. Without them it would have been impossible to produce this book although of course final responsibility rests with the editors.

Section I
Individual, Culture and Society

Section I deals with issues concerning the relationship of the individual to society and the mediating role of culture in that relationship. The reason for starting with this very broad topic is not because we hold to a philosophical position that gives it priority, nor are we unaware of the ideological functions served by the concept 'individualism'. Indeed, it should become clear from the readings in this section that our intention is to confront the individual reader with sociological analyses that call into question, or at least call for reflection on, his or her individuality. As sociologists our concern is to understand the social factors that determine individuals' actions. We are interested in the social forces, and conjunctions of forces, that mould the individual to such an extent that regularities of behaviour occur, enabling us to talk in terms of social types and categories.

Although there is no necessary priority about the question of the relationship of the individual to society, it is not a question that can be ignored for long, nor is it easily disposed of; it constantly returns to haunt sociologists, even when they think they have defined it out of existence or provided sufficient answers. Dennis Wrong's 'The oversocialized conception of man in modern sociology' (Reading 1) provides an example of this. Despite the fact that it was written more than twenty years ago, and was primarily directed at a theory that has lost the dominance it enjoyed at that time, it still has many lessons to teach. (Some of these are brought out in the later Postscript, which we have included with the original article.)

Wrong's original article challenged some question-begging assumptions that had been made in discussions of the relationship between the individual and society. In particular he pointed out the superficiality of some of the answers given by sociologists of the structural-functional school to the question: 'How is social order possible?' or 'How is it that man becomes tractable to social discipline?' His article was notable and ahead of its time for the manner in which he called into question prevailing conceptions of 'man' by contrasting them with Freud's conception. Wrong's contention that, to Freud, 'man is a *social* animal without being entirely a *socialized* animal', still stands as a corrective and a challenge to sociological conceptions that treat the individual as entirely malleable to the impress of social structures.

The issue still arises to confront the newer versions of structuralism, even though these have improved on the older structural-functionalism as far as taking account of structural change and conflict is concerned. When it comes to accounting for the relationship of the individual to social structures, the implicit analogy still seems to be that of the world as a theatre in which individuals act out roles according to a script. Sociological analysis is then limited to decoding the script and, in the case of the structuralist school associated with the name of the French Marxist, Louis Althusser, pointing out the political implications. For all its merits, this approach is little better than structural-functionalism in its treatment of the relationship between human actors and their roles (although it should be added that Althusser does not think it necessary to deal with this issue). But as one critic has put it: 'They cannot be treated as mere "carriers". Their behaviour reminds us continually of the fact that they do treat their roles in a rather *cavalier* way – to the despair of true believers in functionalist sociology as well as in the "Althusserian theatre".'*

Both the structural-functionalist, Talcott Parsons, and Louis Althusser have sought to assimilate some of the challenging ideas of Freud into their theories. We have not space to include excerpts from their works in this book, but rather we have followed the advice of Wrong and returned in the first instance to Freud's own writings. Like Wrong we suspect that Parsons's Freud is a bowdlerized version, and

* Perez-Diaz, Victor M., *State, Bureaucracy and Civil Society*, London: Macmillan, 1978, p. 91.

the same might be said of the result of the selective reading of Freud advocated by Althusser. The excerpts from Freud's works that we have chosen to include will serve to illustrate the challenge that his thought presents to our understanding of the relationship between the individual and society.

The first of these, ' "Civilized" sexual morality and modern nervous illness' (Reading 2), is one of his early papers, published in 1908, which states quite succinctly some of Freud's theses, especially in their relationship to the sexual moral codes of the Judeo-Christian tradition. It connects Freud's interest in understanding neurotic symptoms with wider social and cultural issues. This paper anticipates ideas which were developed further in *Civilization and its Discontents* (1930) and illustrates some of the fundamental continuities in his life's work.

The second, 'Aggression and civilization' (Reading 3), is from the book just mentioned. It focuses not so much on sexual mores as on aggression. This concern had sharpened in Freud's mind after the First World War and led to the formulation of the concept of 'death instincts' in 1920. This piece was written with the later version of the instinct theory, which uses sexual instincts and death instincts as a set of background assumptions.

Although it is true that sociologists have, until recently, faced up to the challenge of Freud only fitfully, an exception should be made of those sociologists associated with the Frankfurt School. The influence of this school of thought, deriving from the Institute for Social Research founded in Frankfurt in 1923, has been consistently in the direction of examining the implications of those writings of Freud and Marx that are concerned with the relationship of the individual to society, and the mediating role of culture in the relationship.

Herbert Marcuse's 'The hidden trend in psychoanalysis' (Reading 4) shows how Freud's ideas were used by one prominent representative of the Frankfurt School. It was a decade after its original publication in the book *Eros and Civilization* that this work, along with other writings of the Frankfurt School, emerged as a central inspiration for the student movement in the West during the Vietnam War period. Its background theme, combining ideas drawn from Marx and Freud, is the repressive effects on individuals of a culture that reflects the structure of domination and control in modern society.

Richard Sennett in 'Destructive Gemeinschaft' (Reading 5) takes up this same theme and examines the changes that have occurred over the last hundred years in individuals' experience of social pressure to feel and behave in culturally approved ways. His chief contention is that it is deceptive to believe there has been a freeing of the individual from social constraints simply because some of the repressions of nineteenth-century bourgeois society have faded; new and equally destructive pressures have taken their place.

One way of tackling the problem of the relationship of the individual to society is to look at examples of deviation from the norm of expected behaviour. Consequently, the study of 'deviants' and 'deviancy' has always been a fruitful field for theorizing in sociology. In 'Sexual stigma: an interactionist account' (Reading 6) Kenneth Plummer contrasts a symbolic interactionist perspective on sexuality with Freudian and Marxist views. His major emphasis is on how sexual meanings are constructed and maintained, rather than on questions of social order and change. While his criticisms of crude biologism take in some tendencies deriving from Freudian sources, there would seem to be room for co-existence between the symbolic interactionists' concerns with the construction of shared, or relatively unshared, meanings about sexuality and gender roles, and Freudian concerns with the links between sexuality, authority and aggression.

Some deviation from the norms of socially acceptable behaviour is defined as criminal in all societies. The study of how this definition occurs and is enforced, how it comes to be accepted even by some of those so labelled, and why some people seem to fall foul of it more than others, forms a large part of the sociology of deviance and is the subject matter of criminology. In 'Working-class criminology' (Reading 7) Jock Young provides a full-blown critique of much of what he calls 'the new deviancy theory', which was itself an attempt to supersede earlier forms of 'positivist' criminology. Young's approach is avowedly radical in both the methodological and the political senses of the term – he sees his primary objective as the creation of a theory of social diversity which can form the basis of 'socialist' criminology. His concern is to free the working class from a slavish commitment to bourgeois values of deviance and criminology which act so as to legitimate inequitable forms of social control. Despite his strong political commitment, an explicit component of his approach, Young provides a very detailed critical model which lays bare the methodological presuppositions of both 'correctionalist criminology' and the more sociologically appealing 'new deviancy theory'.

1. The oversocialized conception of man in modern sociology

Dennis H. Wrong

Gertrude Stein, bed-ridden with a fatal illness, is reported to have suddenly muttered, 'What, then, is the answer?' Pausing, she raised her head, murmured, 'But what is the question?' and died. Miss Stein presumably was pondering the ultimate meaning of human life, but her brief final soliloquy has a broader and humbler relevance. Its point is that answers are meaningless apart from questions. If we forget the questions, even while remembering the answers, our knowledge of them will subtly deteriorate, becoming rigid, formal, and catechistic as the sense of indeterminacy, of rival possibilities, implied by the very putting of a question is lost.

Social theory must be seen primarily as a set of answers to questions we ask of social reality. If the initiating questions are forgotten, we readily misconstrue the task of theory and the answers previous thinkers have given become narrowly confining conceptual prisons, degenerating into little more than a special, professional vocabulary applied to situations and events that can be described with equal or greater precision in ordinary language. Forgetfulness of the questions that are the starting points of inquiry leads us to ignore the substantive assumptions 'buried' in our concepts and commits us to a one-sided view of reality.

Perhaps this is simply an elaborate way of saying that sociological theory can never afford to lose what is usually called a 'sense of significance'; or, as it is sometimes put, that sociological theory must be 'problem-conscious'. I choose instead to speak of theory as a set of answers to questions because reference to 'problems' may seem to suggest too close a linkage with social criticism or reform. My primary

From *American Sociological Review*, 26, 2 (April 1961), pp. 183–93.

reason for insisting on the necessity of holding constantly in mind the questions that our concepts and theories are designed to answer is to preclude defining the goal of sociological theory as the creation of a formal body of knowledge satisfying the logical criteria of scientific theory set up by philosophers and methodologists of natural science. Needless to say, this is the way theory is often defined by contemporary sociologists.

Yet to speak of theory as interrogatory may suggest too self-sufficiently intellectual an enterprise. Cannot questions be satisfactorily answered and then forgotten, the answers becoming the assumptions from which we start in framing new questions? It may convey my view of theory more adequately to say that sociological theory concerns itself with questions arising out of problems that are inherent in the very existence of human societies and that cannot therefore be finally 'solved' in the way that particular social problems perhaps can be. The 'problems' theory concerns itself with are problems *for* human societies which, because of their universality, become intellectually problematic for sociological theorists.

Essentially, the historicist conception of sociological knowledge that is central to the thought of Max Weber and has recently been ably restated by Barrington Moore, Jr, and C. Wright Mills[1] is a sound one. The most fruitful questions for sociology are always questions referring to the realities of a particular historical situation. Yet both of these writers, especially Mills, have a tendency to underemphasize the degree to which we genuinely wish and seek answers to trans-historical and universal questions about the nature of man and society. I do not, let it be clear, have in mind the formalistic quest for social 'laws' or 'universal propositions', nor the even more formalistic effort to construct all-encompassing 'conceptual schemes'. Moore and Mills are rightly critical of such efforts. I am thinking of such questions as, 'How are men capable of uniting to form enduring societies in the first place?'; 'Why and to what degree is change inherent in human societies and what are the sources of change?'; 'How is man's animal nature domesticated by society?'

Such questions – and they are existential as well as intellectual questions – are the *raison d'être* of social theory. They were asked by men long before the rise of sociology. Sociology itself is an effort, under new and unprecedented historical conditions, to find novel answers to them. They are not questions which lend themselves to successively more precise answers as a result of cumulative empirical research, for they remain eternally problematic. Social theory is necessarily an interminable dialogue. 'True understanding', Hannah Arendt has written, 'does not tire of interminable dialogue and "vicious circles" because it trusts that imagination will eventually catch at least a glimpse of the always frightening light of truth.'[2]

I wish briefly to review the answers modern sociological theory offers to one such question, or rather to one aspect of one question. The question may be variously phrased as, 'What are the sources of social cohesion?'; or, 'How is social order possible?'; or, stated in social-psychological terms, 'How is it that man becomes tractable to social discipline?' I shall call this question in its social-psychological aspect the 'Hobbesian question' and in its more strictly sociological aspect the 'Marxist question'. The Hobbesian question asks how men are capable of the guidance by social norms and goals that makes possible an enduring society, while the Marxist question asks how, assuming this capability, complex societies manage to regulate and restrain destructive conflicts between groups. Much of our current theory offers an oversocialized view of man in answering the Hobbesian question and an over-integrated view of society in answering the Marxist question.

A number of writers have recently challenged the over-integrated view of society in contemporary theory. In addition to Moore and Mills, the names of Bendix, Coser, Dahrendorf and Lockwood come to mind.[3] My intention, therefore, is to concentrate on the answers to the Hobbesian question in an effort to disclose the oversocialized view of man which they seem to imply.

Since my view of theory is obviously very different from that of Talcott Parsons and has, in fact, been developed in opposition to his, let me pay tribute to his recognition of the importance of the Hobbesian question – the 'problem of order', as he calls it – at the very beginning of his first book, *The Structure of Social Action*.[4] Parsons correctly credits Hobbes with being the first thinker to see the necessity of explaining why human society is not a 'war of all against all'; why, if man is simply a gifted animal, men refrain from unlimited resort to fraud and violence in pursuit of their ends and maintain a stable society at all. There is even a sense in which, as Coser and Mills have both noted,[5] Parsons's entire work represents an effort to solve the Hobbesian problem of order. His solution, however, has tended to become precisely the kind of elaboration of a set of answers in abstraction from questions that is so characteristic of contemporary sociological theory.

We need not be greatly concerned with Hobbes's own solution to the problem of order he saw with such unsurpassed clarity. Whatever interest his famous theory of the origin of the state may still hold for political scientists, it is clearly inadequate as an explanation of the origin of society. Yet the pattern as opposed to the details of Hobbes's thought bears closer examination.

The polar terms in Hobbes's theory are the state of nature, where the war of all against all prevails, and the authority of Leviathan, created by social contract. But the war of all against all is not simply effaced with the creation of political authority: it remains an ever-present potentiality in human society, at times quiescent, at times erupting into open violence. Whether Hobbes believed that the state of nature and the social contract were ever historical realities – and there is evidence that he was not that simple-minded and un-sociological, even in the seventeenth century – is unimportant; the whole tenor of his thought is to see the war of all against all and Leviathan dialectically, as co-existing and interacting opposites.[6] As R. G. Collingwood has observed, 'According to Hobbes . . . *a body politic is a dialectical thing*, a Heraclitean world in which at any given time there is a negative element.'[7] The first secular social theorist in the history of Western thought, and one of the first clearly to discern and define the problem of order in human society long before Darwinism made awareness of it a commonplace, Hobbes was a dialectical thinker who refused to separate answers from questions, solutions to society's enduring problems from the conditions creating the problems.

What is the answer of contemporary sociological theory to

the Hobbesian question? There are two main answers, each of which has come to be understood in a way that denies the reality and meaningfulness of the question. Together they constitute a model of human nature, sometimes clearly stated, more often implicit in accepted concepts, that pervades modern sociology. The first answer is summed up in the notion of the 'internalization of social norms'. The second, more commonly employed or assumed in empirical research, is the view that man is essentially motivated by the desire to achieve a positive image of self by winning acceptance or status in the eyes of others.

The following statement represents, briefly and broadly, what is probably the most influential contemporary sociological conception – and dismissal – of the Hobbesian problem: 'To a modern sociologist imbued with the conception that action follows institutionalized patterns, opposition of individual and common interests has only a very limited relevance or is thoroughly unsound.'[8] From this writer's perspective, the problem is an unreal one: human conduct is totally shaped by common norms or 'institutionalized patterns'. Sheer ignorance must have led people who were unfortunate enough not to be modern sociologists to ask, 'How is order possible?' A thoughtful bee or ant would never inquire. 'How is the social order of the hive or ant-hill possible?' for the opposite of that order is unimaginable when the instinctive endowment of the insects ensures its stability and built-in harmony between 'individual and common interests'. Human society, we are assured, is not essentially different, although conformity and stability are there maintained by non-instinctive processes. Modern sociologists believe that they have understood these processes and that they have not merely answered but disposed of the Hobbesian question, showing that, far from expressing a valid intimation of the tensions and possibilities of social life, it can only be asked out of ignorance.

It would be hard to find a better illustration of what Collingwood, following Plato, calls *eristical* as opposed to dialectical thinking:[9] the answer destroys the question, or rather destroys the awareness of rival possibilities suggested by the question which accounts for its having been asked in the first place. A reversal of perspective now takes place and we are moved to ask the opposite question: 'How is it that violence, conflict, revolution, and the individual's sense of coercion by society manage to exist at all, if this view is correct?'[10] Whenever a one-sided answer to a question compels us to raise the opposite question, we are caught up in a dialectic of concepts which reflects a dialectic in things. But let us examine the particular processes sociologists appeal to in order to account for the elimination from human society of the war of all against all.

THE CHANGING MEANING OF INTERNALIZATION

A well-known section of *The Structure of Social Action*, devoted to the interpretation of Durkheim's thought, is entitled 'The Changing Meaning of Constraint'.[11] Parsons argues that Durkheim originally conceived of society as controlling the individual from the outside by imposing constraints on him through sanctions, best illustrated by codes of law. But in Durkheim's later work he began to see that social rules do not 'merely regulate "externally" . . . they enter directly into the constitution of the actors' ends themselves'.[12] Constraint, therefore, is more than an environmental obstacle which the actor must take into account in pursuit of his goals in the same way that he takes into account physical laws: it becomes internal, psychological, and self-imposed as well. Parsons developed this view that social norms are constitutive rather than merely regulative of human nature before he was influenced by psychoanalytic theory, but Freud's theory of the superego has become the source and model for the conception of the internalization of social norms that today plays so important a part in sociological thinking. The use some sociologists have made of Freud's idea, however, might well inspire an essay entitled 'The Changing Meaning of Internalization', although, in contrast to the shift in Durkheim's view of constraint, this change has been a change for the worse.

What has happened is that internalization has imperceptibly been equated with 'learning', or even with 'habit-formation' in the simplest sense. Thus when a norm is said to have been 'internalized' by an individual, what is frequently meant is that he habitually both affirms it and conforms to it in his conduct. The whole stress on inner conflict, on the tension between powerful impulses and superego controls, the behavioral outcome of which cannot be prejudged, drops out of the picture. And it is this that is central to Freud's view, for in psychoanalytic terms to say that a norm has been internalized, or introjected to become part of the superego, is to say no more than that a person will suffer guilt-feelings if he fails to live up to it, not that he will in fact live up to it in his behavior.

The relation between internalization and conformity assumed by most sociologists is suggested by the following passage from a recent, highly-praised advanced textbook: 'Conformity to institutionalized norms is, of course, "normal". The actor, having internalized the norms, feels something like a need to conform. His conscience would bother him if he did not.'[13] What is overlooked here is that the person who conforms may be even more 'bothered', that is, subject to guilt and neurosis, than the person who violates what are not only society's norms but his own as well. To Freud, it is precisely the man with the strictest superego, he who has most thoroughly internalized and conformed to the norms of his society, who is most racked with guilt and anxiety.[14]

Paul Kecskemeti, to whose discussion I owe initial recognition of the erroneous view of internalization held by sociologists, argues that the relations between social norms, the individual's selection from them, his conduct, and his feelings about his conduct are far from self-evident. 'It is by no means true', he writes, 'to say that acting counter to one's own norms always or almost always leads to neurosis. One might assume that neurosis develops even more easily in persons who *never* violate the moral code they recognize as valid but repress and frustrate some strong instinctual motive. A person who "succumbs to temptation", feels guilt, and then "purges himself" of his guilt in some reliable way (e.g., by confession) may achieve in this way a better balance, and be less neurotic, than a person who never violates his "norms" and never feels conscious guilt.'[15]

Recent discussions of 'deviant behavior' have been compelled to recognize these distinctions between social demands, personal attitudes towards them, and actual conduct, although they have done so in a laboriously taxonomic fashion.[16] They represent, however, largely the rediscovery of what was always central to the Freudian concept of the superego. The main explanatory function of the concept is to show how people repress themselves, imposing checks on their own desires and thus turning the inner life into a battlefield of conflicting motives, no matter which side 'wins', by successfully dictating overt action. So far as behavior is concerned, the psychoanalytic view of man is less deterministic than the sociological. For psychoanalysis is primarily concerned with the inner life, not with overt behavior, and its most fundamental insight is that the wish, the emotion, and the fantasy are as important as the act in man's experience.

Sociologists have appropriated the superego concept, but have separated it from any equivalent of the Freudian id. So long as most individuals are 'socialized', that is, internalize the norms and conform to them in conduct, the Hobbesian problem is not even perceived as a latent reality. Deviant behavior is accounted for by special circumstances: ambiguous norms, anomie, role conflict, or greater cultural stress on valued goals than on the approved means for attaining them. Tendencies to deviant behavior are not seen as dialectically related to conformity. The presence in man of motivational forces bucking against the hold social discipline has over him is denied.

Nor does the assumption that internalization of norms and roles is the essence of socialization allow for a sufficient range of motives underlying conformity. It fails to allow for variable 'tonicity of the superego', in Kardiner's phrase.[17] The degree to which conformity is frequently the result of coercion rather than conviction is minimized.[18] Either someone has internalized the norms, or he is 'unsocialized', a feral or socially isolated child, or a psychopath. Yet Freud recognized that many people, conceivably a majority, fail to acquire super-egos. 'Such people', he wrote, 'habitually permit themselves to do any bad deed that procures them something they want, if only they are sure that no authority will discover it or make them suffer for it; their anxiety relates only to the possibility of detection. Present-day society has to take into account the prevalence of this state of mind.'[19] The last sentence suggests that Freud was aware of the decline of 'inner-direction', of the Protestant conscience, about which we have heard so much lately. So let us turn to the other elements of human nature that sociologists appeal to in order to explain, or rather explain away, the Hobbesian problem.

MAN THE ACCEPTANCE-SEEKER[20]

The superego concept is too inflexible, too bound to the past and to individual biography, to be of service in relating conduct to the pressures of the immediate situation in which it takes place. Sociologists rely more heavily therefore on an alternative notion, here stated – or, to be fair, overstated – in its baldest form: 'People are so profoundly sensitive to the expectations of others that all action is inevitably guided by these expectations.'[21]

Parsons's model of the 'complementarity of expectations', the view that in social interaction men mutually seek approval from one another by conforming to shared norms, is a formalized version of what has tended to become a distinctive sociological perspective on human motivation. Ralph Linton states it in explicit psychological terms: 'The need for eliciting favourable responses from others is an almost constant component of [personality]. Indeed, it is not too much to say that there is very little organized human behavior which is not directed toward its satisfaction in at least some degree.'[22]

The insistence of sociologists on the importance of 'social factors' easily leads them to stress the priority of such socialized or socializing motives in human behavior.[23] It is frequently the task of the sociologist to call attention to the intensity with which men desire and strive for the good opinion of their immediate associates in a variety of situations, particularly those where received theories or ideologies have unduly emphasized other motives such as financial gain, commitment to ideals, or the effects on energies and aspirations of arduous physical conditions. Thus sociologists have shown that factory workers are more sensitive to the attitudes of their fellow-workers than to purely economic incentives; that voters are more influenced by the preferences of their relatives and friends than by campaign debates on the 'issues'; that soldiers, whatever their ideological commitment to their nation's cause, fight more bravely when their platoons are intact and they stand side by side with their 'buddies'.

It is certainly not my intention to criticize the findings of such studies. My objection is that their particular selective emphasis is generalized – explicitly or, more often, implicitly – to provide apparent empirical support for an extremely one-sided view of human nature. Although sociologists have criticized past efforts to single out one fundamental motive in human conduct, the desire to achieve a favorable self-image by winning approval from others frequently occupies such a position in their own thinking. The following 'theorem' has been, in fact, openly put forward by Hans Zetterberg as 'a strong contender for the position as the major Motivational Theorem in sociology': [24]

> An actor's actions have a tendency to become dispositions that are related to the occurence [*sic*] of favored uniform evaluations of the actor and-or his actions in his action system.[25]

Now Zetterberg is not necessarily maintaining that this theorem is an accurate factual statement of the basic psychological roots of social behavior. He is, characteristically, far too self-conscious about the logic of theorizing and 'concept formation' for that. He goes on to remark that 'the maximization of favorable attitudes from others would thus be the counterpart in sociological theory to the maximization of profit in economic theory'.[26] If by this it is meant that the theorem is to be understood as a heuristic rather than an empirical assumption, that sociology has a selective point of view which is just as abstract and partial as that of economics and the other social sciences, and if his view of theory as a set of logically connected formal propositions is granted provisional acceptance, I am in agreement. (Actually, the view of theory suggested at the beginning of this paper is a quite different one.)

But there is a further point to be made. Ralf Dahrendorf has observed that structural-functional theorists do not 'claim that order *is based on* a general consensus of values, but that it *can be conceived of in terms of* such consensus and that, if it is conceived of in these terms, certain propositions follow which are subject to the test of specific observations'.[27] The same may be said of the assumption that people seek to maximize favorable evaluations by others; indeed, this assumption has already fathered such additional concepts as 'reference group' and 'circle of significant others'. Yet the question must be raised as to whether we really wish to, in effect, define sociology by such partial perspectives. The assumption of the maximization of approval from others is the psychological complement to the sociological assumption of a general value consensus. And the former is as selective and one-sided a way of looking at motivation as Dahrendorf and others have argued the latter to be when it determines our way of looking at social structure. The oversocialized view of man of the one is a counterpart to the over-integrated view of society of the other.

Modern sociology, after all, originated as a protest against the partial views of man contained in such doctrines as utilitarianism, classical economics, social Darwinism, and vulgar Marxism. All of the great nineteenth- and early twentieth-century sociologists[28] saw it as one of their major tasks to expose the unreality of such abstractions as economic man, the gain-seeker of the classical economists; political man, the power-seeker of the Machiavellian tradition in political science; self-preserving man, the security-seeker of Hobbes and Darwin; sexual or libidinal man, the pleasure-seeker of doctrinaire Freudianism; and even religious man, the God-seeker of the theologians. It would be ironical if it should turn out that they have merely contributed to the creation of yet another reified abstraction in socialized man, the status-seeker of our contemporary sociologists.

Of course, such an image of man is, like all the others mentioned, valuable for limited purposes so long as it is not taken for the whole truth. What are some of its deficiencies? To begin with, it neglects the other half of the model of human nature presupposed by current theory: moral man, guided by his built-in superego and beckoning ego-ideal.[29] In recent years sociologists have been less interested than they once were in culture and national character as backgrounds to conduct, partly because stress on the concept of 'role' as the crucial link between the individual and the social structure has directed their attention to the immediate situation in which social interaction takes place. Man is increasingly seen as a 'role-playing' creature, responding eagerly or anxiously to the expectations of other role-players in the multiple group settings in which he finds himself. Such an approach, while valuable in helping us grasp the complexity of a highly differentiated social structure such as our own, is far too often generalized to serve as a kind of *ad hoc* social psychology, easily adaptable to particular sociological purposes.

But it is not enough to concede that men often pursue 'internalized values' remaining indifferent to what others think of them, particularly when, as I have previously argued, the idea of internalization has been 'hollowed out' to make it more useful as an explanation of conformity. What of desire for material and sensual satisfactions? Can we really dispense with the venerable notion of material 'interests' and invariably replace it with the blander, more integrative 'social values'? And what of striving for power, not necessarily for its own sake – that may be rare and pathological – but as a means by which men are able to *impose* a normative definition of reality on others? That material interests, sexual drives, and the quest for power have often been over-estimated as human motives is no reason to deny their reality. To do so is to suppress one term of the dialectic between conformity and rebellion, social norms and their violation, man and social order, as completely as the other term is suppressed by those who deny the reality of man's 'normative orientation' or reduce it to the effect of coercion, rational calculation, or mechanical conditioning.

The view that man is invariably pushed by internalized norms or pulled by the lure of self-validation by others ignores – to speak archaically for a moment – both the highest and the lowest, both beast and angel, in his nature. Durkheim, from whom so much of the modern sociological point of view derives, recognized that the very existence of a social norm implies and even creates the possibility of its violation. This is the meaning of his famous dictum that crime is a 'normal phenomenon'. He maintained that 'for the originality of the idealist whose dreams transcend his century to find expression, it is necessary that the originality of the criminal, who is below the level of his time, shall also be possible. One does not occur without the other.'[30] Yet Durkheim lacked an adequate psychology and formulated his insight in terms of the actor's cognitive awareness rather than in motivational terms. We do not have Durkheim's excuse for falling back on what Homans has called a 'social mold theory' of human nature.[31]

SOCIAL BUT NOT ENTIRELY SOCIALIZED

I have referred to forces in man that are resistant to socialization. It is not my purpose to explore the nature of these forces or to suggest how we ought best conceive of them as sociologists – that would be a most ambitious undertaking. A few remarks will have to suffice. I think we must start with the recognition that *in the beginning there is the* body. As soon as the body is mentioned the specter of 'biological determinism' raises its head and sociologists draw back in fright. And certainly their view of man is sufficiently disembodied and non-materialistic to satisfy Bishop Berkeley, as well as being de-sexualized enough to please Mrs Grundy.

Am I, then, urging us to return to the older view of a human nature divided between a 'social man' and a 'natural man' who is either benevolent, Rousseau's Noble Savage, or sinister and destructive, as Hobbes regarded him? Freud is usually represented, or misrepresented, as the chief modern

35

proponent of this dualistic conception which assigns to the social order the purely negative role of blocking and re-directing man's 'imperious biological drives'.[32] I say 'mis-represented' because although Freud often said things support-ing such an interpretation, other and more fundamental strains in his thinking suggest a different conclusion. John Dollard, certainly not a writer who is oblivious to social and cultural 'factors', saw this twenty-five years ago: 'It is quite clear', he wrote, '. . . that he [Freud] does not regard the instincts as having a fixed social goal; rather, indeed, in the case of the sexual instinct he has stressed the vague but powerful and impulsive nature of the drive and has emphasized that its proper social object is not picked out in advance. His seems to be a drive concept which is not at variance with our knowledge from comparative cultural studies, since his theory does not demand that the "instinct" work itself out with mechanical certainty alike in every varying culture.'[33]

So much for Freud's 'imperious biological drives'. When Freud defined psychoanalysis as the study of the 'vicissitudes of the instincts', he was confirming, not denying, the 'plasticity' of human nature insisted on by social scientists. The drives or 'instincts' of psychoanalysis, far from being fixed dis-positions to behave in a particular way, are utterly subject to social channelling and transformation and could not even reveal themselves in behavior without social molding any more than our vocal chords can produce articulate speech if we have not learned a language. To psychoanalysis man is indeed a social animal; his social nature is profoundly reflected in his bodily structure.[34]

But there is a difference between the Freudian view on the one hand and both sociological and neo-Freudian conceptions of man on the other. To Freud man is a *social* animal without being entirely a *socialized* animal. His very social nature is the source of conflicts and antagonisms that create resistance to socialization by the norms of any of the societies which have existed in the course of human history. 'Socialization' may mean two quite distinct things; when they are confused an oversocialized view of man is the result. On the one hand socialization means that 'transmission of the culture', the particular culture of the society an individual enters at birth;

on the other hand the term is used to mean the 'process of becoming human', of acquiring uniquely human attributes from interaction with others.[35] All men are socialized in the latter sense, but this does not mean that they have been completely molded by the particular norms and values of their culture. All cultures, as Freud contended, do violence to man's socialized bodily drives, but this in no sense means that men could possibly exist without culture or independently of society.[36] From such a standpoint, man may properly be called as Norman Brown has called him, the 'neurotic' or the 'discontented' animal and repression may be seen as the main characteristic of human nature as we have known it in history.[37]

But isn't this psychology and haven't sociologists been taught to foreswear psychology, to look with suspicion on what are called 'psychological variables' in contradistinction to the institutional and historical forces with which they are properly concerned? There is, indeed, as recent critics have complained, too much 'psychologism' in contemporary sociology, largely, I think, because of the bias inherent in our favored research techniques. But I do not see how, at the level of theory, sociologists can fail to make assumptions about human nature.[38] If our assumptions are left implicit, we will inevitably presuppose of a view of man that is tailor-made to our special needs; when our sociological theory overstresses the stability and integration of society we will end up imagining that man is the disembodied, conscience-driven, status-seeking phantom of current theory. We must do better if we really wish to win credit outside of our ranks for special understanding of man, that plausible creature[39] whose wagging tongue so often hides the despair and darkness in his heart.

Postscript 1975

I sometimes reflect ruefully that nothing else I have ever written has attracted anything like as much notice as 'The Oversocialized Conception of Man in Modern Sociology'. The situation is familiar enough for authors of a single successful and influential book but has a certain comic, even humiliating aspect when what is involved is a mere article that hit the target with one resonant phrase. Few people seem aware of the existence of a companion article, for it has never been reprinted and is rarely cited.[40] (It was published, to be sure, in a journal with a far lower circulation among sociologists than the *American Sociological Review*.) 'The Oversocialized Conception of Man', by contrast, has been widely reprinted in several languages; it has contributed a phrase to the vocabulary of sociology; and its major thesis, though inevitably often misrepresented, has by now been virtually absorbed into the conventional wisdom of the discipline. I hope therefore that it will not be thought to be sheer vanity on my part if I attempt a reassessment in light of an intellectual situation in sociology that is very different from the one that prevailed fourteen years ago when the article was first published.

In 1961, structural-functional theory, most frequently associated with the work of Talcott Parsons, who had given it its full name, still seemed to be the dominant mode of sociological theorizing, although a counter-tendency was already fully visible by the end of the 1950s in the work of C. Wright Mills, Barrington Moore, Jr, Ralf Dahrendorf, Reinhard Bendix, Lewis Coser, and several others. This tendency came to be called 'conflict theory' (the label was chiefly Ralf Dahrendorf's) and it obviously had broad affinities with the Marxist tradition. Nevertheless, none of the writers I have mentioned considered himself a Marxist, nor do any of them today, all of them except Mills being alive and still at work. Most of them, including Mills, were more Weberian than Marxist. The now-familiar brunt of their attack on Parsonian

From D. H. Wrong, *Skeptical Sociology*, Columbia University Press, 1976, pp. 47–54.

structural-functionalism was that its view of society minimized the importance of group conflict, coercive power, and material interests and overemphasized consensus, legitimate authority, and moral values.

All these writers were primarily concerned with the macro-social level of group and inter-institutional relations, with 'structure' rather than 'milieu' in Mills's terms. None of them were social psychologists concerned primarily with human nature. Much as I agreed with them in 1961 (and still do), there seemed to be something incomplete about their theorizing, something that failed to go beyond a reaction against the consensual bias of structural-functionalism. Parsons himself rather complacently remarked on this in 1962, observing that 'the "Opposition" has much less of a coherent theory than the "Establishment" '.[41] Structural-functionalism, especially in its Parsonian version, possessed a powerful, well-developed theory of human nature based on the idea that 'the internalization of social norms' is the most important feature of the socialization process, thus linking, as Durkheim had not, a consensual view of society with a conforming and 'role-playing' view of individual personality. Not only did the conflict theorists of the 1950s lack a systematic social psychology of their own, but some of them – notably Gerth and Mills in *Character and Social Structure* – subscribed to conceptions of socialization that scarcely differed from those of Parsons and his fellow functionalists.[42]

I decided, therefore, that the attack by the conflict theorists on the overintegrated conception of society in Parsonian theory needed to be complemented by an attack on the oversocialized conception of man that provided the psychological underpinnings of the theory. I originally conceived of the paper as a kind of companion piece, a social-psychological counterpart, to Ralf Dahrendorf's 'Out of Utopia',[43] and, appropriately enough, the two articles have been reprinted side by side in readers several times. For substance I turned to Freud – not, however, to the bowdlerized Freud of Parsons or of the neo-Freudian psychoanalysts who were so popular among sociologists in the 1930s and 1940s, and on whose writings I had myself been raised intellectually (e.g. Karen Horney, Erich Fromm, Abram Kardiner, Harry Stack Sullivan). The main shaping influences on my 1961 essay were a rereading of Freud himself and three brilliant books of the late 1950s that were critical of the neo-Freudians and that moved in a far wider intellectual and cultural ambience than most previous interpreters of Freud (the majority of whom had been practicing psychoanalysts): Herbert Marcuse's *Eros and Civilization*, Norman Brown's *Life against Death*, and Philip Rieff's *Freud: The Mind of the Moralist*.

So much for the intellectual context of the late 1950s and early 1960s, when 'The Oversocialized Conception of Man' was conceived and written. Today, all has changed: 'the coming crisis of sociology' rather belatedly announced by Alvin Gouldner in 1970 has come and gone; the former sociological 'mainstream' has been diverted into a number of smaller rivulets; the 'Establishment' sociological theory with which Parsons identified himself as late as 1962 has been dis-established, although the victorious 'Opposition' remains as diversified as he then thought it to be. A young British theorist, Herminio Martins, recently observed that 'functional-ism "dies" every year, every Autumn term, being ritually executed for introductory teaching purposes, its life-cycle somewhat resembling the gods of the ancient Near East . . . The demolition of functionalism is almost an initiation rite of passage into sociological adulthood or at least adolescence. If functionalism did not exist – or had not existed – it would have had to be invented.'[44]

Martins goes on to remark on the paradox that none of the competing post-functionalist successor sociologies is innocent of what was almost invariably the major count in the indict-ment of functionalism: its alleged neglect of dynamics, pro-cess, history, and temporality, and its corollary overemphasis on statics, structure, synchrony, and timelessness. Indeed, Martins argues, the successor sociologies are more atemporal and ahistorical than functionalism itself ever was – let alone recent functionalism, which has made attempts in several directions to overcome the defects pointed to by its critics. He mentions Goffman's dramaturgical approach, neo-symbolic interactionism, Homans's neobehaviorism, ethnomethodology, Schutzian social phenomenology, cybernetics systems theory, and French structuralism as the leading cases in point. Most of these schools have two features in common: they exemplify what Martins calls a 'cognitivist revolution' and a 'microscopic reaction'. Adapting his terminology somewhat, one might describe nearly all of them as 'cognitivist microsociologies'.

The major theorizing of these approaches revolves around such concepts as 'receiving and storing information', 'typification', 'reciprocity of perspectives', 'indexicality', 'linguistic codes', 'defining the situation', 'labeling', and 'presentation of self'. All these concepts refer to processes of knowing rather than of desiring, willing, or feeling (or, in Goffman's case, to controlling or manipulating what others can know, 'impression management'). Berger and Luckmann's influential book is subtitled 'A Treatise in the Sociology of Knowledge'.[45] Aaron Cicourel's recent work appears to have moved towards a redefinition of ethnomethodology as 'cognitive sociology'.[46] Back in 1963, in the companion article to 'The Oversocialized Conception of Man', I noted and criticized the cognitivist bias of symbolic interactionism, referring especially to Goffman but also quoting a statement by the father of symbolic interactionism, George Herbert Mead, to the effect that the self is 'essentially a cognitive rather than an emotional phenomenon'.[47]

Most of the new approaches have also largely concerned themselves with microsociological problems, with 'milieu' rather than with 'structure'. They have focused on the world of 'everyday life' and face-to-face interaction; the research they have inspired has explored such circumscribed social situations as the jury room, the doctor's office, fleeting encounters on the street between strangers, and telephone conversations.

A fourfold table suggests itself (at least to anyone who was a graduate student in sociology at Columbia in the late 1940s and early 1950s). One can readily identify current theoretical approaches that are both cognitivist without being microsociological and the reverse. French structuralism, for example, perhaps the most recent entry in the theoretical sweepstakes, is determinedly cognitivist but by no means primarily microsociological. Homans's 'exchange theory' or 'social behaviorism', on the other hand, is microsociological but not exclusively cognitivist in view of its acceptance of a simple hedonistic psychology of motivation.

But what of Marxism, surely the most trendy tendency in the sociological academy today? Whatever else Marxism may be, it can hardly be described in any of its varieties as concerned primarily with the minutiae of face-to-face interaction – with how people break off telephone conversations or reserve seats in bars when they have to go to the bathroom. The conflict theorists of fifteen or twenty years ago, as I have noted, had affinities with Marxism, though usually 'mediated' through Max Weber, and they were unmistakably macrosociological in their concerns. Marxism is obviously a macrosociology, or at least aspires to be. How does it fit into our designation of the post-functional successor sociologies as cognitivist and microsociological?

I think we can find a kinship, if not identity, between the cognitivist character of so much contemporary theory and the prevalent tendency to favor *voluntaristic* versions of Marxism over the deterministic ones that were dominant in the past. One might almost describe the presently fashionable brands of Marxism as 'consciousness raising'. The young Marx rather than the old, the Hegelian Marx rather than the economist, the idealistic Marx (in both the popular and the philosophical meanings of idealism) as against the positivistic and evolutionist Marx are most prominent in contemporary academic Marxism. Perhaps the most resonant phrase among younger sociologists over the past decade has been 'the social construction of reality'. The phrase, of course, is of phenomenological rather than of Marxist origin. The two authors of the book with that name are, it so happens, moderately conservative politically, but as a slogan it crystallizes both the voluntarism and the world-changing aspirations of Western Marxism. The link between Marxism and the apparently quite distinct cognitivist microsociologies now becomes apparent: to Berger and Luckmann 'the social construction of reality' refers to the cognitive meanings and definitions, or 'typifications', used by social actors, and underlines their freedom to *create* such meanings. This freedom manifests itself most directly in the microsocial interactions of 'everyday life'. As

Anthony Giddens has argued:

> The leading forms of social theory, it is asserted, have
> treated man as *homo sociologicus*, the creature rather than
> the creator of society, as a passive recipient of social influ-
> ences rather than as an active, willing agent who injects
> meaning into an otherwise featureless moral universe. If the
> charge is in some degree warranted, the inferences which
> are drawn from it – that the most vital aspects of social
> existence are those relating to the triviata of 'everyday life',
> whereby the individual shapes his phenomenal experience of
> social reality – easily rationalize a withdrawal from basic
> issues involved in the study of macro-structural social forms
> and social processes.[48]

But the emphasis on cognitivism and voluntarism in everyday life carries with it the suggestion that what is true of that
restricted sphere can be extended to the macrosocial world of
institutions, just as in the 1950s some positivist and strongly
empiricist sociologists hoped that a grasp of the laws underlying behavior in small groups might eventually be extended
to apply to – and 'solve' – the problems of war and peace
among nations. If we are free to 'construct' or negotiate over
the social reality we encounter most immediately, then we are
also free to change the world, to conceive of and will into
being a new world closer to our heart's desire, to make the
leap from the Kingdom of Necessity to the Kingdom of
Freedom at the level of 'structure' and not merely 'milieu'.
And the source of our freedom lies in our cognitive powers.

Now, at long last, I am ready to revisit the oversocialized
conception of man. The 1961 paper was, as I have indicated,
intended to complement at the social-psychological level the
attacks on an overintegrated conception of society by the
conflict theorists. Contemporary theory, as Martins and Giddens have stressed, tends to be ahistorical, cognitivist, and
voluntaristic. None of these three attributes can be said to
characterize Freud's thought: he saw biography, or life-
history, as the key to understanding human beings; his theory
is motivational rather than cognitivist; and he was scarcely a

voluntarist, although the famous 'psychic determinism' of his thought has sometimes been overemphasized. (He did, after all, believe that 'where id was, there shall ego be' represented a realistic, attainable goal for men.)

In invoking Freud once more, I have no wish to sanctify every word of the Master as sacred dogma, in the manner of so many of his followers. What is crucial to Freud can, I think, be summed up in three propositions that I am prepared to put forward here as slogans: (1) *Life begins at zero.* (2) *In the beginning is the body.* (This is the only one of the three that was asserted in the 1961 article.) (3) *The child is father to the man.*

No doubt these are a bit vague and flashy, as slogans usually are. With regard to the first, I don't care to specify at what point after conception the 'zero' at which life begins occurs, thus avoiding the possible ire of either, or both, the pro- and antiabortion movements. Nor, obviously, is the slogan meant to rule out the possibility of prenatal influences on personality, a subject long speculated about by both 'old wives' and psychologists. The third proposition or slogan is obviously sexist and might be revised to read *The child is parent to the person*, which is nicely alliterative if lacking the authority of Wordsworth. In further deference to the feminist movement, let me stress that 'in the beginning is the body' is *not* equivalent to the usual understanding of 'anatomy is destiny'.

Psychoanalysis is still alone among social psychologies in taking these three propositions with the absolutely literal seriousness that they require, however doctrinaire and reductive the details of psychoanalytic application of them may be. To the extent that this is so, Herminio Martins's paradox that the successor sociologies to functionalism fail to remedy the alleged major defect of functionalism – its neglect of time and change in society – is paralleled by the failure of the successors to the now-discredited oversocialized conception of man to remedy the defects of that sociological perspective: the neglect of biography, of the motivational depths and complexities of the human heart, and of the somatic, animal roots of our emotional lives.

Notes

1. Barrington Moore, Jr, *Political Power and Social Theory*, Cambridge: Harvard University Press, 1958; C. Wright Mills, *The Sociological Imagination*, New York: Oxford University Press, 1959.

2. Hannah Arendt, 'Understanding and Politics', *Partisan Review*, 20 (July–August 1953), p. 392. For a view of social theory close to the one adumbrated in the present paper, see Theodore Abel, 'The Present Status of Social Theory', *American Sociological Review*, 17 (April 1952), pp. 156–64.

3. Reinhard Bendix and Bennett Berger, 'Images of Society and Problems of Concept Formation in Sociology', in Llewellyn Gross, editor, *Symposium on Sociological Theory*, Evanston, Ill.: Row, Petersen & Co., 1959, pp. 92–118; Lewis A. Coser, *The Functions of Social Conflict*, Glencoe, Ill.: The Free Press, 1956; Ralf Dahrendorf, 'Out of Utopia: Towards a Re-Orientation of Sociological Analysis', *American Journal of Sociology*, 64 (September 1958), pp. 115–27; and *Class and Class Conflict in Industrial Society*, Stanford, Calif.: Stanford University Press, 1959; David Lockwood, 'Some Remarks on "The Social System"', *British Journal of Sociology*, 7 (June 1956), pp. 134–46.

4. Talcott Parsons, *The Structure of Social Action*, New York: McGraw-Hill Book Co., 1937, pp. 89–94.

5. Coser, *op. cit.*, p. 21; Mills, *op. cit.*, p. 44.

6. A recent critic of Parsons follows Hobbes in seeing the relation between the normative order in society and what he calls 'the sub-stratum of social action' and other sociologists have called the 'factual order' as similar to the relation between the war of all against all and the authority of the state. David Lockwood writes: 'The existence of the normative order . . . is in one very important sense inextricably bound up with potential conflicts of interest over scarce resources . . . ; the very existence of a normative order mirrors the continual potentiality of conflict.' Lockwood, *op. cit.*, p. 137.

7. R. G. Collingwood, *The New Leviathan*, Oxford: The Clarendon Press, 1942, p. 183.

8. Francis X. Sutton and others, *The American Business Creed*, Cambridge: Harvard University Press, 1956, p. 304. I have cited this study and, on several occasions, textbooks and fugitive articles

rather than better-known and directly theoretical writings because
I am just as concerned with what sociological concepts and
theories are taken to mean when they are actually used in research,
teaching, and introductory exposition as with their elaboration in
more self-conscious and explicitly theoretical discourse. Since the
model of human nature I am criticizing is partially implicit and
'buried' in our concepts, cruder and less qualified illustrations are
as relevant as the formulations of leading theorists. I am also
aware that some older theorists, notably Cooley and MacIver,
were shrewd and worldly-wise enough to reject the implication
that man is ever fully socialized. Yet they failed to develop
competing images of man which were concise and systematic
enough to counter the appeal of the oversocialized models.

9. Collingwood, *op. cit.*, pp. 181–2.
10. *Cf.* Mills, *op. cit.*, pp. 32–3, 42. While Mills does not discuss
the use of the concept of internalization by Parsonian theorists,
I have argued elsewhere that his view of the relation between
power and values is insufficiently dialectical. See Dennis H. Wrong,
'The Failure of American Sociology', *Commentary*, 28 (November
1959), p. 378.
11. Parsons, *op. cit.*, pp. 378–90.
12. *ibid.*, p. 382.
13. Harry M. Johnson, *Sociology: A Systematic Introduction*, New
York: Harcourt, Brace and Co., 1960, p. 22.
14. Sigmund Freud, *Civilization and Its Discontents*, New York:
Doubleday Anchor Books, 1958, pp. 80–1.
15. Paul Kecskemeti, *Meaning, Communication, and Value*,
Chicago: University of Chicago Press, 1952, pp. 244–5.
16. Robert Dubin, 'Deviant Behavior and Social Structure: Continuities in Social Theory', *American Sociological Review*, 24
(April, 1959), pp. 147–64; Robert K. Merton, 'Social Conformity,
Deviation, and Opportunity Structures: A Comment on the
Contributions of Dubin and Cloward', *ibid.*, pp. 178–89.
17. Abram Kardiner, *The Individual and His Society*, New York:
Columbia University Press, 1939, pp. 65, 72–5.
18. Mills, *op. cit.*, pp. 39–41; Dahrendorf, *Class and Class Conflict in Industrial Society*, pp. 157–65.
19. Freud, *op. cit.*, pp 78–9.
20. In many ways I should prefer to use the neater, more
alliterative phrase 'status-seeker'. However, it has acquired a
narrower meaning than I intend, particularly since Vance Packard
appropriated it, suggesting primarily efforts, which are often consciously deceptive, to give the appearance of personal achievements or qualities worthy of deference. 'Status-seeking' in this

sense is, as Veblen perceived, necessarily confined to relatively impersonal and segmental social relationships. 'Acceptance' or 'approval' convey more adequately what all men are held to seek in both intimate and impersonal relations according to the conception of the self and of motivation dominating contemporary sociology and social psychology. I have, nevertheless, been unable to resist the occasional temptation to use the term 'status' in this broader sense.

21. Sutton and others, *op. cit.*, p. 264. Robert Cooley Angell, in *Free Society and Moral Crisis*, Ann Arbor: University of Michigan Press, 1958, p. 34, points out the ambiguity of the term 'expectations'. It is used, he notes, to mean both a factual prediction and a moral imperative, e.g. 'England expects every man to do his duty.' But this very ambiguity is instructive, for it suggests the process by which behavior that is non-normative and perhaps even 'deviant' but nevertheless 'expected' in the sense of being predictable, acquires over time a normative aura and becomes 'expected' in the second sense of being socially approved or demanded. Thus Parsons's 'interaction paradigm' provides leads to the understanding of social change and need not be confined, as in his use of it, to the explanation of conformity and stability. But this is the subject of another paper I hope to complete shortly.

22. Ralph Linton, *The Cultural Background of Personality*, New York: Appleton-Century Co., 1945, p. 91.

23. When values are 'inferred' from this emphasis and then popularized, it becomes the basis of the ideology of 'groupism' extolling the virtues of 'togetherness' and 'belongingness' that have been attacked and satirized so savagely in recent social criticism. David Riesman and W. H. Whyte, the pioneers of this current of criticism in its contemporary guise, are both aware, as their imitators and epigoni usually are not, of the extent to which the social phenomenon they have described is the result of the diffusion and popularization of sociology itself. See on this point Robert Gutman and Dennis H. Wrong, 'Riesman's Typology of Character' (forthcoming in a symposium on Riesman's work to be edited by Leo Lowenthal and Seymour Martin Lipset), and William H. Whyte, *The Organization Man*, New York: Simon and Schuster, 1956, Chapters 3–5. As a matter of fact, Riesman's 'inner-direction' and 'other-direction' correspond rather closely to the notions of 'internalization' and 'acceptance-seeking' in contemporary sociology as I have described them. Riesman even refers to his concepts initially as characterizations of 'modes of conformity', although he then makes the mistake, as Robert Gutman

and I have argued, of calling them character types. But his view that all men are to some degree both inner-directed and other-directed, a qualification that has been somewhat neglected by critics who have understandably concentrated on his empirical and historical use of his typology, suggests the more generalized conception of forces making for conformity found in current theory. See David Riesman, Nathan Glazer, and Reuel Denny, *The Lonely Crowd*, New York: Doubleday Anchor Books, 1953, pp. 17 ff. However, as Gutman and I have observed: 'In some respects Riesman's conception of character is Freudian rather than neo-Freudian: character is defined by superego mechanisms and, like Freud in *Civilization and Its Discontents*, the socialized individual is defined by what is forbidden him rather than by what society stimulates him to do. Thus in spite of Riesman's generally sanguine attitude towards modern America, implicit in his typology is a view of society as the enemy both of individuality and of basic drive gratification, a view that contrasts with the at least potentially benign role assigned it by neo-Freudian thinkers like Fromm and Horney.' Gutman and Wrong, 'Riesman's Typology of Character', p. 4 (typescript).

24. Hans L. Zetterberg, 'Compliant Actions', *Acta Sociologica*, 2 (1957), p. 189.

25. *ibid*., p. 188.

26. *ibid*., p. 189.

27. Dahrendorf, *Class and Class Conflict in Industrial Society*, p. 158.

28. Much of the work of Thorstein Veblen, now generally regarded as a sociologist (perhaps the greatest America has yet produced), was, of course, a polemic against the rational, calculating *homo economicus* of classical economics and a documentation of the importance in economic life of the quest for status measured by conformity to arbitrary and shifting conventional standards. Early in his first and most famous book Veblen made an observation on human nature resembling that which looms so large in contemporary sociological thinking: 'The usual basis of self-respect', he wrote, 'is the respect accorded by one's neighbors. Only individuals with an aberrant temperament can in the long run retain their self-esteem in the face of the disesteem of their fellows.' *The Theory of the Leisure Class*, New York: Mentor Books, 1953, p. 38. Whatever the inadequacies of his psychological assumptions, Veblen did not, however, overlook other motivations to which he frequently gave equal or greater weight.

29. Robin M. Williams, Jr writes: 'At the present time, the literature of sociology and social psychology contains many refer-

ences to "Conformity" – conforming to norms, "yielding to social pressure" or "adjusting to the requirements of the reference group" . . . ; the implication is easily drawn that the actors in question are *motivated* solely in terms of conformity or non-conformity, rather than in terms of "expressing" or "affirming" internalized values . . .' (his italics). 'Continuity and Change in Sociological Study', *American Sociological Review*, 23 (December 1958), p. 630.

30. Emile Durkheim, *The Rules of Sociological Method*, Chicago: University of Chicago Press, 1938, p. 71.

31. George C. Homans, *The Human Group*, New York: Harcourt, Brace and Company, 1950, pp. 317–19.

32. Robert K. Merton, *Social Theory and Social Structure*, revised and enlarged edition, Glencoe, Ill.: The Free Press, 1957, p. 131. Merton's view is representative of that of most contemporary sociologists. See also Hans Gerth and C. Wright Mills, *Character and Social Structure*, New York: Harcourt, Brace and Company, 1953, pp. 112–13. For a similar view by a 'neo-Freudian', see Erich Fromm, *The Sane Society*, New York: Rinehart and Company, 1955, pp. 74–7.

33. John Dollard, *Criteria for the Life History*, New Haven: Yale University Press, 1935, p. 120. This valuable book has been neglected, presumably because it appears to be a purely methodological effort to set up standards for judging the adequacy of biographical and autobiographical data. Actually, the standards serve as well to evaluate the adequacy of general theories of personality or human nature and even to prescribe in part what a sound theory ought to include.

34. One of the few attempts by a social scientist to relate systematically man's anatomical structure and biological history to his social nature and his unique cultural creativity is Weston La Barre's *The Human Animal*, Chicago: University of Chicago Press, 1954. See especially chapters 4–6, but the entire book is relevant. It is one of the few exceptions to Paul Goodman's observation that anthropologists nowadays 'commence with a chapter on Physical Anthropology and then forget the whole topic and go on to Culture'. See his 'Growing up Absurd', *Dissent*, 7 (Spring 1960), p. 121.

35. Paul Goodman has developed a similar distinction. *Op. cit.*, pp. 123–5.

36. Whether it might be possible to create a society that does not repress the bodily drives is a separate question. See Herbert Marcuse, *Eros and Civilization*, Boston: The Beacon Press, 1955; and Norman O. Brown, *Life Against Death*, New York: Random House, Modern Library Paperbacks, 1960. Neither Marcuse nor

Brown are guilty in their brilliant, provocative and visionary books of assuming a 'natural man' who awaits liberation from social bonds. They differ from such sociological Utopians as Fromm, *op. cit.*, in their lack of sympathy for the de-sexualized man of the neo-Freudians. For the more traditional Freudian view, see Walter A. Weisskopf, 'The "Socialization" of Psychoanalysis in Contemporary America', in Benjamin Nelson (ed.), *Psychoanalysis and the Future*, New York: National Psychological Association for Psychoanalysis, 1957, pp. 51–6; Hans Meyerhoff, 'Freud and the Ambiguity of Culture', *Partisan Review*, 24 (Winter 1957), pp. 117–30.

37. Brown, *op. cit.*, pp. 3–19.

38. 'I would assert that very little sociological analysis is ever done without using at least an implicit psychological theory.' Alex Inkeles, 'Personality and Social Structure', in Robert K. Merton and others (eds), *Sociology Today*, New York: Basic Books, 1959, p. 250.

39. Harry Stack Sullivan once remarked that the most outstanding characteristic of human beings was their 'plausibility'.

40. 'Human Nature and the Perspective of Sociology'.

41. Talcott Parsons, 'Individual Autonomy and Social Pressure: An Answer to Dennis Wrong', *Psychoanalysis and The Psychoanalytic Review*, 49 (Summer 1962), pp. 70–9. This response to my article also seems to be scarcely known, having been published in a lay psychoanalytic rather than sociological journal.

42. Ernest Becker argued, in effect, that Mills held an over-socialized conception of man in 'Mills' Social Psychology and the Great Historical Convergence on the Problem of Alienation', in Irving Louis Horowitz, ed., *The New Sociology*, New York: Oxford University Press, 1964, pp. 112–16.

43. Ralf Dahrendorf, 'Out of Utopia: Towards a Reorientation of Sociological Analysis', *American Journal of Sociology*, 64 (September 1958), pp. 115–27.

44. Herminio Martins, 'Time and Theory in Sociology', in John Rex, ed., *Approaches to Sociology*, London and Boston: Routledge and Kegan Paul, 1974, p. 247. His observation applies to the United States as well as to Britain.

45. Peter L. Berger and Thomas Luckmann, *The Social Construction of Reality*, Garden City, NY: Doubleday, 1966.

46. Aaron Cirourel, *Cognitive Sociology*, New York: The Free Press, 1974.

47. George Herbert Mead, *Mind, Self and Society*, Chicago: University of Chicago Press, 1934, p. 173.

48. Anthony Giddens, *The Class Structure of the Advanced*

The oversocialized conception of man in modern sociology

Societies, London: Hutchinson, 1973, p. 15. The opening sentence of the quotation clearly refers to what has been a widely accepted version of the critique of an oversocialized conception of man. The popularity of this version undoubtedly accounts for the continuing popularity of the phrase.

2. 'Civilized' sexual morality and modern nervous illness

Sigmund Freud

In his recently published book, *Sexual Ethics*, Von Ehrenfels[1] (1907) dwells on the difference between 'natural' and 'civilized' sexual morality. By natural sexual morality we are to understand, according to him, a sexual morality under whose dominance a human stock is able to remain in lasting possession of health and efficiency, while civilized sexual morality is a sexual morality obedience to which, on the other hand, spurs men on to intense and productive cultural activity. This contrast, he thinks, is best illustrated by comparing the innate character of a people with their cultural attainments. I may refer the reader to Von Ehrenfels's own work for a more extensive consideration of this significant line of thought, and I shall extract from it here only as much as I need as a starting-point for my own contribution to the subject.

It is not difficult to suppose that under the domination of a civilized sexual morality the health and efficiency of single individuals may be liable to impairment and that ultimately this injury to them, caused by the sacrifices imposed on them, may reach such a pitch that, by this indirect path, the cultural aim in view will be endangered as well. And Von Ehrenfels does in fact attribute a number of ill-effects to the sexual morality which dominates our Western society today, ill-effects for which he is obliged to make that morality responsible; and, although he fully acknowledges its high aptitude for the furtherance of civilization, he is led to convict it of standing in need of reform. In his view, what is characteristic of the civilized sexual morality that dominates us is that the demands made on women are carried over to

From *The Standard Edition of the Complete Psychological Works of Sigmund Freud*, volume 9, London: The Hogarth Press and the Institute of Psycho-Analysis, 1906–8, pp. 181–204.

the sexual life of men and that all sexual intercourse is prohibited except in monogamous marriage. Nevertheless, consideration of the natural difference between the sexes makes it necessary to visit men's lapses with less severity and thus in fact to admit a *double* morality for them. But a society which accepts this double morality cannot carry 'the love of truth, honesty and humanity' (Von Ehrenfels, *ibid.*, 32ff.) beyond a definite and narrow limit, and is bound to induce in its members concealment of the truth, false optimism, self-deception and deception of others. And civilized sexual morality has still worse effects, for, by glorifying monogamy, it cripples the factor of *selection by virility* – the factor whose influence alone can bring about an improvement . of the individual's innate constitution, since in civilized peoples *selection by vitality* has been reduced to a minimum by humanity and hygiene (*ibid.*, 35).

Among the damaging effects which are here laid at the door of civilized sexual morality, the physician will miss a particular one whose significance will be discussed in detail in the present paper. I refer to the increase traceable to it of modern nervous illness – of the nervous illness, that is, which is rapidly spreading in our present-day society. Occasionally a nervous patient will himself draw the doctor's attention to the part played in the causation of his complaint by the opposition between his constitution and the demands of civilization and will say: 'In our family we've all become neurotic because we wanted to be something better than what, with our origin, we are capable of being.' Often, too, the physician finds food for thought in observing that those who succumb to nervous illness are precisely the offspring of fathers who, having been born of rough but vigorous families, living in simple, healthy, country conditions, had successfully established themselves in the metropolis, and in a short space of time had brought their children to a high level of culture. But, above all, nerve specialists themselves have loudly proclaimed the connection between 'increasing nervous illness' and modern civilized life. The grounds to which they attribute this connection will be shown by a few extracts from statements that have been made by some eminent observers.

W. Erb (1893): 'The original question, then, is whether the

causes of nervous illness that have been put before you are present in modern life to such a heightened degree as to account for a marked increase in that form of illness. The question can be answered without hesitation in the affirmative, as a cursory glance at our present-day existence and its features will show.

'This is already clearly demonstrated by a number of general facts. The extraordinary achievements of modern times, the discoveries and inventions in every sphere, the maintenance of progress in the face of increasing competition – these things have only been gained, and can only be held, by great mental effort. The demands made on the efficiency of the individual in the struggle for existence have greatly increased and it is only by putting out all his mental powers that he can meet them. At the same time, the individual's needs and his demands for the enjoyments of life have increased in all classes; unprecedented luxury has spread to strata of the population who were formerly quite untouched by it; irreligion, discontent and covetousness have grown up in wide social spheres. The immense extension of communications which has been brought about by the network of telegraphs and telephones that encircle the world has completely altered the conditions of trade and commerce. All is hurry and agitation; night is used for travel, day for business, even "holiday trips" have become a strain on the nervous system. Important political, industrial and financial crises carry excitement into far wider circles of people than they used to do; political life is engaged in quite generally; political, religious and social struggles, party-politics, electioneering, and the enormous spread of trade-unionism inflame tempers, place an ever greater strain on the mind, and encroach upon the hours for recreation, sleep and rest. City life is constantly becoming more sophisticated and more restless. The exhausted nerves seek recuperation in increased stimulation and in highly-spiced pleasures, only to become more exhausted than before. Modern literature is predominantly concerned with the most questionable problems which stir up all the passions, and which encourage sensuality and a craving for pleasure, and contempt for every fundamental ethical principle and every ideal. It brings before the reader's mind pathological figures and problems concerned with psychopathic sexuality, and revolutionary and other subjects. Our ears are excited and overstimulated by large doses of noisy and insistent music. The theatres captivate all our senses with their exciting performances. The plastic arts, too, turn by preference to what is repellent, ugly and suggestive, and do not hesitate to set before our eyes with revolting fidelity the most horrible sights that reality has to offer.

'This general description is already enough to indicate a number of dangers presented by the evolution of our modern civilization. Let me now fill in the picture with a few details.'

Binswanger (1896): 'Neurasthenia in particular has been described as an essentially modern disorder, and Beard, to whom we are indebted for a first comprehensive account of it, believed that he had discovered a new nervous disease which had developed specifically on American soil. This supposition was of course a mistaken one; nevertheless, the fact that it was an American physician who was first able to grasp and describe the peculiar features of this illness, as the fruit of a wide experience, indicates, no doubt, the close connections which exist between it and modern life, with its unbridled pursuit of money and possessions, and its immense advances in the field of technology which have rendered illusory every obstacle, whether temporal or spatial, to our means of intercommunication.'

Von Krafft-Ebing (1895): 'The mode of life of countless civilized people exhibits nowadays an abundance of antihygienic factors which make it easy to understand the fateful increase of nervous illness; for those injurious factors take effect first and foremost on the brain. In the course of the last decades changes have taken place in the political and social – and especially in the mercantile, industrial and agricultural – conditions of civilized nations which have brought about great changes in people's occupations, social position and property, and this at the cost of the nervous system, which is called upon to meet the increased social and economic demands by a greater expenditure of energy, often with quite inadequate opportunity for recuperation.'

The fault I have to find with these and many other similarly-worded opinions is not that they are mistaken but that they prove insufficient to explain the details in the picture of nervous disturbances and that they leave out of account precisely the most important of the aetiological factors involved. If we disregard the vaguer ways of being 'nervous' and consider the specific forms of nervous illness, we shall find that the injurious influence of civilization reduces itself in the main to the harmful suppression of the sexual life of civilized peoples (or classes) through the 'civilized' sexual morality prevalent in them.

I have tried to bring forward the evidence for this assertion in a number of technical papers.[2] I cannot repeat it here. I will, however, quote the most important of the arguments arising from my investigations.

Careful clinical observation allows us to distinguish two groups of nervous disorders: the *neuroses* proper and the *psychoneuroses*. In the former the disturbances (the symptoms), whether they show their effects in somatic or mental functioning, appear to be of a *toxic* nature. They behave exactly like the phenomena accompanying an excess or a deprivation of certain nerve poisons. These neuroses – which are commonly grouped together as 'neurasthenia' – can be induced by certain injurious influences in sexual life, without any hereditary taint being necessarily present; indeed, the form taken by the disease corresponds to the nature of these noxae, so that often enough the particular sexual aetiology can at once be deduced from the clinical picture. There is a total absence, on the other hand, of any such regular correspondence between the form of a nervous illness and the other injurious influences of civilization which are blamed by the authorities. We may, therefore, regard the sexual factor as the essential one in the causation of the neuroses proper.

With the psychoneuroses, the influence of heredity is more marked and the causation less transparent. A peculiar method of investigation known as psycho-analysis has, however, enabled us to recognize that the symptoms of these disorders (hysteria, obsessional neurosis, etc.) are *psychogenic* and depend upon the operation of unconscious (repressed) ideational complexes. This same method has also taught us what those unconscious complexes are and has shown that, quite generally speaking, they have a sexual content. They spring from the sexual needs of people who are unsatisfied and represent for them a kind of substitutive satisfaction. We must therefore view all factors which impair sexual life, suppress its activity or distort its aims as being pathogenic factors in the psychoneuroses as well.

The value of a theoretical distinction between toxic and psychogenic neuroses is, of course, not diminished by the fact that, in most people suffering from nervous illness, disturbances arising from both sources are to be observed.

The reader who is prepared to agree with me in looking for the aetiology of nervous illness pre-eminently in influences which damage sexual life, will also be ready to follow the further discussion, which is intended to set the theme of increasing nervous illness in a wider context.

Generally speaking, our civilization is built up on the suppression of instincts. Each individual has surrendered some part of his possessions – some part of the sense of omnipotence or of the aggressive or vindictive inclinations in his personality. From these contributions has grown civilization's common possession of material and ideal property. Besides the exigencies of life, no doubt it has been family feelings, derived from erotism, that have induced the separate individuals to make this renunciation. The renunciation has been a progressive one in the course of the evolution of civilization. The single steps in it were sanctioned by religion; the piece of instinctual satisfaction which each person had renounced was offered to the Deity as a sacrifice, and the communal property thus acquired was declared 'sacred'. The man who, in consequence of his unyielding constitution, cannot fall in with this suppression of instinct, becomes a 'criminal', an 'outlaw',[8] in the face of society – unless his social position or his exceptional capacities enable him to impose himself upon it as a great man, a 'hero'.

The sexual instinct – or, more correctly, the sexual instincts, for analytic investigation teaches us that the sexual instinct is made up of many separate constituents or component instincts – is probably more strongly developed in man than in most of the higher animals; it is certainly more constant, since it has almost entirely overcome the periodicity to which it is tied in animals. It places extraordinarily large amounts of force at the disposal of civilized activity, and it does this in virtue of its especially marked characteristic of being able to displace its aim without materially diminishing in intensity. This capacity to exchange its originally sexual aim for another one, which is no longer sexual but which is psychically related to the first aim, is called the capacity for *sublimation*. In contrast to this displaceability, in which its value for civilization lies, the sexual instinct may also exhibit a particularly obstinate fixation which renders it unserviceable and which sometimes causes it to degenerate into what are described as abnormalities. The original strength of the sexual instinct probably varies in each individual; certainly the proportion of it which is suitable for sublimation varies. It seems to us that it is the innate constitution of each individual which decides in the first instance how large a part of his sexual instinct it will be possible to sublimate and make use of. In addition to this, the effects of experience and the intellectual influences upon his mental apparatus succeed in bringing about the sublimation of a further portion of it. To extend this process of displacement indefinitely is, however, certainly not possible, any more than is the case with the transformation of heat into mechanical energy in our machines. A certain amount of direct sexual satisfaction seems to be indispensable for most organizations, and a deficiency in this amount, which varies from individual to individual, is visited by phenomena which, on account of their detrimental effects on functioning and their subjective quality of unpleasure, must be regarded as an illness.

Further prospects are opened up when we take into consideration the fact that in man the sexual instinct does not originally serve the purposes of reproduction at all, but has as its aim the gaining of particular kinds of pleasure.[4] It manifests itself in this way in human infancy, during which it attains its aim of gaining pleasure not only from the genitals but from other parts of the body (the erotogenic zones), and can therefore disregard any objects other than these convenient ones. We call this stage the stage of *autoerotism*, and the child's upbringing has, in our view, the task of restricting it, because to linger in it would make the sexual instinct uncontrollable and unserviceable later on. The development of the sexual instinct then proceeds from auto-erotism to object-love and from the autonomy of the erotogenic zones to their subordination under the primacy of the genitals, which are put at the service of reproduction. During this development a part of the sexual excitation which is provided by the subject's own body is inhibited as being unserviceable for the reproductive function and in favourable cases is brought to sublimation. The forces that can be employed for cultural activities are thus to a great extent obtained through the suppression of what are known as the *perverse* elements of sexual excitation.

If this evolution of the sexual instinct is borne in mind, three stages of civilization can be distinguished: a first one, in which the sexual instinct may be freely exercised without regard to the aims of reproduction; a second, in which all of the sexual instinct is suppressed except what serves the aims of reproduction; and a third, in which only *legitimate* reproduction is allowed as a sexual aim. The third stage is reflected in our present-day 'civilized' sexual morality.

If we take the second of these stages as an average, we must point out that a number of people are, on account of their organization, not equal to meeting its demands. In whole classes of individuals the development of the sexual instinct, as we have described it above, from auto-erotism to object-love with its aim of uniting the genitals, has not been carried out correctly and sufficiently fully. As a result of these disturbances of development two kinds of harmful deviation from normal sexuality – that is, sexuality which is serviceable to civilization – come about; and the relation between these two is almost that of positive and negative.

In the first place (disregarding people whose sexual instinct is altogether excessive and uninhibitable) there are the different varieties of *perverts*, in whom an infantile fixation to a preliminary sexual aim has prevented the primacy of the reproductive function from being established, and the *homosexuals* or *inverts*, in whom, in a manner that is not yet quite understood, the sexual aim has been deflected away from the opposite sex. If the injurious effects of these two kinds of developmental disturbance are less than might be expected, this mitigation can be ascribed precisely to the complex way in which the sexual instinct is put together, which makes it possible for a person's sexual life to reach a serviceable final form even if one or more components of the instinct have been shut off from development. The constitution of people suffering from inversion – the homosexuals – is, indeed, often distinguished by their sexual instinct's possessing a special aptitude for cultural sublimation.

More pronounced forms of the perversions and of homosexuality, especially if they are exclusive, do, it is true, make those subject to them socially useless and unhappy, so that it must be recognized that the cultural requirements even of the second stage are a source of suffering for a certain proportion of mankind. The fate of these people who differ constitutionally from the rest varies, and depends on whether they have been born with a sexual instinct which by absolute standards is strong or comparatively weak. In the latter case – where the sexual instinct is in general weak – perverts succeed in totally suppressing the inclinations which bring them into conflict with the moral demands of their stage of civilization. But this, from the ideal point of view, is also the only thing they succeed in achieving; for, in order to effect this suppression of their sexual instinct, they use up the forces which they would otherwise employ in cultural activities. They are, as it were, inwardly inhibited and outwardly paralysed. What we shall be saying again later on about the abstinence demanded of men and women in the third stage of civilization applies to them too.

Where the sexual instinct is fairly intense, but perverse, there are two possible outcomes. The first, which we shall not discuss further, is that the person affected remains a pervert and has to put up with the consequences of his deviation from the standard of civilization. The second is far more interesting. It is that, under the influence of education and social demands, a suppression of the perverse instincts is indeed achieved, but it is a kind of suppression which is really no suppression at all. It can better be described as a suppression that has failed. The inhibited sexual instincts are, it is true, no longer expressed as such – and this constitutes the success of the process – but they find expression in other ways, which are quite as injurious to the subject and make him quite as useless for society as satisfaction of the suppressed instincts in an unmodified form would have done. This constitutes the failure of the process, which in the long run more than counterbalances its success. The substitutive phenomena which emerge in consequence of the suppression of the instinct amount to what we call nervous illness, or, more precisely, the psychoneuroses.[5] Neurotics are the class of people who, since they possess a recalcitrant organization, only succeed, under the influence of cultural requirements, in achieving a suppression of their instincts which is *apparent* and which becomes increasingly unsuccessful. They therefore only carry on their collaboration with cultural activities by a great expenditure of force and at the cost of an internal impoverishment, or are obliged at times to interrupt it and fall ill. I have described the neuroses as the 'negative' of the perversions because in the neuroses the perverse impulses, after being repressed, manifest themselves from the unconscious part of the mind – because the neuroses contain the same tendencies, though in a state of 'repression', as do the positive perversions.[6]

Experience teaches us that for most people there is a limit beyond which their constitution cannot comply with the demands of civilization. All who wish to be more noble-minded than their constitution allows fall victims to neurosis; they would have been more healthy if it could have been possible for them to be less good. The discovery that perversions and neuroses stand in the relation of positive and negative is often unmistakably confirmed by observations made on the members of one generation of a family. Quite frequently a brother is a sexual pervert, while his sister, who, being a woman, possesses a weaker sexual instinct, is a neurotic whose symptoms express the same inclinations as the perversions of her sexually more active brother. And correspondingly, in many families the men are healthy, but from a social point of view immoral to an undesirable degree, while the women are high-minded and over-refined, but severely neurotic.

It is one of the obvious social injustices that the standard of civilization should demand from everyone the same conduct of sexual life – conduct which can be followed without any difficulty by some people, thanks to their organization, but which imposes the heaviest psychical sacrifices on others; though, indeed, the injustice is as a rule wiped out by disobedience to the injunctions of morality.

These considerations have been based so far on the requirement laid down by the second of the stages of civilization which we have postulated, the requirement that every sexual activity of the kind described as perverse is prohibited, while what is called normal sexual intercourse is freely permitted. We have found that even when the line between sexual freedom and restriction is drawn at this point, a number of individuals are ruled out as perverts, and a number of others, who make efforts not to be perverts whilst constitutionally they should be so, are forced into nervous illness. It is easy to predict the result that will follow if sexual freedom is still further circumscribed and the requirements of civilization are raised to the level of the third stage, which bans all sexual activity outside legal marriage. The number of strong natures who openly oppose the demands of civilization will increase enormously, and so will the number of weaker ones who, faced with the conflict between the pressure of cultural influences and the resistance of their constitution, take flight into neurotic illness.

Let us now try to answer three questions that arise here:

1. What is the task that is set to the individual by the requirements of the third stage of civilization?

2. Can the legitimate sexual satisfaction that is permissible offer acceptable compensation for the renunciation of all other satisfactions?

3. In what relation do the possible injurious effects of this renunciation stand to its exploitation in the cultural field?

The answer to the first question touches on a problem which has often been discussed and cannot be exhaustively treated here – that of sexual abstinence. Our third stage of civilization demands of individuals of both sexes that they shall practise abstinence until they are married and that all who do not contract a legal marriage shall remain abstinent throughout their lives. The position, agreeable to all the authorities, that sexual abstinence is not harmful and not difficult to maintain, has also been widely supported by the medical profession. It may be asserted, however, that the task of mastering such a powerful impulse as that of the sexual instinct by any other means than satisfying it is one which can call for the whole of a man's forces. Mastering it by sublimation, by deflecting the sexual instinctual forces away from their sexual aim to higher cultural aims, can be achieved by a minority and then only intermittently, and least easily during the period of ardent and vigorous youth. Most of the rest become neurotic or are harmed in one way or another. Experience shows that the majority of the people who make up our society are constitutionally unfit to face the task of abstinence. Those who would have fallen ill under milder sexual restrictions fall ill all the more readily and more severely before the demands of our cultural sexual morality of today; for we know no better safeguard against the threat to normal sexual life offered by defective innate dispositions or disturbances of development than sexual satisfaction itself. The more a person is disposed to neurosis, the less can he tolerate abstinence; instincts which have been withdrawn from normal development, in the sense in which it has been described above, become at the same time all the more uninhibitable. But even those people who would have retained their health under the requirements of the second stage of civilization will now succumb to neurosis in great numbers. For the psychical value of sexual satisfaction increases with its frustration. The dammed-up libido is now put in a position to detect one or other of the weaker spots which are seldom absent in the structure of sexual life, and there to break through and obtain substitutive satisfaction of a neurotic kind in the form of pathological symptoms. Anyone who is able to penetrate the determinants of nervous illness will soon become convinced that its increase in our society arises from the intensification of sexual restrictions.

This brings us to the question whether sexual intercourse in legal marriage can offer full compensation for the restrictions imposed before marriage. There is such an abundance of material supporting a reply in the negative that we can give only the briefest summary of it. It must above all be borne in mind that our cultural sexual morality restricts sexual intercourse even in marriage itself, since it imposes on married couples the necessity of contenting themselves, as a rule, with a very few procreative acts. As a consequence of this consideration, satisfying sexual intercourse in marriage takes place only for a few years; and we must subtract from this, of course, the intervals of abstention necessitated by regard for the wife's health. After these three, four or five years, the marriage becomes a failure in so far as it has promised the satisfaction of sexual needs. For all the devices hitherto invented for preventing conception impair sexual enjoyment, hurt the fine susceptibilities of both partners and even actually cause illness. Fear of the consequences of sexual intercourse first brings the married couple's physical affection to an end; and then, as a remoter result, it usually puts a stop as well to the mental sympathy between them, which should have been the successor to their original passionate love. The spiritual disillusionment and bodily deprivation to which most marriages are thus doomed puts both partners back in the state they were in before their marriage, except for being the poorer by the loss of an illusion, and they must once more have recourse to their fortitude in mastering and deflecting their sexual instinct. We need not enquire how far men, by then in their maturer years, succeed in this task. Experience shows that they very frequently avail themselves of the degree of sexual freedom which is allowed them – although only with reluctance and under a veil of silence – by even the strictest sexual code. The 'double' sexual morality which is valid for men in our society is the plainest admission that society itself does not believe in the possibility of enforcing the precepts which it itself has laid down. But experience shows as well that women, who, as being the actual vehicle of the sexual interests of mankind, are only endowed in a small measure with the gift of sublimating their instincts, and who, though they may find a sufficient substitute for the sexual object in an infant at the breast, do not find one in a growing child – experience shows, I repeat, that women, when they are subjected to the disillusionments of marriage, fall ill of severe neuroses which permanently darken their lives. Under the cultural conditions of today, marriage has long ceased to be a panacea for the nervous troubles of women; and if we doctors still advise marriage in such cases, we are nevertheless aware that, on the contrary, a girl must be very healthy if she is to be able to tolerate it, and we urgently advise our male patients not to marry any girl who has had nervous trouble before marriage. On the contrary, the cure for nervous illness arising from marriage would be marital unfaithfulness. But the more strictly a woman has been brought up and the more sternly she has submitted to the demands of civilization, the more she is afraid of taking this way out; and in the conflict between her desires and her sense of duty, she once more seeks refuge in a neurosis. Nothing protects her virtue as securely as an illness. Thus the married state, which is held out as a consolation to the sexual instinct of the civilized person in his youth, proves to be inadequate even to the demands of the actual period of life covered by it. There is no question of its being able to compensate for the deprivation which precedes it.

But even if the damage done by civilized sexual morality is admitted, it may be argued in reply to our third question that the cultural gain derived from such an extensive restriction of sexuality probably more than balances these sufferings, which, after all, only affect a minority in any severe form. I must confess that I am unable to balance gain against loss correctly on this point, but I could advance a great many more considerations on the side of the loss. Going back to the subject of abstinence, which I have already touched on, I must insist that it brings in its train other noxae besides those involved in the neuroses and that the importance of the neuroses has for the most part not been fully appreciated.

The retardation of sexual development and sexual activity at which our education and civilization aim is certainly not injurious to begin with. It is seen to be a necessity, when one considers the late age at which young people of the educated classes reach independence and are able to earn a living. (This reminds one, incidentally, of the intimate interconnection between all our cultural institutions and of the difficulty of altering any part of them without regard to the whole.) But abstinence continued long after the age of twenty is no longer unobjectionable for a young man; and it leads to other damage even when it does not lead to neurosis. People say, to be sure, that the struggle against such a powerful instinct, and the strengthening of all the ethical and aesthetic forces which are necessary for this struggle, 'steel' the character; and this is true for a few specially favourably organized natures. It must also be admitted that the differentiation of individual character, which is so marked in our day, has only become possible with the existence of sexual restriction. But in the vast majority of cases the struggle against sexuality eats up the energy available in a character and this at the very time when a young man is in need of all his forces in order to win his share and place in society. The relationship between the amount of sublimation possible and the amount of sexual activity necessary naturally varies very much from person to person and even from one calling to another. An abstinent artist is hardly conceivable; but an abstinent young *savant* is certainly no rarity. The latter can, by his self-restraint, liberate forces for his studies; while the former probably finds his artistic achievements powerfully stimulated by his sexual experience. In general I have not gained the impression that sexual abstinence helps to bring about energetic and self-reliant men of action or original thinkers or bold emancipators and reformers. Far more often it goes to produce well-behaved weaklings who later become lost in the great mass of people that tends to follow, unwillingly, the leads given by strong individuals.

The fact that the sexual instinct behaves in general in a self-willed and inflexible fashion is also seen in the results produced by efforts at abstinence. Civilized education may only attempt to suppress the instinct temporarily, till marriage, intending to give it free rein afterwards with the idea of then making use of it. But extreme measures are more successful against it than attempts at moderating it; thus the suppression often goes too far, with the unwished-for result that when the instinct is set free it turns out to be permanently impaired. For this reason complete abstinence in youth is often not the best preparation for marriage for a young man. Women sense this, and prefer among their suitors those who have already proved their masculinity with other women. The harmful results which the strict demand for abstinence before marriage produces in women's natures are quite especially apparent.

It is clear that education is far from underestimating the task of suppressing a girl's sensuality till her marriage, for it makes use of the most drastic measures. Not only does it forbid sexual intercourse and set a high premium on the preservation of female chastity, but it also protects the young woman from temptation as she grows up, by keeping her ignorant of all the facts of the part she is to play and by not tolerating any impulse of love in her which cannot lead to marriage. The result is that when the girl's parental authorities suddenly allow her to fall in love, she is unequal to this psychical achievement and enters marriage uncertain of her own feelings. In consequence of this artificial retardation in her function of love, she has nothing but disappointments to offer the man who has saved up all his desire for her. In her mental feelings she is still attached to her parents, whose authority has brought about the suppression of her sexuality; and in her physical behaviour she shows herself frigid, which deprives the man of any high degree of sexual enjoyment. I do not know whether the anaesthetic type of woman exists apart from civilized education, though I consider it probable. But in any case such education actually breeds it, and these women who conceive without pleasure show little willingness afterwards to face the pains of frequent childbirth. In this way, the preparation for marriage frustrates the aims of marriage itself. When later on the retardation in the wife's development has been overcome and her capacity to love is awakened at the climax of her life as a woman, her relations to her husband have long since been ruined; and, as a reward for her previous docility, she is left with the choice between unappeased desire, unfaithfulness or a neurosis.

The sexual behaviour of a human being often *lays down the pattern* for all his other modes of reacting to life. If a man is energetic in winning the object of his love, we are confident that he will pursue his other aims with an equally unswerving energy; but if, for all sorts of reasons, he refrains from satisfying his strong sexual instincts, his behaviour will be conciliatory and resigned rather than vigorous in other spheres of life as well. A special application of this proposition that sexual life lays down the pattern for the exercise of other functions can easily be recognized in the female sex as a

whole. Their upbringing forbids their concerning themselves
intellectually with sexual problems though they nevertheless
feel extremely curious about them, and frightens them by
condemning such curiosity as unwomanly and a sign of a
sinful disposition. In this way they are scared away from *any*
form of thinking, and knowledge loses its value for them.
The prohibition of thought extends beyond the sexual field,
partly through unavoidable association, partly automatically,
like the prohibition of thought about religion among men,
or the prohibition of thought about loyalty among faithful
subjects. I do not believe that women's 'physiological feeble-
mindedness' is to be explained by a biological opposition
between intellectual work and sexual activity, as Moebius
has asserted in a work which has been widely disputed. I think
that the undoubted intellectual inferiority of so many women
can rather be traced back to the inhibition of thought necessitated by sexual suppression.

In considering the question of abstinence, the distinction
is not nearly strictly enough made between two forms of it
– namely abstention from any sexual activity whatever and
abstention from sexual intercourse with the opposite sex.
Many people who boast of succeeding in being abstinent have
only been able to do so with the help of masturbation and
similar satisfactions which are linked with the auto-erotic
sexual activities of early childhood. But precisely because of
this connection such substitutive means of sexual satisfaction
are by no means harmless; they predispose to the numerous
varieties of neuroses and psychoses which are conditional on
an involution of sexual life to its infantile forms. Masturbation, moreover, is far from meeting the ideal demands of
civilized sexual morality, and consequently drives young
people into the same conflicts with the ideals of education
which they hoped to escape by abstinence. Furthermore, it
vitiates the character through *indulgence*, and this in more
than one way. In the first place, it teaches people to achieve
important aims without taking trouble and by easy paths
instead of through an energetic exertion of force – this is, it
follows the principle that *sexuality lays down the pattern* of
behaviour; secondly, in the phantasies that accompany satisfaction the sexual object is raised to a degree of excellence

which is not easily found again in reality. A witty writer (Karl Kraus in the Vienna Paper *Die Fackel*[7]) once expressed this truth in reverse by cynically remarking: 'Copulation is no more than an unsatisfying substitute for masturbation.'[8]

The sternness of the demands of civilization and the difficulty of the task of abstinence have combined to make avoidance of the union of the genitals of the two opposite sexes into the central point of abstinence and to favour other kinds of sexual activity, which, it might be said, are equivalent to semi-obedience. Since normal intercourse has been so relentlessly persecuted by morality – and also, on account of the possibilities of infection, by hygiene – what are known as the perverse forms of intercourse between the two sexes, in which other parts of the body take over the role of the genitals, have undoubtedly increased in social importance. These activities cannot, however, be regarded as being as harmless as analogous extensions [of the sexual aim][9] in love-relationships. They are ethically objectionable, for they degrade the relationships of love between two human beings from a serious matter to a convenient game, attended by no risk and no spiritual participation. A further consequence of the aggravation of the difficulties of normal sexual life is to be found in the spread of homosexual satisfaction; in addition to all those who are homosexuals in virtue of their organization, or who became so in their childhood, there must be reckoned the great number of those in whom, in their maturer years, a blocking of the main stream of their libido has caused a widening in the side-channel of homosexuality.

All these unavoidable and unintended consequences of the requirement for abstinence converge in the one common result of completely ruining the preparation for marriage – marriage, which civilized sexual morality thinks should be the sole heir to the sexual impulsions. Every man whose libido, as a result of masturbatory or perverse sexual practices, has become habituated to situations and conditions of satisfaction which are not normal, develops diminished potency in marriage. Women, too, who have been able to preserve their virginity with the help of similar measures, show themselves anaesthetic to normal intercourse in marriage. A marriage begun with a reduced capacity to love on both sides succumbs to the process of dissolution even more quickly than others. As a result of the man's weak potency, the woman is not satisfied, and she remains anaesthetic even in cases where her disposition to frigidity, derived from her education, could have been overcome by a powerful sexual experience. A couple like this finds more difficulties, too, in the prevention of children than a healthy one, since the husband's diminished potency tolerates the use of contraceptives badly. In this perplexity, sexual intercourse, as being the source of all their embarrassments, is soon given up, and with this the basis of married life is abandoned.

I ask any well-informed person to bear witness to the fact that I am not exaggerating but that I am describing a state of affairs of which equally bad instances can be observed over and over again. To the uninitiated it is hardly credible how seldom normal potency is to be found in a husband and how often a wife is frigid among married couples who live under the dominance of our civilized sexual morality, what a degree of renunciation, often on both sides, is entailed by marriage, and to what narrow limits married life – the happiness that is so ardently desired – is narrowed down. I have already explained that in these circumstances the most obvious outcome is nervous illness; but I must further point out the way in which a marriage of this kind continues to exercise its influence on the few children, or the only child born of it. At a first glance, it seems to be a case of transmission by inheritance; but closer inspection shows that it is really a question of the effect of powerful infantile impressions. A neurotic wife who is unsatisfied by her husband is, as a mother, over-tender and over-anxious towards her child, on to whom she transfers her need for love; and she awakens it to sexual precocity. The bad relations between its parents, moreover, excite its emotional life and cause it to feel love and hatred to an intense degree while it is still at a very tender age. Its strict upbringing, which tolerates no activity of the sexual life that has been aroused so early, lends support to the suppressing force and this conflict at such an age contains everything necessary for bringing about lifelong nervous illness.

I return now to my earlier assertion that, in judging the

neuroses, their full importance is not as a rule taken into account. I do not mean by this the undervaluation of these states shown in their frivolous dismissal by relatives and in the boasting assurances by doctors that a few weeks of cold-water treatment or a few months of rest and convalescence will cure the condition. These are merely the opinions of quite ignorant doctors and laymen and are mostly no more than words intended to give the sufferer a short-lived consolation. It is, on the contrary, a well-known fact that a chronic neurosis, even if it does not totally put an end to the subject's capacity for existence, represents a severe handicap in his life, of the same order, perhaps, as tuberculosis or a cardiac defect. The situation would even be tolerable if neurotic ill-ness were to exclude from civilized activities only a number of individuals who were in any case of the weaker sort, and allowed the rest to play their part in it at the cost of troubles that were merely subjective. But, far from this being so, I must insist upon the view that neuroses, whatever their extent and wherever they occur, always succeed in frustrating the purposes of civilization, and in that way actually perform the work of the suppressed mental forces that are hostile to civilization. Thus, when society pays for obedience to its far-reaching regulations by an increase in nervous iillness, it cannot claim to have purchased a gain at the price of sacri-fices; it cannot claim a gain at all. Let us, for instance, con-sider the very common case of a woman who does not love her husband, because, owing to the conditions under which she entered marriage, she has no reason to love him, but who very much wants to love him, because that alone corresponds to the ideal of marriage to which she has been brought up. She will in that case suppress every impulse which would express the truth and contradict her endeavours to fulfil her ideal, and she will make special efforts to play the part of a loving, affectionate and attentive wife. The outcome of this self-suppression will be a neurotic illness; and this neurosis will in a short time have taken revenge on the unloved husband and have caused him just as much lack of satis-faction and worry as would have resulted from an acknowl-edgement of the true state of affairs. This example is com-pletely typical of what a neurosis achieves. A similar failure to obtain compensation is to be seen after the suppression of impulses inimical to civilization which are not directly sexual. If a man, for example, has become over-kind as a result of a violent suppression of a constitutional inclination to harshness and cruelty, he often loses so much energy in doing this that he fails to carry out all that his compensatory impulses require, and he may, after all, do less good on the whole than he would have done without the suppression.

Let us add that a restriction of sexual activity in a community is quite generally accompanied by an increase of anxiety about life and of fear of death which interferes with the individual's capacity for enjoyment and does away with his readiness to face death for any purpose. A diminished inclination to beget children is the result, and the community or group of people in question is thus excluded from any share in the future. In view of this, we may well raise the question whether our 'civilized' sexual morality is worth the sacrifice which it imposes on us, especially if we are still so much enslaved to hedonism as to include among the aims of our cultural development a certain amount of satisfaction of individual happiness. It is certainly not a physician's business to come forward with proposals for reform; but it seemed to me that I might support the urgency of such proposals if I were to amplify Von Ehrenfels's description of the injurious effects of our 'civilized' sexual morality[10] by pointing to the important bearing of that morality upon the spread of modern nervous illness.

Notes

1. [See note 10.]
2. See my collection of short papers on the theory of the neuroses (1906) [*Standard Ed.*, 3].
3. [In English in the original.]
4. Cf. my *Three Essays on the Theory of Sexuality* (1905*d*) [*Standard Ed.*, 7, 197].
5. Cf. my introductory remarks above [p. 56].
6. [Freud's first published statement to this effect occurs in the *Three Essays* (1905*d*), *Standard Ed.*, 7, 165. As will be seen,

however, from a footnote to that passage, the notion had been expressed by him many years earlier in his letters to Fliess.]

7. [Karl Kraus (1874–1936), the Austrian journalist and poet, was celebrated for his pugnacious and scathing wit. An anecdote about him is quoted by Freud in his book on jokes (1905c), chapter II, section 11, and is repeated in a footnote to the 'Rat Man' case history (1909d), *Standard Ed.*, 10, 227 n.]

8. [In a much fuller discussion of masturbation some years later (1912f), Freud returned to the points mentioned in this paragraph. See *Standard Ed.*, 12, 251–2.]

9. [See Freud's *Three Essays, Standard Ed.*, 7, 150 ff.]

10. [Christian von Ehrenfels (1859–1932), Professor of Philosophy at Prague, had been praised by Freud for his courageous criticisms of the institution of marriage, in section 3 of chapter III of the book on jokes (1905c).]

3. Aggression and civilization

Sigmund Freud

Psycho-analytic work has shown us that it is precisely these frustrations of sexual life which people known as neurotics cannot tolerate. The neurotic creates substitutive satisfactions for himself in his symptoms, and these either cause him suffering in themselves or become sources of suffering for him by raising difficulties in his relations with his environment and the society he belongs to. The latter fact is easy to understand; the former presents us with a new problem. But civilization demands other sacrifices besides that of sexual satisfaction.

We have treated the difficulty of cultural development as a general difficulty of development by tracing it to the inertia of the libido, to its disinclination to give up an old position for a new one. We are saying much the same thing when we derive the antithesis between civilization and sexuality from the circumstance that sexual love is a relationship between two individuals in which a third can only be superfluous or disturbing, whereas civilization depends on relationships between a considerable number of individuals. When a love-relationship is at its height there is no room for any interest in the environment; a pair of lovers are sufficient to themselves, and do not even need the child they have in common to make them happy. In no other case does Eros so clearly betray the core of his being, his purpose of making one out of more than one; but when he has achieved this in the proverbial way through the love of two human beings, he refuses to go further.

So far, we can quite well imagine a cultural community

From S. Freud, *Civilization and its Discontents*, London: The Hogarth Press and the Institute of Psycho-Analysis, 1930, pp. 45–53.

consisting of double individuals like this, who, libidinally satisfied in themselves, are connected with one another through the bonds of common work and common interests. If this were so, civilization would not have to withdraw any energy from sexuality. But this desirable state of things does not, and never did, exist. Reality shows us that civilization is not content with the ties we have so far allowed it. It aims at binding the members of the community together in a libidinal way as well and employs every means to that end. It favours every path by which strong identifications can be established between the members of the community, and it summons up aim-inhibited libido on the largest scale so as to strengthen the communal bond by relations of friendship. In order for these aims to be fulfilled, a restriction upon sexual life is unavoidable. But we are unable to understand what the necessity is which forces civilization along this path and which causes its antagonism to sexuality. There must be some disturbing factor which we have not yet discovered.

The clue may be supplied by one of the ideal demands, as we have called them, of civilized society. It runs: 'Thou shalt love thy neighbour as thyself.' It is known throughout the world and is undoubtedly older than Christianity, which puts it forward as its proudest claim. Yet it is certainly not very old; even in historical times it was still strange to mankind. Let us adopt a naïve attitude towards it, as though we were hearing it for the first time; we shall be unable then to suppress a feeling of surprise and bewilderment. Why should we do it? What good will it do us? But, above all, how shall we achieve it? How can it be possible? My love is something valuable to me which I ought not to throw away without reflection. It imposes duties on me for whose fulfilment I must be ready to make sacrifices. If I love someone, he must deserve it in some way. (I leave out of account the use he may be to me, and also his possible significance for me as a sexual object, for neither of these two kinds of relationship comes into question where the precept to love my neighbour is concerned.) He deserves it if he is so like me in important ways that I can love myself in him; and he deserves it if he is so much more perfect than myself that I can love my ideal of my own self in him. Again, I have to love him if he is my friend's son, since the pain my friend would feel if any harm came to him would be my pain too – I should have to share it. But if he is a stranger to me and if he cannot attract me by any worth of his own or any significance that he may already have acquired for my emotional life, it will be hard for me to love him. Indeed, I should be wrong to do so, for my love is valued by all my own people as a sign of my preferring them, and it is an injustice to them if I put a stranger on a par with them. But if I am to love him (with this universal love) merely because he, too, is an inhabitant of this earth, like an insect, an earth-worm or a grass-snake, then I fear that only a small modicum of my love will fall to his share – not by any possibility as much as, by the judgement of my reason, I am entitled to retain for myself. What is the point of a precept enunciated with so much solemnity if its fulfilment cannot be recommended as reasonable?

On closer inspection, I find still further difficulties. Not merely is this stranger in general unworthy of my love; I must honestly confess that he has more claim to my hostility and even my hatred. He seems not to have the least trace of love for me and shows me not the slightest consideration. If it will do him any good he has no hesitation in injuring me, nor does he ask himself whether the amount of advantage he gains bears any proportion to the extent of the harm he does to me. Indeed, he need not even obtain an advantage; if he can satisfy any sort of desire by it, he thinks nothing of jeering at me, insulting me, slandering me and showing his superior power; and the more secure he feels and the more helpless I am, the more certainly I can expect him to behave like this to me. If he behaves differently, if he shows me consideration and forbearance as a stranger, I am ready to treat him in the same way, in any case and quite apart from any precept. Indeed, if this grandiose commandment had run 'Love thy neighbour as thy neighbour loves thee', I should not take exception to it. And there is a second commandment, which seems to me even more incomprehensible and arouses still stronger opposition in me. It is 'Love thine enemies'. If I think it over, however, I see that I am wrong in treating it as a greater imposition. At bottom it is the same thing.[1]

I think I can now hear a dignified voice admonishing me:

'It is precisely because your neighbour is not worthy of love, and is on the contrary your enemy, that you should love him as yourself.' I then understand that the case is one like that of *Credo quia absurdum.*[2]

Now it is very probable that my neighbour, when he is enjoined to love me as himself, will answer exactly as I have done and will repel me for the same reasons. I hope he will not have the same objective grounds for doing so, but he will have the same idea as I have. Even so, the behaviour of human beings show differences, which ethics, disregarding the fact that such differences are determined, classifies as 'good' or 'bad'. So long as these undeniable differences have not been removed, obedience to high ethical demands entails damage to the aims of civilization, for it puts a positive premium on being bad. One is irresistibly reminded of an incident in the French Chamber when capital punishment was being debated. A member had been passionately supporting its abolition and his speech was being received with tumultuous applause, when a voice from the hall called out: 'Que messieurs les assassins commencent!'[3]

The element of truth behind all this, which people are so ready to disavow, is that men are not gentle creatures who want to be loved, and who at the most can defend themselves if they are attacked; they are, on the contrary, creatures among whose instinctual endowments is to be reckoned a powerful share of aggressiveness. As a result, their neighbour is for them not only a potential helper or sexual object, but also someone who tempts them to satisfy their aggressiveness on him, to exploit his capacity for work without compensation, to use him sexually without his consent, to seize his possessions, to humiliate him, to cause him pain, to torture and to kill him. *Homo homini lupus.*[4] Who, in the face of all his experience of life and of history, will have the courage to dispute this assertion? As a rule this cruel aggressiveness waits for some provocation or puts itself at the service of some other purpose, whose goal might also have been reached by milder measures. In circumstances that are favourable to it, when the mental counter-forces which ordinarily inhibit it are out of action, it also manifests itself spontaneously and reveals man as a savage beast to whom consideration towards his own kind is something alien. Anyone who calls to mind the atrocities committed during the racial migrations or the invasions of the Huns, or by the people known as Mongols under Jenghiz Khan and Tamerlane, or at the capture of Jerusalem by the pious Crusaders, or even, indeed, the horrors of the recent World War – anyone who calls these things to mind will have to bow humbly before the truth of this view.

The existence of this inclination to aggression, which we can detect in ourselves and justly assume to be present in others, is the factor which disturbs our relations with our neighbour and which forces civilization into such a high expenditure [of energy]. In consequence of this primary mutual hostility of human beings, civilized society is perpetually threatened with disintegration. The interest of work in common would not hold it together; instinctual passions are stronger than reasonable interests. Civilization has to use its utmost efforts in order to set limits to man's aggressive instincts and to hold the manifestations of them in check by psychical reaction-formations. Hence, therefore, the use of methods intended to incite people into identifications and aim-inhibited relationships of love, hence the restriction upon sexual life, and hence too the ideal's commandment to love one's neighbour as oneself – a commandment which is really justified by the fact that nothing else runs so strongly counter to the original nature of man. In spite of every effort, these endeavours of civilization have not so far achieved very much. It hopes to prevent the crudest excesses of brutal violence by itself assuming the right to use violence against criminals, but the law is not able to lay hold of the more cautious and refined manifestations of human aggressiveness. The time comes when each one of us has to give up as illusions the expectations which, in his youth, he pinned upon his fellow-men, and when he may learn how much difficulty and pain has been added to his life by their ill-will. At the same time, it would be unfair to reproach civilization with trying to eliminate strife and competition from human activity. These things are undoubtedly indispensable. But opposition is not necessarily enmity; it is merely misused and made an *occasion* for enmity.

The communists believe that they have found the path to

deliverance from our evils. According to them, man is wholly good and is well-disposed to his neighbour; but the institution of private property has corrupted his nature. The ownership of private wealth gives the individual power, and with it the temptation to ill-treat his neighbour; while the man who is excluded from possession is bound to rebel in hostility against his oppressor. If private property were abolished, all wealth held in common, and everyone allowed to share in the enjoyment of it, ill-will and hostility would disappear among men. Since everyone's needs would be satisfied, no one would have any reason to regard another as his enemy; all would willingly undertake the work that was necessary. I have no concern with any economic criticisms of the communist system; I cannot enquire into whether the abolition of private property is expedient or advantageous.[5] But I am able to recognize that the psychological premises on which the system is based are an untenable illusion. In abolishing private property we deprive the human love of aggression of one of its instruments, certainly a strong one, though certainly not the strongest; but we have in no way altered the differences in power and influence which are misused by aggressiveness, nor have we altered anything in its nature. Aggressiveness was not created by property. It reigned almost without limit in primitive times, when property was still very scanty, and it already shows itself in the nursery almost before property has given up its primal, anal form; it forms the basis of every relation of affection and love among people (with the single exception, perhaps, of the mother's relation to her male child). If we do away with personal rights over material wealth, there still remains prerogative in the field of sexual relationships, which is bound to become the source of the strongest dislike and the most violent hostility among men who in other respects are on an equal footing. If we were to remove this factor, too, by allowing complete freedom of sexual life and thus abolishing the family, the germ-cell of civilization, we cannot, it is true, easily foresee what new paths the development of civilization could take; but one thing we can expect, and that is that this indestructible feature of human nature will follow it there.

It is clearly not easy for men to give up the satisfaction of this inclination to aggression. They do not feel comfortable without it. The advantage which a comparatively small cultural group offers of allowing this instinct an outlet in the form of hostility against intruders is not to be despised. It is always possible to bind together a considerable number of people in love, so long as there are other people left over to receive the manifestations of their aggressiveness. I once discussed the phenomenon that it is precisely communities with adjoining territories, and related to each other in other ways as well, who are engaged in constant feuds and in ridiculing each other – like the Spaniards and Portuguese, for instance, the North Germans and South Germans, the English and Scotch, and so on.[6] I gave this phenomenon the name of 'the narcissism of minor differences', a name which does not do much to explain it. We can now see that it is a convenient and relatively harmless satisfaction of the inclination to aggression, by means of which cohesion between the members of the community is made easier. In this respect the Jewish people, scattered everywhere, have rendered most useful services to the civilizations of the countries that have been their hosts; but unfortunately all the massacres of the Jews in the Middle Ages did not suffice to make that period more peaceful and secure for their Christian fellows. When once the Apostle Paul had posited universal love between men as the foundation of his Christian community, extreme intolerance on the part of Christendom towards those who remained outside it became the inevitable consequence. To the Romans, who had not founded their communal life as a State upon love, religious intolerance was something foreign, although with them religion was a concern of the State and the State was permeated by religion. Neither was it an unaccountable chance that the dream of a Germanic world-dominion called for anti-semitism as its complement; and it is intelligible that the attempt to establish a new, communist civilization in Russia should find its psychological support in the persecution of the bourgeois. One only wonders, with concern, what the Soviets will do after they have wiped out their bourgeois.

If civilization imposes such great sacrifices not only on man's sexuality but on his aggressivity, we can understand better why it is hard for him to be happy in that civilization. In fact, primitive man was better off in knowing no restrictions of instinct. To counterbalance this, his prospects of enjoying this happiness for any length of time were very slender. Civilized man has exchanged a portion of his possibilities of happiness for a portion of security. We must not forget, however, that in the primal family only the head of it enjoyed this instinctual freedom; the rest lived in slavish suppression. In that primal period of civilization, the contrast between a minority who enjoyed the advantages of civilization and a majority who were robbed of those advantages was, therefore, carried to extremes. As regards the primitive people who exist today, careful researches have shown that their instinctual life is by no means to be envied for its freedom. It is subject to restrictions of a different kind but perhaps of greater severity than those attaching to modern civilized man.

When we justly find fault with the present state of our civilization for so inadequately fulfilling our demands for a plan of life that shall make us happy, and for allowing the existence of so much suffering which could probably be avoided – when, with unsparing criticism, we try to uncover the roots of its imperfection, we are undoubtedly exercising a proper right and are not showing ourselves enemies of civilization. We may expect gradually to carry through such alterations in our civilization as will better satisfy our needs and will escape our criticisms. But perhaps we may also familiarize ourselves with the idea that there are difficulties attaching to the nature of civilization which will not yield to any attempt at reform. Over and above the tasks of restricting the instincts, which we are prepared for, there forces itself on our notice the danger of a state of things which might be termed 'the psychological poverty of groups'. This danger is most threatening where the bonds of a society are chiefly constituted by the identification of its members with one another, while individuals of the leader type do not acquire the importance that should fall to them in the formation of a group.[7] The present cultural state of America would give us a good opportunity for studying the damage to civilization which is thus to be feared. But I shall avoid the temptation of entering upon a critique of American civilization; I do not wish to give an impression of wanting myself to employ American methods.

Notes

1. A great imaginative writer may permit himself to give expression – jokingly, at all events – to psychological truths that are severely proscribed. Thus Heine confesses: 'Mine is a most peaceable disposition. My wishes are: a humble cottage with a thatched roof, but a good bed, good food, the freshest milk and butter, flowers before my window, and a few fine trees before my door; and if God wants to make my happiness complete, he will grant me the joy of seeing some six or seven of my enemies hanging from those trees. Before their death I shall, moved in my heart, forgive them all the wrong they did me in their lifetime. One must, it is true, forgive one's enemies – but not before they have been hanged.' (*Gedanken und Einfälle* [Section I].)
2. ['I believe because it is absurd.']
3. ['It's the murderers who should make the first move.']
4. ['Man is a wolf to man.' Derived from Plautus, *Asinaria* II, iv, 88.]
5. Anyone who has tasted the miseries of poverty in his own youth and has experienced the indifference and arrogance of the well-to-do, should be safe from the suspicion of having no understanding or good will towards endeavours to fight against the inequality of wealth among men and all that it leads to. To be sure, if an attempt is made to base this fight upon an abstract demand, in the name of justice, for equality for all men, there is a very obvious objection to be made – that nature, by endowing individuals with extremely unequal physical attributes and mental capacities, has introduced injustices against which there is no remedy.
6. [See Chapter VI of *Group Psychology* (1921), *Standard Ed.*, 18, 101; and 'The Taboo of Virginity' (1918).]
7. Cf. *Group Psychology and the Analysis of the Ego* (1921).

4. The hidden trend in psychoanalysis

Herbert Marcuse

The concept of man that emerges from Freudian theory is
the most irrefutable indictment of Western civilization – and
at the same time the most unshakable defense of this civilization. According to Freud, the history of man is the history
of his repression. Culture constrains not only his societal but
also his biological existence, not only parts of the human
being but his instinctual structure itself. However, such constraint is the very precondition of progress. Left free to pursue
their natural objectives, the basic instincts of man would be
incompatible with all lasting association and preservation:
they would destroy even where they unite. The uncontrolled
Eros is just as fatal as his deadly counterpart, the death
instinct. Their destructive force derives from the fact that they
strive for a gratification which culture cannot grant: gratification as such and as an end in itself, at any moment. The
instincts must therefore be deflected from their goal, inhibited
in their aim. Civilization begins when the primary objective –
namely, integral satisfaction of needs – is effectively renounced.

The vicissitudes of the instincts are the vicissitudes of the
mental apparatus in civilization. The animal drives become
human instincts under the influence of the external reality.
Their original 'location' in the organism and their basic
direction remain the same, but their objectives and their
manifestations are subject to change. All psychoanalytic concepts (sublimation, identification, projection, repression, intro-
jection) connote the mutability of the instincts. But the reality
which shapes the instincts as well as their needs and satisfaction is a socio-historical world. The animal man becomes a
human being only through a fundamental transformation of

From H. Marcuse, *Eros and Civilization*, London: Routledge and
Kegan Paul, 1956, pp. 29–35.

his nature, affecting not only the instinctual aims but also the instinctual 'values' – that is, the principles that govern the attainment of the aims. The change in the governing value system may be tentatively defined as follows:

from:	to:
immediate satisfaction	delayed satisfaction
pleasure	restraint of pleasure
joy (play)	toil (work)
receptiveness	productiveness
absence of repression	security

Freud described this change as the transformation of the *pleasure principle* into the *reality principle*. The interpretation of the 'mental apparatus' in terms of these two principles is basic to Freud's theory and remains so in spite of all modifications of the dualistic conception. It corresponds largely (but not entirely) to the distinction between unconscious and conscious processes. The individual exists, as it were, in two different dimensions, characterized by different mental processes and principles. The difference between these two dimensions is a genetic-historical as well as a structural one: the unconscious, ruled by the pleasure principle, comprises 'the older, primary processes, the residues of a phase of development in which they were the only kind of mental processes'. They strive for nothing but for 'gaining pleasure; from any operation which might arouse unpleasantness ("pain") mental activity draws back'.[1] But the unrestrained pleasure principle comes into conflict with the natural and human environment. The individual comes to the traumatic realization that full and painless gratification of his needs is impossible. And after this experience of disappointment, a new principle of mental functioning gains ascendancy. The reality principle supersedes the pleasure principle: man learns to give up momentary, uncertain, and destructive pleasure for delayed, restrained, but 'assured' pleasure.[2] Because of this lasting gain through renunciation and restraint, according to Freud, the reality principle 'safeguards' rather than 'dethrones', 'modifies' rather than denies, the pleasure principle.

However, the psychoanalytic interpretation reveals that the

reality principle enforces a change not only in the form and timing of pleasure but in its very substance. The adjustment of pleasure to the reality principle implies the subjugation and diversion of the destructive force of instinctual gratification, of its incompatibility with the established societal norms and relations, and, by that token, implies the transubstantiation of pleasure itself.

With the establishment of the reality principle, the human being which, under the pleasure principle, has been hardly more than a bundle of animal drives, has become an organized ego. It strives for 'what is useful' and what can be obtained without damage to itself and to its vital environment. Under the reality principle, the human being develops the function of *reason*: it learns to 'test' the reality, to distinguish between good and bad, true and false, useful and harmful. Man acquires the faculties of attention, memory, and judgment. He becomes a conscious, thinking *subject*, geared to a rationality which is imposed upon him from outside. Only one mode of thought-activity is 'split off' from the new organization of the mental apparatus and remains free from the rule of the reality principle: *phantasy* is 'protected from cultural alterations' and stays committed to the pleasure principle. Otherwise, the mental apparatus is effectively subordinated to the reality principle. The function of 'motor discharge', which, under the supremacy of the pleasure principle, had 'served to unburden the mental apparatus of accretions of stimuli', is now employed in the 'appropriate alteration of reality': it is converted into *action*.[3]

The scope of man's desires and the instrumentalities for their gratification are thus immeasurably increased, and his ability to alter reality consciously in accordance with 'what is useful' seems to promise a gradual removal of extraneous barriers to his gratification. However, neither his desires nor his alteration of reality are henceforth his own: they are now 'organized' by his society. And this 'organization' represses and transubstantiates his original instinctual needs. If absence from repression is the archetype of freedom, then civilization is the struggle against this freedom.

The replacement of the pleasure principle by the reality principle is the great traumatic event in the development of man – in the development of the genus (phylogenesis) as well as of the individual (ontogenesis). According to Freud, this event is not unique but recurs throughout the history of mankind and of every individual. Phylogenetically, it occurs first in the *primal horde*, when the *primal father* monopolizes power and pleasure and enforces renunciation on the part of the sons. Ontogenetically, it occurs during the period of early childhood, and submission to the reality principle is enforced by the parents and other educators. But, both on the generic and on the individual level, submission is continuously reproduced. The rule of the primal father is followed, after the first rebellion, by the rule of the sons, and the brother clan develops into institutionalized social and political domination. The reality principle materializes in a system of institutions. And the individual, growing up within such a system, learns the requirements of the reality principle as those of law and order, and transmits them to the next generation.

The fact that the reality principle has to be re-established continually in the development of man indicates that its triumph over the pleasure principle is never complete and never secure. In the Freudian conception, civilization does not once and for all terminate a 'state of nature'. What civilization masters and represses – the claim of the pleasure principle – continues to exist in civilization itself. The unconscious retains the objectives of the defeated pleasure principle. Turned back by the external reality or even unable to reach it, the full force of the pleasure principle not only survives in the unconscious but also affects in manifold ways the very reality which has superseded the pleasure principle. The *return of the repressed* makes up the tabooed and subterranean history of civilization. And the exploration of this history reveals not only the secret of the individual but also that of civilization. Freud's individual psychology is in its very essence social psychology. Repression is a historical phenomenon. The effective subjugation of the instincts of repressive controls is imposed not by nature but by man. The primal father, as the archetype of domination, initiates the chain reaction of enslavement, rebellion, and reinforced domination which marks the history of civilization. But ever since the first, prehistoric restoration of domination following the first rebellion, repression from without has been supported by repression from within: the unfree individual introjects his masters and their commands into his own mental apparatus. The struggle against freedom reproduces itself in the psyche of man, as the self-repression of the repressed individual, and his self-repression in turn sustains his masters and their institutions. It is this mental dynamic which Freud unfolds as the dynamic of civilization.

According to Freud, the repressive modification of the instincts under the reality principle is enforced and sustained by the 'eternal primordial struggle for existence . . . persisting to the present day'. Scarcity (*Lebensnot*, Ananke) teaches men that they cannot freely gratify their instinctual impulses, that they cannot live under the pleasure principle. Society's motive in enforcing the decisive modification of the instinctual structure is thus 'economic; since it has not means enough to support life for its members without work on their part, it must see to it that the number of these members is restricted and their energies directed away from sexual activities on to their work'.[4]

This conception is as old as civilization and has always provided the most effective rationalization for repression. To a considerable extent, Freud's theory partakes of this rationalization: Freud considers the 'primordial struggle for existence' as 'eternal' and therefore believes that the pleasure principle and the reality principle are 'eternally' antagonistic. The notion that a non-repressive civilization is impossible is a cornerstone of Freudian theory. However, his theory contains elements that break through this rationalization; they shatter the predominant tradition of Western thought and even suggest its reversal. His work is characterized by an uncompromising insistence on showing up the repressive content of the highest values and achievements of culture. In so far as he does this, he denies the equation of reason with repression on which the ideology of culture is built. Freud's metapsychology is an ever-renewed attempt to uncover, and to question, the terrible necessity of the inner connection between civilization and barbarism, progress and suffering, freedom and unhappiness – a connection which reveals itself ultimately as that between Eros and Thanatos. Freud questions culture not from a romanticist or utopian point of view, but on the ground of the suffering and misery which its implementation involves. Cultural freedom thus appears in the light of unfreedom, and cultural progress in the light of constraint. Culture is not thereby refuted; unfreedom and constraint are the price that must be paid.

But as Freud exposes their scope and their depth, he upholds the tabooed aspirations of humanity: the claim for a state where freedom and necessity coincide. Whatever liberty exists in the realm of the developed consciousness, and in the world it has created, is only derivative, compromised freedom, gained at the expense of the full satisfaction of needs. And in so far as the full satisfaction of needs is happiness, freedom in civilization is essentially antagonistic to happiness: it involves the repressive modification (*sublimation*) of happiness. Conversely, the unconscious, the deepest and oldest layer of the mental personality, *is* the drive for integral gratification, which is absence of want and repression. As such it is the immediate identity of necessity and freedom. According to Freud's conception the equation of freedom and happiness tabooed by the conscious is upheld by the unconscious. Its truth, although repelled by consciousness, continues to haunt the mind; it preserves the memory of past stages of individual development at which integral gratification is obtained. And the past continues to claim the future: it generates the wish that the paradise be re-created on the basis of the achievements of civilization.

If memory moves into the center of psychoanalysis as a decisive mode of *cognition*, this is far more than a therapeutic device; the therapeutic role of memory derives from the *truth value* of memory. Its truth value lies in the specific function of memory to preserve promises and potentialities which are betrayed and even outlawed by the mature, civilized individual, but which had once been fulfilled in his dim past and which are never entirely forgotten. The reality principle restrains the cognitive function of memory – its commitment to the past experience of happiness which spurns the desire for its conscious re-creation. The psychoanalytic liberation of memory explodes the rationality of the repressed individual. As cognition gives way to re-cognition, the forbidden images and impulses of childhood begin to tell the truth that reason denies. Regression assumes a progressive function. The rediscovered past yields critical standards which are tabooed by the present. Moreover, the restoration of memory is accompanied by the restoration of the cognitive content of phantasy. Psychoanalytic theory removes these mental faculties from the noncommittal sphere of daydreaming and fiction and recaptures their strict truths. The weight of these discoveries must eventually shatter the framework in which they were made and confined. The liberation of the past does not end in its reconciliation with the present. Against the self-imposed restraint of the discoverer, the orientation on the past tends toward an orientation on the future. The *recherche du temps perdu* becomes the vehicle of future liberation.[5]

The subsequent discussion will be focused on this hidden trend in psychoanalysis.

Freud's analysis of the development of the repressive mental apparatus proceeds on two levels:

(a) Ontogenetic: the growth of the repressed individual from early infancy to his conscious societal existence.
(b) Phylogenetic: the growth of repressive civilization from the primal horde to the fully constituted civilized state.

The two levels are continually interrelated. This interrelation is epitomized in Freud's notion of the return of the repressed in history: the individual re-experiences and re-enacts the great traumatic events in the development of the genus, and the instinctual dynamic reflects throughout the conflict between individual and genus (between particular and universal) as well as the various solutions of this conflict. [. . .]

Notes

1. 'Formulations Regarding the Two Principles in Mental Functioning', in *Collected Papers*, London: Hogarth Press, 1950, IV, p. 14. Quotations are used by permission of the publisher.
2. *ibid.*, p. 18.
3. *ibid.*, p. 16.
4. *A General Introduction to Psychoanalysis*, New York: Garden

City Publishing Co., 1943, p. 273.

5. Ernest G. Schachtel's paper 'On Memory and Childhood Amnesia' gives the only adequate psychoanalytic interpretation of the function of memory at the individual as well as societal level. The paper is entirely focused on the explosive force of memory, and its control and 'conventionalization' by society. It is, in my view, one of the few real contributions to the philosophy of psychoanalysis. Schachtel's paper is in *A Study of Interpersonal Relations*, edited by Patrick Mullahy, New York: Hermitage Press, 1950, pp. 3–49.

5. Destructive Gemeinschaft

Richard Sennett

It is a psychological truism that people experience crises which reinforce the warring elements of their personalities, rather than break up these elements or give one side a victory over the other. Every therapist will have spent hours with clients who are in the grip of emotions which cannot be reconciled. There is a struggle in which the force of the emotions acquires a more powerful hold over the client, the longer he or she attempts to effect a reconciliation. The very origins of the word 'crisis' in Greek link the phenomenon to suffering, to the passive undergoing of and submission to pain, rather than catharsis.

But the truism that crises are agents of reinforcement is alone an inadequate formula, either abstractly or therapeutically, for how people experience reinforcement through a confrontation of warring elements in themselves depends as much on the cultures in which their personalities have developed as it does on interior conflicts in individual experience. All cultures have collective rituals or collective rules which define the understanding people within that culture will have of what 'a crisis' itself is. In this essay I want to describe changes in the definition of crisis which have occurred in bourgeois society from the middle of the nineteenth century to the present time. There has, in fact, occurred a great change in the environment of crisis experience over the course of this hundred-year period. The result of this change is a present-day situation I shall call 'destructive gemeinschaft'. Its chief feature is that it seems to be an environment of liberation from the repressions of nineteenth-century bourgeois society, but in fact is not. New forms of reinforcement of psychic

From N. Birnbaum (ed.), *Beyond the Crisis*, New York: Oxford University Press, 1977, pp. 171–97.

distress have replaced the restrictiveness of former times. This destructive gemeinschaft has arisen from two historical shifts: first, a transmutation of nineteenth-century eroticism into modern sexuality, and second, a transmutation of nineteenth-century terms of privacy into twentieth-century terms of intimacy.

Gemeinschaft, in the sense that the sociologist Ferdinand Tönnies gave it, meant full and open emotional relations with others. In opposing it to gesellschaft, he meant to create a historical, rather than a purely analytic, contrast. Gemeinschaft relations obtained in the precapitalist, preurbanized world of the *ancien régime*; gesellschaft relations, in which people dealt with each other partially and in terms of shared functions, he used to characterize the emotional transactions which prevail in the modern world. Gemeinschaft has been redefined as an idea since Tönnies's time: full disclosure of one's feelings to others has come to identify a moral condition – of authenticity and good faith, rather than a social condition dependent for its maintenance upon personalistic, hierarchic ties. The celebration of gemeinschaft relations today is captured in the ordinary English translation of the word – community. When people are open with each other and expose their feelings to each other, they create a moral-social group, a community. What has occurred with casting this twentieth-century use of gemeinschaft into technical psychological terminology is the celebration of inter-subjectivity as a moral condition.

What I want to show is that this celebration of inter-subjectivity is in fact inter-personally destructive: that is, gemeinschaft relations under the conditions of advanced industrial society are mutually destructive to those who want to be open to each other. My intent is to explain in psychological terms Adorno's critique in philosophy of the cult of authenticity and Lionel Trilling's critique of this same phenomenon in terms of literary culture. In ordinary bourgeois life, gemeinschaft is experienced so that crises of inter-subjectivity arise which cannot be solved within the moral framework of inter-subjective relations themselves.

EROTICISM TRANSFORMED INTO SEXUALITY

When we think of our great-grandparents' experiences of physical love, we are most likely to think about inhibitions and repressions. Victorian bourgeois prudery was so extreme it occasionally acquired an almost surrealist quality: a common practice, for instance, was to cover the legs of grand pianos with leggings, because a bare leg as such was thought 'provocative'. This prudery lay at the root of a number of psychopathologies especially acute at the time, not only hysterias but also what the Victorians called 'complaints', which among women were manifested by such symptoms as uncontrollable vomiting at the sight of menstrual blood and among men by such symptoms as acute attacks of anxiety after the discovery of an ejaculation occurring during sleep.

Certainly, no one today would hope for a continuance or a return of these repressive disorders. Yet it is important to discover the rationale behind the sexual repression and even to comprehend a certain dignity among bourgeois Victorian men and women in these puritanical struggles with themselves, holding on to the repressiveness the Puritans of the seventeenth century had practiced in sexual matters. Within this logic there was a code of eroticism which ruled nineteenth-century bourgeois consciousness, an eroticism composed of three factors.

The first and foremost factor of this erotic code was based on the belief that states of feeling and signs of character show involuntarily. What is deeply felt or deeply rooted is beyond the will to shape or hide, but rather appears unbidden and at moments of vulnerability to betray the person so moved. The involuntary expression of emotion received its greatest theoretical elaboration in Charles Darwin's *The Expression of Emotion in Animals and Man*. Darwin connected the involuntary betrayal of emotion to the necessities of biology which ruled the composition of the human organism. But the same idea had more popular expressions, as in the practice of phrenology and Bertillon measurement: the shape of the skull, hand or foot supposedly revealed the presence of certain characterological traits which a criminal, defective, or salacious

93

person could not disguise. Similarly, neither could more transitory states of feeling be disguised. Depression was supposed to reveal itself by involuntary tension in the cheeks; an episode of masturbation, by the sudden growth of a spot of hair on the palms.

The involuntary expression of character, furthermore, involved a particular system of cognition. Character traits were to be read through details of appearance. The Bertillon measures of criminality concern millimeters of difference between the cranial shape of the criminal and the law-abider. Little details of facial appearance or gesture were taken as signs of a totality of feeling for the more transitory emotional states. And it was the very miniaturization of these involuntary clues of personality that made personality itself so difficult to control; one might control most of one's behavior, and still some little thing would give one away.

Under such conditions anxiety about sexual matters formed part of a larger belief that the expression of all feeling was beyond the will to shape. The only defenses were either to shield oneself as completely as possible, to neutralize one's appearance, as the Victorians did through their clothing, or to attempt to repress feeling itself. After all, if once a transitory emotion is felt, it will be manifest through miniaturized clues to others, security comes only through an attempt to stop feeling in the first place. Concealment and denial, then, are logical consequences of believing in the *immanence* of personality, the necessary presence of inner emotions in appearances made to others, once the emotions are strongly felt by the person himself.

The second factor of the Victorian erotic code was the belief that personality states could be read through miniature clues, 'fetishized' appearances themselves. I use this term more in a Marxian than a Freudian sense to indicate how trivia of appearance could be believed to be signs of a whole human being. This fetishism is the doctrine of immanent disclosure of personality viewed from an opposite perspective; if the self speaks through minutiae of appearance, then every appearance must be a guide to some characterological state. Thus it becomes logical to cover the legs of a piano with skirts, because a leg exposed is the sign of lewdness. This fetishism of appearances was especially strong in the clothing of the Victorian era. For example, a gentleman wearing a drab black broadcloth coat could be distinguished from an ordinary bourgeois wearing almost the same garment, because the buttons on the gentleman's sleeve actually buttoned or unbuttoned. In sex as in class, this fetishism applied, although it was directed more to the dress of women. The differences between the dress of 'loose' women and proper ladies who appeared in *Le Moniteur de la Mode* lay in minor distinctions in the use of color for shawls and hoods, or the length of gloves. Each of these articles of clothing, then, bespeaks a particular mentality, and the minute differences between objects speak of vast differences in feeling between those who wear them.

In the section of the first volume of *Capital* where Marx takes up the subject of fetishized objects, he states that modern capitalism uses this phenomenon of employing objects as class indicators to avoid productive relations, so that the inequities of production, which might be visible if goods were conceived of simply in terms of use, are obscured. Instead, Marx further states, these objects seem to contain mysterious and enticing psychological qualities. Missing in his analysis, however, is a consideration of the psychological consequences of becoming mystified, of believing in minutiae of manmade things as personality omens. The Victorian bourgeois was trying to make logical sense of its daily experience on the basis of an illusion. The result of that effort was a contradictory, tense attempt to read others for signs of their private lives while at the same time one attempted to shield oneself from being read by anyone. This double process of searching and shielding did not permit a simple state of equilibrium or balance between public and private, for the signs of private emotion were continually erupting beyond one's power to control. Nevertheless, an effort to accomplish contradictory ends on this irrational base was made, and even though the sexual dimension may appall us, the enterprise as a whole had a dignity in its very painfulness and seriousness.

The third factor came as a consequence of the first two: sexual relations in the Victorian world had of necessity to be social relations. Today, having an affair with another person does not call into question his or her capacities as a husband or wife or as a parent. For the Victorian bourgeoisie, those connections had to be made. If every act and feeling counts in terms of defining the whole person, then emotional experience in one domain carries unavoidable implications about the character of the person acting in another. Thus evolves the logic that a violation of morality in one sphere means a moral violation in every other: an adulteress cannot be a loving mother; she has betrayed her children in taking a lover, and so on.

I wish to call attention not so much to the brutality of result as to the premise which produced it. The immanence of character in appearances meant for the Victorian that experience of one sort had to be weighed against its relation to and effect upon experiences seemingly quite dissociated. For all the desire to flee the world at large and hide in privatized, isolated places, the acts of the private sphere were still measured in relation to more public acts. This is how a system of social relations was produced.

The Victorians' more social view of their sexuality compared with our contemporary society's can be shown in contrasting the Victorian term 'seduction' with the more modern term 'affair'. A 'seduction' meant to our great-grandfathers breaking down the barriers of moral and social order which one person caused in another. 'Seduction' connoted a concrete, double act of violation, of the other person and of society simultaneously. An 'affair' is something more amorphous; it stands for a sexual relation between two people, but it is a blank term. 'Affair' is a word without a specific imagery which can be shared socially in speech.

People who spoke a language of involuntary expression of feelings and fetishized objects, each of which contained clues to the personality of its wearer or owner and who conceived of their sexual relations as social necessarily inhabited an erotic world. The Victorian culture was a sensual world, over-whelmingly and uncontrollably so, and its logic was to set up attempts at repression and self-discipline which were in fact of the most destructive sort. This eroticized world was the capitalist bourgeoisie in its first epoch of domination in Western society. What has occurred in the present century is that, hoping to escape from Victorian repressiveness, we have overturned the semiotics of that world in such a way that we have substituted a new slavery for the old. We have de-socialized physical love, turning eroticism into the more isolated and inward terms of sexuality. This change from eroticism to sexuality reveals how the processes of destructive gemeinschaft have come to take form in everyday experience.

I may give the impression that the terms of personality in the nineteenth century can be totally divorced from the meanings ascribed to sexual and other personal relations today, but I do not intend that divorce. Rather, the principles of nineteenth-century bourgeois culture have developed to such an extreme point today that a sharp qualitative difference has arisen between past and present. In a very real sense, we remain under the spell of that past culture even as, through a process of taking its principles to an extreme, we have sought to escape its repressive effects. The desocializing of physical love, which has taken place in the present century, is a result of extending to the extreme the principle of personality immanent in appearances. The extreme vision of personality discernible, causally at work, in all kinds of human experiences is that the world soon seems to appear only a mirror of the self. Meanings in the world become psychomorphic; the sense of meaningful and *also* impersonal life disappears.

It is a truism that Americans and American culture tend more to such a psychomorphic view of society, one in which questions of class, race and history are all abolished in favor of explanations which turn on the character and motivation of participants in society. But American society in this view represents a kind of ultimate example of a point of view which is taking hold in Western Europe in the present century as well. Think, for instance, of the foundations on which particular leaders in England, France and West Germany are spoken of as 'legitimate' or 'credible'. These judgments are based not so much on the leader's ideological purity or coherence as on his ability to appeal personally and thus command the votes of those who do not share his ideological interests. The leader legitimates himself as fit to rule in the eyes of the public not by his public position but in terms of his personal appeal. Or think of the increasing tendency of people in the upper working classes and the new *classes moyennes* to view their positions in society as a result of exercising or failing to exercise their personal abilities. This taking of personal responsibility for one's class makes an emotional appeal even as members of these classes may understand in the abstract that their positions result from blind slotting in the class structure.

To view one's experience in the world as a consequence or a mirror of one's personality structure and to measure such questions as political legitimacy in terms of personality both have a specific psychological dimension. It is narcissism. By this is not meant love of self, but rather the tendency to measure the world as a mirror of self. When the principle of immanent personality is extended to such an extreme that all appearances in society come to matter only as manifestations of personality and personal feelings, we are talking about narcissism mobilized as a cultural condition, as a code of meaning.

Let me pin this down more specifically. The psychological disorders which psychotherapists treated most often eighty years ago were hysterias; these hysterias were the raw 'data' upon which psychoanalysis was built. But today, hysteria is a relatively rare complaint, as are the derivative hysterical phobias and compulsion repetitions. Instead what appears most commonly in clinics for treatment are 'character disorders'. The patient feels empty, dead, or dissociated from the people around him but has no objectified neurotic signs, such as an hysteria or a phobia. These 'character disorders' are usually related in treatment to narcissistic deformations; one has this feeling of deadness, of an inability to feel or to relate to other people, because one has begun to conceive of that outside world as a peculiar mirror of self. It exists to fulfill the self; there are no 'human objects' or object relations with a reality all their own. The peculiarity, and the destructiveness, of this narcissistic vision is that the more the environment of the human being is judged in terms of its congruence with or subservience to self-needs, the less fulfilling it becomes. Expectations of the outside grow enormous, the outside becomes a sea in which the self floats without differentiation. For the very reason that expectation of fulfillment becomes at once so vast and amorphous, the possibilities of fulfillment are diminished. Because there are no boundaries between self and other, experiences lose their form; they never seem to have an end or a definition of completion. Concrete experiences with other people, therefore, never seem 'enough'. And because gratification from this oceanic, boundaryless outside never seems enough, the self feels empty and dead. The obvious content of a character disorder is 'I am not feeling'; the hidden narcissistic content is 'the world is failing me, and so I am not feeling'.

The reason that a shift in clinical data has occurred from Freud's generations to the present day is that the society in which therapists work has changed. Today's society has mobilized the forces of narcissism that are potential in all human beings by intensifying the culture of personality immanent in social relations to such a point that those relations now appear only as mirrors of self. The result of this mobilization is to desocialize such personal experiences as sexuality or parentage by erasing the very notion of society itself – 'society' means that different domains of experience are judged in terms of one another, but are not equated as emanating from the same source, and 'society' also means that external, believable constraints operate upon the self, having a reality of their own.

Let me give an example of how this mobilization of narcissism operates in one of the popular ideologies of sexual liberation. A book like Germaine Greer's *The Female Eunuch* starts with a clear and incontestable picture of the domination of men over women in jobs, education, homelife, and so forth. She states that this is because a social 'system' operates in society: men are not tyrants, modern life simply makes them play that role. Well and good. The contention is then made that a woman has to rebel against this system by being able to do anything a man does; she 'deserves' whatever men have. Gradually, as the book unfolds, the idea recedes that a system of social relations created female oppression in the first place. A woman who gets what she 'deserves' in the system plays an oppressor's role so that she has simply changed positions with men in a game of musical chairs. Would the system itself be changed by women entering into the positions of dominance? Such a question is put aside as the author argues that women should try to get 'total gratification' and that they deserve whatever they want. Thus, in the course of making an argument for the equality of the sexes, Greer winds up denying the very social realities which created the problem in the first place. Total gratification of the self becomes the alternative to systematic discrimination against females. In the course of the book, the world, at first seen as concretely unjust, becomes a mirror or resource for the self. This is the process of narcissism at work in an ideology of liberation, defeating the goals of that ideology by gradually blotting out the reality which caused the problem. It must also be said that this conversion of the desire for liberation into the desire for personal liberation well serves to maintain the system as a whole; the social network of inequalities is not altered, although the sex of a few of the players may be changed.

The use of the term 'narcissism' may mislead in that it suggests a culture becoming childish as the mirroring of self in social relations takes an ever stronger hold on people's consciousness. What is truly perverse about narcissistic projections is that they are seldom self-evident, nor do they represent simple demands for pleasure. For example, if a person from the petit bourgeoisie attempts to explain to himself why he has failed to rise to a higher status in society and arrives at the conclusion that some personal failing of his is the cause, he is mirroring the self on to the world, despite all his abstract knowledge that social organization makes it difficult to be mobile the farther down the social ladder one is. This is as much a narcissistic formulation as is the credo that liberation from a subdominant role ought to end up with free gratification of the self through the 'resources' of society.

Elsewhere I have argued that there is a correlation between the increasing bureaucratization of modern capitalism and the mobilization of narcissism in society.[1] Large-scale bureaucratic structures function on a system of promised rewards based on the supposed talent, personal affability and moral character of the employee at work. Reward thus becomes tied to the exercise of personal ability, and failure to gain reward – in fact a systematic necessity since large bureaucracies are sharp pyramids – is increasingly interpreted by those in the lower middle positions as a failure on their own parts to be rewardable, by virtue of their personalities. This explanation complements, rather than underlies, the explanation based on processes of collective consciousness given above: both for functional reasons and as a consequence of the intensified belief in personality immanently disclosed in social relations, narcissism has come to be mobilized.

Therefore, it has become possible to believe, as the Victorian bourgeoisie could not, in a 'protean self'. The American psychiatrist Robert J. Lifton defines a 'protean self' as a belief that one's personality is always undergoing fundamental changes, or is capable of doing so. There is no core of 'innate' human nature or fixed social conditions that defines it. It is a self so totally immanent in the world that it is a creature of immediate appearances and sensations. This selfhood puts an immense premium on 'direct' experiences with other people; it detests reserve or masks behind which other people are felt to lurk, because in being distant they seem to be inauthentic, not taking the immediate moment of human contact as an absolute. Lifton is highly ambivalent about this protean self: he sees it as a pure analytic construct to be valuable, because the vision of an infinitely malleable human nature gets away from the whole problem of ahistorical, innate personality factors. But as a cultural phenomenon, he somewhat fears this protean man. In dedicating oneself so thoroughly to a sensate, direct life of experience, one cannot make long-term commitments, and resistance to immediate moments which are malign or unjust becomes difficult. A protean man may live a rich immediate life, but only at the cost of accommodation to his environment. Differently put, only a sense of something constant in the self produces the will to resist what ought to be resisted in the immediate life-world.

Belief in a protean self follows logically from the erasure of boundaries around the self. If the world of impersonal necessity is erased and reality becomes a matter of feeling, changes in feeling – impression and sensation – seem to be fundamental changes in character. The self is thus fetishized, as objects were a century ago. This totally phenomenological view of the self has had one of its most dramatic expressions in the commune movements of North America and Western Europe during the last decade. These communes were founded not so much on the conviction that new forms of group life would be valuable or pleasureable experiences in and of themselves for their members, as on more millenarian beliefs that they could serve as 'examples' of how the larger society ought to reform itself. That millenarian belief is really the conviction that changes in one's immediate life space are so important – that changes in the quality of feelings between people who become intimate are of such value – that they somehow become emblems of what the whole of society ought to be like, which is really to say that there is no imagination of society as something different from intimate transactions. That changes in immediate feeling are political in character and that these changes have any consequence beyond the boundaries of immediate experience becomes possible to believe only if one believes that the whole of society is made up of creatures whose real being consists of immediate feelings; that is, that society is composed of protean selves waiting for a 'model' of changes in feeling to guide the transformation of the whole.

In the realm of sexuality, this belief in a protean self suggests to people that 'who' they are depends on who their lovers are and how much they experience in love. Lamartine could write as a poetic conceit in the last century that 'who I am depends on whom I love today', but that conceit has been transformed in this century into an all-too-common everyday conviction. Sexuality thus becomes burdened with tasks of self-definition and self-summary which are inappropriate to the physical act of making love with another person. There are now many studies of the anxiety with which people approach the matter of sexual selection of a partner, and there is some evidence that this anxiety has replaced the rather different anxieties of two generations ago about the subsequent experience the partners might have. If the act is freed of repressive checks, the selection of partners seems to carry a different kind of, and perhaps more onerous, burden – choosing someone to sleep with becomes a reflexive act; it tells who you are. Thus, in the Van Burgh researches, there appears a consistent worry about whether 'this person is right for me' over such formulations as 'is he or she attractive' or 'do I like him or her'. Once the self becomes a protean phenomenon, the reality of the other person is erased as an 'other'; he or she becomes another 'resource' of inner development, and loving the other person for his or her differences recedes before a desire to find in another person a definition for oneself.

The belief in protean selfhood produces in its turn a peculiar code of interpersonal interaction. This code treats intimate interchanges as a market of self-revelations. You interact with others according to how much you tell them about yourself; the more 'intimate' you become, the more confessions you have made. When the partners run out of self-revelations, the relation all too often comes to an end; there is nothing more to say, and each takes the other for granted. Making human contact by marketing confessions results in boredom, rather rapidly realized. Psychologists will have had direct experience of this notion of human contact as self-revelation in their training experiences with beginning diagnostic interviewers. The tyro interviewer is convinced that to treat another human being with respect, he must match whatever is revealed to him by some personal experience of a similar sort of his own. This shows he 'understands', he 'sympathizes'. The vision of human interaction as a card game – in which the players match card of identity for card – rules more widely in the culture. It appears in such situations as encounter groups, T groups, and the like. It has become one of the main modes of interaction through which married people experience short-term extramarital affairs, which are initiated by that classic complaint, 'My spouse doesn't understand me.' The market exchange of confession has logic in a society ruled by the fear that one has no self until one tells another person about it; this is the protean man's dilemma.

In therapeutic work with people who harbor a protean sense of themselves, this consciousness poses an extraordinary problem. On the one hand, the therapist and the client operate on the joint assumption that actual changes in personality will occur in therapy; on the other hand, these changes can realistically occur only when the client has abandoned the belief that he must exchange his old, bad, damaged self for an entirely new model. At a social level the same problem holds. Collective change cannot occur so long as the fantasy exists that collective life can instantly change its essence, substituting a 'new' model for the old. And this is why it is no accident that Western bourgeois radicals of the last decade could so easily arrive at a notion of changes in immediate personal relations as 'models' of what should happen to the whole society. That fantasy in no way challenges the structures of domination; it simply sets an asocial alternative against these structures, so life goes on much as before and people dream of a different selfhood.

Let me now summarize the differences in culture which stand behind the nineteenth-century idea of eroticism and the modern idea of sexuality. The repressive eroticism of the nineteenth-century bourgeoisie was the product of three belief structures. The first and most important was that individual personality was immanent in appearances in the public world. The second was that every appearance, every object of use in making an appearance, had by consequence a personalistic meaning so that appearances became fetishized. The third was that for all the desire to retreat from social relations and make securely private the realm of feeling, these intimate emotions like sex remained exposed and judged in societal terms. The belief structure of the modern bourgeoisie is also composed of three parts. The first is the intensification of the idea of immanent personality to such a point that the world becomes a narcissistic mirror of the self. The second is that the self becomes a protean phenomenon. The third is that this immanent, protean self interacts with others and creates the conviction of its own existence by engaging in market transactions of self-revelation. In part the semiotics of twentieth-century personality are only the consequences of the nineteenth-century terms, taken to an extreme; in part also, these modern terms of personality coincide with the increasing bureaucratization of industrial society, for the elaboration of bureaucracy, impersonal as it initially seems, in fact powerfully personalizes the experience of those who live out their adult lives under its terms.

What then are the consequences for the experience of crisis in modern life of these new terms of personality? To answer that question we have to start with the assumption that confrontations as such are unavoidable between human beings, that no matter how tyrannically pure or fraternally utopian the social settings in which they move, differences between people are still going to involve painful encounters, an occasional sense of betrayal, a more usual sense of anger, when these differences are expressed. So that the question really is, What difference do these modern terms of personality make in the unavoidable fact of crises in interpersonal relations?

The difference they make is that today people experience these unavoidable clashes as contests for personal legitimation. The appearance of an unbridgeable difference in another human being becomes a challenge to the worth of one's own self. An unavoidable difference challenges the basic modality of seeing the self mirrored in the world; the processes of mirroring, processes of projection, sharing of similarity, and the like, are shattered. The persons involved are faced with a problem which will not signify according to the terms of immanence, protean self-definition, and market exchange of confidences, which dominate the culture. The experience of interpersonal crises then escalates to a higher question of which person, which side of the difference, should legitimately exist at all.

Let me give a concrete example of the escalation of painful human differences into a crisis of personal legitimacy. Some years ago I interviewed a working-class young adult living in Boston who was recently married. He and his wife were having sexual problems which centered on his disgust of oral-genital sex and her repeated desire for it. As this conflict went on, gradually the issue changed for him from disgust at the act to disgust at his wife as a person who would wish to engage in it. She in turn moved from a sympathy for his reluctance to a feeling that there was something basically weak about him. Each time they made love, whether they engaged in oral-genital sex or not, they began to think of the sexual encounter as a testing of the other person's worth. After a few months, this testing moved out of the bedroom. All sorts of petty signs and behavior were picked up as signals about one or another being 'revolting' or a 'coward'. Their interchanges thus came to be matters of pinning immense characterological labels on each other via smaller and smaller details. At the same time, they both became disturbed that they could no longer talk freely to each other, and what they came back to again and again was the fact of this difference in one part of their sexual tastes indicating some vast chasm which made *any* talk difficult, because all talk seemed burdened with the unbridgeable gap symbolized through the disgust-coward difference in bed. After ten months a separation occurred, and in the period of separation each spoke of their new aloneness as a chance to be at last really a new kind of person, as though the fact of encountering a difference ten months earlier had prohibited each one from being 'authentic' in the presence of the other.

There are two ways to generalize crisis experience of this sort into collective forms. One is simply to write it large; those who talk about the supposedly high rates of divorce now or the equally misleading crisis of the family do so. These images assume that interpersonal crises directly translate into institutional instability, an assumption which later in this essay I shall challenge. The other way to generalize the formation of interpersonal crises as crises of legitimacy is to recognize that there is a continuity in the process of creating meaning from a small to a societal scale. On this ground the modern environment of crises converts conflicts of group, ethnic or class interest into conflicts in group identity.

Just as individuals framing a conflict in terms of legitimacy are struggling over who they are rather than specifically what they want, modern collective units in conflict gradually come to substitute for questions of power, entitlement, and flexibility of action more abstruse, amorphous, and asocial assertions of the moral legitimacy of the group. It has an identity, a collective self, and therefore it deserves to be fed and its demands met. Because the members of the group feel close, feel as one, their claims upon the society are legitimate, no matter what the substance of the claims or the means of their realization. As an extreme example of this, I would cite ethnic-terrorist groups. The fact of having discovered a common self legitimates the means of terror to preserve that end; this is equally true at the opposite end of the political spectrum in Falangist or other modern Fascist groups. If one moves from these political extremes to more ordinary forms of collective conflict, the same process is at work. The locality asserts the integrity of its demands against a central planning organization not on the grounds that the actual practices of the central bureaucracy are unjust *per se*, but rather on the grounds that the solidarity of the locality will be destroyed. It is no accident that local politics conducted on this basis of identity-as-legitimacy so often self-destructs. While the locality fights the outside world for threatening its solidarity, within itself it conducts continual tests of who really belongs and who really expresses the sense and the interests of the collective whole. These tests inevitably lead to fragmentation, intramural struggles over who is an authentic and therefore legitimate members of the group, and so on. Powerlessness is the result of collective action formed out of attempts to define a collective identity, a collective self.

When a crisis escalates to the question of legitimacy of self, a destructive gemeinschaft is created. Openness to others in the hope of sharing feelings is the modern meaning of gemeinschaft. It operates on the principle that selfhood can be generated through mutual confession and revelation, and under the illusion that experiences of power, inequity or domination all have a meaning subsumed in psychological categories. The destructive quality of this gemeinschaft when tested by external or internal conflicts is that questions of unity of impulse become more important than discussion or defense of common interests. If there is not unity of impulse, and given the construction of the human being it is a rare event, then the struggle is in terms of whose impulses are real and legitimate. Thus the community of the marriage or affair becomes a meeting ground for the testing of personalities, rather than an institution with interests of its own; larger communities self-destruct on the same lines. There is withdrawal from others with whom one cannot share. No matter what the scale of modern gemeinschaft, the logic of sharing feelings is that the self is made powerless when feelings cannot be shared. This is why there exists the conviction, now so prevalent among those who come into treatment, that one's real problems are those of the arousal of feeling in the presence of others. Overtly, in individual cases this problem is framed as a matter of self-failure; covertly, in collective as well as individual desires for gemeinschaft relations with others, there is an accusation against the world for not mirroring back to one the finished resources for completing an identity.

In speaking of the psychological semiotics which make of human differences crises in legitimation, I am entering on a domain Jürgen Habermas takes up in much different terms in his *Legitimations-probleme das Spätkapitalismus* (The Problems of Legitimation in Late Capitalism) where he presents a critique of the vision of a better society, one in which interactive processes of communication are free of the problems of societal domination. He advances a theory of cognition (*erkenntnisleitenden*) in which, ideally, distortion-free communication between people is possible. The legitimation problems of modern society are taken by contrast as relevant only to questions of domination and control. I think this view is psychologically naïve. Precisely, the problem of modern culture lies in its assumption that human beings must somehow get away from the issue of domination in order to be communicative and open. To dream of a world in which psychological processes of open communication, processes which are taken to be moral goods, are free from social questions, is to dream of a collective escape from social relations themselves. The preference for psychological canons of openness over the social problematics of power is precisely the dynamic of destructive gemeinschaft. Habermas's work is not so much a critique of the problem of legitimation now faced by the culture as the very embodiment of this problem.

Having outlined the historical processes which have created destructive gemeinschaft relations in modern society, let me turn to the region in which this destructive gemeinschaft operates most powerfully: the family.

PRIVACY TRANSFORMED INTO INTIMACY

Today the phrase 'the private family' seems to connote a single idea, but until the eighteenth century, privacy was not associated with family or intimate life, but rather with secrecy and governmental privilege. There have been numerous attempts to explain the confluence of privacy and family life in the modern period, the most notable and direct being that of Engels. Because of the sterility of human relations in the productive system of capitalism, Engels argued, people displaced their desires for full emotional relations to a single sphere, the home, and tried to make this sphere privileged – that is, exempt from the empty interactions of office or factory. Engels's idea of privatization supplements the process Tönnies saw in the larger society, of a movement from gemeinschaft to gesellschaft relations where the family becomes a miniature gemeinschaft in a largely alien world.

The term 'privatization' has become a cliché today among those who study and write about the family and has taken on two overtones which obscure its meaning. All too often in writings on the private family or its technical form, the isolated nuclear family, it is assumed that privatization can accomplish its own goals, that people who desire to create little hidden regions of open emotional expression in society can actually do so. This is the assumption of the historian Phillippe Aries and those of his school when they talk about the family withdrawing from the world in modern times. Missing in this approach is the sense that what has the power to divide work from family has the power to divide the family itself. If we accept this latter view, as I think we must, then the experience of privatization of the family in the nineteenth century appears as an attempt to make the family a warm, full, emotional unit, but it is an attempt which constantly fails, precisely because the alien world organizes life within the house as much as without it.

Secondly, the cliché 'privatization' misleads by suggesting a static condition – privatized life – which results from the dynamic processes of society. What happens once the family then becomes 'privatized'? In a curious way, those who use the word cannot answer the question. After all, this process of privatization has been at work for two hundred years, and yet its students use fixed emotional states to describe it: 'isolation', 'emotional over-involvement with kin', and the like. Surely the families of *Emma Bovary*, *Buddenbrooks* and *Herzog*, all overtly privatized, are not the same.

It is important, therefore, to construct a picture of changes in the experience of private family life. The changes in the culture of personality between the nineteenth and twentieth centuries outlined above can be used, at least to provide some indication of the profound shifts in family which have occurred within the last four generations and the effects of these shifts in experience of crisis within the family setting.

Let us return for a moment to Engels's view of the pressures creating privatization in the nineteenth century. These are all pressures of displacement; the flow of pressure is in one direction from a work experience more and more empty to a house attempting to provide a forum for the full range of emotional relationships, including those which properly belong and have been displaced from the public world of production. Let us then ask what would set up a contrary pressure so that the family fails in its efforts to provide a refuge, fails to become securely privatized. Critical in setting up this contrary motion were the very semiotics of personality which had crystallized by the 1860s and early 1870s.

In the childrearing manuals which appeared in the 1860s in both France and England, a common, almost monotonous theme appears. For children to grow up with stable characters, they must experience orderly appearances in the family circle; not only must the child, whether boy or girl, act consistently through good 'habits' and 'beneficent rules' but the parents must observe good habits and rules themselves in respect to their children; above all, they must observe these rules *consistently*. This advice about family dynamics was given because of a fear among the Victorian bourgeoisie that if appearances were not routinized in the home, if spontaneity were not suppressed, then personality would never crystallize or the child would not grow emotionally strong. This fear comes out of an equation whose elements we have already uncovered. Personality inheres in appearances, and for personality itself to acquire a form, appearances must be rigidly formed and disciplined.

This code of child-parental behaviour is an instance of the way in which the codes of personality prevalent in the last century pushed family relations, in spite of the desire family members had to withdraw from the terrors of the world into a relaxed warm zone, back into the contradictory impulses of order and immanence which ruled the public world. Between husbands and wives, the same pressure for stabilization of behavior occurred. Love between man and woman in the family was measured precisely by the ability of the partners to conform without deviation to the rules of what love should be. Just as that adherence to a construct of propriety was the necessity for survival in factory or office, it became necessary at home. But the realms of work and home were not therefore identical. In the home changed appearances would threaten the partners' sense that they knew who each other was as a person; a repressive, rigid routine became the means of certifying that the marriage itself was real – just as the child was thought to grow in a healthy way only if he experienced others in terms he could 'trust'. For the Victorians 'trust' meant trust to be the same.

Thus, when we talk about the 'privatization' of the family experience in the nineteenth century, we are on the one hand talking about a belief that the family ought to be removed from the tremors of the outer world and be a moral sphere higher than that outer world, and on the other hand, we are talking about a code of human interaction derived from a belief in immanent personality which thrust the family back out into the very anxieties about order and immanent meaning which ruled public life. *Both* the desire to retreat and the reconstruction of the outer society are elements of privatization; the first would soon have exhausted itself as a desire had not the second so insistently thrust family dynamics back into the public contradiction so that the family's mission of withdrawal always seemed yet to be achieved.

For families of the present generation, privatization on these terms had ceased to exist. Half the equation of pressure has changed. The pressure dividing family experience in people's minds from the experience of work and adult social life does continue. In fact, there is some evidence that in the last forty years the gap has grown wider between the actions which middle-class adults believe make them good parents and the actions which they construe as making them powerful or at least powerful enough to survive in the world. However, because the terms of personality have so altered in this century, the other set of contrary pressures does not obtain. There is no longer a world alien to the self to which the self refers. For example, for the sake of preserving a marriage as a social contract, people today are not willing to make great sacrifices of their immediate feelings and perceptions about the other partner in the marriage. Again we come upon the conundrum that liberation from repression has come to be couched in terms of a liberation from the social dimension itself with rules, restraints, and a logic alien to the logic of human sensibility. What has happened, then, is that the forces creating an ideology of familial withdrawal from the world have persisted, but the contrary force has weakened which nonetheless would refer consciousness of the marital bond back to being judged in terms of other kinds of human bonds.

Given the picture of so many nineteenth-century people imprisoned in loveless, respectable marriages, the breaking of such an equation of pressure may well seem all to the good. The problem is that this change in the terms of privatization has not liberated individuals within the family but, paradoxically, has made the family bond of even greater importance and even more destructive force. When family relations are perceived to be withdrawals from the world and also to have no reference back to nonpsychological conditions, the family group itself is magnified. The family comes to seem, in fact, the terrain on which all emotions are displayed; emotions which are not familial have no reality because the world outside is only instrumental. The more people believe in family relations as a purely psychological matter, the less they can believe that valuable psychological experience ever can exist without reference ultimately to the family. The constraint of convention over sensibility is today being broken down in the family, but in turn the reality of sensibility outside the family is also breaking down.

When people rebel against a bad marriage, it is not usually

to go live alone in the world but rather for the sake of, or in the hope of, finding a newer, more emotionally satisfying mate. When children express anger at their parents, it is not usually because the parents were parents but rather because they were 'inadequate' parents. Because the breaking of the old equation has led to an increasing belief in family relations as a complete universe of psychological relations, the historic change has to be thought of as a movement from the family as an unsuccessfully private institution in the nineteenth-century bourgeois experience to the family as an illusionary psychological category in twentieth-century bourgeois experience.

In this movement from privacy to intimacy, the family has become the domain in which the processes of destructive gemeinschaft are played out. The family defines the territory of a community of feeling. In order to criticize it as such, I want to be as clear as I can about what it means to perceive a family at once socially withdrawn and emotionally complete. It is important to do so because there is so much loose talk about the family as 'in crisis' at the present time, talk of crisis which in fact only serves to reinforce the family as a model of psychological experience in the minds of those who perceive the family falling apart.

What is the rationale of conceiving the family to be socially withdrawn and emotionally complete? The rationale is that of the narcissistic mirror. If the family is withdrawn from crass contingency and morally 'better', then what appears in this particular psychic network has a reality and a purity unsullied by alien contingencies, masks of necessity, and the like. Once freed from the world, the family appears as a disclosure of pure psychological experience. This is then mirrored out beyond the family nexus, and emotional transactions in the world are judged in terms of categories which are familial in their form.

Let me give some concrete examples of this. Patterns of friendship among adults at work today follow a course unlike those of four generations back. The more a friendship between adults at work grows, the more attempts are made to integrate the adults into the respective family circles and form friendships between families. American middle-class workers open the gates to the home rather readily to their friends, French bourgeoisie rather reluctantly, but the path of friendship is the same. One of my students has done a comparative study of friendships between middle-class adults in London and Paris in the 1870s, as these are portrayed in the pulp fiction of the time, and he found something entirely different from this modern pattern. Among males a friend became someone with whom you could escape from the rigors of the family; a friend was someone to take out rather than invite in. Among females, friendship also involved progressive dissociation from family relations; a friend was someone who could become a confidante for grievances against both children and spouse. Because women were incarcerated in the house, female friendships appeared familial, but in fact friends in the house meant a chance to rail against the tyrannies of the home. A century ago, then, friendship was for both sexes a matter of escape from familism; today it is a matter of progressive induction into familism.

Another example is something quite out of the ordinary, and seemingly opposed to the mores of the bourgeois family: the hippie commune. In a study of 1960s-style communes, Rosabeth Moss Kantor found them to be insistently concerned with reliving old family issues and relationships so as to create a higher kind of family. These communes were not formed around work, *per se*, but around shared experiences of survival labor tied to the building of a collective family. She found, indeed, that there was a great problem created for people living in communes when psychological rights were asserted against the collective whole; that is, rights to multiple dimensions of psychological experience outside the commune which could not be absorbed into the higher family or at least made consonant with the commune's values. For example, if you were sleeping with someone not part of the commune, why is it you didn't ask him or her to come live in the commune? The refusal to familize these relations was taken as a betrayal.

The most profound indicator of this new family imagery comes from the realm of ideology. Today, the concept of psychological emancipation which dominates the culture involves liberation of the self rather than liberation from the self. In ordinary speech and desire we use such terms as being able to express one's feelings or feeling free to do so. Habermas's model of open communication has its vulgar counterpart in the belief that social institutions are bad as soon as they get in the way of human expression. One example of that vulgar belief is Greer's *Female Eunuch*; another is the marital break-up outlined in this essay, a case in which both partners came to interpret a sexual conflict as a problem of being able to express themselves rather than interact with each other.

Liberation of one's feelings along these lines is basically a familistic ideal. Liberation from one's feelings is a non-familistic ideal. The first refers to the possibility of experience in which anything one wants and any sensation one has can be received by others; that is, liberation of one's feelings supposes an accepting environment, one in which interest in whatever one does feel will be shown by others and appreciated by them simply because one does have a feeling. This environment can only be that of the child displaying himself to an audience of parents. Liberation from one's feelings refers to the possibility of experience which is impersonal and in which the person observes a convention, plays a role, or participates in a form. Its classic locus is the city; its classic name is cosmopolitanism.

But the contrast cuts further. The display of newly discovered feelings to a fully accepting environment (usually of parents rather than peers) is usually a post-Oedipal phenomenon; that is, it follows upon the child's first consistent declarations of his own independence. The display of play behavior, in which the child participates in a social form with impersonal conventions, is usually a pre-Oedipal experience; it follows upon the child's discovery that he can engage in games. Conservative critics of the modern culture of a 'boundaryless self' usually base their attacks on the notion that this culture is regressive and childish. The real problem is exactly the reverse. The terms of modern bourgeois notions of personality are not regressive *enough*; these notions do not permit the adult to call upon the most fundamental and earliest born of the social impulses, the impulse to play. Play is pleasure in the observance of a form, a convention not dependent on individualized, momentary impulse. The reproach one ought to make to the notion of liberation of the self is that these energies of play remain dormant as the adult celebrates a freedom later apparent in his cycle of maturation, one in which the spontaneous discovery of spontaneous impulses in himself will be received and accepted by others. An ideal of regression only to a post-Oedipal family relation insures that only the most fragile and withdrawn moment of family history becomes enshrined as a cultural ideal.

The distinction between liberation of the self and liberation from the self has a last dimension. The first is a wholly secular belief. In a society harboring any notion of transcendence of the self, it is impossible. Such a society need not be overly religious or have a ritualized creed. The notion that humanity ought to struggle to be liberated from the boundaries of psychological impulse is possible in any culture which perceives the self to be a little cabinet of horrors. In such a society, the goals of social life will be the suppression of these impulses of petty desire, greed and envy for the sake of a sociable existence passed in the company of other people. A vision of society in these terms informed as much of Rousseau's idealism as it did Freud's forbodings. When we speak of a society given over to liberation of the self, we are speaking of a society refusing to take into account the high probability that human beings are capable of destructive feelings which should at least be hidden from the sight of others. This is why a society like ours celebrating the sheer existence of human feeling cannot in the end be called 'privatized', for there is no vision of the social necessity of keeping certain impulses a secret from others, harboring them only in private. Instead, we consider this very necessity for disguise to be only a further proof of the authoritarian injustices of present social arrangements; we are prone to convert discretion and tact into signs of domination. For this reason I cannot see how the word 'liberation' itself denotes a state of progress in the present time from a century past. A hundred years ago, personality was socialized only by ideas of repression; today it is not socialized at all. Surely these are opposite and equal evils.

Let me now conclude with a discussion of the impact of

this familized intimacy on the experience of crises within the family itself. The family as an intimate terrain, a world of its own, a measure of psychic reality, has magnified certain necessary crises which must occur in all kinship systems to such a point that the issues in the crisis become unresolvable, and yet the hold of family life on those caught in these crises is strengthened. The process of destructive gemeinschaft was described at the end of the previous section as a contest for personal legitimacy which arises when psychic conflicts become manifest. On the family terrain, desocialized and a seemingly complete psychological system, conflicts for personal legitimacy with other family members become life-and-death struggles for dominance, struggles based on who has the superior, better or more complete set of feelings.

One of the necessary traumas of family life in which this dynamic rules is the shift from one adult generation to the next. In societies where feudal status is transmitted or in circumstances where adequate amounts of property pass from one generation to the next, intergenerational change in the family is tied to the acquisition of power in the world. When a society contains a bourgeois class occupying for the most part bureaucratic positions which cannot be passed on by inheritance, the correlation between generational change and worldly position breaks down. Or at least it breaks down in a direct way; children from the bourgeois families have a better chance of occupying bourgeois positions than children from lower-class positions, but this is not the same situation as one in which the sheer death of a parent is the means by which the younger generation acquires its power in the world.

Under the circumstances of bureaucratic life, how is a change of generations experienced? We can say it is more purely an emotional matter, but this alone does not take us very far. There are few known societies in which the eclipse of one generation by another is a neutral, smooth, non-traumatic process; feelings of betrayal, loss, and triumph are always involved. The real question is how these traumas are organized. In modern society, the trauma of intergenerational succession is framed in terms of the replacement of an emotionally inferior generation in the family by a new generation with psychological dominance over the past. I think

Simone de Beauvoir is right in her intuitive perception that the aged are abandoned for reasons far beyond the fact that they have become productively useless. They are abandoned because they have become psychologically useless to the next generation. This psychic closure to the generation dying out is in its turn a declaration on the part of those younger that no further psychic transactions with the aged are in the interests of the younger; psychological authority is claimed in the act of surviving. This is why therapists who work with families where three generations occupy the same house find again and again that the aged are tolerated only so long as they behave submissively and why, according to one set of evidence, even the rates of senility are higher in these three-generation households than for the aged who are simply abandoned to live alone.

In a culture where family relations are psychological absolutes, the struggle for legitimation of the self sets up a struggle for psychological dominance over others. It is a zero-sum game in which you cannot feel legitimate in, of, and for yourself unless you de-legitimate someone else in the family. Just as this process leads to a tyranny over the aged, it sets up a profound problem in the relations between adults and their children and among the children themselves.

For a parent to assert a behavior rule under these conditions, the rule itself becomes not a code to be obeyed or rejected in terms of its own value, but rather a symbol of whether the parent is legitimate in his or her own eyes. The child's submission becomes only a means by which the parent reassures him or herself of his worth as a person. Thus, in place of the nineteenth-century fear that the child will do himself harm if he or she does not rigidly adhere to a rule, what one encounters among parents today is a fear that there must be something wrong with themselves if the children do not obey. This fear ought logically to make parents far more disciplinarian than their great-grandparents, but the process works at a deeper level. The parent applies his or her own sense of psychological reality – that one has real feelings when one can express them freely – to the child so that in dimension family relations become what the psychologist Robert Holt has aptly called 'adultomorphic'. At the same time, the parent is faced with the child's need for rules to survive in a world the child cannot yet manage on his or her own. The parent feels he must assert rules for the sake of the child but fears he is violating the child by ruling him. However, in having the child subsequently respond to these rules, the parent confirms his or her own sense of worth. The fact of what the rules are objectively thus gets lost easily in a much subtler but stronger process of asserting the self, guilt over that assertion, and triumph over the child in which the child is only a means to the parent's need for legitimation. If such a process is tangled up, the results are unfortunately all too clear, for these are precisely the means by which a confused sense of object relations is instilled into a growing human being; that is, the means by which a narcissistic character disorder is created. And these character disorders form the dominant class of treatment problems which separate the present time from Freud's generation and its psychic discontents.

Built into the very idea of sibling rivalry is the sense of a zero-sum game; children who compete with each other for parental approval quite naturally believe that attention or rewards given to one child must diminish the rewards given to another. But under cultural conditions in which everyone in the family operates in terms of a zero-sum game, sibling rivalry takes on a peculiar form. The sibs must maximize the differences between themselves in order to have a turf on which they can attract any notice, for they are competing not only with each other but also with their parents. One of the most striking of these patterns of differentiation revolves around the issue of competency and ability. If one child begins to show himself able, another attempts to attract attention via differentiation through systematic failure. The same principle of maximizing differences will be applied to psychological competences, so that one sib reacts to another's emotional strength by accentuating his or her own fear, weakness or passivity.

Certainly sibling rivalry in which failure becomes a means of attention-getting knows no boundaries of time and place. It is a question of how much the specific historical culture reinforces the pattern and on what grounds. What is special about the tendencies to reinforce sibling failure in the modern family is precisely that both male and female sibs are exposed to this principle of differentiation. In societies where girls are taken as ineluctably different from boys, some of the tasks of difference are already established for the sibs without them having to create differentiation through intellectual or psychic failure. The more modern society equalizes its promises, at least of sexual equality, the more the sibling rivalry through failure is spread to all the sibs in the family. It is one of the reasons why the research of Horner and others turns up a pattern among young women of wanting to fail at being independent; if they are independent they will crowd their male sibs' territory and so lose parental love. The answer to such a dilemma is obviously not to restrict again the freedom of women but to change the modern patterns of family life which work against this freedom.

The chances that such crises of family life will transform the family itself seem slim to me. Rather, the reverse seems likely: the kind of crisis experience on this intimate terrain reinforces the dominance of the family as a total field of personal relations at the same time they make members of the modern family suffer. The reason these family relations reinforce is that the premises of personality are not challenged in the family group; rather, the persons in the family appear to be failing to have adequate personalities. It becomes possible, as the communards of the 1960s did, to dream of a higher family in which no one suffers; it becomes possible to think of building more 'meaningful' human relationships by being less competitive, more open, and so forth, but these also are forms of reinforcing the idea of gemeinschaft, which states that significant human experience is intimate and moves on a terrain where people want to know each other's inner feelings. As long as warm intimate relations are given such moral priority, familism will continue, no matter how frequently people divorce and remarry, no matter how unusual their sexual practices, no matter how many affairs they conduct in search of someone who 'understands' them. And as long as this intimate familism prevails, destructive competitions for personal legitimacy will rule. I haven't much hope, therefore, that people can use their intimate experiences as a model for rebuilding society, but rather I think that a new kind of gesellschaft will have to be built in order to change the destructiveness of intimate relations.

Note

1. Richard Sennett and Jonathan Cobb, *The Hidden Injuries of Class*, New York, 1972.

6. Sexual stigma: an interactionist account

Kenneth Plummer

INTRODUCTION: THE PROBLEM OF SEXUALITY IN SOCIOLOGY

Sociologists have failed to study a most important aspect of human social conduct: that of sexuality. Given the prolific outpouring of popular materials on this subject, and given too the folklore that sociologists are men paid thousands of pounds to find their way to the nearest whorehouse, it is a surprise to discover that few sociologists have shown any interest in this field.

The main roads to a knowledge of sexuality lie in the work of Freud, Kinsey and Masters – there were few students before them, and most subsequent work bears the imprint of one or other.[1] Yet although they were not immune from social explanation, they were not sociologists. Freud's interest rested with the innermost emotional development of individuals, Kinsey's lay with the taxonomic classification of behavioural variations, and Masters was engrossed in problems of physiology – a clinician, a zoologist and a gynaecologist respectively.

Those few 'sociologists' who have explored sexuality have done so from viewpoints divorced from sociology. Thus, the pioneer works of Westermarck, Malinowski and Sumner roamed so far from home shores to merit the label 'anthropological', while the work of W. I. Thomas on gender variation roamed so far from the sociological perspective to merit the label 'psychological'. Likewise, the work of men like Marcuse and Reich must be seen as essentially metatheoretical excursions, and at the other extreme, the studies conducted by Schofield, Gorer, Dickinson and others must be seen as social

From K. Plummer, *Sexual Stigma: an Interactionist Account*, London: Routledge and Kegan Paul, 1975, pp. 3–9, 29–41.

surveys and not sociology. These latter studies of social book-keeping – of who does what with whom, how often and where – are the ones most frequently tagged 'sociology': but their authors have rarely been sociologists interested in theory and working in sociological contexts. Dickinson was a medical man, Davis a social worker, Hamilton a psychoanalyst, and Bromley and Britten were journalists. Most of the studies commonly regarded as sociological simply do not meet the criteria of that discipline.

Why has such a neglect within sociology come about?[2] One popular answer is simply that sexuality is a 'taboo' area, in which the practical problems of research are much greater than in other fields. In addition to the problem of getting respondents to talk about such sensitive areas, there are problems of infringing the law, of personal attacks and abuse, of difficulties in authorities co-operating and of public censure (Farberow, 1963: 28; Christenson, 1971: ch. 7; Pomeroy, 1972). Now while there may be some 'special problems' attached to sex research, I agree with Hooker's remark that 'Many of those problems are in no sense unique to the problem area. To treat them as unique or special is to obscure the real issue' (Hooker, 1963: 44). This 'real issue' is that of scientific integrity – that all good scientific work is difficult. It is not enough to account for the neglect of sex research in terms of practical problems because all scientific work has these if performed seriously.[3]

A more fruitful approach to understanding this neglect comes from the sociology of knowledge. As Reiss has hinted, the neglect of sex research has little to do with fieldwork problems and a lot to do with the low place accorded to sex research in the academic hierarchy (Reiss, 1967: 4). Sociologists, fund-granting agencies, publishers and public may all mirror the attitude of a society which devalues and casts suspicion on sex by adopting the same stance towards sex researchers. The person who elects to work in the field of sex becomes morally suspect. If this is true, a change in sexual attitudes in the broader society may be accompanied by the increased output of sex researchers.

The need for a sociology of sex

Whatever the reasons may be for this neglect of sex research in the past, the sociologist continues to ignore it at the peril of both society and his discipline.

On the one hand there is a pressing, practical need for greater understanding of sexual matters in order to resolve both the 'personal problems and public issues' that surround it (Mills, 1970: ch. 1).[4] There is undoubtedly much personal sexual suffering in this society – most of it untapped, and much of it agonizing to the individuals concerned. There are also undoubtedly huge moral and political debates concerning sexuality in this society – the future of marriage, sex education, pornography and censorship, birth control, sexism and feminism, abortion and sex offences, 'permissiveness' and so forth. All these problems are surrounded by such a veil of emotion, dogma, ignorance and blind prejudice that informed debate and humane help remain scarce, while personal suffering and public confusion remain abundant. While in other areas of life, the search for understanding through research is seen as a *sine qua non* of progress, in sexual matters it is decried as irrelevant, dehumanizing and pernicious.[5] I am sure, however, that such research is shunned at great cost.

On the other hand, the sociological analysis of sexuality should also be seen as a worthy subject in its own right and as an important contributor to general sociological theory. Quite apart from the need to describe and explain the multi-faceted nature of sexuality for its own sake, such study also touches upon all those matters that have been of a central and lasting concern to sociologists: the problems of the nature of sociological explanation, order, change and meaning. Theorizing about sexuality would thus have a pay-off in understanding such problems.

First, then, it may clarify the nature of sociological explanation. The problems in such an enterprise become most acute when one examines a phenomenon that is generally considered to be individualistic (organic, psychological). Durkheim's choice of suicide – an 'intensely personal act' – to demonstrate how social phenomena may be explained socially was hardly fortuitous. Likewise, with sexuality a subject is provided which is generally assumed to be a biological invariant with psychological consequences. Yet of all the biological properties of human life, sexuality is one of the most malleable and culturally variable. As Simon and Gagnon (1969: 734) write:

> Undeniably, sexuality is rooted in biological processes, capacities and even needs. But admitting this in no way provides for a greater degree of biological determinism than is true of other areas of corresponding interaction. Indeed, the reverse may be true: the sexual area may be precisely the realm wherein the superordinate position of the socio-cultural over the biological is most complete.

Such a statement gains support from those anthropological, historical and social research materials which indicate that the forms that sexual experiences take are socially organized as well as distributed. This does not deny the role of biological processes in understanding sexuality; on the contrary, the task is to develop detailed studies of the interrelationship between biological invariants of sexual experience and the socially organized forms that it takes. Sociological imperialism is as dangerous as biological tyranny. The problem, however, in developing theories about sexuality that attempt to integrate individual and social factors before an adequate understanding is arrived at of each component part, is the tendency for the field to become merely an eclectic hotchpotch of correlations where genuine theoretical understanding is overlooked. Such, at least, appears to be the plight of the indisciplinary approach to criminology in England, and it would be a pity if the eclectic discipline of 'sexology' moved in the same direction, as it appears to be doing in the United States. The sociological task requires that the sociologist demonstrates the social nature of sexuality while remaining sensitive to the boundaries imposed by biology and psychology.

A second central problem for sociologists is that of order and control, and sexuality is sometimes seen as playing an important part in this order. Either it is argued that through sexuality our social order is channelled, or it is argued that through social order our sexuality is channelled. These two views pose empirically divergent interpretations of sex.

The first view – that sexuality canalizes order – is heavily rooted in the Freudian and biological imagery of an all-powerful 'natural' erupting sexual drive which serves as a shaping influence in the social world. There is both a 'right-wing' and a 'left-wing' version of this view. The former holds that the all-powerful demon of sex needs strong societal regulation for order to be maintained, any chink in the armoury of control leading to rapid moral decay, sexual anarchy and the decline of civilization. In the academic literature such a view is found in the writings of Unwin (1934) and Sorokin (1956) and in the contemporary moral crusades in England of Whitehouse and Longford (Longford, 1972). The 'left-wing' view holds that the powerful drive could be a means of creative self-fulfilment if it was not twisted and repressed by an oppressive state for its own ends: the State regulates the powerful drive through the family in order to rigidify the personality system and render it subservient to the needs of the rulers. In the academic literature such a view is found in the writings of Marcuse (1969) and Reich (1969), and more popularly in the contemporary ideologies of the Gay and Women's Liberation Movements (Altman, 1971; Milligan, 1973). While the right wing sees sexuality as the demon within and the left wing sees sexuality as the great liberator, both credit sexuality with enormous – almost mystical – powers in contributing to social order. Sex becomes the central force upon which civilizations are built up and empires crashed down.

While such views see sexuality as shaping social order, some other theorists suggest that it is society which shapes and orders the sexual experience. In no society does sexuality exist in an inchoate, unstructured form; rather it becomes welded into a system of typifications which render it routinely experienced. As Gagnon and Simon remark (1968a: 121):

All too often the sexual impulse is conceived as a beast held in check only by the application of immense societal sanctions, and much that is both destructive and creative in the human experience is believed to arise from the tension between biological impulse and social contract. Thus the act of freeing the sexual impulse is thought of by some persons as increasing human freedom and by others as creating the conditions for social collapse. In this sense, we have overlooked the meanings and power of sexual acts, and what is likely to be discovered is that the significance of sexuality is exactly in proportion to its perceived significance; that is without the imagery of power and danger, the sexual impulse is no more potent than any other biological component.

This approach leads to a third problem of concern to most sociologists – that of 'meaning'. Indeed, for some it is the central problem of sociology: 'We must take the problem of objectively determining the social meanings of actions to the actors as the fundamental problems of sociology' (Douglas, 1971b: 38). In the sociology of sex, such meanings have not usually been a focus of analysis: rather the sociologist has set about his tasks assuming the everyday, commonsense definitions of sex as given. In his social book-keeping, he has assumed the meanings of sex, orgasm, love and the like; in his cross-cultural comparisons, he has assumed the comparability of 'masturbation', 'homosexuality' and the like; in his metatheorizing, he has taken a series of biological assumptions about man's sexuality and used them as a basis for his theorizing. Throughout the question of how an individual gives meaning to his sexuality has been evaded.

A fourth problem faced by most sociologists – past and present – is that of social change. A number of controversies exist here. First, there is the empirical problem of the nature of sexual change in recent times – some sociologists seeing little change in behaviour patterns over the past fifty years but much change in attitudes (Reiss, 1967; Gagnon and Simon, 1972), others seeing change in behaviour (Christensen and Gregg, 1970) and others envisaging astounding changes occurring or about to occur (Toffler, 1973). Second, there is the theoretical problem of explaining change – some seeing sexuality as a powerful source of change (especially through birth control), while others see sexual changes as the outcome of other societal changes. Third, there is the controversy over the consequences of changing sexuality – some seeing change as leading to the moral decline of society, others seeing it as liberating, and others seeing it as suffering from 'overkill' and saturation. Understanding sexuality as it is linked to social change will tell us a great deal not only about sexuality, but more importantly perhaps about social change.

For sociologists, then, there already exist a series of latent debates surrounding the key issues of sociological theory. On the problem of sociological explanation, some stress sexuality as a biological invariant while others stress its social malleability. On the problem of order, some see it as causal – as a powerful force in shaping society; while others see it as caused – as shaped by social situations. On the problem of meaning, some see it as unproblematic – assuming the meaning of sexuality to be invariable and absolute; while others see it as a social contract relative to time and place. And on the problem of change, some see it as the one great constant over time, others see it as miraculously undergoing rapid change; some see it as precipitating great changes, while others see it as being caused by other changes. In sum, while the sociology of sex may touch upon many great problems of social theory, the answers that have been given so far to these problems can only be seen as a theoretical sea of confusion. It is then from this 'sea of confusion' as well as the 'pressing practical problems' that a need for serious sociological work on matters sexual arises.

Some immediate tasks

Having rejected the view that the sociology of sex is a trivial, titillating indulgence far removed from central sociological concerns, and having been made aware of the paucity of serious work in this field, the sociologist is confronted with a field of seemingly infinite research possibilities. There is simply so much that needs to be done, and so little to build upon. Among the most pressing immediate tasks in building up a serious sociology of sex are the formulation of consistent sociological perspectives, the clarification of the questions that need to be asked through research, and the codification of existing research findings. Without perspectives, work will remain eclectic and unsophisticatedly empirical. Without the formulation of questions, there is no direction or purpose and the field will remain a grand jumble. And without sorting out the existing important findings, and placing them in developed frameworks, work will remain non-cumulative. These are obvious enough points, but points which have not been taken too seriously in the sociology of sex.

This book attempts to address these problems within one limited area of sexual analysis, that of 'deviance' or 'differentiation'. Although deviance can never be understood by divorcing the consensually acceptable from the privately variable, in this book my emphasis is placed upon understanding all those patterns of sexual conduct that occur outside of heterosexual coitus in wedlock. Calling such activities 'deviant' is indeed problematic, and as the argument unfolds it will be apparent that I prefer the terms 'differentiation' and 'variation', while simultaneously acknowledging that some forms of variation by virtue of being stigmatizable are usefully conceived of by sociologists as 'deviance'. Some kinds of sexual experience take on distinctive properties as a consequence of being stigmatizing. [. . .]

DEVIANCE, SEXUALITY AND THE INTERACTIONIST PERSPECTIVE

The interactionist approach to sexuality

The interactionist approach to sexuality takes as one of its fundamental concerns the problematic and socially constructed nature of sexual meanings. In doing this it stands in marked contrast to those accounts of sexuality that assume man's sexuality as able to 'translate itself into a kind of universal knowing or wisdom . . . the assumption that sexuality possesses a magical ability that allows biological drives to seek direct expression in psycho-social and social areas in ways that we do not expect in other biologically rooted behaviour' (Simon and Gagnon, 1969: 735). Such accounts assume a 'magical ability' that is commonly recognized and experienced as similar by society's members. Commonsense and research definitions alike frequently assume that 'everybody-knows-what-sex-is', that 'sex-as-we-know-it' exists independently of its social construction, and that when members talk about 'sex' the categories used are not problematic to the users. But such assumptions cannot be taken-for-granted by the interactionist: for him they become the central data.[6]

The model to be used here thus starts out from an 'open-ended' conception of man, in which he is only marginally restrained in his daily life by the tyranny of biological processes, and then sets about analysing the ways in which sexual meanings are constructed, modified, negotiated, negated and constrained in cojoint action with others. Kuhn, writing in a critique of the reductionist Kinsey approach to sexuality, summed up some of the key points of an interactionist perspective long ago (Kuhn, 1954: 123):

Sex acts, sexual objects, sexual partners (human or otherwise) like all other objects towards which human beings behave are *social objects*; that is they have meanings because meanings are assigned to them by the groups of which human beings are members for there is nothing in the physiology of man which gives any dependable clue as to what pattern of activity will be followed toward them. The meanings of these social objects are mediated to the individual by means of language just as in the case of all other social objects. That the communicators which involve these definition are frequently – at least in our society – surreptitious and characterized by a huge degree of innuendo does not in any wise diminish the truth of this assertion. In short, the sexual motives which human beings have are derived from the social roles they play; like all other motives these would not be possible were not the actions physiologically possible, but the physiology does not supply the motives, designate the partners, invest the objects with preformed passion, nor even dictate the objectives to be achieved.

Drawing from the previous discussion on interactionism, it will be apparent that the interests of clinicians are very different from those of interactionists. Where the clinician highlights man's physiology, interactionism stresses his consciousness and symbol-manipulating ability: 'drives' become subservient to 'meanings'. Where the clinician highlights fairly permanent sexual structures awaiting 'release', the interactionist analyses the often precarious, always emergent task of constructing and modifying sexual meanings: determinism becomes subservient to man's intentionality and points of choice. Where the clinician views sexuality as an independent variable, the interactionist sees it as a dependent variable – one shaped through conjoint action: the social context becomes central for comprehending sexuality as it is commonly experienced in everyday life.

Such a perspective, potentially most illuminating, has been hampered by a lack of empirical research. There are few studies that have inquired into the content of sexual meanings; and knowledge of their forms, nature and range is virtually non-existent. Similarly, little is known about the sources used for building up sexual meanings, and only fractionally more about the learning process involved in the transmission of them. Nor are there studies that attempt to definite the boundaries for constructing sexual meanings – can it really be assumed that man is infinitely plastic, or are there limits to his capacity to develop sexual meanings? Are there deeply regulative rules of sexuality? How are meanings negated, normalized and manipulated in social contexts? Why does any given actor come to hold his particular definition of sexuality and not another? In the absence of detailed information on these points, the following brief discussion is only exploratory and suggestive of a massive research programme.

The nature of sexual meanings

The fundamental axiom of the interactionist approach is simply put: *nothing is sexual but naming makes it so. Sexuality is a social construction learnt in interaction with others.* This is not, of course, to deny the existence of genitals, copulation or orgasms as biological and universal 'facts'; it is simply to assert the sociological commonplace that these things do not have 'sexual meanings' in their own right: these have to be bestowed upon them through social encounters. The 'mind' has to define something as 'sexual' before it is sexual in its consequences. As a simple illustration of this, two extreme cases may be cited: the first involves a woman lying naked while a man fingers her vagina, the second involves a boy watching a football match. If one was asked as an external observer to define which situation was sexual

– by 'universalist, commonsense' definitions – there would be little to query. The first was sexual, the second was not. However, if one ignored the purely behavioural aspects and focused upon the meanings that the actors give to the situation, quite a different picture may emerge. For the man fingering the woman may be shown to be a doctor involved in a vaginal examination; and both actors may have produced clear definitions of the situation as being a medical one (Emerson, 1970; Henslin and Biggs, 1971); while the boy watching the football match may be busily involved in defining the boys playing football as sexual objects, imagining them in sexual acts, and interpreting internal sensations as sexual ones.

This is a very simple example, and there are some obvious difficulties with it – for example, in a vaginal examination members have to work hard to neutralize the 'sexual' elements and thus it may well be that whenever genitals come into a situation, actors associate them with sex unless they can neutralize such meanings away.[7] These real problems notwithstanding, the example could be multiplied many times to make the general point that sexual meanings have to be negotiated and are often problematic.

When a child plays with its genitals, is this 'sexual'? When a person excretes is this sexual? When a man kisses another man publicly, is this sexual? When a couple are naked together, is this sexual? When a girl takes her clothes off in public, is this sexual? When a lavatory attendant wipes down a toilet seat, is this sexual? When a boy has an erection climbing a tree, is this sexual? When a morgue attendant touches a dead body, is this sexual? When a social worker assists her client, is this sexual? When a man and woman copulate out of curiosity or out of duty, is this sexual? The list could be considerably extended; but the point I hope is made. Most of the situations above could be defined as sexual by members; they need not be. Sexual meanings are not universal absolutes, but ambiguous and problematic categories.

A few instances of this problematic nature may be developed here. Thus, for example, a child playing with its genitals may often be linked in adults' minds with sexual experiences it remains unaware of: one of Freud's errors was to equate the sexual meanings constructed by adult men with those of children. What for man may assume the proportion of a learnt sensation of sexual excitement may for the child initially resemble no more than simple bodily play and exploration. There can be little doubt that children both do 'sexual things' (Broderick, 1966) and have 'sexual things' done to them (Gagnon, 1965); but this does not mean that they automatically 'feel' and 'recognize' these experiences in the ways that adults do. Genital play and indecent assault may both be experienced by the child in a totally 'non-sexual' way, because the child has not yet been fully socialized into the motives and feelings that adults routinely come to associate with sexuality: thus the child is merely 'playing', 'being attacked' or 'playing with an adult'. Whatever meanings people come to associate with sexuality, they are always learnt and constructed meanings (Mills, 1940).

This error is also made when considering the sexuality of other cultures and other historical epochs. It cannot be assumed – it is a task for research – that the ancient Greeks' experience of homosexuality was in any way at all like that which we call homosexuality today (Eglinton, 1971), or that the Eskimos' form of wife-exchange can be likened to the contemporary 'wife-swapping, swinging' scene in America (Bartell, 1971). Such assumptions are frequently and quite unjustifiably made in many discussions of sexuality – both lay and academic. Homosexuals, for example, who make a claim to their homosexuality on the grounds that 'the ancient Greeks did it' really highlight the danger of this kind of approach. That sexual meanings change quite dramatically can be found by any brief review of photographic pornography over the past hundred years or so. Positions, postures, 'sexy dress' and so forth change quite rapidly – so as to render what was once 'highly sexy' even ten years ago almost comic, and certainly not 'sexy'. Further, the gamut of sexual meanings in our culture has probably changed dramatically since the advent of Freudian symbolism: a tree used to be a tree, now it is a phallic symbol.

The social sources of sexual meanings

Rather than sexuality determining our social being – as many writers suggest, especially Freudian ones – it is the other way round: social meanings determine and affect our sexuality. Sexuality has no meaning other than that given to it in social situations. The forms and the contents of sexual meanings are another cultural variable, and why certain meanings are learnt and not others is problematic. One important implication of this perspective is the need to analyse sexual activity in our culture for its social origins, the ways in which social experiences become translated into sexual ones. Much sexual behaviour may have 'non-sexual' sources: the health-food faddist may take sex at prescribed regular intervals in the same way as health foods and for the same purpose; the married couple may regularly have sexual activity because they believe the other expects it of them, even when neither wants it; the prostitute employs sex as a means of earning a living – as does the stripper;[8] the man may seek a flow of regular sexual partners in the belief that this may sustain his public image of masculinity; and the student may masturbate out of habit or out of an association with tension-reduction. In each case, sexual experiences are constructed from social motives and settings. Gagnon and Simon (1968b: 28) in one discussion on homosexuality in the prison setting suggest that:

What is occurring in the prison situation for both males and females is not a problem of sexual release, but rather the use of sexual relationships in the service of creating a community of relationships for satisfying needs for which the prison community fails to provide in any other forms. For the male prisoner homosexuality serves as a source of affection, as a source of validation for masculinity, or a source of protection from the problems of institutional life.

Here sex is not merely a 'release' used to structure experiences; rather, the 'sexual world' is itself fashioned by the social needs of the individual. These needs may be centred around the quest for relationships, for validation of gender, or as part of an occupational task. [. . .]

The range of sexual meanings[9]
The ambiguity, relativity and modifiability of each individual actor's socially constructed sexual meanings leads to a seem-

ingly infinite potentiality for the bestowal of such meanings on any object. Having dispensed tentatively with an 'absolute' essentialist definition of sexuality, it is necessary to explore the range of sexual meanings held by actors. In this section my aim is to highlight some of the meanings found in this culture (though there can obviously be no claim to exhaustiveness or systematization in this),[10] while in a subsequent section my aim will be to explain some of the constraints placed upon their construction.

Some current sexual meanings: Presumably, largely as a heritage of the Judaeo-Christian culture, one of the most commonsensical and publicly acknowledged sexual meanings is the *utilitarian one of procreation*: sex is linked intrinsically to processes of child production. Yet, strangely, while this may be a publicly verbalized meaning, it may be statistically the least important and most defunct meaning to actors. Indeed, in some cultures – the Trobrianders studied by Malinowski, for example – it is possible for members to make no mental connection between acts of copulation and procreation (Malinowski, 1929). While it remains a task for research, a suspicion should be voiced that 'sex-as-a-means-of-having-children' as a privatized sexual meaning is statistically unusual. Some recent writers[11] have noted this by distinguishing between procreative and non-procreative sex, suggesting a move in contemporary patterns away from the former towards the latter. In fact, I suspect that throughout history and across cultures it has been rare for individual actors to hold private 'utilitarian' sexual meanings (even when verbalizing them publicly).[12] This view stands in contrast to the 'global, commonsense' views that sexuality, procreation and the family unit are intrinsically linked; and leads to a view which sees sexuality as autonomous from these realms, and open to a wider range of meanings. Some of these I wish to look at briefly.

Perhaps the most significant of these is the *erotic meaning of sexuality*, summed up in everyday language as 'being turned on', 'feeling randy' and 'feeling sexy'. It is a meaning of 'pleasure' constructed to interpret sensations of internal physiological (usually genital) changes 'triggered off' by some stimulus in the outer world. These stimuli seem to have an infinite range; this is most likely to be a member of the opposite sex – but there are many other possibilities. Items of clothing, particular kinds of 'action', books, music, animals and so forth may all trigger erotic meanings for some actors under some situations. Some actors may find a wide range of stimuli which 'turn them on', while others may find few or even none. The research problem here is to analyse how sexual meanings of this kind become attached to variant objects.

Such meanings are generally associated with overt behavioural forms such as masturbation, coitus and orgasm; but they need not be. Further, they are likely to include a number of related components – some 'erotic meanings' are tinged with meanings of 'dirt and filth', others with 'guilt and shame', others with 'danger and excitement', others with 'power and assertiveness'. Moreover such meanings may well be manipulated differently by different socio-economic groupings – if Bernstein's thesis is right, it may well be that middle-class groups are susceptible to a wider range of stimuli for interpretation because of their greater ability at manipulating symbols generally.

These are all issues that need detailed consideration, and I am not arguing that 'erotic meanings' are capable of being captured and bottled in a one-dimensional way. I am merely hinting at one broad category which itself displays a wide range.

Another range of meanings that may be linked with sexuality (and which are themselves clearly linked with the erotic ones described above) could be called *romantic meanings*, caught in phrases like 'he's dreamy', 'I'm in love', 'he gives me goose-pimples'.[18] Such meanings may be publicly declared and announced or they may be secretly pondered upon. This latter category seems to correspond with the privatized sexual meanings discussed by Zetterberg (1966), who suggests the prevalence of a neglected stratification dimension – privatized feelings of emotional overcomeness, demonstrates how their existence may vary in different social contexts and explores some of the dynamics involved in such stratification. According to Zetterberg, most actors may be seen as possessing an erotic ranking – 'the secretly kept probability that he can induce an emotional overcomeness among persons of the opposite sex' – and much tacit interaction in everyday life may be viewed in terms of a secretive ranking and estimating process. An important component of the meanings that Zetterberg discusses flows from their privatized and secretive nature. Making such meanings public dramatically alters the nature of the social relationship; the secret and romantic longing for Johnny becomes a ritualized courtship once the secret is broken and an encounter embarked upon (cf. Aubert, 1965: 201).

A third range of meanings may be seen as linked with *matters of gender*. The very word 'sex' is frequently used as a synonym for 'gender', yet the meaning of sex here, while linked with the others, cannot be equated with them. Garfinkle's discussion of Agnes the hermaphrodite confronted with problems of passing as a 'normal-sexed person' is perhaps the clearest example of research that attempts to stipulate and discuss the socially constructed nature of sexual meanings. For most members of society, sexuality exists as a matter of objective, institutionalized, taken-for-granted knowledge – as a 'natural phenomenon'. Agnes also perceives the world in this way, but through her peculiar location in the social structure as a person of dubious gender identity, she is confronted regularly with situations in which her gender becomes problematic. She thus comes to possess 'uncommonsense knowledge of social structures' through her position as a passing deviant. It is just this kind of knowledge which the researcher needs to possess in the whole spectrum of sexual meanings, and just this kind of knowledge that he currently lacks (Garfinkle, 1967: ch. 5). Apart from analysing some of the problematic situations of passing, which are confronted by Agues – her management of beach attire, dating, sharing flats with girl-friends, visiting hospitals – Garfinkle also presents a ten-point statement on the properties of 'natural, normal sexed persons . . . from the standpoint of adult members of our society'. While there are question marks hanging over his methods, studies of meanings similar to this are crucial to advancing our knowledge in this field.

One further range of sexual meanings could be termed *symbolic*. Here sexuality is seen as a symbol or as being manifested in a symbolic form – it does not have to be seen as procreative, provoke inner feelings of 'sexiness', highlight gender differences, or be infused with notions of love, though it can of course be linked to any of these. Such symbolism may take many forms. In the past it has often been associated with religion and worship, and a number of objects from the male phallus to snakes and food were given a sexual meaning (Ellis and Abarbanel, 1961). Sometimes it has been associated with 'nature' (Watts, 1958). And, since Freud especially, some sexual meanings have become located in a truly diverse range of secular activities from hard work to stealing. While much of this symbolic work may be linked explicitly with the previous categories, some of it exists quite independently of it.

Now these five broad categories – utilitarian, erotic, romantic, gender and symbolic – highlight variations and contrasts in what can be taken for granted in daily used sexual meanings. Such meanings often overlap with each other – a gender meaning may provide many clues as to appropriate erotic and romantic meanings (Kagan, 1964; Simon and Gagnon, 1969), the boy seeing sexuality as linked to aggression and the girl to romance. Further, this brief discussion has not attempted to cover all possible sexual meanings. Two more come to mind from the pages of the journal *Social Problems*: an article (Foote, 1954) suggests that sex is assuming the meaning of 'play', and a later article (Lewis and Brissett, 1967), which, after reviewing marriage manuals, concludes that sex has become 'an activity permeated with the qualities of work'. Many other categories could be added to the above, and in the long run of course it will not be sufficient to simply list the categories of sexual meanings that people construct; analyses will have to be made of the rules used for constructing such meanings and organizing sexual life.

The constraints on sexual meanings

The picture which has so far emerged, and which underlies the interactionist approach to sexuality, is one in which human sexuality is capable of exceptional flexibility and variety and in which man possesses considerable ability at manipulating and developing a wide range of sexual meanings and symbols.

Certainly there is growing historical and cross-cultural evidence of the enormous range, in intensity, incidence, and content, of man's (and woman's) sexuality between groups and cultures. This malleability will thus be taken as axiomatic throughout the book.

But the interactionist's commitment to flexibility and open-endedness should not be taken to imply, as I have commented earlier, a total freedom from constraints. Man may possess a potential for the manipulation of sexual meanings but at many points his 'choice' becomes narrowed, routinized and restricted by a number of factors. It is the task of the interactionist to study these constraints, just as much as it is his task to study the emergent and creative aspects of social life. I cannot deal at any length with such large issues requiring detailed interdisciplinary analysis, but will raise briefly three sets of variables that merit consideration in any discussion of the constraints placed upon man's sexual plasticity. These three variables are (a) biological, (b) cultural and (c) interactive.

(a) *Biological constraints:* An important distinction to make here is between those biological explanations of sexuality which mystify by using obscure reified notions such as 'sexual drives', 'sexual instincts' and 'libido', and those more tangible medical accounts which explore the role of hormones, brain structures, nervous systems, sexual morphology and genetics in the development of sexuality. While the former hinder interactionist understanding, the latter aid it.

The most general biological explanation of sexuality resides in notions of 'instinct'. Now the history of social science can, in one sense, be seen as an ongoing struggle to rescue man from such explanations which constantly reduce him to the level of animals and which constantly stress his instincts as the basis for his action. At one time, every form of human behaviour could be interpreted by evoking the notion of an instinct, but today this status is reserved for a very limited range of man's social activities, with sex to the fore. Now the central point about man's social life – as contrasted with sub-human species – is that it is a symbolic life. This means that man's sexual feelings constantly have to be placed in the context of his symbolic interpretation of them: he does not just act on the basis of biological forces pushing him from within to behave in certain ways; rather he constantly sets about interpreting inner feelings, and making sense of the world around him. To talk of man as having a sexual instinct is a crude reification of a complex symbolic process: rather he has a biological capacity (in the same way as he may have a biological capacity for aggression or cognitive development) which is capable of great variation as he moves and manipulates his symbolic environment. The notion of a drive or instinct builds into the whole idea of sexuality a strength to control human life that I suspect it simply cannot have. It is partly for this reason that a number of psychologists have recently preferred the concept of 'appetite', or 'capacity' to depict the overall biological basis of sexuality (Hardy, 1964; Whalen, 1966; Wright, 1970). Such a concept captures the malleability of sexuality so essential to the interactionist viewpoint.

Many biologists do not simply talk of an instinct – rather they perceive it as a high-pressure drive constituting a closed energy system subject to the laws of the conservation of energy. Such a position is clearly to the fore in Freud's conception of the personality as a complex, intricate but closed energy system in which the libido serves as one great source of energy, which if not channelled into sexual activity will be channelled elsewhere. It is also to be found in Reich's discovery of 'orgone energy', capable of being measured in the orgone accumulator and appearing as a pale blue liquid! Sociologists such as Davis and Polsky also seem to view sexuality as a powerful drive.

The belief, in its crudest terms, suggests that the sexual energy is an absolute force which, if not allowed to manifest itself in its 'natural' state, will break out into other areas of life. Two key concepts here are *repression* and *sublimation*. Thus if 'absolute sexuality' does not develop 'naturally', the energy may be *repressed* – in which case deviations and neuroses are likely to occur through the damming up of libidinal energy; or *sublimation* may arise – in which case libidinal energy may become the source of extra energy in work, especially in such benevolent occupations as nursing, teaching and social work. There are other mechanisms by which the energy may be diverted from its original sexual goal. Freud and others thereby encourage a search for the underlying sexual basis of much social behaviour – one becomes very sceptical of the apparently sexless person and imputes to him all manner of sublimation techniques. Now the concepts of sublimation (along with its recent counterpart 'repressive desublimation'), repression and the libido are all unproven assumptions, which have been absorbed into the 'taken-for-granted' notions of sexuality. They remain 'hypotheses', not 'facts', and if one looks for evidence, there is little that does not hinge around polemics. Two simple hypotheses may be deduced from the broad assumption of an energy system: (1) if a man has little sexual outlet, he must be repressing or sublimating his desires in some manner – and consequently, most likely, exhibiting some form of neurosis; (2) if a man has much sexual outlet, his energy must be sapped away from other things – he is unlikely to be creative, active or productive. In the first case, one wonders what the man can be doing with his sexuality, where it is being sapped to; and, in the second, one becomes concerned with the man's ability to perform well in other spheres of life. For both hypotheses, there is little evidence. The work of Kinsey, however, does suggest that individuals with a high degree of sexual activity can be 'of considerable significance socially' – one of his most sexually active respondents was a 'scholarly and skilled lawyer' who 'averaged over thirty [orgasms] a week for thirty years' (Kinsey, 1948: 195); and others have suggested that 'no genuine tissue or biological needs' are generated by a lack of sexual activity (Beech, in Wright, 1970: 233). The whole area then is one open for empirical debate.

The scepticism which interactionists pour upon mystificatory 'instincts' becomes much less pronounced when applied to specific biological mechanisms such as hormones and nervous systems. These must of course be viewed in relationship with interpretative processes – a hormone may provide a sensation, but it cannot in itself provide a meaning – but the fact that they play a central role is not denied. Simon and Gagnon (1969: 13), interactionists who work harder than most to discredit instinct theorists, comment:

There is much evidence that the early male sexual impulses – initially through masturbation – are linked to physiological changes, to high hormonal inputs during puberty. This produces an organism that, to put it simply, is more easily turned on. Male adolescents report frequent erections, often without apparent stimulation of any kind. Even so, though there is greater biological sensitisation and hence masturbation is more likely, the meanings, organisation, and continuance of this activity still tends to be subordinate to social and psychological factors.

Here the authors refer specifically to 'hormonal input', but other biological factors could also serve as the basis for the social organization of meanings. The nervous system, for example, may provide internal sensations that are innately pleasurable – but the actor has to 'learn' to ascribe meaning to these sensations. The external sexual morphology similarly provides a series of 'cues' as to appropriate gender behaviour, but the actor has to build up appropriate interpretative responses. In each case, a biological foundation provides a source for building up appropriate sexual meanings. But the biological foundation in itself tells us little about the meanings bestowed. And, in cases where there may be cultural confusions about appropriate meanings, or cases where there are biological anomalies not capable of immediate translation, the problematic nature of sexual meanings becomes more apparent.

(b) *Cultural constraints:* While there may be important restrictions placed upon man's sexual capacity by biological factors, cultural constraints are clearly more significant from the point of view of sociologists. As Berger and Luckmann (1967: 67) say:

While man possesses sexual drives that are comparable to those of the other higher mammals, human sexuality is characterised by a very high degree of pliability. It is not only relatively independent of temporal rhythms, it is pliable both in the objects towards which it may be directed and in its modalities of expression. Ethnological evidence shows

that, in sexual matters, man is capable of almost anything
... At the same time, of course, human sexuality is directed,
sometimes rigidly structured, in every particular culture.
Every culture has a distinctive sexual configuration, with
its own specialised patterns of sexual conduct and its own
'anthropological' assumptions in the sexual area. The
empirical relativity of these configurations, their immense
variety, and luxurious inventiveness, indicate that they are
the products of man's own socio-cultural formations rather
than of a biologically fixed human nature.

Man, then, is born into a pre-existing 'sexual world' with
its own laws, norms, values, meanings, typifications on the
cultural level, and its own relationships on the structural level.
This 'world' exists independently of any specific actor, confronts him as massively real, and exerts a tacit power over
him. [. . .] It must be cautioned that I do not propose to
substitute a reified cultural determinism for a reified biological
determinism. The constraints exist but they are not of a simple,
direct nature. [. . .] Each society develops its own configuration of sexual meanings, but actors do not rudely encounter
them. Rather, they are built up by actors in a highly intricate
interactive process over the lifespan. An important set of
constraints on sexual manipulation will thus be the interactive
ones.

(c) *Interactive constraints:* Central to interactionism is a
sensitivity to the potentially enormous range of sexual meanings available to an actor and an awareness of their constantly
negotiated character. Yet it remains an unreal picture if
adequate weight is not also given to the constraints that are
built into action through day-to-day encounters over the lifespan. Such constraints serve to narrow down, restrict, routinize
and order the range of sexual meanings experienced by an
individual. They may be such as to almost totally eliminate
any sexual meanings from an actor's world – as in the portrait
given of an Irish island called Inis Beag (Messenger, 1971).
They may be such as to sensitize an individual to an almost
inexhaustible supply of sexual meanings – as in the case in the
'culture of civility' of San Francisco (Becker and Horowitz,

1970). But, whichever extreme, the sexual world of an individual is never totally emergent – it is also constrained, partially by biology, partially by 'culture', but centrally by interaction itself.

. . . While it is a stimulating picture to imagine man facing each new interactive encounter as if for the first time and evolving new solutions and new meanings, I stressed that this was absurd and false. Through interaction he builds up *commitments, perspectives, 'world-taken-for-granted views'* and a *stable self-conception*, all of which lend a precarious stability to his social world. Such interactive constraints also play a key part in the stabilization of his sexual world. He faces 'problematic sexual situations' and evolves 'perspectives'; he becomes attached to the values of some groups and not others; he comes to view himself as a particular kind of 'sexual being' (or 'non-sexual' being); and he develops a rudimentary, dimly sensed world-view of sexuality. All of these remain subject to constant modification as he encounters new experiences, and faces 'turning points'. But they also serve to restrict his perceived range of alternative choices.[14]

Conclusion

This chapter has outlined some of the problems that an interactionist approach to sexuality raises. What are the kinds of sexual meanings available? How are they constructed? What constraints are placed upon them? These and other questions constitute a large, almost completely unexplored, research programme; and the comments made in this chapter have only been exploratory and suggestive of some paths that could be taken. [. . .]

Notes

1. The interested reader will find useful preliminary statements on the history of sex research in the work of Ellis and Abarbanel (1961), Ehrmann (1964), Brecher (1970) and Sagarin (1971a). A useful compendium of earlier statements is Krich (1963), and a somewhat curious 'Introductory Guide to the Study of Sexual Behaviour' listing thirty-two 'fundamental volumes' is to be found

in Marshall and Suggs (1971).

2. The neglect of sociological perspectives on sexuality needs fuller documentation, but in 1967 Reiss could comment that there were only sixteen sociologists in America heavily involved in the field (Reiss, 1967: 2). The number in England is considerably smaller than this. For example, a review of the 1968 BSA Sociological Register in England (with some four hundred entries) showed nobody who specified human sexuality as a research interest. Likewise, an analysis of the major sociological journals published in England revealed few references to sexuality, and a later analysis did not include sexuality as a variable to be considered (Collinson and Webber, 1971). Further, a review of *Sociology in Britain* by Krausz (1969) makes no reference to sex in the contents or index – though it does devote a few pages to Schofield's important but non-sociological work, and makes passing reference to Comfort. Recently, however, productivity in the field of the sociology of sex has increased – a number of members, for instance, of the National Deviancy Conference of York mention sexuality in the handbook of members' interests. And likewise the literature in America seems to have noticeably increased – quantitatively and qualitatively – in the past few years.

3. For documentation on some of the problems involved in sex research, the reader could consult the work of Bell (1966), Reiss (1967), Marshall and Suggs (1971), Pomeroy (1972) and Douglas (1972).

4. Little has been written on the resolution of practical sexual problems through either social policy or interpersonal intervention, but recent samples of such analysis may be found in Gochros and Schultz (1972) and Resnik and Wolfgang (1972).

5. See for example the diatribe by Holbrook (1972: esp. ch. 8). While I am in sympathy with the broad principles of phenomenology that pervade this work, much of his analysis is dangerously ill-founded. For example, he condemns the Masters and Johnson research as dehumanizing and objectifying. If his condemnation is accepted, the same charge may be levied at all medicine. Medical research into cancer, subnormality and brain disorders are by the same accounts dehumanizing. As is so frequently the case, Holbrook provides one set of criteria to sex, and another to everything else.

6. For example, Chall defined sex as 'the actions of human beings to accomplish sexual union between the male and the female' in 1961 (Ellis and Abarbanel, 1961: 25) and more recently Gebhard defines sexual behaviour as 'those movements, vocalisation, and reactions directly concerned with causing the physiological

responses which constitute, in part, sexual arousal and which – if continued – would ordinarily result in orgasm' (Marshall and Suggs, 1971: 251). These may be helpful as operational definitions, but they also obscure the problem of knowing what sex is.

7. Such a problem leads me to the tentative hypothesis that there are deeply regulative rules surrounding sexuality that link it very firmly to the genitals.

8. Skipper and McCaghy (1970; 1971); McCaghy and Skipper (1969) locate homosexuality among 'strippers' in the occupational structure of stripping and not in the personality structure. They write: 'We found that homosexual behaviour was an important aspect of the culture which apparently stemmed less from any predisposition of the participants than from contingencies of the occupation' (1969: 264). Thus, here the occupation gives the meaning to homosexuality; see also Stewart (1972).

9. The following discussion raises a very important research area worthy of much detailed research. My comments are severely limited, and merely exploratory.

10. A useful introduction to this area is Turner (1970: 319–25), though he uses very different categories: physiological, sacred, secular, serious and casual interpersonal meanings.

11. See the discussion on the 'institutional form of autonomous sexuality' by Sprey (1969).

12. Sjvall (1970: 121) writes: 'Human sexuality is a means of expressing and satisfying individual needs for safety and/or intimacy; on rare occasions such behaviour will also fulfil procreative functions.' See also Kinsey's discussion on total sexual outlet and sexual outlet in marriage (Kinsey *et al.*, 1948; 1953). Note that if it is true that 'sex-as-procreation' is statistically rare, then if a statistical definition of deviancy is accepted (Becker, 1963: ch. 1), then sex-as-procreation becomes deviance. It is ironic that those who use the statistical notions of deviancy are also probably those who see procreative sex as the only normal sex!

13. It is notable that these phrases are put into the feminine person. In the past, I suspect for males sexual meanings have meant *erotic meanings* and for females they have meant *romantic meanings*.

14. There may also be interactive constraints set by 'deeply regulative rules'. The notion of 'deep structures' is borrowed here very loosely from Chomsky and Cicourel's work. In the same way as the capacity for grammatical speech is somehow 'in' the brain, and the grammatical patterns of all languages may be reducible to a finite series of rules – a 'universal grammar' – which locate the principles of all particular grammars, it may well be that the

capacity for sexuality is somehow 'in' the genitals, and there is only a limited finite range of variations possible: a 'universal sexual grammar'.

References

Altman, D. (1971), *Homosexual Oppression and Liberation*, New York: Outerbridge & Dienstfrey.

Aubert, V. (1965), *The Secret Society*, New Jersey: Bedminster.

Bartell, G. D. (1971), *Group Sex: A Scientist's Eyewitness Account of the American Way of Swinging*, New York: P. H. Wyden.

Becker, H. S. (1963), *Outsiders: Studies in the Sociology of Deviance*, London: Macmillan.

Becker, H. S., and Horowitz, I. L. (1970), 'The Culture of Civility', *Trans-Action*, April, pp. 12–19.

Bell, R. R. (1966), *Premarital Sex in a Changing Society*, New Jersey: Prentice-Hall.

Berger, P. L., and Luckmann, T. (1967), *The Social Construction of Reality*, London: Allen Lane: Penguin Press.

Brecher, E. M. (1970), *The Sex Researchers*, London: Andre Deutsch.

Broderick, C. B. (1966), 'Sexual Behaviour of Pre-Adolescents', *Journal of Social Issues*, 22, pp. 6–12.

Christensen, H. T., and Gregg, C. F. (1970), 'Changing Sex Norms in America and Scandinavia', *Journal of Marriage and Family Living*, 32, pp. 611–28.

Christenson, C. V. (1971), *Kinsey: A Biography*, Bloomington: Indiana University Press [4, 211].

Collinson, P., and Webber, S. (1971), 'British Sociology, 1950–70', *Sociological Review*, 19, 521–41.

Douglas, J. D. (1971), *American Social Order: Social Rules in a Pluralistic Society*, London: Collier-Macmillan.

Douglas, J. D. (ed.) (1972), *Research on Deviance*, London: Random House.

Eglinton, J. (1971), *Greek Love* (2nd ed.), London: Spearman.

Ellis, A., and Abarbanel, A. (1961), *The Encyclopaedia of Sexual Behaviour*, 2 vols, New York: Hawthorn Books.

Emerson, J. P. (1970), 'Behaviour in Private Places: Sustaining Definitions of Reality and Gynaecological Examinations'.

Farberow, N. L. (ed.) (1963), *Taboo Topics*, New York: Atheling Books, Atherton Press.

Foote, N. N. (1954), 'Sex as Play', *Social Problems*, 1, pp. 159–63.

Gagnon, J. H. (1965), 'Sexuality and Sexual Learning in the Child', *Psychiatry*, 28, pp. 212–28.

Gagnon, J. H., and Simon, W. S. (1968a), 'Sexual Deviance in Contemporary America', *Annals of the American Academy of Political and Social Science*, 376, pp. 107–22.

Gagnon, J. H., and Simon, W. S. (1968b), 'The Social Meaning of Prison Homosexuality', *Federal Probation 1968*, 32, pp. 23–9.

Gagnon, J. H., and Simon, W. S. (1972), 'Prospects for Change in American Sexual Patterns', in Streib, G. F., *op. cit.* [7, 208].

Garfinkle, H. (1967), *Studies in Ethnomethodology*, New Jersey: Prentice-Hall.

Gochros, H., and Schultz, L. G. (1972), *Human Sexuality and Social Work*, New York: Association Press.

Hardy, K. R. (1964), 'An Appetitional Theory of Sexual Motivation', *Psychological Review*, 71, pp. 1–18.

Henslin, J. M., and Biggs, M. A. (1971), 'Dramaturgical Desexualisation: The Sociology of the Vaginal Examination'.

Holbrook, D. (1972), *Sex and Dehumanization*, London: Pitman.

Hooker, E. (1963), 'Male Homosexuality', in Farberow, *op. cit.*

Kagan, J. (1964), 'Acquisition and Significance of Sex Typing and Sex Role Identity', in Hoffman, M. L., and Hoffman, L. W. (eds), *Child Development Research* (vol. 1), New York: Russell Sage Foundation.

Kinsey, A. C., Gebhard, P., Pomeroy, W. B., and Martin, C. E. (1953), *Sexual Behaviour in the Human Female*, Philadelphia: W. B. Saunders.

Kinsey, A. C., Pomeroy, W. B., and Martin, C. E. (1948), *Sexual Behaviour in the Human Male*, Philadelphia: W. B. Saunders.

Krausz, E. (1969), *Sociology in Britain*, London: Batsford.

Krich, A. (ed.) (1963), *The Sexual Revolution* (2 vols.), New York: Delta Paperbacks.

Kuhn, M. H. (1954), 'Kinsey's View on Human Behaviour', *Social Problems*, 1, pp. 119–25.

Lewis, L. S., and Brissett, D. (1967), 'Sex as Work: A Study of Avocational Counselium', *Social Problems*, 13, pp. 8–18.

Longford, Earl of (1972), *Pornography: The Longford Report*, London: Hodder Paperbacks.

Malinowski, B. (1929), *The Sexual Life of Savages in North Western Melanesia*, New York: Liveright.

Marcuse, H. (1969), *Eros and Civilisation*, London: Sphere Books.

Marshall, D. S., and Suggs, R. C. (1971), *Human Sexual Behaviour*, London: Basic Books.

McCaghy, C. M., & Skipper, J. K. (1969), 'Lesbian Behaviour as an Adaptation to the Occupation of Stripping', *Social Problems*, 17, 262–70.

Sexual stigma: an interactionist account

Messenger, J. C. (1971), 'Sex and Repression in an Irish Folk Community', in Marshall, D. S., and Suggs, R. C., *op. cit.*

Milligan, D. (1973), *The Politics of Homosexuality*, London: Pluto Press Pamphlet.

Mills, C. W. (1940), 'Situated Actions and Vocabularies of Motive', *American Sociological Review*, 5, pp. 904–13.

Mills, C. W. (1970), *The Sociological Imagination*, Harmondsworth: Penguin Books.

Pomeroy, W. B. (1972), *Dr Kinsey and the Institute for Sex Research*, London: Thomas Nelson.

Reich, W. (1969), *The Sexual Revolution: Toward a Self Governing Character Structure* (4th rev. ed.), New York: Farrar, Straus.

Reiss, I. L. (1967), *The Social Context of Premarital Sexual Permissiveness*, New York: Holt, Rinehart & Winston.

Resnik, N. L. P., and Wolfgang, M. (1972), *Sexual Behaviors*, Boston: Little, Brown and Co.

Sagarin, E. (1971), 'An Overview of Sex Research' in J. M. Henslin (ed), *Studies in the Sociology of Sex*, New York: Appleton-Century-Crofts.

Simon, W., and Gagnon, J. H. (1969), 'Psychosexual Development', *Trans-Action*, March, pp. 9–17.

Sjvall, I. (1970), 'Reproduction and Sexuality', in Ciba Foundation Symposia, ed. Elliot, K., *The Family and Its Future*, London.

Skipper, J. K., and McCaghy, C. M. (1970), 'Stripteasers: the Anatomy and Career Contingencies of a Deviant Occupation', *Social Problems*, 17, 391–405.

Sorokin, P. (1956), *The American Sex Revolution*, Massachusetts: Porter Sargent–Extending Horizons.

Sprey, J. (1969), 'On the Institutionalisation of Sexuality', *Journal of Marriage and Family*, 31, 432–40.

Stewart, G. L. (1972), 'On First Being a John', *Urban Life and Culture*, 1, 225–74.

Toffler, A. (1973), *Future Shock*, London: Bodley Head.

Turner, R. H. (1970), Family Interaction, London: Wiley & Sons.

Unwin, J. D. (1934), *Sex and Culture*, London: Oxford U.P.

Watts, A. W. (1958), *Nature, Man and Woman: A New Approach to Sexual Experience*, London: Thames & Hudson.

Whalen, R. E. (1966), 'Sexual Motivation', *Psychological Review*, 73, pp. 151–63.

Wright, D. (1970), 'Sex Instinct or Appetite', *New Society*.

Zetterberg, H. L. (1966), 'The Secret Ranking', *Journal of Marriage and Family Life*, 28, pp. 134–42.

7. Working-class criminology

Jock Young

Those who have wished to emphasize the sober constitutional ancestry of the working-class movement have sometimes minimized its more robust and rowdy features. All
that we can do is to bear the warning in mind. We need
more studies of the social attitudes of criminals, of soldiers,
and sailors, of tavern life; and we should look at the
evidence, not with a moralizing eye ('Christ's poor were not
always pretty'), but with an eye for Brechtian values – the
fatalism, the irony in the fact of Establishment homilies,
the tenacity of self-preservation. And we must also remember the 'underground' of the ballad-singer and the fair-
ground . . . for in these ways the 'inarticulate' conserved
certain values – a spontaneity and capacity for enjoyment
and mutual loyalties – despite the inhibiting pressures of
magistrates, mill-owners and Methodists.

E. P. Thompson, 1968, pp. 63–4

Attacking a theoretical position to which one is opposed often
tends towards the erection of an alternative position which is
merely an inversion of one's opponent's. To avoid this failure,
it is necessary to extract the kernel of an opponent's argument
in order to *transcend* it, encompassing all his data but moving
to a superior position. At the outset, it is essential to be clear
about one's own fundamental tenets (for example, one's conception of human nature, social order and epistemology). To
attack the 'false ideas' of another without being clear about
one's own ideas, merely leads into the construction of theories
which are mirror-images of the false ideas being attacked.

The central contention of this chapter is that the 'new

From I. Taylor, P. Walton and J. Young (eds), *Critical Criminology*, London: Routledge and Kegan Paul, 1975, pp. 63–91.

deviancy theory', originated largely by American sociologists around The Society for the Study of Social Problems in the early 1960s, and developed by the National Deviancy Conference in Britain, fell precisely into this trap. So it was that the attack on the type of positivist criminology, which we characterized in chapter 1 as Fabian, resulted not in an escape from the utilitarian theatre of discourse but merely in a crass inversion of it.

The history of the new deviancy theory is a story of a well-meaning opposition to conservative thinking – leading from a laissez-faire liberalism to a full-blown Romanticism.[1] In its liberal phase, the deviant was seen to be propelled from involvement in a nearly-ubiquitous and innocuous deviancy into an essential and committed membership of hardened criminal subcultures by the clumsy mismanagement of the powerful. In its romantic sequel, the deviant – whether nestling warmly in the tenderloin of the city or making inarticulate but penetrating attacks on the bourgeois order – became a hero for the sociologist of deviancy.[2] The movement led from 'zoo-keeping' of the deviant to a 'moral voyeurism', wherein the 'propinquity of the wicked' sustained our careful dislike of the 'virtuous'.[3]

Let us first examine the basic premises of the correctionalist criminology against which the new deviancy theory reacted, concentrating on two aspects: the specific characteristics of such theories, and their ideological implications.[4]

1. *Consensual view of social order*

Correctional criminology's conception of society postulated an overwhelming agreement over definitions of the conventional and the deviant – the vast majority of individuals acting within this consensus, and a small minority being unambiguously deviant. Thus, we are presented with a 'taken-for-granted' world where social reaction against a particular individual or group was obvious. One does not ask why the burglar or the marihuana smoker should be prosecuted – any reasonable man is seen to be opposed to these activities. The workings of the State and its relationship to law and the judiciary, therefore, are left unexamined. Thus, the *reaction* (against deviance) is declared unproblematic.

2. Homo duplex *conception of human nature*
The deviant individual is seen as a pathological product of undersocialization into the consensus. In its classic form, deviancy is seen as the formless force of the *id* bursting through a hernia in the *superego*. In this way, alternative takes on reality are negated – for meaning has been wrenched from the deviant actor, and he is cast into the realm of the asocial. Thus, the deviant *act* is rendered meaningless.

3. *Determined nature of the deviant act*
The deviant individual is pathological and hence his activities are not those of choice, for no 'normal' individual would ever contemplate them. He is ineluctably propelled into his deviancy. Thus, no normal person would choose to be deviant and the deviant's actions cannot be of his own making.

4. *Primacy of primary socialization*
Deviancy is determined by factors operating in the far past of the individual. There is a split between 'real time' and 'actual time'. Real time has causal significance and is located in the traumas or deprivations of the past which are repeatedly enacted in the future. Actual time is relevant only to the extent that the individual encounters 'precipitating circumstances' which bring out the underlying 'real-time' predispositions. Thus, if we can explain deviant behaviour in terms of events that happened ten years ago we are doing well; if we can explain in the first five years of the actor's life we are doing excellently; but if we can do so in terms of the individual's autonomic nervous system or chromosome structure, that is science! Thus, present circumstances are granted only tangential relevance, and explanation is individualized in the past history of the solitary actor.

5. *Reductionism*
Individual choice and action within the social world is reduced to fixed, psychological, physiological and/or genetic propensities. Deviancy becomes an outcome of these 'essences', and has no meaning outside of an atomized psyche or bodily

structure. This is the ultimate break with the present predicament of the actor.

6. *Scientism*

The necessity for the scientific analysis of the causal factors propelling the deviant allows the expert to speak *ex cathedra*, giving credence to the interpretations of the actor himself only as one of many factors under consideration. This gives scientific respectability to the analysis and assumes the insulated neutrality of the expert from the deviant. Thus, scientific credibility is added to the break that is made with the present predicament.

7. *The therapeutic impact of social reaction*

The expert is seen as having no moral or financial axes to grind; he makes recommendations which manipulate or negate the regressive forces that exist within the deviant actor with a therapeutic purpose and a therapeutic impact. The lay conservative, being more punitively oriented, is presented as one who may potentially exacerbate precipitating factors, which in turn may worsen the deviancy. In contrast, 'scientifically prescribed' social reaction is seen to arise out of neutral assessment, bearing no relationship to the deleterious influence of conservative (or other) ideologies. In this fashion, 'enlightened' or 'rehabilitative' social reaction can be presented as dispassionate and innovative and the expert is dissociated from the ongoing constellation of social reaction forces which maintain the deviant in a stigmatized position.

8. *The divorce of deviant from victim*

The deviant is seen as propelled by his essential propensities into the contemporary world – his victim being the first accidental social atom into which he collides. The suggestion here is that there is little that the deviant might rationally desire of his victim – so that any idea of conflict between deviant and victim is defused.

The ideological significance of these premises in correctionalist criminology is that they achieve a four-fold fracture of reality: first, the actor is severed from his present predicament; second, that predicament is wrenched from the total society (including the 'social reaction' of contemporary society); third, the deviant act itself is separated out from any consciousness of it by the deviant actor; and, finally, the deviant is divorced from his victim.

The central task of the new deviancy theory was to reunite the deviant actor with the contemporary world.[5] The consensual view of the world in correctionalist criminology was replaced by a pluralist view of social action and values. Deviancy was seen as a problematic product of a series of transactions between definer and defined, each in his own social world. Social order was seen, in an extremely pluralistic fashion, as a collection of normative ghettoes, each jostling with the other for elbow-room and for status. One of these groups, however, somehow has more power than others – it is able to impose its own values and conceptions of behaviour on others. Power is stumbled upon, but the reasons for its existence, and for its frequent forays into the plural world (whether in the form of 'the bureaucracy' or Commissioner Anslinger) are not explored, or dissected. Divisions in civil society are found, but their social basis left unexamined. Instead, the call is for a 'culture of civility', wherein the mores of diversity will be respected by all groups.[6] Tolerance will reduce the present war of group against group into a situation of diversity and coexistence – San Francisco and Amsterdam being cited as pointers to a civilized urban future.

The pathological conception of deviancy is overturned: in a pluralistic society, all people are potentially deviant (cf. Douglas, 1971a, chapter 4), all people experience deviant 'impulses', it being the intolerance of power which translates such *normal* action into action which is stigmatized and labelled (cf. Becker, 1963, p. 26). Deviance is not inherent in an action: it is a quality bestowed upon it. So, normal variation in behaviour is transformed by *mismanagement* into behaviour which is seen to be dangerous to the individual and to the wider society.[7] Social reaction against 'the deviant' exacerbates the problems; before that, deviancy is either just the manifestation of the capricious whim of the actor or alternatively an inadequate but rational attempt at problem-solving.[8] Deviancy attempts to solve social problems; social reaction maintains and increases them. There is a fundamental irrationality about State control, for not only does its control activity frequently lead either to 'deviancy amplification' or to the ossification of the actor in his deviant status and position,[9] but also (given that deviant behaviour is ubiquitous throughout the social structure) the State's selection of scapegoats is arbitrary and based, by and large, on the 'false concepts' of policemen, social workers and courts. These false conceptions generate a stereotype of the criminal as lower class – a stereotypical construction which occurs because of the relative powerlessness of the lower class, rather than the fact of greater involvement in criminality as such (cf. Chapman, 1968). Furthermore, these social processes tend to generate the positivist aetiologies under attack, such as the 'broken home' hypothesis, aetiologies which are self-fulfilling in the sense that control agencies select miscreants for apprehension with precisely such criteria to the fore.[10] Criminal statistics, therefore, are seen as fabrications which, at best, can merely give us a head-count of those who have been labelled[11] or, at worst, serve to confirm state mystifications (mystifications which conceal the fact that there is no generalized standard which could meaningfully generate any such figures).[12]

In the new deviancy theory, the present circumstance and the secondary socialization of the deviant take the place of primary socialization and the constellation of determining factors as the focus of investigation. The actor's past is seen largely to be irrelevant – his physical body virtually vanishes, and his self-concept achieves a high degree of continuity with his subcultural environment. For, in the new deviancy theory, the deviant is, above all, a rational, conscious actor, free of the determinants of past events and physical or psychic disturbance, and existing in a homogeneous and normatively-consistent subculture. The concepts of undersocialization and social disorganization as causes of deviancy are replaced by an emphasis on the differential socialization of individuals – dependent on their proximity to one particular normative social organization within the plurality of organizations that make up the total society.

In the new deviancy theory, man's possibilities are open-ended – man does not possess any *essential* features predisposing him towards deviance. The notion of *essence* is associated with an incorrect method of categorization applied by official society in the process of social reaction, notions which sometimes are taken up and acted upon by the actors themselves.[18] Human action is teleological and irreducible to bodily or subconscious processes. Because this is so, the principal method of access to the knowledge necessary for explaining the existence or the content of specific subcultures is experiential and intuitive. The conceptualization of the social universe held to by the actors in question is seen to be of absolutely central importance in explaining their action. 'Insider' information becomes paramount, and the 'outsider' (*qua* sociologist) attempts to return from the particular normative ghetto he has been exploring with a precise image of insider's definitions, untarnished by the outsider-sociologist's own 'middle-class' preconceptions. Conceptual relativism becomes the order of the day, and the sociologist is seen merely to be readjusting 'the hierarchy of credibility' (used to define valid social information) away from its domination by the powerful.[14]

In its attack on the utilitarianism of Fabian criminology [. . .] the new deviancy theory tends to embrace a *romantic* conception of the social universe.[15] That is, the image of a naturally good man – whose goodness would be expressed more extensively were it not for the interference of 'civilized' society – is proposed. Thus, true human expression and authenticity is most likely to be found at the margins of the social world. Elsewhere, official society (whether in the form of the nuclear family, the education system or the social-control agencies) tends to transform the natural round of innocuous diversity (and its beneficent consequences) into a state of intractability and brutalization. On the basis of such a romantic image of man, the new deviancy theorists tend to address their attacks against the utilitarian mismanagement of deviancy, the transformation of the 'useless' into the 'useful' and the incarceration of the intransigent.

Utilitarian crime is of little interest to the new deviancy theory. Indeed, it is engaged in an astonishing accomplishment – the development of a criminology that does not deal with property crime, and a criminology whose subjects live in a world not of work, but of leisure. Expressive deviancy is the centre of attention: marihuana-use rather than burglary, prostitution rather than homicide, 'psychopathy' and 'schizophrenia' rather than 'hysteria' or 'neurosis'. The emphasis is on 'crimes without victims' and the contention, overall, is that a big proportion of crime control involves undue and unnecessary interference in the liberty of the individual.[16] The spectre of John Stuart Mill is here: there is even a suggestion that the non-interventionist catechism be extended to many 'utilitarian' crimes (for example, some forms of juvenile delinquency, on the grounds that they are innocuous prior to reaction) and to homicide, rape and child-molesting (on the grounds that these crimes can involve precipitation by the victim, and hence contain complicity by the victim in the offending activity).

THE THEORY AND PRACTICE OF VOYEURISM

However much there is that is progressive in the idealism of the new deviancy theory (for example, in its attacks on manifestly repressive and mystifying potential of criminological positivism)[17] too many problems remained unsolved. In particular, although there were many texts to delight the connoisseur of deviancy, there were few guide-books to provide pointers to practical struggle. Paradoxically, of course, correctionalist criminology was guilty of no such omission. In its constant endeavour to achieve a staffing position in the management of society and in the disposal of the 'useless', correctionalist criminology has developed a consistently practical concern, and a policy-orientation of considerable sophistication and scope. Indeed, in many criminological texts, the final arbiter of the 'truth' or 'validity' of a theory is its practical utility. The new deviancy theorists have nevertheless been stridently non-interventionist. In the earlier phase, the theorist's attitude to his subject-matter was rather like that of a wild-life conservationist. His message to the State was 'hands off!', reaction and intervention against deviants being seen as unnecessary and exacerbating of the situation. Associated with this avoidance of intervention was what Gouldner

(1968, pp. 121–2) was later to lampoon as the 'Theory and Practice of Cool', a poise of studied neutrality, involving a careful and strictly limited support of their subjects:

> Like the zookeeper, he wishes to protect his collection; he does not want spectators to throw rocks at the animals behind the bars. But neither is he eager to tear down the bars and let the animals go. The attitude of these zoo-keepers of deviance is to create a comfortable and humane Indian Reservation, a protected social space, within which these colourful specimens may be exhibited unmolested and unchanged.

Later, with the rise of more militant and aggressive deviant groups, the tune changed somewhat. For *carefully*, and *theoretically*, the new deviancy theorists delighted in a voyeuristic way in the activities of the new-style deviant. In particular, they relished the overt attack mounted by the new deviants on the 'straight world' – the world of the utilitarian middle class. Whether the deviant in question was a marihuana smoker, a gay, a football hooligan, a sexual deviant, a black-mailer, vandal, greaser or industrial saboteur, the sign was that somebody had sensed that 'society' was 'wrong' and that, moreover, that somebody had the guts to do something about it.[18] A greater contradiction was presented for this later version of the new deviancy theory – for now the message of the deviancy theorist to official society was 'hands off, you'll only make matters worse' but *at the same time* the implicit ideology was 'believe and hope that the new deviant constituencies do represent a genuine threat to the social order'. If an activity was anti-State in any conceivable sense, this was sufficient for it to be celebrated or approved. The project of the new deviancy theory was to show how the reaction of the State to such threats was nevertheless irrational, amplifying deviance whilst at the same time contradicting in the process of reaction its own democratic codes and rule-book.

The problems with this position were two-fold. First, the new deviancy theory was still trapped theoretically – within the confines of an inverted utilitarianism. Second, there was *no* clear conception of practice – power had really been discovered, but there was no desire to dirty one's hands in actual struggles (and certainly no programmes or policies spelt out for those who might so desire).

These two problems were an almost unavoidable feature of an essentially idealist politics: an idealism, that is, which was firmly convinced of the possibility of social change brought on by a demystification of the 'theories' (i.e. the ideologies) of the enlightened middle class, and sustained by the co-operation of diverse and expressive strands within the *marginal* middle and working classes. It was a radical idealism desperately seeking a social base in the wider society. This is not to deny the importance of such marginal groups (as, for example, the new bohemia)[19] – but it is to assert (as these groups were later themselves to discover) that radical ideas by themselves are abortive unless linked to a wider analysis of the total society, and unless tied into a wider struggle in a class society. It should be said that although the organized Left could have contributed a great deal at this point, and raised the level of debate and practice considerably, the response made from that direction was theoretically and practically impoverished. The prevalent attitudes to deviant behaviour on the organized Left fitted largely into two categories, which we can summarize as: the 'After the Revolution' perspective, when, presumably, the activities of deviants would either vanish, or alternatively better 'therapeutic' facilities would be instituted; and the 'Leave 'em alone' perspective, where deviants (like, for example, the homosexual or the marihuana smoker) are seen as irrelevant to the struggle for socialism, and, therefore, to be tolerated. Both of these were strange responses – in the first perspective, an unwillingness (on the part of Marxists) to be involved in discussions as to the real possibilities for a genuine social diversity, and, in the second, an espousal of an essentially liberal and moralistic view of 'tolerance', as a kind of free-floating sentiment to be mobilized irrespective of social context. The tenacity of a utilitarian perspective and culture is clear: the Left is exposed largely to an economistic position, which is atheoretical and grossly limited in its conception of the nature of socialist culture.[20] The Party increasingly focuses, as a result, on bread-and-butter issues and increasingly adopts an *ouvrierist* stance, which uncritically accepts existing working-class attitudes to crime and deviancy (and, hence, to questions of human diversity).

THE PROBLEMS FACING THE NEW DEVIANCE THEORY

In this section, our concern is to examine the empirical problems which confronted the new deviancy theorists, problems which were a direct product of the limited conception of human nature and social order with which they had chosen to work. The object here is to show that although the new deviancy theory was successful in reuniting the fractured man of criminological positivism, in reuniting actor, action and society, it succeeded at the expense of erecting a rational Frankenstein constructed out of the inverted conceptual debris of its positivist opponents.

1. *The problem of consensus*
However much the new deviancy theorist talked of diversity and dissensus in society, the ineluctable reality of a considerable consensus over certain matters could not be wished away. This was particularly noticeable, moreover, in the widespread and uniform social reaction against various forms of deviancy (and, especially, against *crimes* against the person and certain crimes against property).

The positivists had declared there to be a consensus to which all normal men adhered. Deviancy was irrational or meaningless: a product of a pathology that was either individual or social or both. The new deviancy theorists, in contrast, tended to see the social world in pluralistic terms and deviant action itself as problem-solving behaviour. The problem for the new deviancy theory, indeed, was not the extent of crime and deviancy, but the relative lack of it. Given the lack of any clear rationale for consensus in the new deviancy theorist's view of the social world, the problem was that conformity *per se* was irrational. More particularly, in turning to a typical industrial society like Britain, where some 7 per cent of the population own 84 per cent of the wealth, a society not only of palpable material inequality, but also an associated repression of minority groups, and sexual repression, why was there even a shred of consensus, and why did actors not pursue their reasonable interests with even greater vigour and commitment than the reported delinquent of orthodox criminology? Again, why should it be that people are so falsely conscious as to react against crimes which do not directly damage their interests (as, for example, some forms of professional crime and the crimes without victims)? And, moreover, why do people not react more 'rationally' against activities (whether illegal or not) – like the activities of corporations and the powerful in general – which manifestly do disturb their interests?[21]

2. *The problem of statistics*

However dubious the positivist's acceptance of the criminal statistics at face value, the wholesale rejection of the statistics by the new deviancy theorist was equally cavalier. It would be a strange industrial sociologist, for example, who would reject the strike figures on the grounds that they were evidence only of labelling and social reaction – even though he would still be cautious in his interpretations of their significance at a particular time. The rejection of the statistics absurdly disqualifies the new deviancy theorist from contributing to the topical, and politically consequential, debate as to the significance of the crime-rate, whether it is rising and in what way. And the new deviancy theorist is unable either to investigate – on his own admission – questions of comparison over time and across cultures. The new deviancy theorist excludes himself in this important way from the hot questions of crime, the arena of immediate political debate and any kind of intervention in the escalation of control that follows from statistical increases in crime.

Moreover, the new deviancy theorist is left without a conceptual armoury in the discussion of 'unofficial crime-rates'. To argue that the law is a weapon constructed by the powerful in its own interests (that it solves problems confronted by the powerful), hardly enables explanation of the widespread law-breaking currently exposed, and normally institutionalized, in the activities of powerful corporations and political men – law-breaking which, according to Gordon (1971), Pearce (1973) and even Ramsay Clark (1970), is carried out on a scale that makes Al Capone and the Great Train Robbers look like novices. The rule-makers comprise the most ardent of rule-breakers; and, for the new deviancy theorist sensitized to the inequality of the wider society, the problem is that there is far too much rule-breaking amongst the powerful for his simple conception of law to make sense. On the one hand, then, the new deviancy theory is unable to cope with the relatively infrequent and unextensive amount of working-class deviancy in a divided society; and, on the other, it cannot explain the prevalence and persistence of the criminality of the powerful.

3. *The problem of social disorganization*
The new deviancy theorists accused those who operated with notions of social disorganization of belittling, or denying the authenticity, of alternative forms of social organization developed in pursuit of other than dominant goals, However important this accusation may have been in pointing to the plurality of social organizations in a divided society, the fact remains that certain ecological areas *are* disorganized; and that this disorganization relates both to the external and internal forces acting on such areas (for example, on skid-row, or in 'hippie' communities). And it is absurd to deny that phenomena like marital breakdown are irrelevant, at the micro-level of interaction, in the aetiology of deviant behaviour. To accord a sub-cultural solution authenticity is not equivalent to endowing it with health.

4. *The problem of irrationality*
Why should men act in certain ways that, according to the tenets of the new deviancy theory, were patently irrational? Why, for example, should men behave in ways which suggested determination of precisely the kind described by the positivists (in terms of childhood experience, in predictable fashion, as if determined by the facts of bodily reality)? Why should some behaviour appear random, meaningless and unrelated to specifiable human motivation? Why do some people describe themselves as being sick and determined? Why should

some people opt for manifestly untenable solutions to their problems, solutions that were clearly against their own interests? Why should men behave as if afraid of freedom (limiting their own solutions and possibilities in a variety of ways)? Why should the powerful, also, act in such a way as to increase and exacerbate the problems *they* faced (for example, in their attempts to control others)? Why, indeed, do individuals appear to resist the presumably liberative ideas and strategies thrown up by the new deviancy theorists and by other social and political movements at large?

Specifically, it would be instructive to know why Howard Becker and Irving Horowitz's much-vaunted 'culture of civility' (a culture of mutual tolerance, and a social contract of genuine liberality) should not exist except (briefly) in a small area and in a period of high prosperity. Why, indeed, is the reader they produced on *Culture and Civility* prefaced by a eulogy to the tolerance existing in San Francisco at the time, but then followed by a series of essays detailing the defensive formation of Red Guards by the young Chinese, the repeated racism of the police in its attacks on the black community, the frightening destruction of the hippie colony and the continuing immiseration of the ghetto?

5. *The problem of psychic disturbance*

Where the new deviancy theorist portrays his deviant as an open-minded, calm, rational actor, we are beholden to explain the social realities of guilt as a universal form of human experience, the ongoing reverence for authority (which often intensifies to the point of rendering anti-authoritative action impossible), the existence of internal contradictions in individual desires, values and needs, and (for the deviancy theorist as well as for the deviant) the prevalence of situations in which one knows 'what ought to be done' but feels unable to carry through the necessary solutions.

6. *The problem of bodily discomfort*

The tendency in the new deviancy theory was to ignore the fact that the human actors under discussion possessed a human body. Thus, there was violation of evidence confirming the experience of bodily anxiety produced at the 'invitational edge' of criminality – the activity of the autonomic nervous system that does occur as one's hands move towards the 'goodies'. Additionally, little or no discussion was given the existence of hysteria and other psychologically-induced ill-nesses or psychosomatic complaints.

7. *The problem of objectivity*

Attributing rationality to deviant decisions, asserting the differential tenability of various human acts, and denying the reality of consensus implies the existence not of a totally relative world, but of an elusive though complex standard (a standard that is not recognized or portrayed in law or in dominant social norms). In other words, there is some standard somewhere, whereby one is able to talk of appro-priate and, most importantly, of inappropriate responses to problem-situations. The spectre of normality and pathology, once exorcized, re-emerges. Only by holding to some standard of normality is it possible, indeed, to talk of lapses in rationality on the part of an individual, a group or even on the part of a total society. But this standard need not be simply a description of what human nature and social order are, under existing social arrangements, but, crucially, can be statements about what they *might* be – statements, that is, about their potentiality. To talk in terms of objectivity, more-over, demands that one relates the notion of deviance to conformity within a total system. The alternatives are either to adopt the positivist's identification of deviance as a depar-ture from the existing arrangements of interest and power, and to use these arrangements as a standard of objectivity and rationality, *or* to analyse society in terms of a conflict between classes, the falsely conscious nature of much working-class behaviour, and the illusory nature of appeals to a consensus.

THE PARAMETERS OF NORMALITY

What inducement has the proletariat not to steal? It is all very pretty and very agreeable to the ear of the bourgeois to hear the 'sacredness of property' asserted; but for him who has none, the sacredness of property dies out of itself.

Money is the god of this world. The bourgeois takes the proletarian's money from him and so makes a practical atheist of him (Engels, 1969, p. 145)

As we have indicated earlier, a central problem facing the new deviancy theorists was the irrational irresistance of individuals to crime, the psychic and bodily weightings towards conformity, and the apparently senseless commitment of the subordinate to consensual values. In a society where the producers of wealth remain relatively impoverished – where real poverty is widespread and where the worker in 'decent' employment still finds it difficult to budget – this conformity is all the more difficult to explain. Yet crime is not so obvious a decision as Engels might have us believe. The continuing respect for property in grossly inequitable societies underlines two inter-related questions: in the immediate situation, why is there *not* a widespread and rational pursuit of criminal careers, and why in the long-term is there not the obvious pursuit of socialism? Why is property respected and why is the working-class involved in supporting political ideas which manifestly fail to meet or are opposed to their interests? The 'problem of order' and the tenacity of 'order' generates the same kinds of questions within deviancy theory and within socialist theory. A British libertarian socialist magazine poses the question most pointedly: [22]

> Let us consider for a moment – and not through rose-tinted spectacles – the average British middle-aged working-class voter today. He is probably hierarchy-conscious, xenophobic, racially-prejudiced, pro-monarchy, pro-capital punishment, pro-law and order, anti-demonstrator, anti-longhaired students and anti-drop-out.

Attempts to explain this travesty of consciousness, the *Solidarity* article continues, have typically taken three forms:

1. *Betrayal of left-wing leaders*
No doubt such betrayals have occurred, but *why* are repeated betrayals tolerated, and *why* are left-wing leaders so timid? Is it really simply that such leaders would exchange a bottle

of brandy and a handshake with Princess Anne for the realization of a new society, the actualization of a dream?

2. *The mass media*

The argument here is the media have successfully instilled in the population an all-pervasive respect for property and an abhorrence of criminality. No doubt the media *does* attempt to spread such messages, but, again, *why* should the distorted media messages find such an eager audience? Why are the televisions left on, the newspapers read so avidly? Why do the ideas slot so easily into the heads of the viewing population? Ideas must have some meaning, some response for their audience and life situation, or else other – more radical – ideas would find their audience more readily.[23] At this juncture, *Solidarity*, like many other libertarian socialist groups, plumps for a third alternative.

3. *Long-standing conditioning: distorted character structure set up in infancy through sexual repression*

In this perspective, Fascism in Germany, working-class quiescence, respect for property and prudery are all seen to be functions of rigid and repressive parents, and hence child-rearing itself is seen as a product and a producer of an authoritarian system. Or, as Wilhelm Reich (1946, pp. 25–6) put it:

Suppression of the natural sexuality of the child, particularly of its genital sexuality, makes the child apprehensive, shy, obedient, afraid of authority, 'good' and 'adjusted' in the authoritarian sense; it paralyzes the rebellious forces because any rebellion is laden with anxiety, it produces by inhibiting sexual curiosity and sexual thinking in the child a general inhibition of thinking and of critical faculties. In brief, the goal of sexual repression is that of producing an individual who is adjusted to the authoritarian order and who will submit to it in spite of all misery and degradation . . . The result is fear of freedom, and a conservative, reactionary mentality. Sexual repression aids political reaction, not only through this process which makes the mass individual passive and unpolitical, but also by creating in his structure an interest in actively supporting the authoritarian order.

Earlier, we noted how the attack on positivism from the new deviancy theory resulted merely in its inversion (into idealism) and how left-wing explanations of criminality often simply replicated bourgeois accounts. If we reverse the problematic from 'why do people deviate?' to 'why do people conform?' – as in Reich – we obtain a similar result. All of the three 'socialist' explanations for the widespread respect for property and the consensus are mirror-images, only, of conventional explanations of criminality.

The *corrupt leadership* theory is the precise counterpart of the notion of 'bad company' and the corruptor-corruptee relationship in conventional criminological explanation; the understanding here being that no deviant would act in the way that he did unless he were sick, under the influence or corrupted. The same understanding is extended, in left-wing accounts, to the activities of the left-wing leader, and to his effect on those whom allegedly he represents.

The *baleful image of the mass media* theory is idealist, in that it assumes that people are in some way motivated by ideas, *irrespective* of their material circumstances. Any ideas can be 'caught' from the media, provided that they are marketed with sufficient intensity and duration. The parallels with differential association theory in orthodox criminology as an account of the learning of norms and values are apparent.

The *authoritarian character armour* theory of Reich, of course, is an exact replica of theories of undersocialization in both psychological and sociological positivism.

All three theories – whether phrased in left-wing or right-wing rhetoric, and whether developed for the purposes of control or liberation – tend to ignore the material situation of the individual and his present social predicament. All three of them rely on the idea of a passive, non-reflective individual who is prey, without significant defences, to external or internal 'malignant' influences. No doubt each of them contains a kernel of truth but to accord them primacy, as explanations of working-class passivity, over explanations located in the real social and material situation of working-class members is unjustified, and is disastrous for understanding both working-class politics and working-class crime. To understand the material situation of the working-class criminal, it is necessary to examine the ideological underpinning of social-control activity (in the widest possible sense). The project here is to understand how the precepts of bourgeois ideology (a) contain within them a sufficient though distorted degree of truth as to be rationally, if mistakenly, believed, (b) act upon and provide some measure of reassurance for the very real problems of justice and order confronting the working class, (c) are presented with a high degree of unanimity and with a denial of any existing alternative so as to don a 'natural' appearance, and (d) are maintained by means of an entirely real and contemporary social-control apparatus that does operate with a view to controlling and checking the deviation of, in particular, threatening working-class behaviours.

These four features of bourgeois ideology will be examined in greater detail.

1. DISTORTED TRUTH

Engels (1969, pp. 144–5) wrote:

> There is . . . no cause for surprise if the workers, treated as brutes, actually become such; or if they can maintain their consciousness of manhood only by cherishing the most glowing hatred, the most unbroken inward rebellion against the bourgeoisie in power. They are men so long only as they burn with wrath against the reigning class. They become brutes the moment they bend in patience under the yoke, and merely strive to make life endurable while abandoning the effort to break the yoke.

For Engels, the working man faced with economic deprivation had four alternatives. He could, firstly, become so brutalized as to be, in effect, a determined feature, 'as much a thing without volition as water' (1969, p. 159), giving way to the disorganizing social forces that beset him. Or, secondly, he could accept the prevalent mores of capitalist society, and enter into a war of all against all (1969, p. 161): [24]

> In this country, social war is under full headway, everyone stands for himself against all comers, and whether or not he shall injure all the others who are his declared foes, depends upon a cynical calculation as to what is most advantageous for himself.

Thirdly, the working man could steal the property of the rich (1969, p. 240):

> It was not clear to his mind why he, who did more for society than the rich idler, should be the one to suffer under these conditions. Want conquered his inherited respect for the sacredness of property, and he stole . . . Theft was the most primitive form of protest.

And, finally, of course, Engels argued, the working man could struggle for socialism.

However crude this 'typology' and however much Engels confused these options elsewhere, the classification of options, coined in 1845, has obvious advantages over the welter of schema developed from 1938 onwards as criminological typologies, typologies which have become the bugbear and the source of mystification for generations of students in criminology and deviance. Crime can be a product of the thoroughgoing brutalization of social forces impinging upon the actor, it can involve the voluntarism of competitive individualism, or it can be an individualized and primitive form of consciousness, easily broken by the 'social reaction' of the ruling class.

In the first instance, the positivist's conception of criminality as 'determined' is correct – though the explanation of this (as a matter of human nature or essential criminality) is not. The determination of criminality is more a matter of human (mis)fortune. In the second case, the criminal, like the rate-buster on the factory floor, is acting divisively; he is acting against the interests of the work-group and the class as a

169

whole. In the third, a measure of consciousness is involved which presages the developed form of rationality of the final instance: the collective struggle for socialism. If we confuse these categories, we are unable to be discriminate in our attitudes to crime[25] – i.e., we either condemn it out of hand or we romanticize it. Either way, we accept legal categories at face value and neglect to study criminal phenomena from the perspective of class interests and socialist principles. For the working class does have a real stake in a genuine social order, however much it may be that conservative 'law and order' campaigns are a sham behind which particular interests advance themselves, and proclaim themselves to be acting in the interests of all. It is a simple fact that the majority of working-class crime is *intra-* and not *inter*-class in its choice of target, area of activity and distribution. Working-class people suffer from crime, confront daily the experience of material desperation, undergo the ravages of disorganization and competitive individualism. The ideology that plays on this – bourgeois ideology – contains an element of truth, and touches on the genuine interests of the class – albeit in a distorted fashion.

2. MORAL INDIGNATION

Members of the working class also have a considerable stake in the notion (and the achievement) of social justice; they want a fair return for their labour, and are antagonistic towards those who obtain easy money parasitically upon the work of others. Bourgeois ideology plays upon this genuine fear, arguing that all will be rewarded according to their utility and merit, and that those who cheat at these rules will be punished. In this way, ideology aspires to acceptance as a universal interest, although in reality it conceals the rampant particular interests of the ruling class as displayed in both their legal *and* illegal aspects. The thoroughly meritocratic society of social utilitarianism is impossible in the context of existing property relationships, and thus the exhortation in bourgeois ideology towards free competition with the inducement of success for those who do is both an illusion and a mystification. The moral indignation of the powerless against those who succeed in material self-aggrandisement, in such circumstances, flows out of an entirely correct sense of malaise, an accurate reading of real possibilities for self in such a society. It is, however, a moral indignation that is directed at the visible criminals in the media, rather than the invisible criminals within bourgeois society's 'institutions of privacy'.[26] The criminal is an enormously useful scapegoat – to be put to use as a target for the sense of injustice of the powerless – and he is realistically a target in the sense that he often does act against class interests, yet unrealistically so in that his 'villainy' pales once set against that of the powers that be.

There is, however, a rather more profound sense in which moral indignation is played upon by ideology. Cattier's biography of Reich contains the following insight (Cattier, cited in *Solidarity*, 1969, p. 22):

> It would be wrong to believe that working people fail to revolt because they lack information about the mechanisms of economic exploitation. In fact revolutionary propaganda which seeks to explain to the masses the social injustice and irrationality of the economic system falls on deaf ears. Those who get up at 5 in the morning to work in a factory, and have on top of it to spend 2 hours of every day on underground or suburban trains have to adapt to these conditions by eliminating from their mind anything that might put such conditions in question again . . . revolutionary ideas slither off the character armour of the masses because such ideas are appealing to everything that people have had to smother within themselves in order to put up with their own brutalization.

To make sense of hardship, men must attempt to believe in an ultimate justice, however much their daily experience constantly belies it. Without embracing Reichian notions of 'character armour', and also without exaggerating the availability of revolutionary alternatives, we must be aware of the power of resistance to rational social action. This does not demand, as we shall see, a focus on childhood socialization, but it is certainly a crucial element in the social reaction against deviant behaviour and 'unconventional' ideas.[27]

Ideological displacement

Ideology is not, then, merely a set of false notions slotted into men's heads irrespective of their own real needs and desires. Ideology involves some degree of attention to men's felt needs and the world-views with which they attempt to live in the world. This is seen even more clearly in the case of what we may call 'ideological displacement'.

Donald Cressey, in his famous book on the Mafia, *Theft of the Nation*, notes how a tight-knit group of criminal families with a clearly differentiated hierarchy of function, exerts a pervasive and parasitic influence throughout the American economy. These families are thieving the wealth of the nation – every time an American eats a hamburger, buys milk, real estate or whatever, a certain percentage accrues to the Mafia. What is more, they do not even pay taxes! Now whereas the existence of such an all-pervasive and hierarchically organized group of families is doubtful (and Albini [1971] argues powerfully that it does not [exist]), organized crime in America is a reality. It is more diffused and localized, however, than the 'octopus with tentacles reaching to all parts of the country' as in Mickey Spillane or the romantic villainy of *The Godfather*, and ideological fantasies of the internal enemy repeatedly evoked by the Kennedy–Johnson administration. This is not to suggest that organized crime does not harm working-class interests, but it is to argue that it does so much less than the illegal (and, of course, the legal) activities of corporations in America (cf. Pearce, 1973). The extraordinary point is that the picture of the Mafia portrayed in Cressey, and also (importantly) in the media, is a direct parallel of the structure of family control over the 'legitimate' American economy. It is as if the reality of bourgeois domination was taken up and projected as a social image on to a conveniently caricatured and alien outgroup. Similar processes occurred, of course, in pre-war Germany, where if one erased the word Jew in 'Left' Nazi propaganda and replaced it with 'bourgeoisie', one would be left with something looking remarkably like a crude Marxist tract. As Peter Sedgwick notes in his analysis of fascism in Germany (1970, p. 33):

> What has to be determined is the function of anti-Semitism and anti-Slavism in the belief-system of the National Socialist movement as a whole. For, despite the programmatic timidity and opportunism of all wings of Nazism, from Hitler to the so-called 'Left Nazis' like the Strassers, the 'Socialism' of 'National Socialism' has to be taken very seriously. All the militancy and sacrifice, all the hatred of privilege and corruption, all the determination to make a better and cleaner world, which among revolutionary Socialists is attached to a class perspective upon society, was present among the Nazi pioneers, only linked to a racial vision. Demagogy and conscious deception were practised constantly and consciously, but within the limits of a terrible sincerity. *Pessima corruptio optimi*: the worst vices come through the corruption of the noblest instincts – and the worst cruelties through the deflection of class-militancy upon a non-class target . . . no movement without some kind of ideological parallel to Marxism could have hoped to master a society like Germany in which the contours of class-division were so deeply graven.

3. THE NATURAL APPEARANCE OF IDEOLOGY

Lukács, in *History and Class Consciousness* (1971, p. 262) points to the vital role of ideology in the functioning of a social system, noting that although 'the coercive measures taken by society in individual cases are often hard and brutally materialistic . . . the strength of every society is in the last resort a spiritual issue'. The State is seen as a 'natural' entity outside of man's own creation (1971, p. 257):

> That is to say, the organs of authority harmonize to such an extent with the [economic] laws governing men's lives, or seem so overwhelmingly superior that men experience them as natural forces, as the necessary environment for their existence. As a result they submit to them *freely* [which is not to say that they *approve* of them].

Thus, the criminal in his isolated violation of laws still feels guilty and, moreover, even in periods of revolution, when this 'natural' environment is disturbed the 'instincts' of the average man are so deeply violated 'that he regards it as a catastrophic threat to *life as such*, it appears to him to be a blind force of nature like a flood or an earthquake' (Lukács, 1971, p. 258).

Especially in Anglo-Saxon countries, where revolutionary alternatives are minuscule and radical rhetoric largely absent, the consensus appears as a monolith. Proponents of diversity forget that this consensus throughout society corresponds to the uniformity of the mode of production dominating the social order. Far from being 'problematic', it is all too palpable – it is, as Lukács describes it, a fact of nature.

4. THE SOFT MACHINE

The control system in such societies works not through beatings or paddy wagons (though these are always present as an ultimate arsenal, at the terminus of social control), nor indeed by beliefs and ideologies marketed as natural and uncontestable, but by a judicial distribution of rewards tied into a thousand pinpricks of punishment in the work-place that is society. These pinpricks act on the personality structure set up in childhood. The family itself is the product of such personality constructions, and is in turn geared to producing more children to undergo such character-training. Thus, a certain personality set is maintained throughout life in aspic. Both the individual, and the working-class culture of which he is a member, are dominated by memories of the costs to be paid for deviation and dissent. Such a culture contains and relays knowledge of the inhumanity of unemployment, the gross stigma of prison (and its *real* social consequences – in terms of job chances *and* personal isolation), and is acquainted with the poverty and despair of the lumpenproletariat. At the same time, it has knowledge of the contemporary and continuing mechanisms of the soft machine of control: the perks of conformity, the incessant minutiae of punishment for rebellion in the job situation. Cudgels and baton charges are unnecessary in the maintenance of this aspect of control. *The real locus of social control is in the work situation.*[28] In this respect, it should be noted that the degree of freedom experienced by particular segments of the population (i.e. in being immunized from the 'social reaction' of the powerful) contains its own rationality. The deviation of those without real social power is tolerated. It is a thousand times easier to become a radical academic than a militant shop steward: the first course of action leads to Penguin Books Ltd and the second to the blacklist. The irony of socialist ideology gaining headway amongst the intelligentsia is the lack of any power in the intellectual groups; but, of course, tolerance even for 'academic socialism' is withdrawn when the economic climate changes and radical ideas find ready ears.

The hard edge of the soft machine is directed largely at those beyond the systems and rewards of the work-place – towards the 'disorganized', 'unproductive' or idle. The criminal statistics, in this sense, are indicative of the dispersal of power deemed necessary to create a control situation. It would be absurd to punish all offenders; the object is to create a symbolic group who are physically and materially degraded in order to define a hard parameter to the workings of the soft machine of control.

The effectiveness of the soft machine is most clearly seen in the context of the post-war period of prosperity, moving ahead, until recently, apparently without hindrance. The extent of conformity amongst privileged sections of the working class in a period when those sections remembered the experience of unemployment, and could compare it to the relatively beneficent present, is hardly surprising and certainly not irrational. Similarly, the response of the German working class to fascism, however disagreeable, was not a product of madness nor merely the consequence of the compilation of authoritarian personalities. Sedgwick puts this well (1970, p. 33):

Marxism, the most dedicated and developed social theory that human civilisation has attained, has nothing to contribute towards our understanding of Nazism's politics of race murder. The very use of expressions like 'barbarism' and 'medieval' by Marxists at this point testifies to the replacement of analysis by horror. It is little wonder that so many on the Left have resorted to psychological explanation as the first available alternative to the Marxist vacuum . . . The 'Frankfurt School' of FreudoMarxists has extracted a variety of psychoanalyses from the mass unconscious: thus, mass society expresses either the submissiveness engendered by an authoritarian pattern of family upbringing (Adorno, Reich) or alternatively the confusion produced when these patterns get relaxed and replaced by permissiveness (Marcuse). Apart from their contradictory nature, these are answers to a false question, namely: 'Why did the Germans follow Hitler?' But on looking at the various phases and sources of mass support for Nazism, it becomes hard to believe that one requires any special psychological factors, other than those which explain, e.g. why the masses supported Churchill or Wilson. Nazi society was not a 'mass society' of atomized, hypnotized individuals: underneath the totalitarian armour, it was a typical advanced industrial society displaying all the sectors of varying and colliding class consciousness. It doesn't need Freud to tell us why people cheer a politician who stops unemployment, or why they fight savagely when their homes are bombed.

This is not to deny the physiological and psychological components of conformity, and neither is it to say that individual biographies are irrelevant. Rather, it is to argue that the autonomic nervous system and the conformist, quiescent personality are not simply products of childhood conditioning, but that they are maintained *in stasio* by the continuing system of 'opportunity', social control and ideological domination. To say that there is continuity in personality structures over time is to say no more than that the social situation has remained largely unchanged.

Show me a man whose social situation is changed markedly, and you will see a change in personality; show me a class which has successfully clarified its situation in an act of praxis and then you will have massive changes in personality. Show me a man who has been typed as of lower intelligence and placed in a job deemed suitable for his level, and you will observe a constant (and) low level of intelligence being maintained. Or a man brutalized into psychopathy, further brutalized by prison, and returned to his initial and stultifying milieu – there is the constant psychopath. It is at the desperate end of the social spectrum where the overwhelming milieu precipitates men into highly determined roles wherein the tyranny of the organism is best displayed, and where the psychologist or the biologist comes into his own. But this is a product of historical time and place – it is *not* a part of 'human nature'; of 'man's essence' in the way that psychologists might have us believe. The correlations of psychological positivists, between the organic and the social, may indeed hold water in a period where the possession of certain organic attributes (for example, the XYY chromosome) is related to the moral careers made available for those with organic afflictions: such correlations *describe* the power-invested processes so established; they do little to undermine the idea that such processes are necessary and inevitable.[29]

SOCIAL AND PSYCHIC CONFLICT

Western man exists constantly in a state of contradiction. On the one hand, he is dominated by a conservative ideology which is monolithic and largely unopposed, legitimized by its very continuity and sustained by a social-control apparatus directed at the containment of those who may deviate. And, as we have argued, this ideology also draws strength from the fact that it plays on real needs, and justifiable fears. On the other hand, the individual's knowledge of reality contradicts the ideology – he is anxious that the world is not what it purports to be, he is troubled by the injustice of the system, and he is racked by alienation in the work-place. These contradictions are expressed in a *consensus* (about fundamentals, on which we are all agreed) and a diversity of values and opinions about the attainment, the expression or the experience of these fundamentals. On the psychological level, this contradiction can lead to intra-psychic conflict[30] of a sort which leads to moral indignation, to conservatism, to negativistic violence and destruction, to a guilt and neurosis, and, at times, when the opportunities arise, to vast changes in attitudes (changes, incidentally, which become inexplicable in an empiricist sociology). But neither psychic tension nor contradictions in attitude occur in a vacuum: it is the task of a critical criminology to situate them historically and to study the ways in which such tensions and contradictions can be resolved and removed.

DEMANDS

A radical criminology, like radicalism in general, has to develop a programme of demands. Amongst these demands must be a concern for the following:

1. *Power and class*

The scholar or scientist's way of becoming partially blind is, inadvertently perhaps, to structure fields of enquiry in such a way as to obscure obvious connections or take the connections for granted and leave the matter at that. The great task of disconnection – it was arduous and time consuming – fell to the positive school of criminology. Among their most notable accomplishments, the criminological positivists succeeded in what would seem the impossible. They separated the study of crime from the workings and the theory of the state (Matza, 1969, pp. 143–4).

In *Becoming Deviant*, Matza describes the fifty-year 'task of disconnection' in positivist criminology in detail, and we shall not repeat the story. From the late 1960s, however, criminologists have become increasingly aware of the fact of power. Yet at no time have they wanted to be involved in power. They have pointed increasingly to the fact of class inequalities in apprehension and 'labelling', but have stopped short of working out policies in terms of working-class interests. Thus, Edwin Schur writes (1969, p. 337):

All available evidence indicates that crime in America will not be effectively reduced until we make basic changes in the structure and quality of American life. Respect for law and order will not be restored until respect for the nature of our society is restored. Our confrontation with crime cannot be successful if we persist in viewing it as a battle with some alien force. Since America's crime problems are largely of our own creation, we have it well within our power to modify them and bring them within reasonable control.

The use of the royal 'we' is preposterous here. It is unclear to this writer how *we* have created crime, and news to all of us, indeed, that *we* have the power to bring it under control.

The task facing socialist criminologists is to replace paradigms of this kind, with their continual reference to hypothetical publics and national problems, with paradigms developed around the interests of the class. Such a paradigm will reveal what demands are in fact revisionist, what demands we can pose as interim measures, and what strategic confrontations make sense politically. We will need to examine the relationship of organized Left parties and the class in terms of deviant behaviour, in the process attempting to substitute a conception of socialist diversity for the pluralism of the idealist tradition. Methodologically, we shall have to reject the bland formulation of 'participant observation', with its insistence on retaining a subculture or social situation unchanged. The only scenario where such a programme would ever have made sense would have been in a mortuary. In order to understand a subculture in the fullest possible sense, it is essential to understand its potentialities – that is, how it can *change*. The researcher, therefore, must be involved in the subculture – not afraid to argue, not refraining from exercising influence, and not resistant to change in himself.

2. *Statistics*

The criminal statistics represent the end-result of the deployment of social-control agencies by the powerful. The policeman on the beat, the courts, the social workers are all geared into this process in the sense that their areas of discretion are usually within the parameters their bureaucratic controllers permit. It is only in atypical situations that the idiosyncratic values and ideologies of particular social-control agencies

assume *paramount* importance. To see each sector as conflicting over fundamentals is misleading, and is a product of the
kind of pluralism which cannot distinguish differences of
emphasis from differences in objective position. The statistics
provide us with a blurred but useful picture of the degree of
respect for property and the extent of social disorganization
and conflict in the society in question. The categories represented in the statistics, however, must be interpreted with
extreme caution, for given their legal basis they do not capture
the meanings of crime for the actor, nor indeed the aetiological
context of the act. For example, we are not so much concerned with the amount of property stolen as we are with the
targets of property theft (and hence the motives informing
such crimes). The criminal statistics are subject to the same
good use, and the same problems of interpretation, as the
strike statistics; but they form the basis for a socialist analysis
of the development of contradictions and conflict in a
propertied society.

3. *Freedom*

What state, what time and under what conditions? It
depends. I work not with abstractions, only with realities
(Leon Trotsky, 1973b, p. 28, on asked whether the press
would be free under socialism).

The idealist tradition in criminology (which we discussed
earlier as 'anti-utilitarian' criminology) refused consistently to
be involved itself with power. Indeed, it went close to arguing
that power corrupts (or 'amplifies') the very deviants the
powerful wish to control or to 'purify'. So, idealist criminologists were led into an unconditional support for freedom.
Marihuana-smoking, heroin-use, prostitution and gambling
were activities which individuals freely chose – and they should
have the right to pursue these activities unimpeded. But the
meanings of such activities and their objective significance
varies with time and place. There is nothing implicit in the
heroin molecule which is either progressive or reactionary,
but heroin addiction, for example, in the black ghettoes is
without doubt an insidious expression of exploitation, and an
agency for passivity and defeat. To call for absolute freedom

in a population driven to the edge of desperation is to invite the exercise of the laws of the laissez-faire market and the continuing rule of the powerful. Who is to say that the Black October group, who made it a part of their programme to eliminate heroin-pushers in the black slums of the USA, were not acting progressively?

The tendency to see heroism in the adaptive deviancy of those suffering most from the vagaries of capitalism is closely related to this appeal for freedom. As Joe Warrington argued bitterly in his critique of Laing's approach to schizophrenia (1973, p. 15):

> But expressing X ≠ understanding Y. Some people do learn valuable things from abnormal experiences; some even escape from the coils of the system but many, probably most, are wrecked . . . The gut thing about schizophrenia is dreadful, dreadful unhappiness. Encouragement to wallowing in some vapid 'special status' is like encouraging a compulsive gambler in his solitary romanticization of the betting shop when one has no betting problems oneself. I regard this kind of weird, surrogate vampirism of another's terrible experience as being gravely immoral.

The development of social responsibility in the criminologist demands that he discriminate, that he does not merely collect exotica, that he separates out desperation from solution, and that he relates the deviant solution to its effects on others (situating it historically in terms of a class struggle). This requires a radical paradigm change in the study of deviancy. It does not rule out interim demands but it insists that such demands be part of an overall strategy. Thus, it does not lecture social workers and mental nurses that their function is *necessarily* as an instrument of social control, nor does it deny intermediate solutions, tentative graspings for survival on the part of the deviant. To do this would be utopian – it would be to suggest that men are necessarily either fully conscious revolutionaries or alternatively altogether reactionary. Rather it suggests that it is only through struggle, however limited at first, that consciousness is realized.

4. *Neo-correctionalism*

The idealists argued that social control was impossible in terms of the elimination of deviancy. They maintained that the requirement was a radical programme of decriminalization. Such a programme neglects to acknowledge that the process of decriminalization has important and ineradicable control functions within capitalist society, and that decriminalization, where it has occurred, is a product more of bureaucratic strategies evolved to deal with an overloading of inmates or social work cases than it is a genuine attempt to create a society free of the necessity to criminalize. Appeals to the powerful, however idealistically phrased, tend to be taken up in terms of the powerful's own interests, in order to serve ruling-class interests rather than those of the oppressed.[81]

It is unrealistic to suggest that the problem of crimes like mugging is merely the problem of miscategorization and concomitant moral panics. If we choose to embrace this liberal position, we leave the political arena open to conservative campaigns for law and order – for, however exaggerated and distorted the arguments conservatives may marshal, the reality of crime in the streets *can be* the reality of human suffering and personal disaster. We have to argue, therefore, strategically, for the exercise of social control, but also to argue that such control must be exercised within the working-class community and not by external policing agencies. The control of crime on the streets, like the control of rate-busting on the factory floor, can only be achieved *effectively* by the community immediately involved. Working-class organizations have eventually to combat the war of all against all that is the *modus vivendi* of civil society. Further, it is only in the process of struggle for control that the community can evolve out of its frequently disorganized and disintegrated state. The radical criminologist's task is to aid and inform such struggles and projects. His task is not to help the courts to work, nor to design better prisons. The problems of social control are problems for those who want to control *existing* social arrangements.

Radical criminological strategy is not to argue for legality and the rule of law but it is to show up the law, in its true colour, as the instrument of a ruling class, and *tactically* to demonstrate that the State will break its own laws, that its legitimacy is a sham, and that the rule-makers are also the greatest of rule-breakers. The law may be used where there are advantages in so doing, without succumbing to the notion that the law can universally be so useful. For it is precisely the nature of law to conceal particular interests behind universalistic ideology and rhetoric. The task is not to romanticize illegality: it is, as Lukács suggests, to judge deviant action in terms of its relationship to the struggle, ignoring the classifications of legality and illegality created by the powerful in *their* struggle against the powerless.

5. Socialist diversity

The ultimate goal in such a struggle must be a socialist culture which is diverse and expressive – that is, a culture which takes up the progressive components in pluralism, whilst rejecting those activities which are directly the product of the brutalizations of existing society (however diverse, expressive or idiosyncratic their manifestation). This involves a fight on two fronts: first, against the existing class society; and, secondly, against those tendencies within the socialist movement and the working class which would gravitate towards a strictly economistic interpretation of the socialist revolution. We argued earlier that capitalism is successful in creating a rubric of personal repression to which individuals do adapt: and hence it is clear that great resistance will occur against the achievement of a diverse and expressive society. There will, indeed, be a 'fear of freedom'. Just as it is now a truism to say that Women's Liberation, Gay Liberation and the new bohemia need to evolve out of a 'politics of subjectivity' into a fully socialist analysis, so it is also correct that the organized Left needs its own healthy transfusion from these movements.

CONCLUSION

Whereas the positivist ascribed deviant behaviour to a series of determining forces which excluded human choice and reason, the idealist vacillated towards a theory which portrayed deviancy as a product of reason bereft of time and place, a pure form impeded only by the clumsy administration of the State. Both stances ignored the material rubric and biographical frameworks within which human choice occurs and is moulded.[32] We have seen how the material circumstances of the criminal and his subjective assessment of the situation are affected by the stick and carrot of social control, and obfuscated by the domination of a highly persuasive ideology. We have argued that the biographical characteristics that lead to psychic conflicts and resistance are ossified by the ongoing institutions of the social-control apparatus, and by the lack of any real moral or material alternatives. Choice occurs within a cage, whose bars are obscured and glimpsed with certainty only at the terminal points of the social-control process. It is the role of the radical criminologist to demystify control, and to join with those movements which seek to provide tangible alternatives and areas of choice.

Crime and deviancy from a socialist perspective are terms which encompass an uneven array of activities and behaviours – at times, behaviours which are quite inimical to socialism; at other times, rebellions against property and repression which are as justifiable in their consequences as they are primitive in this conception. Forms of illegality exist within the working class which are adaptive, collective in their accomplishment and progressive in their function (objects 'fall off the backs of lorries', factory property metamorphosizes as bric-à-brac within the home). Forms of deviancy occur as attempts to create unhampered and liveable space, the tyranny of the work-place and conventional sexuality being left momentarily behind. Marihuana and booze, pub-life and gay-bars, black music and white rhythm-and-blues – a tender-loin of the city where a sense of 'the possible' breaks through the facticity of what is. But just as one must discriminate actively between crimes which are cultural adaptations of the people, and crimes which derive from the brutalization of criminal and community alike, so we must clearly distinguish the contradictory nature of many of these adaptive manifestations. Deviant sexuality, for instance, will contain both positive and negative moments: the breakthrough from repression is distorted and beguiled by the reality from which it sprang. The intellectual task of a socialist criminology is to provide a materialist analysis of deviancy, and strategy which will link such theory to a real social practice. The goal is a socialism of diversity, the problems enormous but the goal even more so.

Notes

1 For a discussion of the place of romantic thought in deviancy theory, see Young (1972c).

2. For a description of the 'control perspective' as an organizing theme in the early work of the National Deviancy Conference, see chapter 1 of Taylor, Walton and Young (eds), *Critical Criminology* (1975) .

3. The discerning reader will note how the moral voyeurism of the enlightened middle-class sociologist was an inversion of the state of moral indignation which Albert Cohen (1965) succinctly defined by asking 'what effect does the propinquity of the wicked have on the peace of mind of the virtuous'.

4. In Chapter 3 of *The Drugtakers* (Young, 1971a), I examine in detail the characteristics of such theories and their use as a conflict weapon. Suffice it to say that there are tendencies towards the kind of relativism which is criticized here. The ideological implications of correctional theory are to be developed in the introduction to *Myths of Crime* (Rock and Young, eds, 1975) and are touched on in Young (1973a).

5. This characterization of the new deviancy theory is presented in a highly articulated, ideal-typical fashion. It is, obviously, true that individual writers will often present a superior position on a few of these theoretical themes. The task is not, however, to pause over the limited features of difference within a general tradition, but to focus on a coherent theory which embodies this tradition. The difficulty here is that theoretical products are very rarely presented as a total theory. Protestations as to the limited nature of one's project, accompanied by a rapid change of emphasis, are not thereby rendered defensible, however (cf. Becker, 1974). One exception to this is Jack Douglas (1971a), who allows us to glimpse a vision of where such theoretical relativism might lead, if a way to break the relativism is not found in time.

6. The best examples of such a social contract are Becker and Horowitz (1971), in the essay on 'Culture and Civility', Becker

(1968) in his comments on the solution to campus drug problems (campus authorities are to ignore them in order to avoid public scandal, in exchange for which the student should play it cool) and Jack Douglas (1971b) in *Crime and Justice in American Society*.

7. For a criticism of the mismanagement thesis, see Gouldner (1968). An excellent example of the thesis in action, in the drugs field, is Duster (1970), which I criticized in detail elsewhere (Young, 1972d). One of Gouldner's contentions – that reason for the critique of mismanagement was the desire for research-funding from federal agencies – is, however, misconceived. Labelling theory was mounted in opposition to all official social-control agencies – it was only as the theory was taken up and ideologically transformed that the position castigated by Gouldner ensued. This transformation was accompanied by a rejection of the Romanticism of labelling theory (where official intervention led to the corruption and degeneration of the 'natural deviant') to a positivism and an absorption into Fabian criminology which saw in stigmatization and social reaction merely another factor to be reckoned with in the *management* of deviancy. A concrete example of this is the government White Paper, *Children in Trouble*, Cmnd. 3601 (London: HMSO, 1968).

8. Idealism opposes two 'aetiologies' to positivism: capriciousness (as in Becker, 1963) or rational problem-solving (as in Lemert, 1972, especially chapter 3). Either way, the actor is detached from his structural position (and hence his problems) and apparently decides, in a social vacuum, the course of action which would best suit his needs.

9. This is the reverse of the positivistic 'correctional' approach which sees as its prime task the elimination of crime. For the idealists, the elimination of crime was seen as impossible, and indeed, social reaction merely buttressed and amplified crime or deviant behaviour.

10. See Cicourel (1968) for a discussion of the self-fulfilling nature of the 'broken-home' hypothesis.

11. See Kitsuse and Cicourel (1963) for an attack on positivistic uses of the criminal statistics from a phenomenological perspective (tied into the social-reaction approach).

12. See Jack Douglas (1971a, chapter 4) for a thorough advocacy of this position.

13. See Everett Hughes's discussion of the notion of master status, as the identity which men may be ascribed and simultaneously embrace (Hughes, 1958). The idea is developed in Becker (1963), Duster (1970) and Douglas (1971a).

14. For the idea of the 'hierarchy of credibility', see Becker (1967).

15. The relationship between labelling theory and Romanticism is discussed by Gouldner (1968) and Young (1974a).

16. For the development of the debate over 'crimes without victims', see Schur (1965; 1969), Duster (1970) and Douglas (1971b).

17. To attack the new deviancy theory is not to deny the very real advances such a theoretical tradition achieved. E.g., interactionist work on the mentally subnormal and the physically handicapped has produced devastating yet neglected arguments against the genetic determinist theories, which currently appear to be experiencing a revival.

18. For essays illustrating this approach, see the two volumes emanating from the work of the National Deviancy Conference: Cohen (1971) and Taylor and Taylor (1973).

19. For a critique of the idealism of the hippie movement, alongside an appraisal of its potential importance, see Young (1973b).

20. And in stark contrast to the work of earlier Marxist thinkers, see Trotsky (1973a).

21. See Pearce (1973) for a discussion of the comparative cost of burglary, organized crime, tax evasion and illegal profit.

22. See *Solidarity*, pamphlet No. 33 (1969).

23. For an analysis of the reasons for the appeal of the mass media, see Young (1974b).

24. This is, of course, similar to the 'competitive individualism' ('institutionalized de-institutionalization') which Durkheim (for entirely different political purposes) attacked. See Young (1974b).

25. However confused Engels sometimes was in his use of these 'categories', he frequently distinguished between crimes which are the product of a total determinism and those which involve an element of voluntarism (extending as far as the point of a primitive class-consciousness). It is important to note that when Hirst (in chapter 8) cites Engels in his argument he quotes from the well-known passage (1844, p. 159), wherein crime appears in its totally determined form. This is not the only aetiology of crime identified by Engels.

26. An important contribution to our understanding of the ways in which the powerful immunize themselves from view (of the public in general, as well as from social control) is Stinchcombe's (1963) discussion of the development of public and private areas of space and living.

27. For a discussion of the concept of moral indignation in this

light, illustrating the ways in which the mass media play on such deeply-felt needs, see Young (1974c).

28. The importance of the work of Richard Cloward and his associates, from *Delinquency and Opportunity* (Cloward and Ohlin, 1960) to *Regulating The Poor* (Piven and Cloward, 1972) is that they accord work (and opportunity) such a central place in their discussion of social control and social order, and the ways in which the State uses opportunity (together with welfare and relief) to maintain such 'order'.

29. For examination of contradictions in attitudes and sudden changes in attitudes in the course of action, see Blackburn (1969).

30. The work of Albert Cohen, particularly in his development of the notions of 'reaction-formation' (1955) and 'moral indignation' (1965), is, in part, an attempt to relate social and psychic conflicts.

31. See the discussion by Cohen (1974a) of the politics of de-penalization, and in particular the point that reductions in the prison population are more likely in the context of economizing on the cost of maintaining 'high-security' prisons than they are as a result of any genuinely liberal attempts to eliminate prisons.

32. Gordon (1973) takes up an option which we might call 'Left rationalism' – where crime is seen as an obvious *economic* choice, given the disparities of wealth in the USA. It should be clear that the present analysis focuses on the problems of the seeming *irrationality* of crime and conformism.

References

Albini, Joseph L. (1971), *The American Mafia: Genesis of a Legend*, New York: Appleton-Century-Crofts.

Becker, Howard S. (1963), *Outsiders: Studies in the Sociology of Deviance*, New York: Free Press.

Becker, Howard S. (1967), 'Whose side are we on?' *Social Problems*, 14, 3, pp. 239–47.

Becker, Howard S. (1968), 'Ending campus drug incidents', *Trans-Action*, 5, April, pp. 4–5.

Becker, Howard S. (1974), 'Labelling theory reconsidered', in Paul Rock and Mary McIntosh (eds), *Deviance and Social Control*, London: Tavistock Publications.

Becker, Howard S, and Horowitz, Irving L. (1971), 'The culture of civility', in H. S. Becker (ed.), *Culture and Civility in San Francisco*, Chicago: Aldine.

Blackburn, Robin (1969), 'A brief guide to bourgeois ideology', in

Alexander Cockburn and Robin Blackburn (eds), *Student Power*, Harmondsworth: Penguin.

Cattier, Michel (1969), *La Vie et L'Oeuvre du Docteur Wilhelm Reich*, Lausanne: La Cité.

Chapman, Dennis (1968), *Sociology and the Stereotype of the Criminal*, London: Tavistock Publications.

Cicourel, Aaron V. (1968), *The Social Organization of Juvenile Justice*, New York: John Wiley.

Clark, Ramsay (1970), *Crime in America*, New York: Simon & Schuster.

Cloward, Richard, and Ohlin, Lloyd (1960), *Delinquency and Opportunity: A Theory of Delinquent Gangs*, New York: Free Press.

Cohen, Albert K. (1955), *Delinquent Boys: The Culture of the Gang*, Chicago: Free Press.

Cohen, Albert K. (1965), 'The sociology of the deviant act; anomie theory and beyond', *American Sociological Review*, 30, 1, pp. 5–14.

Cohen, Stanley (ed.) (1971), *Images of Deviance*, Harmondsworth: Penguin.

Cohen, Stanley (1974a), 'Criminology and the sociology of deviance in Britain: a recent history and a current report', in Paul Rock and Mary McIntosh (eds), *Deviance and Social Control*, London: Tavistock Publications.

Cressey, Donald R. (1969), *Theft of the Nation: The Structure and Operations of Organized Crime in America*, New York: Harper & Row.

Douglas, Jack D. (1971a), 'Crime and justice in America', in J. D. Douglas (ed.), *Crime and Justice in American Society*, Indianapolis: Bobbs-Merrill.

Douglas, Jack D. (1971b), *The American Social Order*, New York: Free Press.

Duster, Troy (1970), *The Legislation of Morality*, New York: Free Press.

Engels, Frederick (1969), *The Condition of the Working Class in England in 1844*, Harmondsworth: Penguin.

Gordon, David M. (1971), 'Class and the economics of crime', *Review of Radical Political Economics*, 3, 3.

Gordon, David M. (1973), 'Capitalism, class and crime in America', *Crime and Delinquency*, 19, April, pp. 163–86.

Gouldner, Alvin W. (1968), 'The sociologist as partisan: sociology and the welfare state', *The American Sociologist*, 3, May, pp. 103–16; reprinted in J. D. Douglas (ed.), *The Relevance of Sociology*, New York: Appleton-Century-Crofts, 1970; also in

A. W. Gouldner (1973).

Home Office (1968), *Children in Trouble*, London: HMSO, Cmnd. 3601.

Hughes, Everett C. (1958), *Men and their Work*, Chicago: Free Press.

Kitsuse, John I., and Cicourel, Aaron V. (1963), 'A note on the uses of official statistics', *Social Problems*, 11, pp. 131–9.

Lemert, Edwin M. (1972), *Human Deviance, Social Problems and Social Control*, 2nd ed., Englewood Cliffs, NJ: Prentice-Hall.

Lukács, Georg (1971), *History and Class Consciousness*, Cambridge, Mass.: MIT Press; also London: Allen Lane.

Matza, David (1969), *Becoming Deviant*, Englewood Cliffs, NJ: Prentice-Hall.

Pearce, Frank (1973), 'Crime, corporations and the American social order', in I. Taylor and L. Taylor (eds) (1973).

Piven, Frances F., and Cloward, Richard A. (1972), *Regulating the Poor*, London: Tavistock Publications.

Reich, Wilhelm (1946), *The Mass Psychology of Fascism*, New York: Orgone Institute Press; also London: Souvenir Press, 1972.

Rock, Paul, and Young, Jock (eds) (1975), *The Myths of Crime*, London: Routledge & Kegan Paul.

Schur, Edwin M. (1965), *Crimes Without Victims*, Englewood Cliffs, NJ: Prentice-Hall.

Schur, Edwin M. (1969), *Our Criminal Society*, Englewood Cliffs, NJ: Prentice-Hall.

Sedgwick, Peter (1970), 'The problem of fascism', *International Socialism*, 42, February–March, pp. 31–4.

Solidarity (1969), *The Irrational in Politics*, London: Solidarity pamphlet No. 33.

Stinchcombe, A. (1963), 'Institutions of privacy in the determination of police practice', *American Journal of Sociology*, 69, pp. 150–60.

Taylor, Ian, and Taylor, Laurie (eds) (1973), *Politics and Deviance: Papers from the National Deviancy Conference*, Harmondsworth: Penguin.

Thompson, Edward P. (1968), *The Making of the English Working Class*, Harmondsworth: Penguin.

Trotsky, Leon (1973a), *Problems of Everyday Life*, New York: Menad Press.

Trotsky, Leon (1973b), *On the Freedom of the Press*, ed. V. Karalasingham, Colombo: International Publishers.

Warrington, Joe (1973), 'A critique of R. D. Laing's social philosophy', *Radical Philosophy*, 5, pp. 10–16.

Young, Jock (1971a), *The Drugtakers: The Social Meaning of Drug Use*, London: MacGibbon & Kee/Paladin.

Young, Jock (1972c), 'Romantics, Keynesians and beyond: a social history of the new deviancy theory', paper given at the 11th National Deviancy Conference, University of York, 18–19 September 1972.

Young, Jock (1972d), Review of Troy Duster's *The Legislation of Morality*, in *British Journal of Criminology*, Winter, 12, pp. 300–4.

Young, Jock (1973a), 'Drug use as problem-solving behaviour', in *Proceedings of the Anglo-American Conference on Drug Abuse*, London: Royal Society of Medicine.

Young, Jock (1973b), 'Student drug use and middle class delinquency', in Roy Bailey and Jock Young (eds), *Contemporary Social Problems in Britain*, Farnborough, Hampshire: Saxon House.

Young, Jock (1974a), 'New directions in subcultural theory', in John Rex (ed.), *Contributions to Sociology*, London: Routledge & Kegan Paul.

Young, Jock (1974b), 'Mass media, drugs and deviance', in Paul Rock and Mary McIntosh (eds) (1974).

Young, Jock (1975), 'The myths of crime', in Paul Rock and Jock Young (eds) (1974).

Section II
Class Structure and Society

Section II consists of readings which address themselves to a recurrent issue in the history of sociological thought – that of social structure. What is the nature of the dominant institutions of a particular society? What are the most significant social groups? How do they relate to other aspects of the social structure? What role is there for the individual in effecting significant social change? The responses which have been given are legion and they vary with the kind of society to which such questions are addressed. All of the extracts selected are concerned primarily with that form of society dominant in Western Europe and North America, capitalism, and all begin, in one way or another, from the work of its foremost theorist Karl Marx.

In 'The "political" and the "economic" in Marx's theory of classes' (Reading 8) Stuart Hall seeks to demonstrate that the Marxist theory of the capitalist mode of production is far from the unilinear, monocausal economic theory which both proponents and critics often present. Illustrating the complexities and nuances of Marx's writings, and charting its marked shifts in emphasis over time, he shows that what is meant by 'the economic' is much wider than is generally understood. In particular, Hall makes it clear that Marx's concerns, far from being static and unchanging, were primarily with the subtleties of transformed and transforming social relations and that, in his analysis of these, he constantly returned to the independent effects of political and ideological factors, though within a structure broadly determined by the economic.

Such interpretation of Marxist class theory is still far from fully developed and in 'The class structure of advanced capitalist societies' (Reading 9) – Erik Olin Wright investigates the important contribution of Nicos Poulantzas to this field.

Summarizing in detail Poulantzas's work, which argues that economic position alone does not necessarily determine class, Wright goes on to suggest, with points drawn from Marx's theory of the capitalist mode of production, some of the difficulties involved in this analysis. Wright demonstrates here the importance of conceptual critique for the development of theory and shows how discussions conducted from within an acceptance of a particular analytical framework leave room for constructive debate.

However, not all social theorists have accepted the validity of Marxist theory and in 'Some later theories' (Reading 10) Anthony Giddens provides us with a succinct and lucid account of the work of three such recent authors. Documenting how Dahrendorf, Aron and Ossowski each begins from an appreciation of the writings of Marx, he shows how each, nevertheless, citing conceptual confusion and historical inadequacies in the original work, reject Marxist theory. Giddens summarizes the alternative conclusions reached by each author, conclusions which are united in the necessity of recognizing a plurality of significant groupings within the social structure.

One area in which the strengths of such a pluralist approach has long been argued is that of explaining a society divided along racial or national lines. In 'Immigrant workers and class structure' (Reading 11) Stephen Castles and Godula Kosack advance the contrary claims of Marxist class analysis. As the conclusion to a detailed analysis of the position of migrant labour in four Western European societies – France, Germany, Switzerland and Great Britain – they contend that such workers must be seen, not only as a major group in their own right, but more fundamentally as an integral part of the class structure. They are, Castles and Kosack suggest, to be located within the working class of such societies, but in a particular form of working class, one riven by internal divisions and rivalries, founded on conflicting interests and different historical experiences.

The final contribution to this section, 'State and society under liberalism and after' (Reading 12) by Gianfranco Poggi, similarly poses analytical and historical issues. Dealing with broad trends in the relationship between state and society, it traces the increasing involvement of government and quasi-government agencies in all spheres of social life and shows how this development must significantly affect our understanding of social structure. Poggi stresses that such fundamental changes affect the balances of power within society and, in so doing, modify the commitment of social groups to the existing social order. This concern emphasizes a theme informing each of the contributions to this section. Social structure must not only be seen as relatively immutable, as determining the forms of action and belief of particular groups and individuals, but also as relatively fluid, for a social order may be changed through the conscious efforts of its participants. Sociology is concerned to chart and to understand this relationship – that of the dialectic between social action and social structure.

8. The 'political' and the 'economic' in Marx's theory of classes

Stuart Hall

I

The Communist Manifesto was drafted by Marx and Engels for the Communist League 'to make plain to all the true nature of the "spectre" that was supposed to be haunting Europe'. It was published on the eve of the great revolutionary upsurge of 1848 – by the time it appeared, Marx was already in Paris at the invitation of the liberal-radical government which had overthrown Louis-Philippe. It was explicitly designed as a revolutionary tocsin; many, if not all, of its simplifications must be understood in that light. By the summer of 1848, the counter-revolution had begun to unroll; Marx and Engels were forced to admit that they had misread the birth-pangs of bourgeois society as its death-knell. Marx changed his mind – about many more things than the speed at which the revolutionary showdown would be enacted. Gwyn Williams (Williams, 1976) has brilliantly demonstrated how this 'break' in perspective – a *political* break – registers inside the *theoretical* structure of one of Marx's most critical texts, *The Eighteenth Brumaire of Louis Bonaparte*. Indeed, without simplifying the connection, we could say that the historical collapse of the 1848 Revolutions produced a theoretical advance of the first order in Marx's understanding of the complex question of classes and their relation to political struggle. One way of assessing the distance he travelled and the discoveries he made can be measured in terms of the *differences* – and convergences – between the way he writes about classes in the *Manifesto* (1847) and the essays on *The*

From A. Hunt (ed.), *Class and Class Structure*, London: Lawrence and Wishart, 1978, pp. 19–54.

Eighteenth Brumaire and *The Class Struggles in France*, drafted between 1850 and 1852.

> The history of all hitherto existing society is the history of class struggles. Freeman and slave, patrician and plebian, lord and serf, guild-master and journeyman, in a word, oppressor and oppressed, stood in constant opposition to one another, carried on an uninterrupted, now hidden, now open fight, a fight that each time ended in a revolutionary reconstruction of society at large, or in the common ruin of the contending classes.
>
> ... With the development of industry the proletariat not only increases in number; it becomes concentrated in greater masses, its strength grows and it feels that strength more. The various interests are more and more equalised, in proportion as machinery obliterates all distinctions of labour, and nearly everywhere reduces wages to the same low level. The growing competition among the bourgeois ... makes their livelihood more and more precarious; the collision between individual workmen and individual bourgeois takes more and more the character of collision between two classes. Thereupon the workers begin to form combinations (trade unions) against the bourgeois ... This organisation of the proletarians into a class, and consequently into a political party, is continually being upset by the competition between the workers themselves. But it ever rises up again, stronger, firmer and mightier. It compels legislative recognition of particular interests of workers, by taking advantage of divisions among the bourgeoisie itself. Thus the Ten Hours Bill in England. (*MESW* (1), pp. 35ff.)

What is so fatally seductive about this text is its simplifying revolutionary sweep: its *élan*, coupled with the optimistic sureness of its grasp on the unrolling, unstoppable tide of revolutionary struggle and proletarian victory; above all, its unmodified sense of historical inevitability. That note sits uneasily with our much refined sense of the revolution's infinitely 'long delay' – and of how much more complex, how less inevitable, its denouement has proved to be. And this is connected with a rejection of one of the central propositions which appears to power and sustain this unrolling-through-revolution: the progressive simplification of class antagonisms, articulated along a linear path of historical time, into *basically* two hostile camps – bourgeoisie and proletarians, facing one another in a 'process of dissolution of . . . a violent and glaring character'. The whole logic of this part of the text is over-determined by the historical conjuncture in which it was drafted. Undoubtedly, classes are constructed in the text historically, in the simple sense: the dissolution of feudalism; the revolutionary role of the emergent bourgeoisie; 'free competition' and 'free labour' – Marx's two preconditions for the installation of a capitalist mode of production on an expanded scale; the gigantic development of capital's productive capacities; then, industrial and commercial crises; progressive immiseration, class polarisation, revolutionary rupture and overthrow.

This *linearity*, this undisguised historical evolutionism, is interrupted or displaced by the play of, essentially, only a single antagonism: between the developing forces of production, and the 'fettering' relations of production in which the former are embedded. It is this fundamental contradiction which provides the basic punctuation of the class struggle in the capitalist mode. Its course is subject, of course, to delays; but its essential tendency is forwards – towards 'collision'. This is because the two levels are directly harnessed – the class struggle 'matures' as capitalism 'develops'. Indeed, the latter develops and matures the former: capitalism is its own grave-digger. Capitalism thus produces its own 'negation' – the oppressed classes whose rising struggles propel that phase to its conclusion, and drive society forwards to the next stage of its development. Since bourgeois versus proletarians is the most 'universal' of the class struggles to date – the proletariat is the last class to be emancipated; that which 'has nothing to lose but its chains' – the proletarian revolution entails the emancipation of all classes, or the abolition of class society *as such.*

The basic problematic of the *Manifesto* is hardly in doubt. Its presence is luminously rendered in the transparency of the writing – a transparency of style which recapitulates the way the relations and connections dealt with in the text are grasped and driven forwards. It treats classes as 'whole' subjects – collective subjects or actors. It deals with the transposition of the class struggle from the economic to the political level unproblematically. They are interchangeable: the one leads, inexorably, to the other. They are connected by means of what Althusser has called a 'transitive causality'. It treats history as an unfolding sequence of struggles – arranged into epochs, punctuated by *the* class struggle, which is its motor. It conceives a capitalist social formation as, essentially, a simple structure – a structure whose immediate forms may be complex, but whose dynamic and articulation is simple and essentialist: its articulation is basically 'given' by the terms of a single contradiction (forces/relations of production) which unrolls unproblematically from the economic 'base', evenly throughout all its different levels, 'indifferently'. A break at one level therefore gives rise, sooner or later, to a parallel break at the other levels. This has been defined as a 'historicist' conception (Althusser, 1969) because it deals with a social formation as what Althusser calls an 'expressive totality'. There is even, behind this 'historicism', the trace of an earlier problematic: that which conceives of the proletarian revolution as the liberation of all humanity, the 'moment' of the installation of the rule of Reason in History – one which recalls the humanist thrust of, say, the section 'On Communism' of the *1844 Manuscripts*, with its undisguised Feuerbachean and Hegelian overtones. It is a heroic, humanist vision. But it is flawed, both in its substantive predictions and in its mode of conceptualisation.

The most decisive and definitive dismantling of this whole problematic is certainly to be found in Althusser's seminal essay, 'Contradiction And Over-determination' in *For Marx*. The *Manifesto* must now be read in the light of that intervention. Briefly, in it, Althusser argues that in the concrete analysis of any specific historical moment, although the principal contradiction of the capitalist mode of production – that between the forces of production and the 'fettering' relations of production – provides the 'final' determinacy, the terms of this contradiction, alone, are not sufficient for analysing the way *different levels of class struggle* lead to a revolutionary rupture. Because the levels of a social formation are not neatly aligned in the way the *Manifesto* suggests, contradictions do not immediately and unmediatedly unroll from the economic base, producing a rupture or break at all the different levels simultaneously. Indeed, as Lenin indicated with respect to 1917, the crucial question is rather how 'absolutely dissimilar currents, absolutely heterogeneous class interests, absolutely contrary political and social strivings have merged . . . in a strikingly "harmonious" manner' as the result of an 'extremely unique historical situation'. These dissimilar currents cannot, then, be reduced to the determinacy of the 'laws' of the economic base. 'The Capital-Labour contradiction is never simple, but always specified by the historically con-crete forms and circumstances in which it is exercised. It is specified by the forms of the superstructure . . . by the internal and external historical situation . . . many of these phenomena deriving from the "law of uneven development" in the Leninist sense' (Althusser, 1969).

This requires us to conceive of different contradictions, each with its own specificity, its own tempo of development, internal history, and its own conditions of existence – at once 'deter-mined and determining': in short, it poses the question of the relative autonomy and the specific effectivity of the different levels of a social formation. If this is to be combined with the cardinal principle of Marxism – that without which it is theoretically indistinguishable from any other 'sociology' – namely, 'determination in the last instance by the (economic) mode of production', then a decisive turn in the relations of forces in a social formation cannot be adequately 'thought' in terms of a *reduction* of all the secondary contradictions to the terms of the principal contradiction. In short, Marxism requires a form of determinacy which is *not* equivalent to an economic reductionism. The 'merging' of these 'heterogeneous currents', Althusser suggests, is better 'thought', not as a reduction but as a *complex effect* – an accumulation of all the instances and effects, a merger, a rupture – an 'over-determin-ation'. It follows from this argument that a social formation is not a 'totality' of the essentialist type, in which there is a simple 'identity' between its different levels, with the super-structural levels the mere 'epiphenomena' of the objective laws governing 'the economic base'. It is, rather, a unity of a necessarily complex type – an 'ensemble' which is always the result of many determinations: a unity, moreover, which is characterised by its *unevenness*.

In his 1857 *Introduction* to the *Grundrisse* Marx argued that, though Capital, in its prolonged circuit, requires both production, distribution and exchange, these must not be thought of as 'equivalents', but as different 'moments' of a circuit, *articulated into* a 'unity' – a unity which does not efface their necessary differences but must be 'thought' rather 'in terms of their differences'. And though 'production' does exert a final determinacy over the circuit as a whole, each 'moment' has its own determinateness, plays its necessary, non-reducible role in the self-expanding value of capital, obeying its own conditions of existence. The relation, specifically, of the economic to the political must, similarly, be conceptualised as articulated into a unity, through their necessary differences and displacements. There is therefore *no necessary immediate correspondence* between the 'economic' and the 'political' constitution of classes. The terms in which their 'complex unity' could be thought, of course, remained to be developed. But there can be little doubt that these developments decisively mark out as radically different the terrain of Marx's subsequent work from that so lucidly prescribed in the *Manifesto*.

Important as it is to mark the line which separates the phase of Marx's thought which finds a definitive statement in the *Manifesto* from his subsequent development, it is also necessary to remind ourselves of what cannot be left behind – of what has already been gained, what is irreducible in it. This becomes clearer provided we detach the *Manifesto* a little from its immediate location, and reconsider its 'advances', as I have tried to phrase it, 'in the light of *Capital*'. The declaration that 'the history of all hitherto existing society is the history of class struggles', for example, is as fundamental to Marxism as it was to appear a 'startling premiss' when first enunciated. Marxism is unthinkable without it. The emphasis on 'classes' there is almost as fundamental as the emphasis on 'struggles'. The brief articulation of this proposition which immediately follows – freemen and slave, lord and serf, bourgeois and proletarian – though in no sense an *adequate* account of the complex class structures of the modes of production to which they refer (and therefore the site of a continuing difficulty) – is an absolutely necessary starting point. The idea that 'men' first appear as biological individuals, or as the 'bare individuals' of market society, and only then are coalesced into classes – class as, so to speak, a secondary formation – is not a reading supportable from this text or anything in Marx which follows it. This premiss therefore foreshadows the many later passages in which Marx dethrones the apparently natural and obvious reference back to 'individuals' as the basis for a theory of classes.

From the standpoint of Marxism, 'men' are always preconstituted by the antagonistic class relations into which they are cast. Historically, they are always articulated, not in their profound and unique individuality, but *by* 'the ensemble of social relations' – that is as the supports for class relations. It is this prior constitution which produces, under specific conditions, as its *results*, a specific type of individuality: the possessive individual of bourgeois political theory, the needy individual of market society, the contracting individual of the society of 'free labour'. Outside these relations, the individual – this 'Robinson Crusoe' of classical political economy, self-sufficient in a world surveyed only from the standpoint of 'his' needs and wants – which has formed the natural, de-historicised point of origin of bourgeois society and theory, is not a possible theoretical starting point at all. It is only the 'product of many determinations'. The history of its production, Marx once remarked (in *Capital* I, p. 715) 'is written in the annals of mankind in letters of blood and fire'. As he subsequently argued:

Society is not merely an aggregate of individuals; it is the sum of relations in which individuals stand to one another. It is as though someone were to say that, from the point of view of society, slaves and citizens do not exist; they are all men. In fact, this is rather what they are outside society. Being a slave or a citizen is a socially determined relation between individual A and individual B. Individual A is not as such a slave. He is only a slave in and through society (*Grundrisse*, p. 265).

Like all its predecessors, the capitalist process of production proceeds under definite material conditions which, are, however, simultaneously the bearers of definite social relations entered into by individuals in the process of reproducing their life. Those conditions, like these relations, are on the one hand pre-requisites, on the other hand results . . . of the capitalist process of production; they are produced and reproduced by it (*Capital*, III, pp. 818–19).

Almost everything which passes for a sort of sociological 'common sense' about social classes is contradicted and forbidden by those formulations: and their essential point is already implicit in the *Manifesto*.

Second, there is the premiss which Marx himself noted as the nub of his own contribution (Marx to Weydemeyer, 5 March 1852: *MESC*, p. 69) and which is reaffirmed again by Marx and Engels in their joint Preface to the 1872 German edition of the *Manifesto*: the premiss that 'the existence of classes is only bound up with particular phases in the development of production'. It is the conditions and relations of production, made specific to different phases in the contradictory development of capital, which provides the basic and essential framework for a Marxist theory of classes. It is this premiss which divides Marxism as a 'scientific' theory from all previous and subsequent forms of Utopian Socialism. Henceforth the class struggle was no longer a moral assertion about the inhumanity of the capitalist system, nor was capitalism's destruction projected on to the system from the outside by an exercise of will or hope.

Capitalism, in this sense, produces and reproduces itself *as* an antagonistic structure of class relations: it remorselessly divides the 'population', again and again, into its antagonistic classes. Note, at the same time, that it is the phases in the development of the *mode of production* which provides the necessary, though not the sufficient, condition for a Marxist theory of classes: it is not 'the economic' in some more obvious sense, which 'determines'. Marx is absolutely consistent about this, from the first formulations of the question in *The German Ideology*, through to the end. But so powerful is the grasp of bourgeois common-sense, and so persistently does it return to exert its influence even at the heart of Marxist theory itself, that it is worth repeating. It is the material and social relations within which men produce and reproduce their material conditions of existence which 'determines' – *how* remains to be elucidated. The unequal distribution of economic wealth, goods and power, which forms the basis for a 'socio-economic' conception of 'social classes' is, for Marx, not the basis but the *result* of the *prior* distribution of the agents of capitalist production into classes and class relations, and the prior distribution of the means of production as between its 'possessors' and its 'dispossessed'.

The simplification of classes, which appears to be a fundamental thesis of the *Manifesto* is also not as simple an argument as it at first appears. In arguing that, under capitalism bourgeois versus proletarians is the fundamental form of the class struggle, the *Manifesto* does not – as is sometimes supposed – neglect the presence of other classes and class fractions. Indeed, it contains a summary judgement on the revolutionary potential of *inter alia* 'the lower middle classes, the small manufacturer, the shopkeeper, the artisan, the peasant' as well as 'the dangerous class, the social scum', from which Marx never departed. What it argues is that 'of all the classes that stand face to face with the bourgeoisie today, the proletariat alone is the really revolutionary class'. This is a difficult point, requiring further examination.

Marx comes to the assertion on the basis of the objective position which the proletariat has in a mode of production, based on the latter's expropriation from the means of production and the exploitation of its labour power. In *this* sense the proposition stands – the revolutionary *position* of the proletariat being, in this sense, 'given' (specified) by its location in a specific mode. This does, however, tend to treat the proletariat as an unfractured and undifferentiated 'class subject' – a subject with a role *in* history but no internal, contradictory history of its own, at least within the capitalist epoch. This is a premiss which Marx subsequently modified and which we must reject. But the passage could also be read as if it asserted that, *because* the proletariat has an objectively revolutionary *position* in the economic structure of capitalist production, *therefore* it also and always must exhibit empirically a revolutionary political consciousness and form of political organisation. It is just this further 'move' which Lukács makes in *History and Class Consciousness*; and when he is obliged to recognise that this proletariat does not 'empirically' always live up to its appointed form of consciousness, he treats it 'abstractly' as if this is its ascribed destiny – its 'potential consciousness' – from which its actual, concrete historical divergences are but temporary lapses. The enormous historical problem, for Marxism, of the 'economism' of trade union consciousness, and of the containment of the Western European working-class movements within the confines of social democratic reformism, cannot be systematically elucidated from this position. We come back, then, to one of the critical weaknesses – it recurs in one form or another throughout the text – of the *Manifesto*: a weakness which can now be summarily stated.

The *Manifesto* is correct in its (obviously and necessarily schematic) discussion of the economic constitution of classes in terms of the phases of development of the mode of production. But it is fatally flawed in treating, systematically, the relation between the economic and the political. To this question the *Manifesto* either returns an unsatisfactory answer (i.e. they are more or less aligned, more or less 'corresponding'); or it leaves a *space*, a gap, through which the abstract error of a Lukácsean historicism constantly escapes. In short, all that is necessary to think the specificity of the political class struggle and its relation to the economic level – on which our ability to expound 'the ensemble' as a whole depends – is not yet present as usable concepts in Marx's thought. These further concepts are, indeed, *forced into discovery* by the historical and political conjuncture they were required to explain: the collapse of the 1848 revolutions. Thus, precisely, their clearest and most substantial formulation occurs in the essays and studies which immediately follow – the writings on France, especially, more fleetingly (and less satisfactorily) the asides on Britain: texts which, so to speak, appear in the light of theoretical reflection and clarification cast by a moment of revolutionary defeat. Here we are on the terrain of real discoveries, of a theoretically revolutionary *break-through*. This break-through occurs 'in thought', certainly: but it can hardly be adequately understood as 'epistemological'.

Still, we have not fully plumbed the depth of that brilliantly-surfaced text, the *Manifesto*. Why and how did Marx and Engels envisage the 'simplification' of classes (with its profound consequences for deciphering the rhythm of the class struggle) to be *implicit* in the unfolding of capitalist development?

II

It is the increasing size and scale of capitalist production which precipitates this 'simplification'. The circumstances which, first, produce the proletariat, then develop it, then drive all the intermediary class strata into its growing ranks are worth briefly detailing: (a) the formation of a class, expropriated from the ownership of the means of production, with only its labour power to sell, exposed to the 'vicissitudes of competition and all the fluctuations of the market'; (b) the division of labour consequent on the extensive use of machinery which 'deskills' the worker, reducing him to an appendage of the machine; (c) the growing exploitation of labour power 'whether by prolongation of the working day in a given time or by increased speed of the machinery, etc.'; (d) the organisation of labour into an 'industrial army' in factory conditions under the command of capital's 'officers and sergeants'; (e) the *dilution* of labour through the lowering of the value of labour power – the employment, at lower wages, of women and children; (f) the exposure of the class to exploitation in the market for subsistence goods – by the landlord, the shop-keeper, the pawn-broker. In this context arises (g) the thesis that the lower strata of the middle class 'sink gradually into the proletariat' – partly through their losing battle with (h) large-scale, concentrated 'big' capital. The intermediary strata are what Gramsci would call 'subaltern' fractions of the middle classes. They are intrinsically conservative, reactionary in outlook – trying to 'roll back the wheel of history'. They are or become 'revolutionary' only face to face with their 'impending transfer into the proletariat' – their 'proletarianisation'.

The attentive reader will recognise at once that all of these sketchy ideas reappear, and are subject to a major development, above all in Marx's seminal Chapter XV on 'Machinery and Modern Industry' in *Capital* I. The formation, historically, of a class of 'free labour', with nothing to sell but its labour-power, out of the matrix of feudal relations, is constantly returned to in *Capital* as its 'historic basis'. The progressive reduction of the worker to an 'appendage of the machine' is central to Marx's description of the capitalist labour process, and to his qualitative distinction between the phase of 'machinery' and the phase of 'modern industry'. The growing exploitation of labour power foreshadows the critical distinction in *Capital* between Absolute (the prolongation of the working day) and Relative (the increase of the ratio of 'dead' to 'living' labour) surplus value. The growing hierarchisation and 'despotism' of capital's command leads on to Marx's distinction between the 'formal' and the 'real' subsumption of labour. The 'dilution' of skilled labour and the formation of a 'reserve army' are two of the critical 'counter-acting tendencies' to the tendency of the rate of profit to fall, discussed both in *Capital* I (for example, Chapter XXV) and again in *Capital* III, where the processes leading to the growing concentration and centralisation of capitals are more fully described. In this context, also there arises the description of the emergence of the modern 'collective worker' and the first hints at the *expansion* of the *new* intermediary classes, consequent on a developing division of labour, as the older petty-bourgeoisie and its material basis in 'small' and trading capital is eroded. In the context of this major theoretical development, the sketchy outline of the *Manifesto*, which contains little but an *indication* of how the organisation of capitalist production provides the basis for this *formation* and *recomposition* of classes, is both expanded and transformed. Again, both continuities and the breaks necessary for their theoretical development must be observed.

When in *Capital* Marx sets out to resume, in a condensed form, the general overall tendency of this whole development, the terms he employs are *strikingly similar* to those he employed in the *Manifesto*. One has only to turn to the summary review contained in the brief Chapter XXXII of *Capital* I to hear again the familiar phrases:

> At a certain stage of development it brings forth the material agencies of its own dissolution. From that moment new forces and new passions spring up in the bosom of society: but the old organisation fetters them and keeps them down . . . As soon as this process of transformation has sufficiently decomposed the old society from top to bottom, as soon as the labourers are turned into proletarians, their means of labour into capital, as soon as the capitalist mode of production stands on its own feet, then the further socialisation of labour . . . takes a new form . . . This expropriation is accomplished by the action of the immanent laws of capitalist production itself, by the centralisation of capital . . . Hand in hand with this centralisation, or this expropriation of many capitals by few, develop, on an ever-extending scale, the co-operative form of the labour-process, the conscious technical application of science, the methodological cultivation of the soil, the transformation of the instruments of labour into instruments of labour only usable in common, the economising of all means of production by their use as the means of production of combined, socialised labour, the entanglement of all peoples in the net of the world market . . . but with this too grows the revolt of the working-class, a class always increasing in numbers, and disciplined, united, organised by the very mechanism of the process of capitalist production itself (*Capital* I, 714–15).

This is the echo, the 'voice' of the *Manifesto*, inside *Capital*. But side by side with this résumé, we must set the detail, but more significantly the *method*, by which the simple sketch of the *Manifesto* is transformed into the terms and concepts of *Capital*'s investigation. It is impossible within the scope of this paper to provide the 'reading' which would substantiate in detail the nature of this theoretical transformation. But some examples can be taken in order to demonstrate how the sketch of the process in the *Manifesto* – structured largely on a linear development, punctuated by the rising tempo of class struggle – is *thoroughly transformed*, in its reworking in *Capital*, by really setting to work the concept of *contradiction* and the notion of dialectical development.

Two examples will have to suffice. In the opening section of Chapter XV, Marx established the technical difference between the nature of the instruments of production (and the consequent division of labour in the labour process itself) which characterises the *first* phase of capitalist development – the era of Machinery – and that further qualitative development – 'machinery organised into a system', where the machine 'uses' the worker rather than the reverse – which marks out the period of 'Modern Industry'. In the section on 'The Factory' Marx then explores the complex and contradictory effects of this transformation of capitalism's material basis. He comments, *inter alia*, on the decomposition of the traditional skills of the class, as these skills are increasingly 'passing over' into the machine itself: here, he notes, the *tendency* towards the equalisation and reduction of skills 'to one and the same level of every kind of work'. But this has consequences, at once, for the *social* organisation of production: it brings in its train the recomposition of the elements of production into 'the head workman' and his 'mere attendants': and, alongside this, the new 'superior class of workmen, some of them scientifically educated' who look after the whole of the machinery itself and repair it.

As the machine begins to dictate the organisation of the labour process, it brings further contradictory developments with it: the greater ease of substituting one labour force for another; the introduction of continuous production and the shift system (the 'relay system'); the dilution of labour and the erosion of traditional skills born of an earlier division of labour – 'traditional habits' now 'systematically remoulded'. In the annexation of worker to the machine, the systematic 'pumping dry' of living labour by dead labour proceeds at an enormous pace – the 'special skills of each individual factory operator vanishes as an infinitesimal quantity before the science, the gigantic physical forces and the mass of labour that are embodied in the factory mechanism'. But this has further consequences, too, for the nature of factory discipline, hierarchy and command – redividing workers into 'operatives and overlookers' (the 'private soldiers and sergeants of an industrial army') – and for the administration of a more detailed and coercive labour regime. Dr Andrew Ure, the 'poet' of Modern Industry, himself saw how the revolution in the means of production both *required* and *made possible* the withdrawal of any process requiring particular skill and dexterity from the 'cunning workman . . . prone to irregularities' to the 'self-regulating mechanism' which even the child can superintend. Thus the 'technical' revolution in the means of production produces an unlooked-for effect in the regulation of labour and the repression of the strikes and other 'periodic revolts' of the working class against its conditions of life. Again, as Marx, quoting Ure, observes: when 'capital enlists science into her service, the refractory hand of labour will always be taught docility'.

In this Section alone we see how what, in the *Manifesto*, appears to be organised around a simple antagonism, is articulated into a complex and contradictory one: the necessary terms are *effects*, not intended, which nevertheless have contradictory outcomes: effects at *levels* where no result was calculated: *tendencies*, immediately cross-cut by their opposite: advances which produce, elsewhere, regressive results. Above all, what was in the earlier text represented as an essentially homogeneous force – the proletariat – is now itself constantly and ceaselessly acted upon, redefined, recomposed, 'remoulded' by the operation of capital's contradictory law. Already in the *Manifesto* Marx had foreseen how the growing cohesion of the proletariat, in the conditions of factory labour, was constantly interrupted by the tendency towards 'competition between workers'. But it is only when the process of development which lays the foundation for that growing cohesion is investigated in depth that we can see *why* it is that capital produces, of necessity, *both* the massification and the 'simplification' of labour, as one of its tendencies; but also, equally 'necessarily', the internal divisions between skilled and the unskilled, the distribution of skills into different branches of production, as 'Modern Industry' seizes on them and transforms them *unevenly*: how the 'dilution' of the traditional work-force by the employment on a large scale of women and children (a development made possible only by the revolution in the nature of the labour process itself) sets one group of workers against another, introducing as a further contradiction 'the natural differences of age and sex' – i.e. the sexual division of labour into its social division: and how capital comes to be in a position to exploit these new elements in the division of labour (or the parallel one between supervisors, the 'superior class of workmen' and the machine-minders) to its political advantage. In short how the production of two, opposite *tendencies* in capital's contradictory development decisively *intervenes* between any simple notion of the 'inevitable cohesion of the proletariat' and its actual realisation under the new conditions of capital's historic organisation.

Something absolutely central about the form and character of the class struggle under modern conditions of production is already present in the deceptively simple remark, by Marx, that:

> So far as division of labour reappears in the factory it is primarily a distribution of the workmen among the specialised machines; and of masses of workmen, not however organised into groups, among the various departments of the factory, in each of which they work at a number of similar machines placed together; their co-operation therefore is only simple. The organised group, peculiar to manufacture, is replaced by the connexion between the head workman and his few assistants (*Capital* I, p. 396).

This tendency does not obliterate the earlier one: it represents both the expanding base for the 'socialisation of labour' and the technical interdependence of the various branches of capitalist production: as well as the social basis for the formation of a modern proletariat. The development of capitalism reproduces *both* tendencies at once: in short, in driving itself forward through one of its 'technical' limits, in overcoming one of the material barriers to its revolutionising self-expansion, capital produces new contradictions at a higher level of development. Its advance – quite contrary to the dominant impression of the *Manifesto* – is, in the *full* sense, dialectical.

We can see this at work in another instance, where also there are apparently straight 'echoes' of the *Manifesto*. Marx noted in that text the two 'paths' open to capital – prolongation of the working day, and the 'increase of the work exacted in a given time . . . the increased speed of machinery, etc'. He also noted, but in another context, the growing political strength of the proletariat – 'it ever rises up again, stronger, firmer, mightier' – compelling a recognition of the 'particular interests of the workers'; in this latter context he cites the 'Ten Hour bill'. Again, it is striking to observe how deeply and thoroughly these ideas are transformed as they reappear in *Capital*. The enlarged application of machinery has the effect of increasing the productivity of labour – 'shortening the working-time required in the production of a commodity'. But it also has the effect of reducing the resistance of the workers to the prolongation of the working day. Here, at once, is a contradiction, 'since of the two factors of the surplus-value created by a given amount of capital, one, the rate of surplus-value, cannot be increased except by diminishing the other, the number of workmen'. The effects are, therefore, as contradictory as they are 'unconscious' (p. 407, fn. i). If it extends the working day, 'changes the method of labour, as also the character of the social working organism, in such a manner as to break down all opposition to this tendency', it also 'produces, partly by opening out to the capitalist new strata of the working class . . . partly by setting free the labourers it supplants, a surplus working population'. It is this unfettered exploitation of labour power which provokes 'a reaction' on the part of a section of the ruling class – a reaction leading to 'divisions among the bourgeoisie itself' which the workers' struggle takes advantage of, forcing through the Factory legislation, with its statutory limits to the working day. Marx subsequently notes that the capitalists oppose this limit, politically, vigorously: they declare production to be 'impossible' under such conditions. Yet it is precisely the imposition of this limit – which 'the surging revolt of the working class compelled [on] Parliament' – which *drives* capital forward to 'raising the productive power of the workman, so as to enable him to produce more in a given time with the same expenditure of labour'. This is the enormous – the uneven and unplanned – threshold which capital crosses, from the epoch of Absolute to that of Relative surplus value.

Its effects are immense: the rise in the organic composition of capital; the lowering of the value component of every commodity; the intensification of the labour process; the 'filling up of the pores of the working day'; the 'increasing tension of labour power'; the speed-up of the production process; the great stimulus to technical advance and the application of science as a material force; and the gain in the administration of a regime of 'regularity, uniformity, order, continuity' in labour – these are only *some* of the consequences Marx outlines. By 1858, Marx notes, the Factory Inspector is reporting that 'the great improvements made in machines of every kind have raised their productive power very much . . . Without any doubt, the shortening of the hours of labour . . . gave the impulse to these improvements'. Towards the end of Chapter XV, Marx returns again to the complex outcome of the mid-century Factory legislation, dealing now more fully both with its technical and its social (education, children, the family) consequences. Thus what appears in the *Manifesto* as a simple disconnection between the levels of the mode of production and of political struggle, is brought together into a contradictory 'unity': a unity which shows how, while the law of value obtains, capital advances, blindly, unconsciously – as Brecht would say, 'from its bad side': how it is impelled to advance itself by contravening the very limits and barriers it establishes for itself: how its 'political' consciousness is often at variance with its inner drive and necessities. It illustrates vividly capital's powers of *recuperation*: how it constantly is forced to weave together its own contradictory impulses into forms of social and economic organisation which it can bend and force to advance its own 'logic'. It shows how, in order to master and contain within its framework those 'particular' advances which the working class is able to force upon it, capital develops a different *repertoire*; it discovers new 'solutions'. Any idea that the 'logic of capital' is a simple and straightforward functional 'unfolding', or that its logic is one which can be separated from the 'logic of class struggle' – two disconnected threads – is definitively disposed of in this Chapter.

Out of this historical-analytic exposition Marx detaches the seminal theoretical argument, which is then presented (in the following chapter) in its 'purer' theoretical form: the concepts of 'The Production of Absolute and of Relative Surplus Value'. The whole tendential direction is thus concisely summarised: the 'general extension of factory legislation to all trades for the purpose of protecting the working class' – the outcome of an immediate political struggle – also 'hastens on the general conversion of numerous isolated small industries into a few combined industries . . . it therefore accelerates the concentration of capital and the exclusive predominance of the factory system'. It 'destroys ancient and transitional forms behind which the domination of capital is still in part concealed, and replaces them by the direct and open sway of capital; but thereby it also generalises the direct opposition to this sway'. It enforces uniformity, regularity, order and economy, and provides the spur to technical improvement, the intensity of labour and the 'competition of machinery with the worker'. It destroys the material basis of petty and domestic production. 'By maturing the material conditions and the combination on a social scale of the processes of production, it matures the contradictions and antagonisms of the capitalist form of production' (*Capital* I, p. 503). If this appears to make a last-hour return to the terrain of the *Manifesto*, it is only in so far as the contradictory double-thrust of capitalist development and its intrinsically antagonistic nature lies at the heart of both conceptions. From the vantage point of *Capital*, the so-called 'simplification of classes and the class struggle' – or what we must now call the *complex simplification* of classes and the logic of class struggle within the 'logic' of capital's historic development – has been thoroughly and irreversibly transformed. In terms of the Marxist 'theory of classes', we have entered quite new territory.

III

As we have seen, one of the critical points left in an unsatis-factory state by the *Manifesto* is the relations between the economic and the political aspects of class struggle. Marx does pose the question of 'this organisation of the proletarians into a class . . . and consequently into a party': as if the political aspects were simply a more advanced form of the 'economic', requiring no alteration of terms or extension of conceptual framework. In *The German Ideology*, Marx says of the capitalist class that 'the separate individuals form a class in so far as they have to carry on a common battle against another class; otherwise they are on hostile terms with one another as competitors' (*German Ideology*, p. 69). In *The Poverty of Philosophy* Marx speaks of Utopian Socialism as typical of a period in which 'the proletariat is not sufficiently developed to constitute itself into a class' and consequently, 'the very struggle of the proletariat with the bourgeoisie has not yet assumed a political character' (*MECW*, vol. 6, p. 177). He calls the proletariat 'this mass which is already a class in opposition to capital but not yet a class for itself'. In *The Eighteenth Brumaire*, Marx writes:

> In so far as millions of families live under economic con-ditions of existence that separate their mode of life, their interests and their culture from those of other classes and put them in hostile opposition to the latter, they form a class. In so far as there is merely a local interconnection among these small-holding peasants and the identity of their interests begets no community, no national bond, no political organisation amongst them, they do not form a class. They are consequently incapable of enforcing their class interests in their own name.

In 1871, in a Letter to Friedrich Bolte, which touches again the Factory legislation discussed above, Marx writes:

> The ultimate object of the political movement of the work-ing class is, of course, the conquest of political power for

this class, and this naturally requires that the organisation of the working class, and the organisation which arises from its economic struggles should previously reach a certain level of development. On the other hand, however, every movement in which the working class as a *class* confronts the ruling classes and tries to constrain them by pressure from without is a political movement. For instance the attempt by strikes, etc., in a particular factory or even in a particular trade to compel individual capitalists to reduce the working day, is a purely economic movement. On the other hand, the movement to force through an eight hour, etc., *law* is a *political* movement. And in this way, out of the separate economic movements of the workers there grows up everywhere a *political* movement, that is to say, a *class*, movement, with the object of enforcing its interests in a general form, in a form possessing general, socially coercive force. While these movements presuppose a certain degree of previous organisation, they are in turn equally a means of developing this organisation (23 November 1871, *MESC*, pp. 254–5).

Marx was writing here to clarify certain theses of the General Council of the International whose Rules he had formulated. A few days later Engels was to write in very similar terms for a very similar purpose to the Turin newspaper, *Il Proletario Italiano*:

> The economical emancipation of the working classes is . . . the great end to which every political movement ought to be subordinated as a means . . . in the struggle of the working class its economic movement and its political action are indissolubly united (29 November 1871, *MESC*, p. 255).

Here we find Marx and Engels rethinking precisely what is too simply proposed and glossed in the *Manifesto*: the necessary displacements as well as the conjunctures in the relation between the political and economic forms of the class struggle. The span of time is a lengthy one – from *The Poverty of Philosophy* to the Paris Commune; and in that period Marx's thought on this critical topic underwent what has been called 'further fluctuations' (Poulantzas, 1973, p. 58). These 'fluctuations' need to be treated with care.

The distinction drawn in the *Poverty of Philosophy* passage between class 'in itself' and class 'for itself' has, subsequently, hardened into a sort of pat formula. It appears to pose the economic/political relation in an incorrect manner. It suggests that there comes a moment when the proletariat as a whole develops the form of revolutionary class consciousness ascribed for it in its given, objective economic determination; and that only then does the class exist *at all* at the level of political struggle. We have indicated earlier the weakness which lies behind this too-neat bifurcation; which seems exclusively to reserve for such a moment of fulfilled consciousness the ascription 'political class struggle'; which derives it too neatly from the economic determinations of class; which makes the achievement of an 'autonomous' form of consciousness the only test of the political existence of a class; and which treats classes as unified historical subjects.

The 'in itself/for itself' distinction *is* useful as a way of defining different moments and forms of class consciousness, and perhaps even as a very rough way of marking the development out of a 'corporate' form of class struggle. But this would in fact require us to develop Marx's passing observation in a manner which is at odds with where it is pointing in this passage: for the distinction between 'corporate' and what Marx later calls a struggle which possesses 'general, socially coercive force' is *not* a distinction between the presence/absence of political struggle and its 'appropriate' forms of class consciousness, but precisely the opposite: a distinction between *two different forms* of the class struggle, two modes of class consciousness, each with its own determinate conditions in the material circumstances of the classes under capitalism. As both Marx and Engels observed, and as Lenin remarked even more extensively, working class reformism and 'trade union consciousness' – or what Lenin in *What Is To Be Done?* calls specifically 'working class bourgeois politics' (*CW*, vol. 5, p. 437) – has its own conditions of existence, its own material base in the economic conditions of the working class under capitalism: far from being a level or form of class struggle, so to speak 'below' the horizon of politics, it could be said to be the natural (or as Lenin called it, the 'spontaneous') form of working class struggle, in conditions where the means of raising that struggle to its more 'general' form are absent. But what those conditions might be, through which the forms of economic and political struggle can be heightened to their 'general' form, is not given in the in itself/for itself distinction.

The Letter to Bolte, on the other hand, has quite a different purchase. The phrase 'the conquest of political power for this class' has behind it the force of Marx's observations about the necessity of breaking the political power of the state erected by the bourgeoisie; and his stress on the 'dictatorship of the proletariat', which arose from his analysis of the Paris Commune, was embodied in *The Civil War in France*. More interestingly, the terms 'economic' and 'political' appear to be used, here, to designate *where*, in any specific conjuncture, the class struggle appears to have pertinent effects. The organisation by the proletariat within production to constrain capital's efforts to intensify the exploitation of labour by prolongation of the working day is defined as an 'economic movement' which attempts to modify the law governing the limitation of the working day (whose object must therefore be the bourgeois state itself) and constitutes a 'political movement'. Here, everything is translated to the level of the concrete conjuncture of a specific historical moment in which the class struggle 'takes effect'. Every trace of automatism in the movements between these two levels has been obliterated. What all the passages quoted put on the agenda, however, is the question of what the further conditions are, and what are the forms, by means of which the antagonistic relations of production of the capitalist mode can appear at, and have such pertinent effects in, the 'theatre' of politics. It is above all in the *Class Struggles in France* and in *The Eighteenth Brumaire* that the concepts begin to emerge which enable us to grasp the sources and the mechanisms of the 'relative autonomy' of the political level of the class struggle from the economic.

The first sections of *The Class Struggles in France* were composed in the immediate aftermath of 1848. Though already convinced that the proletariat was still too 'immature' to carry the day, this part of Marx's analysis is concentrated by the way the bourgeois political forces are driven by their own internal contradictions to destroy the basis of their own 'mature' political rule – universal suffrage – and consequently come gradually to confront the stark alternatives: retreat under the protection of Napoleon's bayonets, or proletarian revolution. The final Section was, however, drafted and published later: and there is a major and irreversible 'break' between the two perspectives. Fernbach has called it 'perhaps the most important [break] during his entire political work as a communist'. The nature of that break is resumed by Gwyn Williams: 'In the summer of 1850 Marx returned to his economic studies which were to immerse him in the British Museum for so many years. He came to the conclusion that the 1848 cycle of revolution had been set in train by a particular crisis in the new capitalist society ... that the return of prosperity made a new wave of revolutions exceedingly unlikely and, more important, that no proletarian revolution was possible on the continent until capitalist economy and capitalist relations of production had been much more fully developed ... His new perspective was grounded in a much fuller and more structural analysis, the analysis which was in fact to reach its climax in *Capital* seventeen years later' (Williams, 1976, p. 112).

The difference – most profoundly, then, registered in the analysis Marx offers in *The Eighteenth Brumaire* – does *not* differ from the schemas of the *Manifesto* in the sense of emphasising 'politics' at the expense of the 'objective conditions' constituted by the level of development of the forces and relations of capitalism. Quite the reverse. The objective determinations and the limits of what solutions were, and were not 'possible' at the political level are, in the later work, if anything *more* rigorously formulated, more structurally conceived and more systematically enforced than in the earlier texts. The elaboration of the 'practical concepts' of the political, for which *The Eighteenth Brumaire* is justly famous, is structured, through and through, by this unrelenting application of the 'determinations' which objective conditions place over the political resolutions. What Marx breaks with is any lingering assumption that the two levels exactly correspond: that the terms and contents of the one are fully given in the conditions and limits of the other. What he does, in the detailed and provocative tracing out of the forms which the class struggle assumes in what Gramsci calls 'its passage to the level of the complex superstructure' (Gramsci, 1971), is to put into place, for the first time, those concepts which alone enable us to 'think' *the specificity of the political*.

Briefly, then, in its overall tendency and trajectory, the crisis of 1851 is fundamentally and decisively over-determined by the objective development of French capitalism. It is this which establishes the outer limits, the determinations, the horizon within which the forms of the political arise and appear. Relatively, the French social formation is still at an early stage of its capitalist development. The proletariat, with its slogans and demands, is already 'on stage'; but it cannot as yet play the decisive role, and, above all, it cannot play an autonomous role. The bourgeoisie is already fully formed, articulated in politics through its major fractions, each fraction playing now one, now another of the political parties and factions, trying now one, now another of the available solutions. But *its* historic role is not anywhere near completion: above all, it has no means as yet 'netted' those classes which arose in earlier modes of production within its hegemonic sway. The bourgeoisie is therefore not yet in a position where it can, on its own feet and in its own terms, lay hold of French society and 'conform' its civil and political structures to the needs of the developing capitalist mode. The Republic thus totters from one unstable coalition to another; it runs through the entire repertoire of republican and democratic forms – constitutional assembly, parliamentary democracy, bourgeois-republican, republican-socialist. Each 'form' represents the attempt by a fraction – always in a temporary *alliance* – to secure political hegemony. As each alliance is exhausted or defeated, the social base to a possible solution narrows: in each the proletariat is either a pertinent but subordinate partner, or – as the end approaches – the force which is isolated. Finally, when all the possible solutions are exhausted, the unstable equilibrium of political forces on stage falls into the keeping of Napoleon Bonaparte, who 'would like to appear as the patriarchal benefactor of all classes' but only because he has already *broken them*: 'Above all things,

France requires tranquillity.'

We must restrict ourselves here to only two aspects of this demonstration: the question of the classes and their political 'forms of appearance', and the problem of the 'determination in the last instance' of the economic mode of production over the forms and outcomes of the political struggle.

The first thing to notice is that, though the entire exposition is framed with the structural analysis of the fundamental classes of the capitalist mode constantly in mind as its *analytic framework* – it is this which provides the whole, dazzling, dramatic narrative with its mastering logic – there are no 'whole classes' on stage here. The proletariat is the class which is most frequently treated as a 'bloc' – and even here the designation of a specific and critical role to the 'lumpen-proletariat' intersects the tendency to present the proletariat in the clash of positions as an 'integral' force. For capital, Marx always distinguishes its dominant *fractions* – 'big landed property'; 'high finance, large-scale industry, large-scale trade'; capital's 'two great interests', 'financial aristocracy', 'industrial bourgeoisie', etc. The petty-bourgeoisie – 'a transitional class in which the interests of the two classes meet and become blurred' – is given, in fact, a pivotal role and position. When Marx comes finally to the class characterization of Napoleon, he signals the presence of a class which was in fact a declining historical force – and differentiates its key fraction: the 'small peasant proprietors'.

The second thing is to note that none of these fractions ever functions on the political stage in isolation. The key concept which connects the particular class fractions with the political and constitutional forms is the term – or, rather, the shifting and constantly reconstituted terms of the alliance or class bloc. The first constitutional form of the 'crisis' is that of the *bourgeois republic*. The republic is hoisted to power by the June insurrection of the Paris proletariat: but though this is the class which bears the brunt of the struggle, it is a *subordinate* party to the alliance. Temporarily, the *leading fractions* in the alliance are the republican elements of the financial aristocracy and the industrial bourgeoisie, with the support of the petty bourgeoisie.

There are other critical forces on the political stage –

political forces to which no clear class designation corresponds, though their role and support is pivotal: the army, the press, the intellectual celebrities, the priests, the rural population. Occasionally, Marx hints at the class content of these supporting strata and coteries – for example, he calls the Mobile Guard 'the organised lumpen-proletariat'. This is the last moment when the Paris proletariat appears as a decisive actor; thereafter, the matter is settled 'behind the back of society'. But already it is in an alliance whose dominant fraction lies elsewhere. The republic thus reveals 'only the unrestricted despotism of one class over other classes'. This unstable political form then has, nevertheless, a structural and historical function: it is the classic 'political form for revolutionising of bourgeois society'. Its history in this moment is the short-lived 'history of the domination and dissolution of the republican fraction of the bourgeoisie'. Opposed to it is the 'Party of Order' – rallied behind the ancient slogans: property, family, religion, order. This alliance, in the conjuncture, appears in its double royalist disguise – Bourbon Legitimists and Orleanists. But this unstable bloc has its class composition too: behind the 'different shades of royalism' cluster 'big landed property', with *its* coterie and forces (priests and lackeys), and 'high finance, large-scale industry, large-scale trade, i.e. *capital*, with its retinue of advocates, professors and fine speech-makers'. Here, too, the struggle for predominance is masked by the need for unity in the face of the Party of Anarchy. What essentially divides them – driving each to 'restore its own supremacy and the subordination of the other interest' – is *not exclusively* their material conditions of existence ('two distinct sorts of property') but also the ideological traditions in which each has been formed. This is one of the many places where Marx demonstrates the pertinent, and the specific effectivity, of the *ideological* dimension of the class struggle upon the political, adding yet a further level of complexity: 'A whole superstructure of different and specifically formed interests and feelings, illusions, modes of thought and views of life arises on the basis of the different forms of property, of the social conditions of existence.' One must make, Marx adds, a sharp distinction 'between the phrases and fantasies of the parties and their real organisation and real interests, between their conceptions of themselves and what they really are'. In the conjuncture of May, what these fractions 'thought' of themselves, though referrable in the last instance to the material basis of their existence, had real and pertinent effects – as *The Eighteenth Brumaire* dramatically demonstrates. Marx performs the same kind of analysis – the formation of complex alliances, based on class fractions, their internal contradictions, the 'necessity' of the political positions, temporary programmes and ideological forms in which those 'interests' appear – for each 'moment' of the conjuncture of *Brumaire*.

The third point to note is the question of how these political fractions and strata achieve *political representation* in the course of the struggle. The two major fractions of the big bourgeoisie appear on the political stage in their respective royalist liveries: but the restoration of their respective ruling dynasties is not the objective 'work' which this alliance performs. Their union into and representation through the Party of Order brings on the question of the rule of the class 'as a whole', rather than the predominance of one fraction over another. Objectively, it is this temporary and unholy union which makes them the 'representatives of the bourgeois world order'. Time and again Marx returns to this central question of 'class content' and its *means of political representation*. It is not simply that the representation of class interests through political alliances and 'parties' is never a straightforward matter. It is also that the political interests of one class fraction can be represented through the role which another fraction plays on the political or the ideological stage. One excellent example is where Marx discussed the coalition of the proletariat and the petty-bourgeoisie into the 'so-called social democratic party'. This 'party' has its immediate determinations: it advances, temporarily, the interests of those left aside by the forceful regrouping of bourgeois forces. It has its contradictory internal structure: through their subordination within it the proletariat lose 'their revolutionary point' and gain 'a democratic twist'. Social democracy also has its objective *political* content: 'weakening the antagonism between capital and wage labour and transforming it into a harmony' (*MESW* (3), I, pp. 423–4). It is 'democratic' reform within the limits of bourgeois society.

It is in this precise context that Marx warns us about a too *reductive* conception of political representation. This temporary 'solution' is not petty-bourgeois because it advances the narrow interests of that transitional class. Its 'representatives' cannot be analysed in terms of the reduction to the narrow terms of their class designation – they are not all 'shop-keepers'. The *position* of this alliance is 'petty-bourgeois' in character because, temporarily, the *general* resolution to the crisis it proposes and endorses corresponds to the objective limits of the *particular* material interests and social situation of the petty bourgeois as a class. The political representatives, whoever they are and whatever their particular material designation, assume for the moment a petty-bourgeois political *position*, play a petty-bourgeois political role, propose a petty-bourgeois political resolution. It is the convergence, from different starting points, around those objective limits which – Marx argues – provides the basis for deciphering the 'general relationship between the political and literary representatives of a class and the class they represent' (*MESW* (3), I, p. 424). Thus, though the social and material limits and the objective class content set the terms and provide the horizon within which a 'petty-bourgeois' resolution to the crisis can appear, at a specific conjuncture, everything turns on the means and conditions which permit such a solution to surface and take a concrete shape as a *political force* in the theatre of the crisis.

It is this concept – of the *re-presentation* of the objective class content of the forces arrayed and the means and conditions of the political struggle, a struggle with its own forms of appearance, its own specific effectivity – which allows Marx to propose a dazzling solution to the central question which shadows *The Eighteenth Brumaire*. What does Napoleon, who does this exceptional suspension of the struggle through the execution of the coup d'état, *represent*? We know the solution for which Marx settled: he 'represents' the small-holding peasant – the conservative not the revolutionary peasant, the peasant who wants to consolidate, not the one who wants to strike out beyond the *status quo*.

We can only summarise in the barest outline how this

'solution' is constructed. It entails, first, an analysis of the specific mode of peasant production – based on the small holding – and of the form of social life which arises from it: the peasantry's isolation from mutual intercourse, its enforced self-sufficiency, the structure of village communities, its lack of diversity in development or wealth of social relationships. It traces the crucial transformation in the peasantry's economic role – from semi-serfdom into free landed proprietors – accomplished under the aegis of the first Napoleon. It relates the immediate consequences of this uneven transformation: the fragmentation of peasant property, the penetration of free competition and the market, the role in this backward and traditional sector of the money-lender, the mortgage and debt. Here the ravages of the disorganisation of peasant society by the capitalist invasion of the countryside is detailed. It is this which provides the basis of the developing antagonism between the peasantry and the bourgeoisie – an antagonism which gives Napoleon his 'independence'. Not only are the small-holding peasantry plunged into indebtedness; but the hidden burden of taxation fatally connects their immiseration with the swollen arms of the government and the executive apparatus of the state.

To this Marx adds a brilliant exposition of how the *ideological* outlook of the peasantry now finds, not a correspondence so much as a resonant *complementarity*, with the ideology of Louis Napoleon – 'Napoleon's ideas'. Napoleon's ideas are, in their objective content, nothing but 'the ideas of the underdeveloped small holding in its heyday'. There is a 'homology of forms' between them. Does this mean that the Napoleonic solution has, after all, no correspondence with France's developing mode of production, no life-line to the bourgeoisie? It remains the fact, Marx suggests, that Napoleon can no longer directly represent any particular section of the bourgeoisie, for he has come to power only as the result of the successive defeat or retreat of each of its major fractions. This progressive liquidation founds the coup d'état on insecure and contradictory foundations. It is this which drives Napoleon to rest his political claims, finally, on a class which 'cannot represent themselves, they must be represented. Their representative must appear simultaneously as their master, as an authority over them, an unrestricted governmental power that protects them from the other classes and sends them rain and sunshine from above' (*MESW* (3), I, p. 479). But it is just here – where a whole class fraction appears politically only through the exceptional political form of a one-man dictatorship – that Marx executes the final ironic twist. For this makes the small-holding peasantry dependent, through Napoleon, directly on the executive – on *the state*.

It is in the maturing of state power, the creation of a swollen but 'independent' state machine, perfected through Napoleon's regime, and resting on the contradictory basis of his 'independence', that Bonaparte comes finally to do some service, not for this or that fraction of the bourgeoisie, but for the maturing of capitalist relations in France. 'The material interest of the French bourgeoisie is most intimately imbricated precisely with the maintenance of that extensive and highly ramified state machine. It is that machine which provides its surplus population with jobs, and makes up through state salaries for what it cannot pocket in the form of profits, interest, rent and fees. Its *political* interests equally compelled it daily to increase the repression, and therefore to increase the resources and personnel of state power . . . The French bourgeoisie was thus compelled by its class position both to liquidate the conditions of existence of all parliamentary power, including its own, and to make its opponent, the executive, irresistible.' This is the long-term 'work' which through its reversals and detours, its advances and retreats, the 'crisis' of 1851 perfects and matures on behalf of the developing capitalist forces of French society. This is the objective labour which the revolution performs 'on its journey through purgatory' (*MESW* (3), I, p. 476).

The level of the political class struggle, then, has its own efficacy, its own forms, its specific conditions of existence, its own momentum, tempo and direction, its own contradictions internal to it, its 'peculiar' outcomes and results. If everything is, here, governed in the last instance by the stage of development of the material and social relations through which the prevailing mode of production (and the subordinate or surviving modes of production which appear combined with it in any concrete society) reproduces itself, very little of the actual

227

shifts in the political relations of class forces can be deciphered by reducing them back to the abstract terms of the 'principal contradiction'. The political *is* articulated with the level of the economic; and *both* (to make the distinction absolutely clear) are in a critical sense over-determined (constituted fundamentally by, and limited in the possible variants or outcomes) by the forces and relations combined within the 'mode of production'.

To suggest that they are not articulated, that there is no 'correspondence' of any kind, is to forfeit the first principle of historical materialism: the principle of social formations as a 'complex unity', as an 'ensemble of relations'. But that articulation is accomplished only through a series of displacements and disarticulations. Between the classes constituted in the economic relations of production, either in their 'pure' form (when the mode of production functions as an analytic framework) or in their concrete historical form (where they appear in complex forms, together with the formations of earlier modes) there intervenes a set of forms, processes, conditions and terms, graspable by a distinctive set of concepts – non-reducible concepts – which 'fill out' the level of the political in a social formation. The re-presentation of the 'economic' at the level of 'the political' must pass through these representational forms and processes. This is a process, a complex set of practices – the practices of the political class struggle; without them there would be no 'political' level at all. And once the class struggle is subject to the process of 'representation' in the theatre of political class struggle, that articulation is permanent: it obeys, as well as the determinations upon it, its own internal dynamic; it respects its own, distinctive and specific conditions of existence. It cannot be reversed. It is this transformation which produces and sustains the necessary level of appearance of the political. Once the class forces appear as political class forces, they have consequent political results; they generate 'solutions' – results, outcomes, consequences – which cannot be *translated back* into their original terms.

It is, of course, the 'raw materials' of the social relations of production – at the mode of production level – which provide the political class struggle with its elements. And the political results and conclusions 'won' or secured at the level of the political not only serve to articulate 'the political' as a permanent practice in any social formation – one which can *never* thereafter be an 'empty space' – they also have consequences for the manner in which the forces and relations of the material conditions of existence themselves develop. That is, they react, retrospectively, upon that which constitutes them – they have pertinent effects. The precise political form in which the 'compromise' of the 1851 coup d'état was struck is important both for the pace and for the character of capitalist development in France. It affects both the political and the economic life of French society. That 'reciprocal action' – if you like, of the political-ideological superstructures on the 'base' – does not operate in a 'free space'. Yet the precise direction and tendency of that reaction is not given exclusively by the forces and relations of the base: it is *also* given by the forces and relations of the political and the ideological struggle, and by all that is specific – relatively autonomous – to them. The superstructural results can 'react' upon the base by either favouring or hindering its development. Althusser noted that 'an over-determined contradiction may be either overdetermined in the direction of a historical inhibition, a real block . . . or in the direction of a revolutionary rupture, but in neither condition is it ever found in the "pure" state' (Althusser, 1969, p. 106).

Engels, in his famous Letter to Schmidt, in which he dealt with this very question, suggested that:

> The retroaction of the state power upon economic development can be one of three kinds: it can proceed in the same direction, and then things move more rapidly; it can move in the opposite direction . . . or it can prevent the economic development from proceeding along certain lines, and prescribe other lines (27 October 1890, *MESC*, p. 399).

This, Althusser comments, 'well suggests the character of the two limit positions' (Althusser, 1969, p. 106, fn. 23). (It is important to note that this concept of 'determination' differs from the full-blown but more 'formal' notion of determination through 'structural causality' which Althusser and Balibar adopted for the exposition of *Reading Capital*. Its absence from the more formalist conception was one of the principal sources of the latter's 'theoreticist deviation'.)

Marx noted in the Introduction to the *Grundrisse* that, once we cease to think the relation between the different 'moments' of a process as *identical*, we are of necessity into the terrain of *articulation*. Articulation marks the forms of the relationship through which two processes, which remain distinct – obeying their own conditions of existence – are drawn together to form a 'complex unity'. This unity is therefore the result of 'many determinations', where the conditions of existence of the one does not coincide exactly with that of the other (politics to economic, circulation to production) *even if* the former is the 'determinate effect' of the latter; and that is because the former also have their own internal 'determinations'.

The concepts which Marx begins to elaborate and operate in *The Eighteenth Brumaire* – alliances, blocs, constitutional forms, regime, political representatives, political ideologies or 'ideas', fractions, factions, etc – are the concepts which enable us to 'think' the complexity of this double determination. Since these political forms and relations are themselves constituted by the antagonistic class relations of the capitalist mode in which they appear, they are the concrete objects of the practices of class struggle – the class struggle in 'the theatre of politics'. The very term 'theatre' and the sustained dramaturgical nature of Marx's style of exposition in the *Eighteenth Brumaire* underlines the *representational* aspect of this relation. This level is always present – it is always 'filled out' in one way or another – in any developed social formation. It performs a 'function' for the social formation as a whole, in that, at this instance there appears the forms and relations of the political through which the various fractions of capital and its political allies can contend, both among themselves and with the subordinate classes, so as to dominate the class struggle and to draw civil society, politics, ideology and the State into conformity with the broad underlying 'needs' of the developing mode of production. But those 'needs' never appear in their 'pure state'. Indeed, as Marx was obliged to observe in relation to Britain, the fundamental classes of capital never emerge full-blown and united and 'take charge of the social formation' in their own name and persona, 'for capital'. The distinction between the 'economically dominant class' and the 'politically leading or ruling caste', in Marx's and Engels's writings on Britain, recapitulates in miniature the distinctions, drawn *in extenso*, in *The Eighteenth Brumaire*, and provided the key to deciphering the class struggle in Britain: 'The governing caste ... is by no means identical with the ruling class . . .' ('Parties and Cliques', in *Surveys from Exile*, p. 279). The political level therefore also provides the necessary space of representation where those bargains, coalitions, 'unstable equilibria', are struck and dissolved which, *alone*, allow the 'laws of capital' to have pertinent effects.

It is consequently also in this 'space' – but also through its specific forms and relations – that the working class can struggle to contain the sway of capital in the form of its political representatives and forces, and, under a favourable conjuncture, to transform the *economic* structure of society by taking as its object the point where that structure is *condensed*: in the form of bourgeois state – i.e. *political* – power. It follows that we cannot conceive of 'the class struggle' as if classes were simply and homogeneously constituted at the level of the economic, and only then fractured at the level of the political. The political level is 'dependent' – determinate – because its 'raw materials' are given by the mode of production *as a whole*; a process of 'representation' must have something to represent. But classes are *complexly constituted* at each of the levels of the social formation – the economic, the political and the ideological. To grasp the 'state of play' in the relations of class forces in a concrete historical formation at a particular conjuncture *is* to grasp the necessary complexity and displacements of this 'unity'. It is only in the very exceptional conditions of a revolutionary rupture that the instances of these different levels will ever correspond. Thus to grasp the 'unity' of the class struggle, so constituted, is of necessity to grasp the question of classes *in its contradictory form*.

IV

Twenty years separate *The Eighteenth Brumaire* from *The Civil War in France*, in which Marx most directly extends some of the concepts elaborated in the former. It is a text whose conceptual developments are worked through directly in relation to a revolutionary political conjuncture requiring serious analysis (the Paris Commune), and is considerably influenced by Marx's and Engels's renewed political work in the context of the International (including the struggle against Bakunin and the Anarchists). Only three significant points can be indicated here from a body of political writing which is far too little studied and reflected upon in the Marxist movement.

The first concerns the indispensable necessity for the working class to constitute itself 'into a party': its aim being the 'conquest of the political power', its object, the rupture of the state and state power, 'the national power of capital over labour . . . a public force organised for social enslavement . . . an engine of class despotism'. In the Preface to the reissue of the *Manifesto* which Marx and Engels published in 1872, this 'lesson' was vividly enshrined: 'One thing especially was proved by the Commune, viz. that "the working class cannot simply lay hold of the ready-made state machinery and wield it for its own purpose".' The detailed analysis of the Commune not only constitutes Marx's most extended writing on the forms of proletarian political power, but contains the critical argument for what, in *The Critique of the Gotha Programme*, he calls 'a revolutionary dictatorship of the proletariat' as the only and necessary form in which the working class will 'have to pass through long struggles, through a series of historic processes, transforming circumstances and men' (*MESW*, pp. 327 and 291).

It is in this context that Marx returns to the question, already posed in *The Eighteenth Brumaire*, as to what class forces the figure and formation of the Napoleonic state represents, and the relation of the Napoleonic 'solution' to the economic development of capitalism in France. Here in *The Civil War in France* (*MESW*, pp. 285–6), Marx considerably elaborates on the growing autonomisation of the 'centralised power of the state'; he resumes the constitutional forms of the 1851 crisis through which this state power is matured and developed – the 'objective work' of the revolution; and the political work of domination over the under-developed fractions which they allowed Napoleon to accomplish. Here lies the basis for that theory of the state as a 'class state', of the state as the 'résumé of man's practical conflicts', the state as the relation of *political condensation*, which Lenin was subsequently to bring to a high order of importance (through his commentary on the fragmentary insights on this question of Marx and Engels in *State and Revolution*). One consequence of this emergent theory for our understanding of the relation between the political and economic aspects of the class struggle we will take up in a moment.

But first, Marx returns to the question of 'representation'. Napoleon, he now argues, 'professed to rest upon the peasantry, the large mass of producers not directly involved in the struggle of capital and labour' (*MESW* (3), II, p. 219). This class interest, apparently outside the direct play between the fundamental classes, served to substantiate the apparent 'autonomy' of Napoleon from the immediate terms of the struggle – it secured for his *coup* the appearance of autonomy. It thus enabled him to project his political intervention – a classic ideological function of the state – as incarnating the 'general interest', the 'representative' of all the classes (because it represented none), of 'the nation'. 'It professed to unite all classes by reviving for all the chimera of national glory' (*ibid.*).

Marx suggests how and why this form of political resolution related to the immediate relations of forces in the central arena of struggle – related to it, but *indirectly*, as a representation, *as a postponement of it.* 'In reality, it was the only form of government possible at a time when the bourgeoisie had already lost, and the working class had not yet acquired the faculty of ruling the nation' (*ibid.*). The 'postponement' of a political resolution – appearing in the political domain as the temporary but displaced 'rule' of an *absent* class – a class which could not appear in its own name – was a *form* which corresponded (but in no sense 'immediately') to the precise state of under-development of the class relations of capitalist production in France. But this 'unstable equilibrium' is also the condition which provides precisely the space through which the state drifts 'apparently soaring high above society' – incarnating but also at the same time *masking* the class struggle. And it is in this form – the form of 'the national power of capital over labour' (*ibid.*) – that capitalism in France *develops* – develops, of course, with its contradictory effects. Those effects are still to be seen in the peculiar form of 'étatisme' which capitalist development manifests in the French social formation. The demonstration could hardly be clearer of how powerful are the consequences of the political *for* the economic. Just as it could hardly be more evident that the political and the economic are *coupled* but not *as an identity relation*.

In this context, it is noteworthy that Marx returns to a passage in the *Manifesto* which we have previously discussed, and offers a clarification which is (in the light of *The Eighteenth Brumaire*) a necessary correction. In *The Critique of the Gotha Programme* Marx takes up Lassalle's misinterpretation of his assertion that, face to face with the working class, 'all other classes are a single reactionary mass' (i.e. the theses of the 'simplification of the classes' in political struggle). He makes two points of clarification. First, he reiterates that what made the bourgeoisie *the* revolutionary class *vis-à-vis* the feudal classes was its historic role as 'the bringer of large-scale industry'. It is this objective condition which also gives to the proletariat its revolutionary position. But this does not mean *collapsing* the other classes into a single mass. The remnants of feudal classes may play an objectively reactionary role, but 'these do not form a single reactionary mass together with the bourgeoisie' (*MESW* (3), III, p. 20). In short, the political analysis is now definitively identified as *requiring* a theory of the complex formation of class fractions in class alliances. These – not some indistinguishable fusion of whole classes – constitute the terms of the political class struggle.

Time and again, especially in the subsidiary writings of this period, both Marx and Engels return, on the basis of the theses of the International, to reaffirm the necessity of 'the political movement' as the means to the 'economical emancipation of the working class' (Speech on the Anniversary of the International, Fernbach, 1973–4, *The First International and After*, p. 271). The more the theory of the state and the centrality of state power to the expansion of capitalism is developed, the more central becomes the role of the political struggle at the forefront of 'the social revolution'. It is true, as Fernbach observes, that Marx and Engels never work their way through to a fully developed theory of the corporate forms of working-class economic and political struggle: and he is right to attribute their failure, on the whole, to grasp the nature of the working-class movement in Britain to this theoretical lacuna (Fernbach, 1973, *Surveys from Exile*, pp. 22–4). One has to turn to Lenin's polemic against Martynov and the 'economists' for an adequate theorisation of this tendency. This debate cannot be presented here; but the whole Chapter on 'Trade Union Politics and Social-Democratic Politics', in Lenin's *What Is To Be Done?*, needs to be read in the context of this question: for the confusions which Lenin confronts there remain to plague us, with greatly augmented force, today (Lenin, *CW*, vol. 5, pp. 397–440). The view that, because the economic relations and foundations determine, in the last instance, the forms and outcomes of the class struggle, therefore the struggle *waged at the level of the economic* is (as Martynov declared) 'the most widely applicable method' of struggle, is dismantled by Lenin with all the cogency of his polemical force. He calls the proposition 'the quintessence of Economism'; and this designation leads him into an analysis of the corporate character of a struggle limited to the battle 'for better terms in the sale of their labour power, for better conditions of life and labour', which takes us, in turn, directly to the heart of social-democratic reformism and 'economism' – to 'the soundly scientific (and "soundly" opportunist) Mr and Mrs Webb and . . . the British Trade unions' (*What Is To Be Done?*, *CW*, vol. 5, p. 404). What Lenin's intervention (and its subsequent development in the setting of his theory of imperialism) brings out far more sharply than Marx does, is the *damage* which has been wrought by the use, by Marx and Marxists after him, of the same *term* – the 'economic' – to designate *two* quite different things: the relations and forces of the mode of production and the site of those practices and forms of struggle which have economic relations (e.g. conditions of work, or wages) as their specific object. [. . .]

References and abbreviations

Althusser, 1969, *For Marx*, London: Allen Lane, 1969.

Fernbach, 1973–4, Introductions to Marx, *Surveys from Exile* and *The First International and After*, Harmondsworth: Penguin, 1973, 1974.

Gramsci, 1971, *Prison Notebooks*, London: Lawrence and Wishart, 1971.

Lenin, *CW*: *Collected Works* (45 vols), London: Lawrence and Wishart, 1960–70.

Lukács, *History and Class Consciousness*, London: Merlin Press, 1971.

MECW: *Marx–Engels Collected Works*, London: Lawrence and Wishart, 1975ff.

MESW (1): *Marx–Engels Selected Works* (in 1 vol.), London: Lawrence and Wishart, 1970.

MESW (3): *Marx–Engels Selected Works* (in 3 vols), Moscow: Progress, 1969–70.

MESC: *Marx–Engels Selected Correspondence*, Moscow: Progress, 1975.

German Ideology: Marx and Engels, *The German Ideology*, London: Lawrence and Wishart, 1965.

Capital I: Marx, *Capital* I, London: Lawrence and Wishart, 1970.

Capital III: Marx, *Capital* III, London: Lawrence and Wishart, 1972.

Civil War: Marx, *The Civil War in France*, *MESW* (1 vol.), London: Lawrence and Wishart, 1970.

Class Struggles in France: Marx, *The Class Struggles in France 1848 to 1850*, *MESW* (3 vols).

Gotha Programme: Marx, *Critique of the Gotha Programme*, *MESW* (1 vol.).

Eighteenth Brumaire: Marx, *The Eighteenth Brumaire of Louis Bonaparte*, *MESW* (3 vols).

Poverty of Philosophy: Marx, *The Poverty of Philosophy*, *MECW*, vol. 6, pp. 105–212.

Communist Manifesto: Marx and Engels, *The Manifesto of the Communist Party*, *MESW* (1 vol.), pp. 35–63; and *The Revol-*

utions of 1848, Harmondsworth: Penguin, 1973.

Grundrisse: Marx, *Grundrisse*, Harmondsworth: Penguin, 1973.

Poulantzas, 1973: *Political Power and Social Classes*, London: New Left Books, 1973.

Williams, 1976, *France 1848–1851*, Open University (A321, Units 5–8).

9. The class structure of advanced capitalist societies

Erik Olin Wright

All Marxists agree that manual workers directly engaged in the production of physical commodities for private capital fall into the working class. While there may be disagreement about the political and ideological significance of such workers in advanced capitalism, everyone acknowledges that they are in fact workers. There is no such agreement about any other category of wage-earners. Some Marxists have argued that only productive manual workers should be considered part of the proletariat.[1] Others have argued that the working class includes low-level, routinized white-collar employees as well.[2] Still others have argued that virtually all wage-labourers should be considered part of the working class.[3] If this disagreement were just a question of esoteric academic debates over how best to pigeon-hole different social positions, then it would matter little how these issues were eventually resolved. But classes are not merely analytical abstractions in Marxist theory; they are real social forces and they have real consequences. It matters a great deal for our understanding of class struggle and social change exactly how classes are conceptualized and which categories of social positions are placed in which classes. Above all, it matters for developing a viable socialist politics how narrow or broad the working class is seen to be and how its relationship to other classes is understood.

This chapter will explore the problem of understanding class boundaries in advanced capitalist society. Rather than review the wide range of approaches Marxists have adopted in defining classes, I will focus primarily on the work of Nicos Poulantzas, in particular on his book. This work is, to my knowledge, the most systematic and thorough attempt to

From Erik Olin Wright, *Class, Crisis and the State*, London: New Left Books, 1978, pp. 30–61.

understand precisely the Marxist criteria for classes in capitalist society. While there are many points in Poulantzas's argument with which I disagree, his work has the considerable merit of sharply posing the problem of defining classes in advanced capitalism and of providing some stimulating solutions. A critical discussion of Poulantzas's work can, therefore, provide a very useful starting-point for the development of an explicit theory of classes in contemporary capitalism.

The first section below presents an outline exposition of Poulantzas's theory of the structural determination of class. Poulantzas's basic conclusion is that only manual, non-supervisory workers who produce surplus-value directly (productive labour) should be included in the proletariat. Other categories of wage-labourers (unproductive employees, mental labour, supervisory labour) must be placed in a separate class – either the 'new' petty bourgeoisie, or in the case of managers, the bourgeoisie itself. This exposition of Poulantzas will be followed in the second section by a general assessment and critique of his argument. [. . .]

POULANTZAS'S THEORY OF THE STRUCTURAL DETERMINATION OF CLASS

The following presentation of Poulantzas's ideas will necessarily be schematic and incomplete. I will discuss only the essential elements of his views on class boundaries and not deal with a variety of other important issues which he raises (such as class fractions, the relationship of classes to state apparatuses, etc.). While the exposition will lose many of the nuances of Poulantzas's analysis, I hope that the basic contours of his argument will stand out. Critical comments will be kept to a minimum in this section.

GENERAL FRAMEWORK

Poulantzas's analysis of social classes rests on three basic premises. 1. *Classes cannot be defined outside of class struggle.* This is a fundamental point. Classes are not 'things', nor are they pigeon-holes in a static social structure. 'Classes', Poulantzas writes, 'involve in one and the same process both class contradictions and class struggle; social classes do not firstly exist as such and only then enter into class struggle. Social classes coincide with class practices, i.e. the class struggle, and are only defined in their mutual opposition.'⁴ Poulantzas does not mean by this proposition that classes can only be understood in terms of class *consciousness*. Class struggle, in Poulantzas's analysis, does not refer to the conscious self-organization of a class as a social force, but rather to the antagonistic, contradictory quality of the social relations which comprise the social division of labour. Class struggle exists even when classes are disorganized. 2. *Classes designate objective positions in the social division of labour.* These objective positions, Poulantzas stresses, 'are independent of the will of these agents'.⁵ It is crucial not to confuse the analysis of the structure of these objective class positions with the analysis of the individuals (*agents* in Poulantzas's terminology) who occupy those positions. While both analyses are important, Poulantzas insists that 'the question of who occupies a given position, i.e. who is or becomes a bourgeois, proletarian, petty bourgeois, poor peasant, etc., and how and when he does, *is subordinate to the first aspect* – the reproduction of the actual positions occupied by the social classes'.⁶ Poulantzas refers to the reproduction of these objective positions within the social division of labour as the 'structural determination of class'. These first two propositions taken together imply that in order to define classes it is necessary to unravel the objective positions within the antagonistic social relations comprising the social division of labour. 3. *Classes are structurally determined not only at the economic level, but at the political and ideological levels as well.* This is perhaps the most distinctive (and problematic) part of Poulantzas's analysis. While it is true that 'the economic place of the social agents has a

240

principal role in determining social classes',[7] their position in ideological and political relations of domination and subordination may be equally important: 'It must be emphasized that ideological and political relations, i.e. the places of political and ideological domination and subordination, are themselves part of the structural determination of class: there is no question of the objective place being the result only of economic place within the relations of production, while political and ideological elements belong only to [class struggle].'[8] Political and ideological factors cannot be relegated to the transformation of a 'class-in-itself' into a 'class-for-itself', but lie at the heart of the very determination of class positions.[9] Given these premises, the basic theoretical strategy Poulantzas adopts for analysing class boundaries centres on elaborating the economic, political and ideological criteria which determine objective class positions within the social division of labour. We will first examine how Poulantzas does this for the working class and the new petty bourgeoisie, and then for the bourgeoisie.

STRUCTURAL DETERMINATION OF WORKING CLASS AND NEW PETTY BOURGEOISIE

In the course of capitalist development the traditional petty bourgeoisie – independent artisans, small shopkeepers, etc. – has steadily dwindled. In its place there has arisen what Poulantzas calls the 'new petty bourgeoisie', consisting of white-collar employees, technicians, supervisors, civil servants, etc. Under conditions of advanced capitalism, the crucial question for understanding the structural determination of the working class, Poulantzas argues, centres on analysing the boundary between the working class and this new segment of the petty bourgeoisie.

Poulantzas's argument proceeds in two steps. First, he discusses the economic, political and ideological criteria which separate the proletariat from the new petty bourgeoisie. The basic economic criterion he advances is the distinction between productive and unproductive labour. The basic political criterion is the distinction between non-supervisory and supervisory positions. The core ideological criterion is the division between mental and manual labour. Secondly, Poulantzas discusses why this 'new' petty bourgeoisie belongs to the same class as the traditional petty bourgeoisie. He argues that, although they appear quite different at the economic level, both the old and new petty bourgeoisie bear the same ideological relationship to the class struggle between the proletariat and the bourgeoisie, and this common ideological relationship is sufficient to merge them into a single class. The first argument explains why certain categories of wage-labourers should be excluded from the working class; the second explains why they should be considered members of a common class, the petty bourgeoisie. We will examine the first of these arguments in some detail, the second more briefly.

Economic criteria

Poulantzas argues that the distinction between productive and unproductive labour defines the boundary between the working class and the new petty bourgeoisie at the economic level. All workers are productive labourers and all unproductive labourers are new petty bourgeois (as we shall see, some productive labourers are also petty bourgeois). Poulantzas thus decisively rejects wage-labour *per se* as an appropriate criterion for the working class: 'It is not wages that define the working class economically: wages are a form of distribution of the social product, corresponding to market relations and the forms of "contract" governing the purchase and sale of labour power. Although every worker is a wage-earner, every wage-earner is certainly not a worker, for not every wage-earner is engaged in productive labour.'[10]

Poulantzas defines productive labour in a somewhat more restrictive way than most Marxist writers: 'Productive labour, in the capitalist mode of production, is labour that produces surplus-value *while directly reproducing the material elements that serve as the substratum of the relation of exploitation: labour that is directly involved in material production by producing use-values that increase material wealth*.'[11] The conventional definition of productive labour by Marxists does not explicitly restrict it to labour directly implicated in material production. Poulantzas, however, argues that 'labour producing surplus-value is broadly equivalent to the process of material production in its capitalist form of existence and reproduction'.[12] He insists that this definition is consistent with Marx's usage of the concept of productive labour, since Marx always associated surplus-value creation with commodity production, and commodity production (according to Poulantzas) is always material production.

Given this definition of productive labour under capitalism, Poulantzas argues that unproductive wage-earners must be excluded from the ranks of the proletariat because they lie outside the basic capitalist relation of exploitation. In discussing commercial employees as an example of unproductive labour, Poulantzas writes: 'Of course, these wage-earners are themselves exploited, and their wages correspond to the reproduction of their labour-power. "The commercial worker . . . adds to the capitalist's income by helping him to reduce the cost of realizing surplus-value, inasmuch as he performs partly unpaid labour." Surplus labour is thus extorted from wage-earners in commerce, but these are not directly exploited in the form of the dominant capitalist relation of exploitation, the creation of surplus-value.'[13] The working class is defined by the fundamental class antagonism within capitalism between direct producers, who are separated from the means of production and produce the social surplus product in the form of surplus-value, and the bourgeoisie, which owns the means of production and appropriates surplus-value. Unproductive wage-earners, while clearly not members of the bourgeoisie, do not contribute to the production of the surplus product. Thus they are not directly exploited in the form of the dominant capitalist relation of exploitation and so, Poulantzas argues, cannot be included in the working class.

Political criteria

As Poulantzas stresses time and time again, economic criteria alone are not sufficient to define the structural determination of class. In particular, political and/or ideological criteria exclude certain categories of productive wage-earners from the working class. The use of political criteria is especially important in Poulantzas's analysis of the class position of managerial and supervisory labour. Within the process of material production, supervisory labour is unquestionably productive because of its role in co-ordinating and integrating the production process. But within the *social* division of labour, supervisory activity represents the political domination of capital over the working class: 'In a word, the despotism of the factory is precisely the form taken by the domination of the technical division of labour by the social, such as this exists under capitalism. The work of management and supervision, under capitalism, is the direct reproduction, within the process of production itself, of the political relations between the capitalist class and the working class.'[14]

How then does Poulantzas reconcile these competing criteria? At the economic level, supervisory labour in commodity production is exploited in the same way that manual labour is exploited; but at the political level, supervisory labour participates in the domination of the working class. Poulantzas solves this problem by turning to the distinction between the *social division of labour* and the *technical division of labour*. While he never explicitly defines the differences between the two, the general sense is that the technical division of labour represents structural positions derived from the particular technologies used in production (or forces of production), whereas the social division of labour is derived from the social organization of production (or relations of production). Now, it is a basic proposition of Marxist theory that 'in the actual organization of the labour process, the social division of labour, directly dependent upon the relations of production, dominates the technical division'.[15] Poulantzas then argues that the position of supervisors as exploited productive labour reflects their role in the purely technical division of labour, whereas their position of political domination of the working class defines their role in the social division of labour. Given this assertion, he concludes that supervisors' 'principal function is that of extracting surplus-value from the workers', and on this basis they must be excluded from the working class altogether.[16]

Supervisors, however, are also excluded from the bourgeoisie, for while they politically dominate the working class they are also politically dominated by capital itself. This specific position within political relations of domination and subordination – subordinated to capital while dominating the proletariat – defines the political criteria for the new petty bourgeoisie.

Ideological criteria

The working class is not only exploited economically and dominated politically, it is also dominated ideologically. The central axis of this ideological domination within the social division of labour is the division between *mental* and *manual* labour.[17] Poulantzas argues that the mental/manual division excludes the working class from the 'secret knowledge' of the production process, and that this exclusion is necessary for the reproduction of capitalist social relations. 'Experts' of various sorts at all stages of the production process help to legitimize the subordination of labour to capital, by making it appear natural that workers are incapable of organizing production themselves. The division between mental and manual labour thus represents the ideological prop for the exclusion of workers from the planning and direction of the production process.[18] Experts are the direct carriers of this ideological domination; thus, like supervisors, they are excluded from the working class.

This ideological criterion is especially important in determining the class position of certain categories of engineers and technicians. Engineers and technicians are generally productive wage-earners, and although many of them occupy positions within the supervisory structure (and thus are new petty bourgeois because of political criteria), there are subaltern technicians who do not directly supervise anyone. Nevertheless, Poulantzas argues, because of the primacy of the social division of labour over the technical division, and because within the social division of labour even subaltern technicians (as mental labour) occupy a position of ideological domination over the working class, they must be excluded from the proletariat and considered part of the new petty bourgeoisie. The mental/manual division is central to the determination of the class position of all mental labourers, not just technicians, engineers and the like. White-collar workers in general participate, if only in residual ways, in the

245

elevated status of mental labour, and thus participate in the ideological domination of the working class. Even low-level clerks and secretaries, Poulantzas insists, share in the ideological position of mental labour and thus belong to the new petty bourgeoisie rather than the proletariat.[19]

As in the case of political criteria, capital dominates the new petty bourgeoisie ideologically. The division between mental and manual labour simultaneously supports the ideological domination of manual labour by mental labour and the ideological subordination of mental labour to capital. Experts may participate in the 'secret knowledge' of production, but that knowledge is always fragmented and dominated by the requirements of capitalist production and reproduction.

The class unity of the new and traditional petty bourgeoisie
Poulantzas admits that it might seem strange to categorize the new and traditional petty bourgeoisie in a single class. He even agrees that the traditional petty bourgeoisie 'does not belong to the capitalist mode of production, but to the simple commodity form which was historically the form of transition from the feudal to the capitalist mode'.[20] How then can two groupings which are rooted in such utterly different economic situations be amalgamated into a single class? Poulantzas argues that this class unity is a consequence of the relationship of both the traditional and the new bourgeoisie to the class struggle between the bourgeoisie and the proletariat: 'If the traditional and the new petty bourgeoisie can be considered as belonging to the same class, this is because social classes are only determined in the class struggle, and because these groupings are precisely both polarized in relationship to the bourgeoisie and the proletariat.'[21] This common polarization with respect to the bourgeoisie and the proletariat has the consequence of forging a rough ideological unity between the traditional and the new petty bourgeoisie. It is this ideological unity, Poulantzas maintains, which justifies placing both the traditional and the new petty bourgeoisie in the same class: 'The structural determination of the new petty bourgeoisie in the social division of labour has certain effects on the ideology of its agents, which directly influences its class position . . .

these ideological effects on the new petty bourgeoisie exhibit a remarkable affinity to those which the specific class determination of the traditional petty bourgeoisie has on the latter, thus justifying their attribution to one and the same class, the petty bourgeoisie.'[22]

The core elements of this common petty-bourgeois ideology include reformism, individualism, and power fetishism. *Reformism*: Petty-bourgeois ideology tends to be anticapitalist, but regards the problems of capitalism as solvable through institutional reform rather than revolutionary change. *Individualism*: 'Afraid of proletarianization below, attracted towards the bourgeoisie above, the new petty bourgeoisie often aspires to promotion, a "career", to "upward mobility".'[23] The same individualism characterizes the traditional petty bourgeois, but takes the form of mobility through his becoming a successful small businessman. *Power Fetishism*: 'As a result of the situation of the petty bourgeoisie as an intermediate class . . . this class has a strong tendency to see the state as an inherently neutral force whose role is that of arbitrating between the various social classes.'[24] While Poulantzas admits that in certain respects the ideologies of the two petty bourgeoisies are different, he insists that the unity is sufficiently strong as to warrant considering them a single class.

THE STRUCTURAL DETERMINATION OF THE BOURGEOISIE

Whereas in his discussion of the boundary between the working class and the new petty bourgeoisie Poulantzas focuses on political and ideological criteria, in the discussion of the bourgeoisie he concentrates on the strictly economic level. His basic argument is that the bourgeoisie must be defined not in terms of formal legal categories of property ownership, but in terms of the substantive dimensions which characterize the social relations of production. Two such dimensions are particularly important. *Economic Ownership*: This refers to the 'real economic control of the means of production, i.e. the power to assign the means of production to given uses and so to dispose of the products obtained'.[25] Such economic ownership must not be confused with legal title to productive property: 'This ownership is to be understood as real economic ownership, control of the means of production, to be distinguished from legal ownership, which is sanctioned by law and belongs to the superstructure. The law, of course, generally ratifies economic ownership, but it is possible for the forms of legal ownership not to coincide with real economic ownership.'[26] *Possession*: This is defined as 'the capacity to put the means of production into operation'.[27] This refers to the actual control over the physical operation of production. In feudal society, the peasant generally retained possession of the means of production while the feudal ruling class maintained economic ownership; in capitalist society, on the other hand, the bourgeoisie has both economic ownership and possession of the means of production. The working class is separated from control not only over the product of labour, but over the very process of labour itself.

These two dimensions of social relations of production – economic ownership and possession – are particularly important in analysing the class position of managers.[28] Poulantzas argues that since these agents fulfil the *functions* of capital, they occupy the *place* of capital. Thus they belong to the bourgeoisie, regardless of any legal definitions of ownership: 'It is the place of capital, defined as the articulation of relationships that bear certain powers, that determines the class memberships of the agents who fulfil these "functions". This refers us to two inter-connected aspects of the problem: (a) the powers involving either utilization of resources, allocation of the means of production to this or that use, or the direction of the labour process, are bound up with the relationships of economic ownership and possession, and these relationships define one particular place the place of capital; (b) the directing agents who directly exercise these powers and who fulfil the 'functions of capital' occupy the place of capital and thus beyond to the bourgeois class even if they do not hold formal legal ownership. *In all cases, therefore, the managers are an integral section of the bourgeois class.*'[29]

Poulantzas recognizes that the precise relationship between economic ownership and possession is not immutably fixed in capitalism. In particular, the process of centralization and concentration of capital characteristic of the development of monopoly capitalism generates a partial 'dissociation' of economic ownership and possession. Especially in the developed monopoly corporation, where very heterogeneous production units are often united under a single economic ownership, managers of particular units will generally have possession of the means of production of that unit without directly having economic ownership.[30] Nevertheless, Poulantzas insists that the 'dissociations that we have analysed between the relationships of economic ownership and possession (i.e. the direction of the labour process) do not in any way mean that the latter, exercised by the managers, has become separated from the place of capital'.[31] Capital remains a *unitary structural position* within class relations even if the *functions* of capital have become differentiated. It is this structural position which fundamentally determines the class location of managers as part of the bourgeoisie.

Poulantzas has very little to say about the specific ideological and political criteria defining the bourgeoisie, other than that they occupy the position of ideological and political domination in the social division of labour. The most important context in which Poulantzas explicitly treats such criteria is in the discussion of the heads of state apparatuses. Such positions belong in the bourgeoisie, Poulantzas argues, not because they directly occupy the place of capital at the economic level, but because 'in a capitalist state, they manage the state functions in the service of capital'.[32] The class position of such agents is thus not defined directly by their immediate social relations of production, but rather indirectly by the relationship of the state itself to the capitalist class.

ASSESSMENT AND CRITIQUE OF POULANTZAS'S ANALYSIS

The following critique of Poulantzas's analysis will parallel the foregoing exposition.[33] First, the logic of his analysis of the boundary between the working class and the new petty bourgeoisie is examined. The discussion focuses on two criticisms: 1. that there is little basis for regarding the distinction between productive and unproductive labour as determining the boundary of the working class at the economic level; 2. that Poulantzas's use of political and ideological factors effectively undermines the primacy of economic relations in determining class position. Secondly, Poulantzas's claim that the traditional and new petty bourgeois are members of the same class is criticized on two grounds: 1. the ideological divisions between the two categories are at least as profound as the commonalities; 2. while ideological relations may play a part in the determination of class position, they cannot neutralize divergent class positions determined at the economic level. Finally, there is a brief examination of Poulantzas's treatment of the boundary of the bourgeoisie. The main criticism made here is that not all managers should be considered an integral part of the bourgeoisie, even if they participate in certain aspects of relations of possession.

THE BOUNDARY BETWEEN WORKING CLASS AND NEW PETTY BOURGEOISIE

It will be helpful in our discussion of Poulantzas's perspective to present schematically the criteria he uses in analysing the structural determination of classes. Table 1 presents the criteria by which he defines in the most general way the working class, the traditional and new petty bourgeoisie and the capitalist class. Table 2 examines in greater detail the various combinations of criteria which define different sub-categories within the new petty bourgeoisie. It is important not to interpret the categories in these typologies as constituting discrete, empirical 'groups'. This would certainly be a violation of Poulantzas's view of social classes. The purpose of the typologies is to highlight the relationships among the various criteria, not to turn the analysis of classes and class struggle into a static exercise in categorization.

Let us now turn to the question of Poulantzas's use of the productive/unproductive labour distinction in his analysis of the boundary of the working class, and then to the logic of his use of political and ideological factors as criteria for class. Once these two tasks are completed, we will examine some statistical data on the size of the proletariat in the United States using Poulantzas's criteria.

Productive and unproductive labour

There are three basic difficulties in Poulantzas's discussion of productive and unproductive labour: 1. problems in his definition of productive labour; 2. the lack of correspondence between the productive/unproductive labour distinction and actual positions in the labour process; 3. – and most significantly – the lack of fundamentally different economic interests between productive and unproductive workers.[34]

Productive labour, to Poulantzas, is restricted to labour which both produces surplus-value and is directly involved in the process of material production. This definition rests on the claim that surplus-value is only generated in the production of physical commodities. This is an arbitrary assumption. If use-values take the form of services, and if those services are produced for the market, then there is no reason why surplus-value cannot be generated in non-material production as well as the production of physical commodities.[35]

The second difficulty with Poulantzas's use of productive/ unproductive labour concerns the relationship of this distinction to positions in the social division of labour. If actual positions generally contain a mix of productive and unproductive activities, then the distinction between productive and unproductive labour becomes much less useful as a criterion for the class determination of those positions. A good example is grocery-store clerks. To the extent that clerks place commodities on shelves (and thus perform the last stage of the transportation of commodities), then they are productive; but to the extent that they operate cash registers, then they are unproductive. This dual quality of social positions as both productive and unproductive is not restricted to the circulation of commodities, but exists directly within the process of material production itself. Consider the case of the material production of the packaging for a commodity. Packaging serves two distinct functions. On the one hand, it is part of the use-value of a commodity. One can hardly drink milk

251

TABLE 1. GENERAL CRITERIA FOR CLASS IN POULANTZAS'S ANALYSIS

	Economic criteria			Political criteria		Ideological criteria	
	Exploiter		Exploited*	Domination	Subordination	Domination	Subordination
	Appropriates surplus-value	Surplus labour extorted	Surplus-value extorted				
Bourgeoisie	+	−	−	+	−	+	−
Proletariat	−	+	+	−	+	−	+
New petty bourgeoisie	−	+	−/+	+/−	+	+/−	+
Old petty bourgeoisie	−	−	−	−	+	+	+

+ criterion present   +/− criterion usually present, but sometimes absent
− criterion absent   −/+ criterion usually absent, but sometimes present

*To say that 'surplus labour' is extorted from a wage-labourer, but not surplus-value, means that the worker performs unpaid labour for the capitalist, but does not produce actual commodities for exchange on the market. The worker is thus not formally productive, but nevertheless is exploited.

TABLE 2. VARIOUS COMBINATIONS OF CRITERIA FOR THE NEW PETTY BOURGEOISIE

	Economic criteria			Political criteria		Ideological criteria	
	Exploiter	Exploited					
	Appropriates surplus-value	Surplus-labour extorted	Surplus-value extorted	Domination	Subordination	Domination	Subordination
Unproductive labour							
Supervisors in circulation and realization	–	++	–	+	++	++	++
Subaltern mental labour	–	+	–	–	+	–	+
Unproductive manual labour*	–		–	–			
Productive labour							
Supervisors in material production	–	+	+	+	+	+	+
Technicians and engineers in material production (who are not also supervisors)	–	+	+	–	+	+	+

*This category is not explicitly discussed by Poulantzas, but it is clearly a possibility (e.g. a janitor in a bank).

without placing it in a transportable container. But packaging is also part of realization costs under capitalism, since much of the labour embodied in packaging goes into producing advertising. Such labour cannot be considered productive, because it does not produce any use-values (and thus cannot produce surplus-value). This is not a question of any historical normative judgement on the goodness of the labour. Labour which produces the most pointless luxuries can still be productive. But labour which merely serves to facilitate the realization of surplus-value is not, and at least part of the labour-time that is embodied in packaging falls into this category.[86]

While Poulantzas does admit that some labour has this dual productive/unproductive character, he sidesteps this problem in his analysis of classes by saying that labour is tendentially one or the other. In fact, a large proportion of labour in capitalist society has both productive and unproductive aspects, and there is no reason to assume that such mixed forms of labour are becoming less frequent. The productive/unproductive labour distinction should thus be thought of as reflecting two dimensions of labour activity rather than two types of labourers.

The most fundamental objection, however, to Poulantzas's use of the productive/unproductive distinction goes beyond questions of definition or the conceptual status of the distinction. For two positions within the social division of labour to be placed in different classes on the basis of economic criteria implies that they have fundamentally different class *interests* at the economic level.[87] Let us assume for the moment that the productive/unproductive labour distinction generally does correspond to different actual positions in the social division of labour. The key question then becomes whether this distinction represents a significant division of class interests. If we assume that the fundamental class interest of the proletariat is the destruction of capitalist relations of production and the construction of socialism, then the question becomes whether productive and unproductive workers have a different interest with respect to socialism. More precisely, do unproductive workers in general lack a class interest in socialism? One possible argument could be that many unproductive jobs would disappear in a socialist society and thus unproductive workers would be opposed to socialism. Aside from the problem that this argument confuses occupation with class, many jobs that are quite productive under capitalism would also disappear in a socialist society, while many unproductive jobs in capitalist society – doctors employed by the state, for example – would not.

It could also be argued that since unproductive workers produce no surplus-value, they live off the surplus-value produced by productive workers and thus indirectly participate in the exploitation of those workers. Taking the argument one step further, it is sometimes claimed that unproductive workers have a stake in increasing the social rate of exploitation, since this would make it easier for them to improve their own wages. This kind of argument is perhaps clearest in the case of state workers who are paid directly out of taxes. Since taxation comes at least partially out of surplus-value, it appears that state workers live off the exploitation of productive labour. There is no question that there is some truth in this claim. Certainly in terms of immediate economic interests, state workers are often in conflict with private-sector workers over questions of taxation. The bourgeois media have made much of this issue and have clearly used it as a divisive force in the labour movement. However, the question is not whether divisions of immediate interests exist between productive and unproductive workers, but whether such divisions generate different objective interests in socialism. Many divisions of immediate economic interest exist within the working class – between monopoly and competitive sector workers, between black and white workers, between workers in imperialist countries and workers in the third world, etc. But none of these divisions implies that the 'privileged' group of workers has an interest in perpetuating the system of capitalist exploitation. None of these divisions changes the fundamental fact that all workers, by virtue of their position within the social relations of production, have a basic interest in socialism. I would argue that this is true for most unproductive workers as well.

Poulantzas agrees that, in general, both productive and unproductive workers are exploited; both have unpaid labour extorted from them. The only difference is that in the case of productive labour, unpaid labour time is appropriated as surplus-value; whereas in the case of unproductive labour, unpaid labour merely reduces the costs to the capitalist of appropriating part of the surplus-value produced elsewhere. In both cases, the capitalist will try to keep the wage bill as low as possible; in both cases, the capitalist will try to increase productivity by getting workers to work harder; in both cases, workers will be dispossessed of control over their labour process. In both cases, socialism is a prerequisite for ending exploitation. It is hard to see where a fundamental divergence of economic interests emerges from the positions of unproductive and productive labour in capitalist relations of production. Certainly Poulantzas has not demonstrated that such a divergence exists. He has stated that the formal mechanisms of exploitation are different for the two types of workers; but he has not shown why this formal difference generates a difference in basic interests and thus can be considered a determinant of a class boundary.[88]

Another way of looking at this issue is from the point of view of capital. No one has ever suggested that the distinction between productive and unproductive capital represents a class boundary between the capitalist class and some other grouping. Typically, the productive/unproductive capital distinction is treated as one element defining a fractional boundary within the bourgeoisie (such as between banking and industrial capital). However, it could be argued, in much the same fashion as Poulantzas argues for the working class, that unproductive capital lies 'outside the dominant capitalist relation of exploitation' and thus agents occupying the place of unproductive capital should not be considered members of the capitalist class. This argument, of course, would be absurd, because it is obvious that whatever short-run conflicts of interests there might be between productive and unproductive capital, their fundamental class interests are the same. The same can be said for the distinction between productive and unproductive labour.[89]

Political and ideological criteria

Poulantzas insists that while ideological and political criteria are important, economic criteria still play the principal role in determining classes.[40] If we look at Tables 1 and 2, this does not appear to be the case. As can be seen from the tables, the working class represents the polar opposite of the bourgeoisie: on every criterion they have opposite signs. *Any* deviation from the criteria which define the working class is enough to exclude an agent from the working class in Poulantzas's analysis. Thus, an agent who was like a worker on the economic and political criteria, but deviated on the ideological criteria, would on this basis alone be excluded from the proletariat (this is the case for subaltern technicians). In practice, therefore, the ideological and political criteria become co-equal with the economic criteria, since they can *always* pre-empt the structural determination of class at the economic level. (This is quite separate from the question of the correctness of the economic criteria themselves as discussed above.) It is difficult to see how, under these circumstances, this perspective maintains the primacy of economic relations in the definition of classes.

The treatment of ideological and political criteria as effectively co-equal with economic criteria stems, at least in part, from Poulantzas's usage of the notion of the 'technical' division of labour. Poulantzas very correctly stresses that the social division of labour has primacy over the technical division. But he incorrectly identifies the technical division of labour with economic criteria whenever he discusses the role of political and ideological factors. For example, in the discussion of technicians Poulantzas writes: 'We have . . . seen the importance of the mental/manual labour division for the supervisory staff and for engineers and technicians. This played a decisive role in so far as, by way of the primacy of the social division of labour over the technical, it excluded these groupings from the working class despite the fact that they too perform "capitalist productive labour".'[41] Poulantzas in effect equates the performance of productive labour with the technical division of labour. But if the 'dominant capitalist relation of exploitation' constitutes the essential definition of productive labour, then it is unreasonable to treat productive

257

labour as strictly a technical category. More generally, rather than viewing economic criteria as being rooted in the technical division of labour and political-ideological criteria in the social division, both should be considered dimensions of the social division of labour. If this is granted, then it is no longer at all obvious that ideological and political criteria should always pre-empt economic criteria in the structural determination of class. On the contrary: if economic criteria within the social division of labour are to be treated as the principal determinants of class, then they should generally pre-empt the ideological and political criteria.

Aside from undermining the economic basis of the theory of class, Poulantzas's use of political and ideological criteria has other difficulties. Especially in his discussion of political criteria, it is sometimes questionable whether these criteria are really 'political' at all. The core political criterion Poulantzas emphasizes in his discussion of the new petty bourgeoisie is position within the supervisory hierarchy. Now, apart from the issue of supervision as technical co-ordination, there are two ways in which supervision can be conceptualized. Following Poulantzas, supervision can be conceived as the 'direct reproduction, within the process of production itself, of the political relations between the capitalist class and the working class'.[42] Alternatively, supervision can be seen as one aspect of the structural dissociation between economic ownership and possession at the economic level itself. That is, possession, as an aspect of the ownership of the means of production, involves (to use Poulantzas's own formulation) control over the labour process. In the development of monopoly capitalism, possession has become dissociated from economic ownership. But equally, possession has become internally differentiated, so that control over the entire labour process (top managers) has become separated from the immediate control of labour activity (supervision). Unless possession itself is to be considered an aspect of political relations, there is no reason to consider supervision a reflection of political relations within the social division of labour rather than a differentiated element of economic relations.[43]

In Poulantzas's use of ideological criteria, it is never clear exactly why the mental/manual division should be considered a determinant of an actual class boundary, rather than simply an internal division within the working class. It is also not clear why this particular ideological dimension was chosen over a variety of others as the essential axis of ideological domination/subordination within the social division of labour. For example, sexism, by identifying certain jobs as 'women's work' and of inferior status to men's work, is also a dimension of ideological domination/subordination within the social division of labour. This puts men as a whole in a position of ideological domination, and yet this hardly makes a male worker not a worker. The same can be said of racism, nationalism and other ideologies of domination. All of these create important divisions within the proletariat; but, unless they correspond to different actual relations of production, they do not constitute criteria for class boundaries in their own right.

The size of the proletariat using Poulantzas's criteria

The upshot of Poulantzas's use of economic, political and ideological criteria is that the working class in the United States becomes a very small proportion of the total population. Of course, the validity of a conceptualization of class relations can hardly be judged by the number of people that fall into the working class. Nevertheless, since it is of considerable political importance how large or small the working class is seen to be, it is worth attempting to estimate the distribution of the population into classes using different criteria for class position.

While census data are of relatively little use in estimating the size of the working class, since they are not collected in terms of Marxist categories, there are other sources of data which are more useful. In particular, the University of Michigan Survey Research Center conducted a survey in 1969 on working conditions throughout the United States which included a number of questions which make it possible to reach a reasonably good estimate of the size of the working class using a variety of criteria. The survey contains data on: the respondent's occupation and the industry in which he/she works; whether or not the respondent has subordinates on the job whom he/she supervises; whether or not the respondent is self-employed, and if so, how many employees, if any, the respondent has.[44] On the basis of these questions, we can estimate the size of the working class according to Poulantzas's criteria if we make some rough assumptions about the relationship of occupational titles to the mental/manual labour division and the relationship of industrial categories to the productive/unproductive labour distinction.

For present purposes, we will use the following definitions: 1. *Mental Labour*: professionals, technicians, managers (by occupational title), clerks and salespeople. 2. *Manual Labour*: craftsmen, operatives, labourers, transportation and services (i.e. janitors, barbers, cooks, etc.). 3. *Unproductive sectors*: wholesale and retail trade, finance, insurance, real-estate, services and government. 4. *Productive sectors*: agriculture, fishing, mining, construction, manufacturing, transportation and communications.

This set of categories is not perfect, both because of limitations of the data and because the complex reality of class relations can only be approximated by statistical data. By Poulantzas's definition of mental labour, there are certainly some craftsmen who should be considered mental labourers (i.e. they are not separated from the 'secret knowledge' of production and use it in their labour process). There are also positions in trade and government which are clearly productive by any definition, and some positions in productive sector industries which are unproductive. Nevertheless, these categories can give us a pretty good idea of the size of the proletariat based on Poulantzas's analysis.

The results appear in Tables 3–5. Table 3 presents the proportion of the total economically active population (i.e. people working twenty hours a week or more) that fall into each combination of the criteria for class. (None of the results differs significantly if the analysis is restricted to full-time workers.) The working class – non-supervisory, manual wage-earners in the productive sector – constitutes less than 20 per cent of the American labour force. The new petty bourgeoisie, on the other hand, swells to a mammoth 70 per cent of the economically active population. Table 4 gives these same results for men and women separately. Less than 15 per cent of the economically active women in the American population are working class according to Poulantzas's criteria, while among men the figure is still only 23 per cent.[45] Finally, Table 5 gives the proportion of the population which is working class using a variety of different combinations of Poulantzas's criteria. If the productive/unproductive labour distinction is dropped, but the other criteria kept, the working

TABLE 3. DISTRIBUTION OF THE ACTIVE LABOUR FORCE BY CLASS CRITERIA (UNITED STATES NATIONAL RANDOM SAMPLE TAKEN IN 1969)

| | *Self-employed* | | *Wage-earners* | | |
	Employers	Petty bourgeoisie	Supervisors	Non-supervisors	TOTALS
Mental labour					
Unproductive sector	3·3%	1·9%	15·6%	16·5%	37·2%
Productive sector	2·5%	0·4%	4·4%	4·5%	11·9%
Manual labour					
Unproductive sector	0·3%	0·3%	5·3%	11·2%	17·2%
Productive sector	1·3%	1·8%	10·7%	19·7%	33·6%
TOTALS	7·5%	4·5%	36·1%	51·9%	100·0%
Number in sample	110	65	526	758	1459

SOURCE: 1969 Survey of Working Conditions, Institute of Social Research, University of Michigan (for a detailed discussion of the sample, see my 'Class Structure and Income Inequality', unpublished Ph.D Dissertation, Department of Sociology, University of California, Berkeley. Available from University Microfilms, Ann Arbor, Michigan).

DEFINITIONS:
Mental labour: professionals, technicians, managers (by occupational title), clerks, sales
Manual labour: craftsmen, operatives, labourers, transportation, services (i.e. janitors, etc.)
Unproductive sectors: wholesale and retail trade, finance, insurance, real estate, services, government
Productive sectors: agriculture, mining, fishing, construction, manufacturing, transportation, communications

class increases to over 30 per cent of the population. If the manual/mental labour distinction is dropped, but the supervisory labour criterion kept, the proportion rises to over 50 per cent of the population (67 per cent for women). The important point in the present context is that it makes a tremendous difference which criteria are used to define the proletariat, and that using Poulantzas's criteria reduces the American working class to a small minority.

TABLE 4. DISTRIBUTION OF ACTIVE LABOUR FORCE BY CLASS CRITERIA FOR MEN AND FOR WOMEN (1969)

MEN	*Self-employed*		*Wage-earners*		
	Employers	Petty bourgeoisie	Supervisors	Non-supervisors	TOTALS
Mental labour					
Unproductive sector	4·0%	1·7%	14·3%	9·0%	29·0%
Productive sector	4·0%	0·6%	5·6%	3·0%	13·2%
Manual labour					
Unproductive sector	0·4%	0·2%	5·6%	8·7%	14·9%
Productive sector	2·1%	2·7%	15·4%	22·7%	42·9%
TOTALS	10·5%	5·3%	40·8%	43·4%	100·0%
Number in sample	98	49	380	404	931

WOMEN	*Self-employed*		*Wage-earners*		
	Employers	Petty bourgeoisie	Supervisors	Non-supervisors	TOTALS
Mental labour					
Unproductive sector	2·2%	2·0%	18·1%	30·9%	53·1%
Productive sector	0·0%	0·2%	2·4%	7·1%	9·6%
Manual labour					
Unproductive sector	0·2%	0·4%	5·1%	15·2%	20·9%
Productive sector	0·0%	0·0%	1·8%	14·6%	16·3%
TOTALS	2·4%	2·6%	27·4%	67·7%	100·0%
Number in sample	12	13	129	344	508

(See Table 3 for definitions of the categories)

TABLE 5. THE SIZE OF THE AMERICAN WORKING CLASS BY DIFFERENT CRITERIA (1969)

Criteria for the working class	Percentage of the economically active population which is working class by given criteria		
	TOTAL	MEN ONLY	WOMEN ONLY
All wage-earners	88·0%	83·6%	95·1%
All wage-earners who are not supervisors	51·9%	43·4%	67·7%
Blue-collar wage-earners (including blue-collar supervisors)	46·8%	52·4%	36·7%
Blue-collar, non-supervisory wage-earners	31·0%	31·4%	29·8%
Productive, non-supervisory manual labour (the working class in Poulantzas's analysis)	19·7%	22·7%	14·6%

SOURCE: Same as Table 3

THE CLASS UNITY OF THE NEW AND TRADITIONAL PETTY BOURGEOISIE

The relationship of economic to political and ideological criteria is even more important in Poulantzas's argument about the class unity of the old and new petty bourgeoisie than it is in his analysis of who should be excluded from the working class in the first place. At the economic level not only are the old and new petty bourgeoisie characterized by different economic situations, but those situations are in many ways fundamentally opposed to each other. In particular, the old petty bourgeoisie is constantly threatened by the growth of monopoly capitalism, while the new petty bourgeoisie is clearly dependent upon monopoly capital for its reproduction. At the political level their interests are also opposed: the new petty bourgeoisie in general has an interest in the expansion of the state; the old petty bourgeoisie is generally opposed to big government and large state budgets.

In order for these opposing interests of the old and new petty bourgeoisie at the economic and political levels to be neutralized by the ideological level, the ideological bonds between the old and new petty bourgeoisie would have to be very powerful indeed. In fact, Poulantzas provides a partial view of the ideologies of the old and new petty bourgeoisie, and it is equally plausible to characterize them as opposed at this level as well as at the economic and political levels. While it is true that individualism characterizes the ideology of both the new and old petty bourgeoisie, the individualism of the two categories is extremely different. The individualism of the old petty bourgeoisie stresses individual autonomy, be your own boss, control your own destiny, etc. The individualism of the new petty bourgeoisie, on the other hand, is a careerist individualism, an individualism geared towards organizational mobility. The archetypal new petty bourgeois is the 'organization man', whose individualism is structured around the requirements of bureaucratic advancement; the archetypal traditional petty bourgeois is the 'rugged individualist', who makes his/her own way outside of the external demands of organizations. To call both of these 'petty-bourgeois individualism' is to gloss over important distinctions.

The basic problem with Poulantzas's discussion of the old and new petty bourgeoisie, however, does not concern these ideological divisions between them. Even if the two categories could be said to have identical ideologies, it would still be very questionable on this basis to call them a single class. In what sense can the economic level be considered the 'principal' determinant of class relations if two groups of agents with contradictory positions at the economic level – in fact, who exist in different modes of production at the economic level – can, on the basis of ideology alone, be grouped into a single class? In the end, the procedure Poulantzas adopts makes ideology itself the decisive criterion for class.

THE CLASS BOUNDARY OF THE BOURGEOISIE

Table 6 presents the various combinations of criteria Poulantzas uses to define the bourgeoisie. The most valuable aspects of his discussion are the emphasis on the need to go below legal categories of ownership and the analysis of the historical transformations and dissociations of economic ownership and possession.

Poulantzas's discussion of the class position of managers, however, is inadequate. When a manager occupies a position in the relations of production that is characterized by *both* economic ownership and possession, it is certainly reasonable to categorize the manager as part of the bourgeoisie. The problem arises when a manager occupies a position characterized by possession but not economic ownership. Poulantzas's solution to this situation is to argue that, in spite of the structural differentiation of different functions of capital, the positions remain unitary parts of capital as such. Thus, occupying any such position is sufficient to define the manager as bourgeois. This is an arbitrary solution. It is equally plausible to argue that exclusion from economic ownership defines non-capitalists in capitalist society, and thus managers who are 'mere' possessors of the means of production should be excluded from the bourgeoisie. A third possibility is to argue that there are positions in the social division of labour which are *objectively contradictory*. Managers who are excluded from any economic ownership would constitute such a category, even if they retain partial possession of the means of production.

A second problem with Poulantzas's analysis of the bourgeoisie is that he tends to regard economic ownership and possession as all-or-nothing categories. A position either does or does not have real economic control of the means of production (economic ownership), or does or does not have the capacity to put those means of production into operation (possession). In fact, many managerial positions must be characterized as having limited forms of both ownership and

TABLE 6. DETAILED CRITERIA FOR THE BOURGEOISIE AND FOR DIFFERENTIATION OF BOURGEOISIE AND PETTY BOURGEOISIE

	Economic criteria			Political criteria			Ideological criteria	
	Legal ownership	Economic ownership	Possession	Direct producer	Domination	Subordination	Domination	Subordination
Traditional entrepreneurial capitalists	+	+	+	−	+	−	+	−
Top corporate executives	−	+	+	−	+	−	+	−
Managers	−	−	+	−	+	−	+	−
Heads of state apparatuses	−	−	−	−	+	−	+	−
Traditional petty bourgeoisie	+	+	+	+	−	+	−	+

possession. Some managers may have substantial control over one small segment of the total production process; others may have fairly limited control over a broader range of the production process. While it is clear that an agent whose control is so attenuated that he/she merely executes decisions made from above should be excluded from the bourgeoisie, there is considerable ambiguity how middle-level managers of various sorts should be treated. Poulantzas's apparent solution is to argue that 'In all cases, therefore, the managers are an integral section of the bourgeois class'.[46] Again, an alternative solution is to treat contradictory cases as contradictory cases rather than to collapse them artificially into one class or another.

Notes

1. For example, Nicos Poulantzas in 'On Social Classes', *New Left Review* 78, and in *Classes in Contemporary Capitalism*, London: NLB, 1975.
2. For example, Al Szymanski, 'Trends in the American Working Class', *Socialist Revolution* No. 10.
3. For example, Francesca Freedman, 'The Internal Structure of the Proletariat', *Socialist Revolution* No. 26.
4. *Classes in Contemporary Capitalism*, p. 14.
5. *ibid.*
6. 'On Social Classes', pp. 49–50.
7. *Classes in Contemporary Capitalism*, p. 14.
8. *ibid.*, p. 16. In this particular passage, Poulantzas uses the expression 'class position' rather than 'class struggle' at the end. By class position in this context, Poulantzas refers to the concrete situation of a class in a specific historical conjuncture. Thus, for example, under certain historical circumstances, the labour aristocracy may assume the class position of the bourgeoisie, without actually changing its objective place in the class structure. This is a confusing use of the word 'position' and Poulantzas himself is not always consistent in the way he uses it (note the quote under proposition 2 above). At any rate, throughout this discussion I will use the expression 'class position' to refer to objective class location.
9. Poulantzas writes: 'The analyses presented here have nothing

in common with the Hegelian schema with its class-in-itself (economic class situation, uniquely objective determination of class by the process of production) and a class-for-itself (class endowed with its own "class consciousness" and an autonomous political organization=class struggle), which in the Marxist tradition is associated with Lukács.' (*ibid.*)

10. *ibid.*, p. 20.
11. *ibid.*, p. 216. Italics in original.
12. *ibid.*, p. 221.
13. *ibid.*, p. 212.
14. *ibid.*, pp. 227–8.
15. *ibid.*, p. 225.
16. *ibid.*, p. 228.
17. In defining the mental/manual labour division, Poulantzas writes: 'We could thus say that every form of work that takes the form of knowledge from which the direct producers are excluded, falls on the mental labour side of the capitalist production process, irrespective of its empirical/natural content; and that this is so whether the direct producers actually do know how to perform this work but do not do so (again not by chance), or whether they in fact do not know how to perform it (since they are systematically kept away from it) or whether again there is simply nothing that needs to be known.' (*ibid.*, p. 238.) Poulantzas is thus very careful not to define mental labour as 'brain work' and manual labour as 'hand work'. While there is a rough correspondence between these two distinctions, the mental/manual division must be considered an aspect of the social division of labour and not a technical fact of whether muscle or brain is primarily engaged in the labour process.
18. It is important to note that ideological domination, in Poulantzas's framework, has nothing to do with the consciousness of workers. Ideology is a material practice, not a belief system within the heads of workers. To say that the division of labour between mental and manual activities constitutes the ideological domination of the working class means that the material reality of this division excludes workers from the knowledge necessary for the direction of the production process. Of course, such an exclusion has consequences on consciousness – workers may come to believe that they are utterly incapable of gaining the necessary knowledge to organize production – but the ideological domination is real irrespective of the beliefs of workers.
19. This does not mean that Poulantzas regards the mental/manual division as operating uniformly on all categories of wage-labourers within the new petty bourgeoisie. He stresses that the mental/

manual division is reproduced within the new petty bourgeoisie itself, and that many new petty bourgeoisie are themselves subordinated to mental labour within the category of mental labour: 'The mental labour aspect does not affect the new petty bourgeoisie in an undifferentiated manner. Certain sections of it are affected directly. Others, subjected to the reproduction of the mental/manual division within mental labour itself, are only affected indirectly; and while these sections are still affected by the effects of the basic division, they also experience a hierarchy within mental labour itself.' (*ibid.*, p. 256.)

20. *ibid.*, pp. 285–6.

21. *ibid.*, p. 294.

22. *ibid.*, p. 287. Note that here Poulantzas is talking about the ideology *of* a class rather than the position of the class in the social division of labour at the ideological level. While it may be true that the traditional petty bourgeoisie occupies the place of mental labour in the mental/manual division (i.e. the old petty bourgeoisie is not separated from the 'secret knowledge' of production even though many petty bourgeois artisans would be classified *technically* as manual labourers), Poulantzas is more concerned here with certain features of the ideology of agents within the petty bourgeoisie.

23. *ibid.*, p. 291.

24. *ibid.*, p. 292.

25. *ibid.*, p. 18.

26. *ibid.*, p. 19.

27. Loc. cit.

28. When Poulantzas uses the term 'managers', he is explicitly discussing those managerial personnel who directly participate in economic ownership and/or possession. When he discusses lower-level positions within the managerial hierarchy, he uses expressions like 'the work of management and supervision', or simply 'supervisors'.

29. *ibid.*, p. 180. Italics added.

30. Poulantzas provides an extremely interesting discussion of the transformations of the dissociation of economic ownership and possession in the course of the development of monopoly capitalism (*ibid.*, pp. 116–30). He argues that during the initial stages of monopoly concentration, economic ownership became concentrated more rapidly than the labour process actually became centralized (i.e. under unified direction). The result was that during this initial phase of concentration, monopoly capital itself was characterized by economic ownership of the means of production with only partial powers of possession. It was not until what Poulantzas calls

the restructuring period of monopoly capitalism that economic ownership and possession were fully reintegrated within monopoly capital itself.

31. *ibid.*, p. 181.

32. *ibid.*, p. 187.

33. This assessment of Poulantzas's analysis of classes will focus on the actual criteria he uses to understand classes in contemporary capitalism, rather than on the epistemological assumptions which underlie his analysis. I will thus not deal with the problem of his general concept of 'class struggle' and his categorical rejection of 'consciousness' as a useful category in a Marxist analysis. While it is important to deal with these issues (indeed, most reviews of Poulantzas's work are preoccupied with these questions rather than the substance of his argument), I feel that it is more useful at this point to engage Poulantzas's work at a lower level of abstraction.

34. Many of the ideas for this section on productive and unproductive labour come directly from James O'Connor's very important essay 'Productive and Unproductive Labor', in *Politics and Society*, Vol. 5, No. 2, and from numerous discussions within the San Francisco Bay Area *Kapitalistate* collective.

35. Marx's famous comparison of teaching factories and sausage factories makes this precise point: 'The only worker who is productive is one who produces surplus-value for the capitalist, or in other words contributes towards the self-valorization of capital. If we may take an example from outside the sphere of material production, a schoolmaster is a productive worker when, in addition to belabouring the heads of his pupils, he works himself into the ground to enrich the owner of the school. That the latter has laid out his capital in a teaching factory, instead of a sausage factory, makes no difference to the relation.' (*Capital*, Vol. I, London: Penguin/NLR, 1976, p. 644.) It would be hard to imagine a clearer statement that Marx did not restrict the concept of productive labour to labour directly involved in material production. It is surprising that Poulantzas never discusses this quotation, especially since he does cite Marx heavily to support his own use of the concept of productive labour.

36. Admittedly, such advertising-packaging labour is socially necessary labour time under capitalism and contributes to the costs of production of commodities. But this can be said about most realization labour, not just realization labour that becomes physically embodied in a material aspect of the commodity. Advertising labour should therefore be categorized as a *faux frais* of capitalist production, along with many other kinds of unproductive labour.

For a discussion of advertising labour, see Baran and Sweezy's analysis of the interpenetration of sales and production in monopoly capitalism: *Monopoly Capital*, New York, 1966, chapter 6.

37. The expression 'fundamental' or 'ultimate' class interests refers to interests involving the very structure of social relations; 'immediate' class interests, on the other hand, refers to interests within a given structure of social relations. Expressed in slightly different terms, immediate class interests are interests defined within a mode of production, whereas ultimate class interests are interests defined between modes of production.

38. A concrete example may help to illustrate the argument. By every definition of unproductive labour, a janitor in a bank is unproductive. No surplus-value is produced in a bank and thus the labour of all bank employees is unproductive. A janitor in a factory, however, is productive, since cleaning up a work area is part of the socially necessary labour time in the actual production of commodities. Is it reasonable to say that these two janitors have a different class interest in socialism? Unless this is the case, it is arbitrary to place one janitor in the working class and the other in the new petty bourgeoisie. (See G. Carchedi, 'On the Economic Identification of the New Middle Class', *Economy and Society*, Vol. IV (1975), No. 1, p. 19, for a similar critique of unproductive labour as a criterion for class.)

39. This critique of Poulantzas's use of the productive/unproductive labour distinction as a class criterion does not imply that the distinction has no relevance for Marxist theory in general. In particular, the distinction between productive and unproductive labour may play a central part in the analysis of the accumulation process and crisis tendencies in advanced capitalism.

40. In reading this critique of Poulantzas's use of political and ideological criteria in the definition of classes, it is important to remember the political and ideological context in which Poulantzas has developed his analysis. In a personal communication, Poulantzas writes: 'I think that one of our most serious politico-theoretical adversaries is *economism*, which *always* pretends, as soon as we try (with all the theoretical difficulties we encounter here) to stress the importance of the politico-ideological, that we "abandon the primacy of economics".' Poulantzas is absolutely correct in attacking economism and in attempting to integrate political and ideological considerations into the logic of a Marxist class analysis. The difficulty, as we shall see, is that he does not develop a clear criterion for the use of ideological and political criteria, and thus in practice they assume an almost equal footing with economic relations.

41. *Classes in Contemporary Capitalism*, p. 251.

42. *ibid.*, p. 228.

43. It is one thing to say that supervision has a political dimension and another to say that supervision is itself political relations within production. The former seems correct and is analogous to saying that possession and even economic ownership have political dimensions. The latter considerably expands the notion of the 'political' and must, of necessity, make possession of the means of production itself part of the 'reproduction of political relations within production'.

44. See my 'Class Structure and Income Inequality', unpublished PhD Dissertation, Department of Sociology, University of California, Berkeley (available from University Microfilms, Ann Arbor, Michigan), for a detailed discussion of the survey.

45. A reasonable objection could be raised that the estimates according to Poulantzas's criteria are unrealistically low because I have used such a broad definition of supervision. Undoubtedly, some individuals say that they 'supervise others on the job' when in fact they are simply the chief of a work team and have virtually no actual power within the labour process. As a result of the vagueness of the criterion for supervision, the estimates in Tables 1 and 2 indicate that well over a third of the labour force are supervisors. A second set of data enables us to adopt a more refined criterion for supervision. (However, the data set in question, the ISR Panel Study of Income Dynamics, is much less of a representative sample than the survey used in the above Tables, and thus is less adequate to gain a picture of the overall shape of the class structure.) In this second survey, individuals who said that they were supervisors were also asked if they had 'any say in the pay and promotions of their subordinates'. Approximately 65 per cent of all male blue-collar supervisors said that they did *not* have any say in pay and promotions (the data are not available for female supervisors). If we assume that all of these individuals should be classified as workers by Poulantzas's criteria, then the proportion of males in the working class increases from 23 per cent in Table 2 to about 33 per cent. Undoubtedly, the true proportion is somewhere in between these two estimates. In any event, even using this narrower definition of supervision, the working class remains a decided minority in Poulantzas's framework.

46. *ibid.*, p. 180.

10. Some later theories

Anthony Giddens

1. DAHRENDORF: CLASSES IN POST-CAPITALIST SOCIETY

Dahrendorf's theory of class and class conflict, as described particularly in his *Class and Class Conflict in Industrial Society*, treats themes previously developed by Geiger and others, but elaborates upon them in a different way. While he couches his ideas in terms of a 'positive critique' of Marx, he eventually reaches a theoretical position which departs very substantially from the one established by that thinker.[1] Like Geiger (and, of course, Weber before him), Dahrendorf offers two related sets of criticisms of Marx, concerning supposed conceptual weaknesses in Marx's notions of 'classes' and 'class conflict' on the one hand, and in his (abstract) model of capitalist development on the other.

According to Dahrendorf, Marx's works are based upon an illegitimate fusion of 'sociological' and 'philosophical' elements. We must draw a strict separation between those of Marx's propositions which are, in Dahrendorf's terms, 'empirical and falsifiable' and those which belong to a 'philosophy of history'. Propositions such as 'class conflict generates social change' are of the first type, while statements such as 'capitalist society is the final class society in history', or 'socialism leads to a complete realisation of human freedom' are not capable of either verification or falsification by reference to documented fact.[2] The task of the sociologist is to sift out those of Marx's ideas which can be embodied within an empirically verifiable theory of classes.

In Dahrendorf's view, the conjunction of 'sociological' and

From A. Giddens, *The Class Structure of the Advanced Societies*, London: Hutchinson, 1973, pp. 53–68.

'philosophical' elements in Marx's writings serves to mask a fundamental weakness in the connection which he makes between classes and private property. 'Property' can be conceived of in two ways: in a broad sense, as *control* of the means of production, regardless of the specific manner in which that control is exercised; or, more narrowly, as the legally recognised right of ownership. 'Property' is not *what* is owned, but refers to the rights relating to the object. In the broad sense of property, these rights are defined in a generalised manner, and hence it can be said that property is a 'special case of authority'. In this sense, the manager of an industrial enterprise in a society in which private ownership of capital has been abolished, in so far as he has directive *control* of the enterprise, may be said to exercise 'property rights'. In the narrower meaning, by contrast, authority is a 'special case of property': i.e. the authority structure of the enterprise is dependent upon 'who owns the means of production' in the legal sense. According to Dahrendorf, Marx's analysis of classes and private property turns upon the latter, 'narrow' definition of 'property'. The existence of classes and, correspondingly, the disappearance of classes in socialist society, in Marx's formulations, are tied to social conditions in which legal title to property ownership is in the hands of a minority of individuals. In a society in which legal ownership of property by private individuals is abolished, there can – by definition – be no classes.

It is only because Marx employs the narrow conception of property that he is able to integrate, in an apparently plausible way, the 'sociological' with the 'philosophical' aspects of his theory:

By asserting the dependence of classes on relations of domination and subjection, and the dependence of these relations on the possession of or exclusion from effective private capital, he makes on the one hand empirically private property, on the other hand philosophically social classes, the central factor of his analysis. One can retrace step by step the thought process to which Marx has succumbed at this point. It is not the thought process of the empirical scientist who seeks only piecemeal knowledge and expects only piecemeal progress, but that of the system builder who suddenly finds that everything fits! For if private property disappears (empirical hypothesis), then there are no longer classes (trick of definition)! If there are no longer any classes, there is no alienation (speculative postulate). The realm of liberty is realised on earth (philosophical idea).[3]

The confusions inherent in this reasoning disqualify Marx's conception of classes, in unmodified form, as a viable scheme for analysing the class structure of modern societies. This is demonstrated further by the inadequacy of Marx's analysis in the face of the changes which have affected capitalism since the close of the nineteenth century. 'Capitalism', as Marx knew it, has become transformed: not through a process of revolution, however, and not in the direction which he anticipated. Here Dahrendorf introduces the conception of 'industrial society', of which capitalism is only one sub-type. Capitalism is that form of industrial society which is distinguished by the coincidence of the legal ownership of private property, in the hands of the entrepreneur, and actual *control* of the means of production. In this type of society, the two senses of 'property' overlap with one another – which explains Marx's failure to distinguish between them on the theoretical level. The modern form of society no longer preserves this characteristic, and is thus quite different from capitalism as Marx knew it: while it is still an 'industrial society', it is also a 'post-capitalist' society.

Dahrendorf details the following changes as being the most significant in the transformation of capitalism: (1) The decomposition of capital. Although, in the third volume of *Capital*, Marx discussed the growth of joint-stock companies, and the 'functional irrelevance of the capitalist', he failed to discern their true significance. In Dahrendorf's view, this has to be understood as a process of role differentiation, whereby the blanket category of 'capitalist' has become separated into the two categories of 'shareholder' and 'manager'. This process does not represent an enclave of socialism within capitalism; rather, it constitutes a progressive separation between the two forms of 'property' which were temporarily united in capitalist society. The authority of the managerial executive does not rest upon legal property rights. Since the interests of managers are not wholly convergent with those of shareholders, it follows that the real outcome of the development of joint-stock companies is the fragmentation of the unitary 'capitalist class'. (2) The decomposition of labour. Marx held that the mechanisation entailed by the growing maturity of capitalist production leads to the elimination of skilled labour, and thus to the increasing internal homogeneity of the working class. In fact, this has not occurred. On the contrary, the trend has been towards the maintenance, and even the expansion, of skilled labour; and the 'semi-skilled' category has intruded between the skilled and the unskilled. Far from becoming increasingly homogeneous, the working class has become more diversified: the differences in skill-level serve as a basis for divisions of interest which cut across the unity of the class as a whole. Thus the internal differentiation at the lower levels of post-capitalist society complements that which occurs in the upper echelons with the decomposition of the capitalist class.

(3) The growth of the 'new middle class'. The expansion of administrative or non-manual occupations is again a phenomenon unanticipated by Marx. But while the decomposition of capital and wage-labour is a consequence of social changes which have disaggregated these previous coherent classes, 'the "new middle class" was born decomposed'.[4] The so-called new middle class, according to Dahrendorf, is not in fact a distinct class at all, but consists of two parts: those workers who are part of an administrative chain of authority ('bureaucrats'), and those who occupy positions outside such hierarchies (such as shop assistants). The bureaucrat, whether high-placed or lowly, shares in the exercise of authority, and thus his position is directly linked to that of the dominant groups in society; those workers in the second type of situation, on the other hand, are closer to the position of manual workers. But these two sectors of the 'new middle class' therefore add to the diversification in the structure of post-capitalist society already implied by the twin processes of the decomposition of the capitalist and the working class.

(4) The increase in rates of social mobility, which Dahrendorf regards as one of the principal characteristics of indus-

trial society. The effects of widespread inter- and intra-generational mobility are twofold. First, these act to diminish the boundaries between classes, and thus to corrode any rigid barriers which might otherwise grow up between them. Secondly, the existence of high rates of social mobility serves to 'translate' group conflict into individual competition.[5] Group antagonisms – class conflicts – become dissolved into a competitive struggle between individuals for valued positions within the occupational system. (5) The achievement of 'citizenship rights', as embodied in universal suffrage and welfare legislation, for the mass of the population. These are not simply formal privileges, but have had real effects in undercutting the extremes of political and economic disparity found in nineteenth-century capitalism. The Marxian anticipation of a polarisation between the economic fortunes of capital and wage-labour is again quite at variance with the actual trend of development: 'by institutionalising certain citizenship rights, post-capitalist society has developed a type of social structure that excludes both "absolute" and many milder forms of privilege and deprivation'.[6] (6) The 'institutionalisation of class conflict', in the form of recognised procedures of industrial arbitration. The recognition of the right to strike, together with the existence of mutually accepted methods of resolving differences, has had the effect of confining conflicts to the sphere of industry itself, preventing them from ramifying into class conflicts.

These changes can only be adequately understood by abandoning an orthodox Marxian standpoint. Nonetheless, Dahrendorf argues, certain elements of Marx's conception must also be retained. The most important of these concerns Marx's emphasis that every (class) society incorporates conflicts which create a pressure towards internal change: there is an inherent connection between conflict and change. Secondly, Marx rightly assumes that social conflict must be understood in terms of a two-party model: a theory of class conflict must be founded upon recognition that, in any situation of antagonism, the struggle devolves upon two primary classes. While there may be coalitions, there are always two main positions in a conflict situation. But having accepted these formal properties of Marx's model, Dahrendorf explicitly repudiates most of the substantive content of the Marxian view. Marx's conception of class, as both a 'sociological' and 'philosophical' notion, is tied to his fusion of the two senses of 'property'. If the 'sociological' part of this conjunction has any validity, it is limited to nineteenth-century European capitalism. For the purpose of his theory of history, Marx universalises a particular – the connection between private property (narrow sense) and authoritative control (broad sense) which existed in the nineteenth century. A more adequate theory of class and class conflict, Dahrendorf suggests, must reverse this relation. That is to say, rather than class being defined in terms of ownership of private property (narrowly conceived), the tie between private property and authority, given such prominence by Marx, should be seen as a special case of a much broader relationship between class and authority. Marx's 'private property' should be seen as only a specific instance of authoritative right of control more generally. 'Class', therefore, should be defined in terms of authority relationships: rather than ownership versus non-ownership of property, class should be taken to refer to *possession of, or exclusion from, authority*:

in every social organisation some positions are entrusted with a right to exercise control over other positions in order to ensure effective coercion . . . in other words . . . there is a differential distribution of power and authority . . . this differential distribution of authority invariably becomes the determining factor of systematic social conflicts of a type that is germane to class conflicts in the traditional (Marxian) sense of the term. The structural origin of such group conflicts must be sought in the arrangement of social roles endowed with expectations of domination and subjection.[7]

'Authority', following Weber, is defined as the legitimate right to issue commands to others: 'domination' represents the possession of these rights, while 'subjection' is exclusion from them. Within 'imperatively co-ordinated associations' – i.e. groups which possess a definite authority structure (e.g. the state, an industrial enterprise) – possession of, and exclusion from, authority generates opposing interests. These interests may not be perceived by those involved: a 'quasi-group', in

Dahrendorf's terminology, is any collectivity whose members share latent interests, but who do not organise to further them. Where a collectivity does organise itself for this purpose, it becomes an 'interest group'.

The utility of this *schema*, in Dahrendorf's view, is not limited in its application to post-capitalist societies: it can also be used to cover the characteristics of the class structure of capitalism as described, in different terms, by Marx. Thus the development of nineteenth-century capitalist enterprise may be said to have stimulated the emergence of two quasi-groups, capital and labour. The specific character of capitalist society, however, derived from the fact that industrial and political conflict were 'superimposed' upon one another. The conflict between capital and labour was not confined to industry, but extended to the political sphere, since political authority was largely conterminous with economic domination. As a result of this superimposition of interest divisions, class conflict became particularly intensive as organised interest groups began to form to represent the divergent claims of capital and wage-labour. But the very appearance of these interest groups, and the concrete changes which they have helped to bring into being, have undermined the possibility of the revolutionary upheaval foreseen by Marx.[8]

According to Dahrendorf's conceptual scheme, it follows that 'post-capitalist' society is necessarily a class society. But, no less obviously, its class system is very different from that of capitalism. The most far-reaching of the various changes in terms of which Dahrendorf seeks to distinguish 'capitalism' from 'post-capitalism' is the institutional separation of industrial and political conflict – a phenomenon which derives from the connected processes of the establishment of collective bargaining in industry and the attainment of universal franchise in the political sphere. This is manifest in the fact that the occurrence of industrial conflict, in the main, has no direct repercussions upon political action. According to Dahrendorf, 'the notion of a workers' party has lost its political meaning'.[9] There is no integral connection between trade unions and 'labour' parties in the Western countries: those links which still exist are merely the residue of tradition. The same is true at the higher levels. The position of authority occupied by the manager in the enterprise yields no direct political influence: the latter is allocated independently of relationships pertaining in the industrial sphere.

2. ARON: INDUSTRIAL SOCIETY

Rather than being directed solely to a critique of Marx, Aron's various writings on the development of 'industrial society' are focused upon a comparative assessment of Marx and Tocqueville.[10] In common with Saint-Simon, of course, Tocqueville saw occurring in the newly emerging social order of postfeudal Europe, not the establishment of a new set of conflicting classes, but the development of tendencies towards democratisation and levelling. How far does the subsequent movement of society since the nineteenth century bear out the vision of Marx, in tending towards the polarisation of classes and the growing intensity of class conflict? Alternatively, how far has Tocqueville's anticipation of a growth in social differentiation, accompanied by the progressive impetus towards the eradication of inequalities, been realised?

These questions cannot be answered, Aron stresses, without taking account of the fact that there have been two 'paths' of social development in the modern world – one confined to the internal evolution of capitalism itself, and the other, although not originating within the advanced capitalist societies, claiming to represent the supersession of capitalism. The contrasts between these two forms of society, capitalist and socialist, cannot be understood, however, without recognising that they also share certain important elements in common as types of industrial society. The simplest abstract definition of 'industrial society' involves three principal characteristics: where the vast majority of the labour force is concentrated in the secondary and tertiary sectors; where there exists a constant impulsion, in contrast to the relatively static character of traditional societies, to expand productivity; and, consequently, where there is a rapid rate of technological innovation.[11] If this elementary definition of industrial society be adopted, Aron argues, it follows that certain formulae in Marx's analysis of capitalism apply also to the contemporary socialist or 'Soviet-type' societies:

> Marx considered that one of the main characteristics of capitalism was the accumulation of capital. We know today, from factual evidence, that this is a characteristic of all industrial societies to the degree to which, obsessed by the anxiety to heighten production, they are obliged to invest a growing volume of capital in machinery. In the same way, Marx considered that the worker was exploited because he did not receive, in the form of wages, the whole of the value produced by his labour. But, whatever the regime, this is obviously necessary, since a proportion of the value that is created must be reinvested . . . In both societies (capitalist and socialist), certain individuals are privileged: that is to say, they have higher incomes than those of workers at the bottom of the hierarchy. The phenomenon of capital accumulation or 'exploitation' is common to both types of industrial society, and not characteristic of one type in contrast to the other.[12]

This 'exploitation' of the worker occurs within societies committed to ideals of democratic egalitarianism. All contemporary industrial societies proclaim the rule of the 'common man'; but at the same time as they do so, they generate inequalities which contradict their professed ideals. But this 'contradiction' is closer to that which might be envisaged following certain of the ideas of Tocqueville than those deriving from Marx.

Like Dahrendorf, Aron distinguishes two aspects of Marx's theory of classes: 'factual propositions' and 'philosophical propositions' which are intertwined in Marx's writings. Only the factual assertions – e.g. 'the material and moral suffering of the working class becomes worsened, and as a consequence of this worsening the workers become more revolutionary'[13] – can be examined in relation to empirically observable developments which have occurred in society since Marx's time, and are necessarily of a different order to statements which express a metaphysical philosophy of history. This

281

distinction is directly relevant to Marx's concept of class, for there are, according to Aron, two definitions of 'class' in Marx. The first is that which treats 'class' as referring to the place of a grouping of individuals within the process of production, a conceptualisation which might be acceptable to a sociologist who is not of a Marxist persuasion. The second, however, ties the notion of class to (unrealisable) goals, such as that the 'domination of man by man' can be transcended with the supersession of capitalism by socialism – conceptions which are not acceptable unless one embraces Marx's theory *in toto*. It is the conjunction of these two elements in Marx's writing, Aron emphasises, which helps to explain the continuing fascination of social thinkers with the notion of class. But this is, in turn, bound up with the attraction exerted by Marxism itself – a phenomenon which Aron explains in 'Tocquevillean' terms. Modern societies, in so far as they are 'democratic', are exposed to the 'contradiction' between their declared faith that all men are equal and the manifest political and economic inequalities which exist within them. 'The industrial democracies proclaim the equality of individuals, in work and in the realm of politics. Now the fact is that there is great inequality in incomes and in modes of life.'[14] The constant tension between the ideal and the reality, and the vision of a society in which this is dissolved – through the revolutionary action of a deprived class – explains the passionate commitment which Marxism can stimulate.

It follows that, for Aron, while Marx's ideas express certain of the aspirations generated by this inherent tension within industrial society, they do not provide a satisfactory analysis of its sources – even if we neglect Marx's 'philosophy of history', and confine ourselves to his 'factual propositions' about classes and class conflict. Marx's theory of class, Aron suggests, drew heavily upon observations which relate primarily to the proletariat, the 'class *par excellence*'. In nineteenth-century Europe, during the early phases of industrialisation, the proletariat, excluded from political power, working and living in uniformly degrading circumstances, appeared as the type-case of an oppressed class. But no other class conforms to this degree to the criteria of distinctiveness which Marx sought to apply. The 'bourgeoisie', for example, has never been such a clearly identifiable grouping, if it is defined as including everyone above the (not clearly demarcated) category of 'small property owner'. According to Aron, any theory of class must come to terms with the indefinite character of social reality *itself*: 'classes' are rarely such distinct and clearly identifiable groupings as was the nineteenth-century proletariat. The ambiguity of conceptual discussions of class since Marx reflects an actual condition in reality. This 'uncertainty in social reality', Aron argues, must 'be the point of departure of any enquiry into social classes'.[15] Social thinkers in the Western societies have been obsessed with the problems of class, but have been incapable of reaching acceptable definitions of the phenomenon. The paradox is resolved in terms of the preceding analysis: industrial societies (of both types, capitalist and socialist) continually generate inequalities, whilst at the same time removing many of the forms of manifest discrimination that characterised previous types of society which were not influenced by democratic ideas. Legally prescribed relationships of inequality, for example, such as existed in the medieval estates, have been abolished; the hierarchical structures of industrial societies are more fluid and less clearly delineated. Moreover, these structures are of a complicated kind, involving a multiplicity of phenomena.

Under what conditions, therefore, Aron asks, can we speak of the existence of distinguishable classes? There are three sets of circumstances in which we may *not* do so: (1) Where the main principle of hierarchical differentiation is not economic, but religious or racial. (2) Where the fate or the 'life-chances' of the individual do not depend primarily upon the group to which he belongs within society, but exclusively upon himself: in other words, where something close to full equality of opportunity prevails. (3) Where the socio-economic conditions of everyone are fundamentally similar. None of these three sets of circumstances obtains within the industrial societies, and consequently 'it is not illegitimate to speak of social classes, socio-economic categories (*ensembles*) defined by a plurality of criteria and constituting more or less real groups, within the total society'.[16] The equivocation 'more or less real' is deliberate. If classes were, as Marx implied, clearly defined groupings, normally producing a consciousness of class unity, there would be no problem. But of the four major classes which are often recognised by sociologists as existing within capitalist societies, there is none which takes a clear-cut form. The 'bourgeoisie' is 'not a coherent unity'; the 'middle class' (or, as is frequently said, 'middle *classes*') constitutes 'a kind of hold-all' in which individuals are placed if they cannot be put into any of the other classes; the 'peasantry' is sometimes described as a single class, and on other occasions is treated as composed of two classes in relation to the ownership of property (farm owners and agricultural workers). Even the working class, which approximates most closely to the notion of a distinguishable and unified class group, is far from being a homogeneous entity, as measured either by socio-economic criteria or by political affiliation.

Marx was correct, Aron agrees, in believing that classes only become important agencies in history to the degree that they manifest a unified group consciousness, expressed particularly in the context of a struggle with other classes. While the working class may be characterised by shared objective and subjective traits, it does not manifest, in modern capitalist societies, the form of class consciousness necessary to provide the impulsion towards effecting a fundamental change in society. The role of 'class messianism', as set out in Marxism, has been a paradoxical one. It has undoubtedly played a major part in recent history, and thus in one sense has been endorsed by social developments since Marx's time; but it has been invalidated at the same time, because those who have adopted it, according to the theory, should not have done so. The influence of Marxism, as an organising political catechism, has been in inverse relation to capitalist development. On the whole, the working class has been less revolutionary the more advanced the capitalist forces of production. Marxism has become an influence promoting the industrialisation process in the less developed countries, rather than expressing the demands of mature capitalist society. The 'socialist' countries are those which have followed a different route to industrial society than that taken by the countries of Western Europe.

The development of industrial society, Aron argues, should be understood in terms of a distinction between 'stages of economic growth' and 'modes of industrialisation'. At each stage of economic growth we find the emergence of different forms of 'contradiction' which can be resolved according to divergent modes of social and political control. In the initial phase of industrialisation, for example, it is necessary to promote rapid capital accumulation and investment, which can only be accomplished by some form of authoritative regime that restricts consumption on the part of the mass of the population. The 'contradiction' here is that the advance of (future) prosperity depends upon the self-abnegation of the present generation. The form which this took in the early development of capitalism in Western Europe, however, differs considerably from that which, legitimised within the framework of Marxist socialism, it assumed in the Soviet Union.

In a developed industrial society, whether 'capitalist' or 'socialist', the need for the authoritative or forced imposition of self-denial upon the population diminishes. But the 'Tocquevillean dilemma' assumes a burgeoning importance: the new 'contradiction' is between the democratic demand for 'levelling' and the continuing existence of inequalities.

3. OSSOWSKI: IMAGES AND CONCEPTS OF CLASS

Ossowski's *Class Structure in the Social Consciousness* attempts a general examination of the criteria which have been used, both in popular thought and in more systematic sociological analysis, to identify forms of 'class' (and forms of 'classlessness').[17] The language of 'class', Ossowski points out, is permeated with spatial metaphor, representing society in terms of a 'vertical' order of divisions or 'layers' piled upon one another. But this vertical representation has assumed a variety of types, and it is the objective of Ossowski's work to analyse these.

The simplest type is the 'dichotomic' conception of class structure. The conception of a polar division between two main classes in society, Ossowski shows, is one which constantly appears in history. There are three principal modes in which this representation occurs, corresponding to the sorts of privilege according to which advantages are distributed: (1) The 'rulers and the ruled': a division of power or authority, centred upon a separation between those who command and those who obey (Dahrendorf's conception of 'class', of course, falls into this category). (2) The 'rich and the poor': an economic differentiation, dividing those who own wealth or property from those who do not. (3) Those 'for whom others labour' and those who are the 'labouring class': a separation emphasising the *exploitation* of one group by another. These three modes of representing a dichotomous class division are not, of course, mutually exclusive, although where they are found together one of them tends to be treated as dominant and as determining the others. Most socialist thinkers of the nineteenth and twentieth centuries, according to Ossowski, have regarded the third category ('exploitation') as being conditional upon one or other of the first two, and consequently have looked to the abolition of the former as the medium for the elimination of exploitative class relationships. But there have been important exceptions to this, among whom may be placed Saint-Simon. Since Saint-Simon's 'working class' includes all the 'real producers', industrialists as well as propertyless wage-labourers, his 'classless society' is quite compatible with major differentials in power and wealth.[18]

The existence of 'middle classes' is sometimes recognised in dichotomic schemes, but these are always seen as secondary groupings which are appendages of one or other of the two major class groups. What Ossowski calls 'schemes of gradation', the second main type of representation of class structure, differ from dichotomous conceptions in that a middle class (or classes) is often regarded as the most basic class, the position of other classes being determined in relation to it. In dichotomic forms of class imagery, moreover, each class is defined in terms of its dependence upon the other. In gradation schemes, on the other hand, the relationship between classes is one of ordering rather than dependence: this sort of conception is normally applied in a descriptive rather than an explanatory manner. Ossowski distinguishes two types of gradation scheme: the 'simple' and the 'synthetic'. In the former, a representation of class structure is made according to a single criterion, such as income. This was the case, for example, with the original Roman census categories: under the Republic, citizens were divided into six income classes. Synthetic schemes involve a similar rank ordering of classes, but apply a combination of criteria to effect the ranking. This is the typical conception of social class, Ossowski suggests, adopted by most contemporary American sociologists. Thus Warner's studies, for instance, set up a synthetic gradation scheme yielding six major classes in American society.[19]

The third principal form of class imagery Ossowski calls the 'functional scheme'. Here society is seen as being divided into functionally interrelated groupings in the division of labour. This conception usually recognises a plurality of classes; rather than being perceived as antagonistic groups, as tends to be the case in dichotomic representations, or as a set of ranked divisions as in gradation schemes, classes are considered to be interdependent and co-operative agencies. Certain contemporary sociological interpretations of class systems are of this kind: for example, those which identify a set of functionally interdependent classes such as 'managers', 'clerical workers', 'skilled workers', etc. – or, on a more ideological level, Stalin's conception of 'non-antagonistic classes' in the Soviet Union. Such classes are not measured in terms of uniform gradations on a scale: a given class differs from a second in respects which are distinct from those by which the second class differs from a third.

The significance of Marx's theory of classes is that it ties together strands drawn from each of the three modes of representation of class structure within a single, coherent theory: 'the writings of Marx form some sort of immense lens which concentrates the rays coming from different directions, and which is sensitive both to the heritage of past generations and to the creative resources of modern science.'[20] Marx's writings integrate the inherent revolutionary appeal of the dichotomic scheme with a systematic analysis of other properties of class relationships as these existed in the contemporary European societies of his time. The dichotomous conception, according to Ossowski, is most prominent in Marx's more propagandist writings, in which he sought to stimulate the development of a revolutionary consciousness. In his more scholarly writings, however, he was forced to blunt the clarity of the dichotomic perspective by introducing 'intermediate' classes, and managed to arrive at a descriptive assessment of class relationships in historical societies. Thus while, according to Ossowski, Marx's works embody each of the three main ways of representing class structure – the dichotomic, gradation and functional schemes – these are conceived in a new way, in terms of the intersection of two or more dichotomous class divisions.[21]

In Marx's writings, of course, the class societies of the present are counterposed to the classless order of the future. The concept of 'classlessness' in fact, Ossowski points out, has as long a history as that of 'class'. Just as images of class have differed, so have notions of classlessness. In the modern world, however, there are two versions of classlessness which are particularly important as political ideologies. One of these simply involves a stress upon a functional scheme as against any competing modes of interpreting class relationships. Unlike the dichotomic and gradation schemes, which stress the asymmetry of class divisions, the functional conception involves the idea that classes are mutually supportive. Concentration upon functional connections, therefore (as in the notion of 'non-antagonistic classes'), can serve as a means of reducing the apparent significance of class divisions – not by lessening inequalities of wealth or power, but by emphasising the co-operative nature of classes. This conception differs radically from Marx's version of 'classlessness', since the latter presupposes a much more profound dissolution of class relationships. But it is a development of the functional interpretation of classlessness which has actually come to predominate in modern political ideology – and not only in the Western societies, committed to liberal democratic ideals, but also the socialist countries, nominally committed to Marx's classless society.

The American image of 'non-egalitarian classlessness', according to Ossowski, is formed primarily around the notion of equality of opportunity: everyone, regardless of origins, is presumed to have the same chance, if he possesses the appropriate capacities, of reaching the highest levels in the occupational system. The structure of Soviet society, as portrayed in Marxist orthodoxy, might appear to be quite different from this. In fact, there are very close similarities:

The socialist principle 'to each according to his needs' is in harmony with the tenets of the American creed, which holds that each man is the master of his fate, and that a man's status is fixed by an order of merit. The socialist principle allows of the conclusion that there are unlimited opportunities for social advancement and social demotion; this is similar to the American concept of 'vertical social mobility'. The arguments directed against *uravnilovka* [equalisation of wages] coincide with the arguments put forward on the other side of the Atlantic by those who justify the necessity for economic inequalities in a democratic society.[22]

The main difference between the two ideological standpoints, Ossowski suggests, is that, according to the socialist view, 'non-egalitarian classlessness' is only a temporary phase. Nevertheless, while the ultimate objective is different, the distinction here is not a radical one. For, according to socialist theory, the transition to 'egalitarian classlessness' is to be a progressive, not a revolutionary, process – and liberal democracy also envisages a continual advance towards the further realisation of the principle of equality of opportunity.

The conception of 'non-egalitarian classlessness', in common with any sort of function scheme, tends to appeal to those who wish to defend an existing social order. Dichotomic representations, on the other hand, often have a revolutionary connotation, since they tend to perceive class relationships as antagonistic in character. Gradation schemes, being primarily descriptive, are more neutral than either of the other two. The fact that these three types of imagery reappear throughout history, and are to be traced in both ideological thought as well as in the more systematic conceptions of modern sociology, Ossowski stresses, demonstrates the ubiquity of the social interests which generate them. This does not mean, however, that the formulations of sociology can be directly equated with popular images of class structure. Rather, the older conceptions form the background against which concern with class as a sociological concept came to dominate social thought from the turn of the nineteenth century onwards. Marx's theory, in particular, drew upon deeply engrained themes in the European cultural heritage, and connected the revolutionary appeal of the dichotomic conception to a concrete analysis of the class relationships in nineteenth-century capitalism.

But, like Dahrendorf and others, Ossowski sees the relevance of Marx's conception of class as largely limited to a form of society (i.e. 'early capitalism') in which economic power was the mainspring of social and political organisation. This type of society, as Marx anticipated, proved to be a transitory one. The social changes which have occurred since the nineteenth century, however, while they have partly been shaped by Marx's ideas, have departed from the line of development he foresaw. Socialism, in one sense, has diverged from capitalism, because it has not sprung, as Marx believed it must do, from the latter; but, in another sense, the two forms of society, capitalism and socialism, have evolved in a similar direction. The Marxian conception, in its 'classical' formulation, can today be no more usefully applied to the analysis of the class structure of the Western societies, which have moved far away from a situation in which private property 'rules', than it can be to those societies in which private property has been formally abolished:

> In situations where the political authorities can overtly and effectively change the class structure; where the privileges that are most essential for social status, including that of a higher share in the national income, are conferred by a decision of the political authorities; where a large part or even the majority of the population is included in a stratification of the type to be found in a bureaucratic hierarchy – the nineteenth-century concept of class becomes more or less an anachronism, and class conflicts give way to other forms of social antagonism.[23]

Notes

1. The German edition of *Class and Class Conflict* was published in 1957. See also, Dahrendorf, *Marx in Perspektive: die Idee des Gerechten im Denken von Karl Marx* (Hanover, 1953, doctoral dissertation).
2. *Class and Class Conflict*, pp. 28ff.
3. *ibid.*, pp. 30–1.
4. *ibid.*, p. 56.
5. See Dahrendorf, *Conflict after Class*, Noël Buxton lecture (Essex, 1967).
6. *Class and Class Conflict*, p. 62. Here I adopt the practice of using the adjective 'Marxian' with reference to what I take to be Marx's own ideas and contributions; I use the terms 'Marxist' and 'Marxism' to refer generically to the writings of subsequent authors who are self-professed followers of Marx.
7. *ibid.*, p. 165.
8. Dahrendorf recognizes, however, that 'The Changes that separate capitalist and post-capitalist society are not wholly due to the effects of class conflict, nor have they merely been changes in the patterns of conflict.' (*ibid.*, pp. 245–6.)
9. *ibid.*, p. 275.
10. Raymond Aron, *Democracy and Totalitarianism* (London, 1968); *18 Lectures on Industrial Society* (London, 1968); *Progress and Disillusion* (New York, 1968); and especially *La lutte des classes* (Paris, 1964).
11. *La lutte des classes*, pp. 22–3; cf. also *18 Lectures on Industrial Society*, pp. 73–6.
12. *La lutte des classes*, pp. 23–4.
13. *ibid.*, pp. 51–2.
14. *ibid.*, p. 95.
15. *ibid.*, p. 78. See also Aron, 'La classe comme représentation et comme volonté', in *Les classes sociales dans le monde d'aujourd'hui, Cahiers internationaux de sociologie* 38 (1965).
16. *ibid.*, p. 356.
17. Stanislaw Ossowski, *Class Structure in the Social Consciousness* (London, 1963).
18. *ibid.*, p. 27.
19. W. L. Warner and P. S. Lunt, *The Social Life of a Modern*

Community (New Haven, 1941).
20. Ossowski, *op. cit.*, p. 70.
21. *ibid.*, pp. 69ff.
22. *ibid.*, p. 114.
23. *ibid.*, p. 184.

11. Immigrant workers and class structure

Stephen Castles and Godula Kosack

Every industrial and commercial centre in England now possesses a working class *divided* into two *hostile* camps, English proletarians and Irish proletarians. The ordinary English worker hates the Irish worker as a competitor who lowers his standard of life. In relation to the Irish worker he feels himself a member of the *ruling* nation and so turns himself into a tool of the aristocrats and capitalists of his country *against Ireland*, thus strengthening their domination over himself. He cherishes religious, social and national prejudices against the Irish worker. His attitude towards him is much the same as that of the 'poor whites' to the 'niggers' in the former slave states of the USA. The Irishman pays him back with interest in his own money. He sees in the English worker at once the accomplice and the stupid tool of the *English domination in Ireland*.

This antagonism is artificially kept alive and intensified by the press, the pulpit, the comic papers, in short, by all the means at the disposal of the ruling classes. This *antagonism* is the *secret of the impotence of the English working class*, despite their organization. It is the secret by which the capitalist class maintains its power. And that class is fully aware of it.

Karl Marx[1]

1. THE CONCEPT OF CLASS STRUCTURE

The presence of immigrant workers is a long-term feature of

From S. Castles and G. Kosack, *Immigrant Workers and Class Structure in Western Europe*, Oxford University Press for the Institute of Race Relations, 1973, pp. 461–82.

Western European society. The economic, demographic and social factors which originally brought about migration are still effective. During 1970, more immigrant workers entered Germany and France than in any previous year. Even Switzerland, which has taken stringent measures to control immigration, had a slight increase in the immigrant labour force and a considerable increase in the immigrant population in 1969. Only Britain, with her stagnant economy, has not had any significant immigration in the last few years. In all four countries, immigrant workers have become an integral part of the production system: their concentration in certain industries and occupations makes their presence indispensable for the functioning of the economy. In the unlikely event of the sudden removal of the immigrant labour force, the resulting disorganization would inevitably lead to economic crisis.

It is often argued that there is a basic difference between the type of immigration experienced by Britain since the war, and the type prevailing in Continental Europe. In the former case, the overwhelming majority of immigrants are permanent settlers, while in the latter they typically come for a few years only and then return home. This postulated dichotomy between permanent and temporary migration does not correspond with the true situation. In France, Germany and Switzerland an ever-growing number of immigrants have been there for over five years. Many of them may be expected to remain permanently, even though few had this intention when they first arrived. Increasing numbers of workers are bringing their families to join them – an important indication of their stabilization. Nor is all migration to Britain of a permanent type. European and Irish workers often remain for a few years only. Even New Commonwealth immigrants frequently return home after some years in Britain. At present departures of West Indians exceed new arrivals. Moreover, many New Commonwealth immigrants did not intend to remain permanently when they first arrived. The decision to stay permanently came only after some time, when it became evident that no possibilities of adequate employment were likely to become available at home. It was not until the 1962 Commonwealth Immigrants Act, which stopped the entry of workers, but allowed in the families of those already present, that permanent immigration finally superseded temporary immigration as the dominant form. Thus the differences between migratory patterns in the various countries are not absolute, but only gradual.

Furthermore, even if permanent immigration predominates in one case and temporary in the other, the effects on society are similar in both. In Britain, most immigrants have settled permanently, but because those from the New Commonwealth are coloured, they remain identifiable. This applies equally to the original immigrants' children, who may have largely adopted the language, values and customs of the receiving society. It has been shown that there is considerable prejudice against coloured school-leavers, even if their entire upbringing has been in Britain. Discrimination ensures that second-generation coloured immigrants remain in the same subordinate position as their parents. In the other three countries, on the other hand, most immigrants are not racially distinct from the indigenous populations. Second-generation immigrants will probably stay in a low social position due to the specific educational problems which they experience, but they do not remain an identifiable separate group. Once they learn the language and adopt local customs and styles of dress, they will become more or less integrated into the population. But the new immigrant workers who continue to come into these countries will always be a distinct group, with problems of language and of adaptation to industrial work and urban life. They will continue to be given the worst jobs, to be concentrated into the poorest housing and to suffer various social problems. Thus there is a permanent immigrant group with *rotating membership*. This rotation ensures that the group remains separate and subordinate. Rotation has the same effect on the position of immigrants in Germany, France and Switzerland as does colour prejudice in Britain. In both cases immigrants continue to be the group with the worst jobs and social conditions long after the migratory movement first started. [. . .]

Some observers designate the immigrants as a new proletariat, separate from the indigenous working class. For instance Albert Delpérée, General Secretary of the Belgian Ministry of Social Welfare, has said:

> Of course there is frequent talk of equal rights, human dignity, workers' solidarity. But in practice there remain unavoidable conditions of discrimination, inequality, handicaps. Foreign employees are often the true proletarians of this second half of the twentieth century.[2]

Similarly, an article in the organ of the German Social Democratic Party asserts:

> The foreign workers can be designated as a new proletariat because they live on the margins of our society, increasingly form its 'lowest class' and because they suffer social discrimination through being given mainly the most physically demanding manual jobs. They enjoy neither political nor social equality – this is hindered by the natural obstacle that they are not German citizens. Another special characteristic of the new proletariat is its isolation with regard to both language and housing.[3]

But many social scientists would disagree with such popular views. For instance, Henri Bartoli writes: 'Rather than the birth of a new working class, we are witnessing a restructuring of the working class between a sub-proletariat (external and internal migrants) and a proletariat with a higher standard of living, but with depersonalized living and working conditions.'[4] The discussion here does not involve any disagreement on the fact that immigrant workers have the lowest social position, but rather on the nature of class structure and on the criteria which should be used to designate and to distinguish social classes. Before proceeding, it is therefore necessary to examine the concept of class structure.

Much of modern sociological discussion on class structure has been a debate with Marx. In the Marxian theory of society, classes are of vital importance – class conflict is regarded as the motor of history. But it is only in capitalist society that classes exist in their essential form. In previous societies the direct economic distinctions between different social groups were concealed and overlaid by religious, legal and political factors.[5] A man's social position was fixed irrevocably by law and custom. Such societies were based on castes or estates rather than on classes. Only after the victorious industrial bourgeoisie had ripped away the veils of personal dependence and destroyed the myth of god-given natural authority, subjugating all human relationships to the laws of the world market, could classes in their modern, primarily economically determined form, come into being. In Marx's class theory, an individual's class position is judged according to his ownership or exclusion from ownership of the means of production. Society has two basic classes: the capitalists or bourgeoisie, and the proletariat or working class. According to Marx, class structure was becoming polarized in the nineteenth century: 'Society as a whole is more and more splitting up into two great hostile camps, into two great classes directly facing each other: Bourgeoisie and Proletariat.'[6] Marx did not ignore other groups of society, which did not fall into these two classes. Considerable attention was devoted in various writings to the *petit-bourgeoisie* – small merchants, artisans, shopkeepers – and to small independent peasants. Such groups tend to identify with the bourgeoisie in its defence of the rights of property, but objectively they are condemned to lose their independent existence and to sink into the proletariat, 'partly because their diminutive capital does not suffice for the scale on which modern industry is carried on, and is swamped in the competition with the large capitalists, partly because their specialized skill is rendered worthless by new methods of production'.[7] They are remnants of pre-industrial society and have no place in the new capitalist order. As members of the *petit-bourgeoisie* lose their livelihood, they degenerate into the *lumpenproletariat*, 'the social scum, that passively rotting mass thrown off by the lowest layers of old society'.[8] The *lumpenproletariat* is an unstable group, which is likely to be bribed into taking a reactionary position in the event of a revolution.

Besides these strata which do not fall into the bourgeoisie or the proletariat, the existence of stratification within the two main classes is recognized. The bourgeoisie is composed of landowners, industrialists, financiers and merchants[9] – the leading role being increasingly taken by the industrialists. The proletariat is divided into agricultural workers and industrial workers. But within each class, the various strata share the same essential relationship to the means of production – either ownership or exclusion from it – and the same long-term interests. In capitalist society, the conflict between bourgeoisie and proletariat is the basic determinant of social conditions and social change. The strata outside the two main classes, on the other hand, play only a subsidiary role. Their own interests are unattainable, and serve only to conceal from them the true nature of social relationships. These strata ally themselves with one or other of the main classes at different times, but have no stable political position.

Although an individual's class position is determined in the first place by his position in the production process, it would be wrong to think that the objective, economic factor is the only determinant. On the contrary, considerable emphasis is put on the subjective factor in the formation of class consciousness. Common economic conditions and interests determine that a group of people objectively form a class ('class in itself'). But they can act as a class only when they come to realize their common interests, and that there are other classes with different – usually opposing – interests. The development of class consciousness is the precondition for true class existence ('class for itself'), and this is only possible when the relationships of dependence and exploitation with other classes are understood. Classes do not exist independently, but only in relation to each other. Class consciousness inevitably leads to political organization and class struggle. But class consciousness does not develop mechanically out of material conditions according to some abstract sociological law. It is the result of diverse cultural and historical factors, which may have different effects in different historical phases of the conflict between labour and capital.

The Marxian class theory is most commonly attacked on the grounds that the predicted polarization of society into two antagonistic classes has not in fact taken place. For instance Ralf Dahrendorf writes:

Already before the turn of the century a structural change

298

began in all industrial societies, which directly counteracted the polarization of society into bourgeois and proletarians. Although the old middle strata of peasants, artisans, small tradespeople, shopkeepers, continued to shrink (and Marx was right to this extent) a 'new middle class' of salaried employees and officials developed, at first in industry itself, later in public administration and in commerce. It was far from clear that these people belonged to one of the two classes.[10]

If there is a 'new middle class' of this type, the criteria given by Marx for judging class position lose their validity. The salaried employees and officials are not owners of the means of production – they are dependent workers who receive wages. As such they would appear to be members of the working class according to the Marxian theory. But in fact many observers regard them as a separate class. According to T. B. Bottomore,

> . . . most sociologists would probably agree in recognizing the existence of an upper class (comprising the owners of the major part of the economic resources of a society), a working class (chiefly the industrial wage-earners), and a middle class, or middle classes (a more amorphous group, often treated as a residual category, but including most white-collar workers and most members of the liberal professions).[11]

Ownership or exclusion from ownership of the means of production ceases to be the main criterion for class assignation. It is replaced by other factors: a person's position in the occupational structure, his income level, social status, life-style, and his aspirations for himself and his children. The functionalist school explain social stratification in the following way:

> Starting from the proposition that no society is 'classless', or unstratified, an effort is made to explain, in functional terms, the universal necessity which calls forth stratification

in any social system . . . The main functional necessity
explaining the universal presence of stratification is . . . the
requirement faced by any society of placing and motivating
individuals in the social structure . . . Social inequality is
thus an unconsciously evolved device by which societies
ensure that the most important positions are conscientiously
filled by the most qualified persons.[12]

Social inequality is regarded not only as inevitable, but also
as being in the general interest. Since the hierarchical nature
of society is not based on exploitation or on conflicting
interests, there are no grounds for class struggle.

The logical consequence of the functionalist theory of
stratification is the complete displacement of classes based on
position in the production process, and the substitution of a
hierarchy of 'status-groups'. These are 'aggregates of individuals of equal social prestige, based on similarities which
are not exclusively economic, and whose relations to each
other are not primarily antagonistic but are partly competitive and partly emulative'.[13] A society consisting of such status
groups would appear to be based on consensus rather than
conflict, and to be relatively stable, rather than holding the
potential of basic changes.

However, since the Second World War, the main currents
of sociological thought in Western Europe have not altogether
followed the functionalist theory. Rather the tendency has
been to acknowledge the relative accuracy of Marx's description of the situation at the time at which he was writing, but
to contend that his economic predictions on the development
of capitalism were wrong, and that therefore social structure
has evolved in an unexpected direction. Theories of the
embourgeoisement of the working class are a product of the
long period of prosperity and full employment following the
war.[14] They argue that manual workers are increasingly taking
on middle-class values and life-styles, and that their political
views are accordingly tending to become more conservative
and individualistic. Three main causes are advanced for this
change: firstly, increasing numbers of workers are receiving
higher wages, which are often comparable to those of white-

collar workers in the 'middle-income' bracket. Secondly, advanced technology reduces the physical effort involved in work, so that workers become technicians who are paid for their knowledge and ability to control processes, rather than for manual exertion. This tends to break down the barrier between management and men: repressive authority is replaced by team-work. Thirdly, rural–urban migration and the move of many workers into new suburbs break down the traditional working-class communities. This helps destroy working-class culture with its emphasis on solidaristic ideals and action.[15]

The *embourgeoisement* theory asserts that Western European society is moving towards a new social structure. The old 'pyramid' with a broad working class at the base, a smaller middle class, and a very small ruling or upper class at the apex, is being replaced by a 'diamond-shaped' distribution. At the bottom are 'marginal groups' – a sort of *lumpenproletariat* of criminals, permanently unemployed, chronic sick, semi-illiterates, and so on – then come the middle strata consisting of both manual and white-collar workers, on top is a small elite of top managers, financiers, politicians, etc. The middle groups share certain common features: adequate income, consumer orientation, individualistic rather than collective values – but are stratified according to differences in occupational status, income, and education. Thus in the new model, class is related to economic factors (amongst others) but does not depend on ownership or non-ownership of the means of production. Conflict between different social groups or strata is possible, but it is not class conflict in the traditional sense. It is about day-to-day interests and does not pose a threat to the ongoing social order.

Embourgeoisement theories usually point to a trend rather than to a state of affairs. Few people would claim that the traditional working class has already ceased to exist. Rather, it is asserted that the most advanced sections (i.e. those in the new high-technology industries) are moving towards a middle-class way of life, and that this points to the future development which will be followed by the others. But many social scientists deny that this development is in fact taking place. P. Jostock, for instance, remarks: 'How one can speak of the disappearance of class differences as long as the land and the other means of production are still the private property of a minority, while the majority of the people remain propertyless, is incomprehensible.'[16] The traditional characteristics of the proletariat are the following: they are personally free (unlike slaves or serfs) but they do not own the tools they work with. They are therefore forced to work for the capitalist who owns the means of production. They do not determine the way in which they work nor do they control the product. Their position is one of insecurity and they may easily be thrown out of work. Their wages are only high enough to cover the necessities of life so that they are unable to save enough to become independent. The proletarian's dependent position is inherited by his children.[17] According to such criteria, present-day workers should still be regarded as proletarians, for their basic lack of property and their dependent position still persist[18] – in fact an ever-increasing proportion of the labour force are becoming dependent employees, rather than independent farmers, artisans or professionals.

But apart from a few sociologists – notably in Eastern Europe – who follow a dogmatic and mechanistic application of the Marxian theory, most critics of the *embourgeoisement* thesis would agree that there have been important changes in the character and position of the working class in recent decades. However, there is disagreement with the proponents of the *embourgeoisement* thesis on the exact nature of these changes and the interpretation to be put upon them. Firstly, although there has been an absolute increase in the incomes of many manual workers, they still remain clearly differentiated from white-collar workers in many respects. As Goldthorpe *et al.* point out:

. . . the work situation of white-collar employees is still generally superior to that of manual wage earners in terms of working conditions and amenities, continuity of employment, fringe benefits, long-term income prospects and promotion chances. Class position is not merely a matter of consumer power: the function and status of a group within the social division of labour must still be regarded as being of basic importance.[19]

Although manual workers may sometimes have high earnings for a period, their long-term earning chances and their security are greatly inferior to those of white-collar employees, whose earnings usually rise steadily throughout their careers.

Secondly, it is far from certain that the changes in working methods brought about by new technology actually improve conditions and reduce alienation for the worker. On the contrary, production-line work and other advanced methods tend to reduce work to a mere repetition of single monotonous tasks. Moreover the worker remains in his basically subordinate position, with no control over the production process or over that which is produced. The alienation of the worker is thus as great if not greater than it used to be. In addition, alienation at work is reflected by the worker's alienation as a consumer, using his income to satisfy false needs imposed upon him by advertisements, mass media and educational institutions.[20]

Thirdly, where workers move out of traditional communities – the 'urban villages' of the older industrial centres – into new suburbs, this does not necessarily mean that their lifestyle becomes middle class. Patterns of social relationships do indeed change in the new environment, but the change is an adaptation to the new conditions, rather than an emulation of middle-class behaviour. Even when they move into middle-class areas, working-class people have little contact with middle-class people.[21]

If it is accepted that the working class remains a distinct class, characterized by its lack of property, its economic insecurity, and its separate culture and institutions, both political and social, it becomes necessary to ask why this class does not use its numerical superiority to gain power and to improve its living conditions. This question was posed already by Marx and Engels. The former mentioned the division of the working class on national lines as one cause for its political impotence, as we saw in the quotation at the beginning of this chapter. Engels spoke of the 'bourgeois "respectability" bred into the bones of the workers'.[22] In another place he mentions the advantages that English workers gained from the immense expansion of industry and from English dominance of the world market.[23] Where, despite the objective existence of a

303

class with distinct interests, the members of that class do not unite to struggle against other classes, Marxists speak of 'false consciousness'. Because it controls the means of production, the ruling class also has considerable control over the production and diffusion of culture through the schools and other educational instruments, through the mass media, through literature and the arts. The ideological dominance of the ruling class, which extends to the socialization process itself, allows it to control the working class, and to create competition between its members, when their true interest lies in solidarity. Thus workers' consciousness does not always correspond with their social conditions, and they may support political aims and parties which are in fact against their interests.

The greatest problem for a class theory based on relationship to the means of production is the position of the evermore important group of the white-collar workers. Such employees have better working conditions, greater economic security, and usually higher earnings than manual workers. More important still, they tend to have different values and customs, forms of social relationships, and consumer habits. Their aspirations are higher, both for themselves and for their children. Especially important is their expectation of individual promotion – work is regarded as a career with steady promotion within a hierarchy.[24] But are these characteristics sufficient to justify regarding the white-collar workers as an independent middle class?

The original white-collar employees in industry and commerce may have had some justification in feeling themselves quite distinct from the manual workers. Not only was their work clearly mental rather than manual, in addition they formed part of the chain which helped to pass orders down from the employers to the manual workers. They may not have possessed authority, but they helped to exercise it. Today the situation of many white-collar workers has changed. They too tend to work in large groups under supervision, and with no personal share in the exercise of authority. Moreover the difference between their work and that of manual workers is becoming blurred, as both groups become more and more operators of machines. The mental demands made on skilled manual workers or technicians are often far higher than those made on white-collar employees. Basically, the white-collar employee is just a dependent worker. His work is alienated in that it is controlled by somebody else. His earnings and security are only marginally better than those of the manual worker.[25] The desperate attempt to safeguard the higher status traditionally accorded to white-collar employees appears as a form of 'false consciousness' and is doomed to failure in the face of objective developments. Indeed, there is evidence of changes in the consciousness of this group, for instance the growth of white-collar trade unionism, and the increasing willingness of white-collar employees (even professionals) to take strike action to achieve industrial aims. In this context it is interesting to note that the authors of *The Affluent Worker in the Class Structure* find that rather than an *embourgeoisement* of the working class, there has been a

> . . . 'normative convergence' between certain manual and non-manual groups . . . This process was seen as chiefly involving in the case of white-collar workers a shift away from their traditional individualism towards greater reliance on collective means of pursuing their economic objectives; and in the case of manual workers, a shift away from a community-orientated form of social life towards recognition of the conjugal family and its fortunes as concerns of over-riding importance.[26]

Our answer to the question of the class position of white-collar workers must be that their basic position is similar to that of the manual workers. Their economic privileges are not large enough to justify regarding them as a distinct class, and are in any case declining. In so far as they still see themselves as members of a special social group with interests similar to those of their employers, they are victims of a false assessment of their own position. But increasingly, they are thinking in collectivist terms, and although they generally feel no identity with the manual workers, patterns of thought and behaviour are coming closer together.

On the basis of the above analysis, class structure appears to be still essentially dichotomic, with two basic classes: on the one hand the working class, on the other the ruling class. The working class consists not only of manual workers, but also of white-collar workers and professionals, in fact of everyone who is compelled to sell his labour and who does not control how he works and what is produced. The ruling class consists not only of the owners of the means of production: in addition there is an increasingly important group of managers whose material rewards are so high that their interests are identical with those of the owners; power and control over the means of production makes up for lack of ownership. In fact the line between managers and owners is fluid, with frequent movement of persons from one function to the other. The basic determinant of class is still relationship to the means of production, but today exercise of control or exclusion from it, is as important as ownership or non-ownership.

In addition to the two major classes, there are certain other strata. Vestiges of the groups whose disappearance was predicted by Marx still persist: small independent peasants, craftsmen, shopkeepers, and the like. On the whole such groups are shrinking rapidly, but some elements may survive if they are able to offer specialized services in fields which are not profitable for big business. One might also speak of a *lumpenproletariat* – casualties of the welfare state, who may more conveniently be left to rot in poverty than be brought into the production process through costly social welfare measures.

2. THE IMPACT OF IMMIGRATION

We may now return to the questions of immigrant workers' position in the class structure and the effect of immigration upon society in general. [. . .] Immigrant workers in all the countries concerned share the same basic position: they have the poorest conditions and lowest status in every social sphere.

On the labour market, which is the key area for determination of class position, immigrants are highly concentrated in a limited range of occupations and industries: those offering the lowest pay, the worst working conditions, and the lowest degree of security. An analysis of socio-economic status showed that immigrant workers are considerably over-represented in the lowest categories. The overwhelming majority are manual workers – mainly unskilled or semi-skilled – and very few are employed in white-collar occupations. Immigrant workers tend to suffer more severely than their indigenous colleagues from unemployment at times of recession.

Immigrants have a similar disadvantageous position outside work. They experience great difficulty in obtaining housing, and generally have to pay high rents for run-down accommodation seriously lacking in amenities. In some countries, there are special housing schemes for immigrant workers. These are insufficient to meet the demand, and often do not provide satisfactory material conditions, particularly when the housing is provided at the expense of the employer. Moreover, such housing tends to segregate immigrants from the rest of the population, and may expose them to the risk of pressure from the employer during industrial disputes. In France the housing situation is so acute that large shanty-towns have developed. Despite the atrocious conditions prevailing, these form the only refuge for tens of thousands of immigrants. Here there is a clear tendency to ghetto-formation, but elsewhere as well immigrant enclaves are becoming established in the older slum areas of large cities, and in the cellars, attics and shacks which form typical immigrant habitations.

Such housing conditions are reflected in serious health problems. Tuberculosis, rickets and other diseases associated with poverty are much more prevalent among immigrants in all four countries than among the rest of the populations. Other difficulties encountered by immigrants, with regard to education, leisure activities and family life, are also closely related to their economic and social conditions.

Low income, insecurity, bad housing, social problems; these characteristics of immigrants were also regarded as typical of the nineteenth-century European proletariat. Does this justify classifying immigrant workers as a separate class, a new sub-proletariat or *lumpenproletariat*? The answer depends on the concept of class structure which is adopted. In the functionalist model, in which classes are replaced by a profusion of 'status groups', immigrant workers would form one such group. Because of their inferior occupational position, the low material standards which characterize their 'life-style', and their lack of prestige, they would be regarded as one of the lowest status groups. In terms of functionalist theory, the presence of an immigrant group occupying such a subordinate position could be regarded as a rational feature of society. Immigrants would fulfil a necessary societal function by providing essential labour for menial tasks. Their remaining in this position could thus be seen as a necessary and more or less permanent feature of social stratification, although upward social mobility might be possible for the most talented individuals.

A representative of the *embourgeoisement* theory might regard immigrant workers as a new proletariat. While the indigenous workers have achieved incomes comparable to those of the middle class, and have accordingly taken on middle-class consumer habits, values and aspirations, the immigrants have characteristics similar to those of the proletarians in the period immediately following industrialization. But for the *embourgeoisement* theory, the inferior position of immigrants is only an irregularity in the overall process of the workers' advancement and integration into the middle class. Immigrants fill the gaps left by indigenous workers who have gained promotion out of low-paid and unpleasant jobs. Technological progress may be expected to eliminate such jobs, and the type of labour at present provided by immigrants will cease to be necessary. Large-scale immigration may then be expected to stop, and those immigrants already present who decide to stay will participate in the general upward mobility.

But according to the concept of class structure which we have argued to be the correct one, immigrant workers cannot be regarded as a distinct class. A group which makes up 10, 20 or even 30 per cent of the industrial labour force is neither marginal nor extraneous to society and certainly does not constitute a *lumpenproletariat*. Nor are immigrant workers a 'new proletariat' or a 'sub-proletariat'. The first term implies that the indigenous workers have ceased to be proletarians and have been replaced by the immigrants in this social position. The second postulates that immigrant workers have a different relationship to the means of production from that traditionally characteristic of the proletariat. All workers, whether immigrant or indigenous, manual or non-manual, possess the basic characteristics of a proletariat: they do not own or control the means of production, they work under the directions of others and in the interests of others, and they have no control over the product of their work. The basic long-term interests of immigrant and indigenous workers are common ones: the collective improvement of the living and working conditions of all workers, and the abolition of a capitalist system which creates distinctions between different categories of workers which assists in maintaining its own domination.

Immigrant workers and indigenous workers together form the working class in contemporary Western Europe, but it is a divided class. The immigrants have become concentrated in the unskilled occupations and the indigenous workers have tended to leave such jobs. Immigrants have lower incomes and inferior housing and social conditions. The two groups are more or less isolated from each other, through differing positions and short-term interests. This objective split is reproduced in the subjective sphere: a large proportion of indigenous workers have prejudiced and hostile attitudes towards immigrants. They lack solidarity with their immigrant colleagues and favour discriminatory practices. Often immigrants find themselves isolated and unsupported when they take collective action to improve their conditions. We may therefore speak of two strata within the working class: the indigenous workers, with generally better conditions and the feeling of no longer being right at the bottom of society, form the higher stratum. The immigrants, who are the most under-privileged and exploited group of society, form the lower stratum.

It is not to be expected that immigrants will rapidly gain promotion to better occupations and thus cease to form the lowest stratum. The labour market developments of the last two decades show that modern industrial expansion creates demand for both skilled and unskilled workers. Many menial jobs cannot readily be eliminated by mechanization. Even where this possibility exists, it may be more profitable to continue labour-intensive forms of work-organization, particularly where immigration tends to keep down the wages for unskilled labour. In this situation, promotion is most likely to be offered to indigenous workers, partly because of their better education and greater industrial experience, partly because of discrimination. [. . .] Discriminatory laws and practices are important in maintaining the inferior occupational position of immigrants in all four countries.

The key to promotion for immigrants is therefore twofold: firstly promotion requires the end of discrimination. Secondly, it presupposes the provision of adequate educational and vocational training facilities for immigrant workers and their children. But [. . .] the educational opportunities offered to immigrants are extremely restricted. Immigrant workers rarely get any vocational training permitting promotion beyond the semi-skilled level. Immigrant children also face educational difficulties, and most of them are unlikely to reach the same educational standard as the majority of indigenous children [. . .] Most immigrant children thus become manual workers. Obviously, it is not in the interests of the ruling class to follow policies which would encourage the promotion of immigrant workers and their children, as this would remove the supply of cheap unskilled labour which is at present so profitable.

The restructuring of the working class into an indigenous stratum and an immigrant stratum is immigration's most important impact on society. It is through this restructuring that the principal societal effects of immigration are mediated. These effects may be divided into three categories.

Firstly, there are economic effects. [. . .] The existence of an industrial reserve army in underdeveloped areas, which can be brought in to take unskilled jobs in Western Europe, tends to hold back increases in the wages for unskilled work. This effect may be great enough to hold down the general wage rate for the whole economy. In this case, immigration brings considerable gains for capitalists: in a situation of expansion, stagnant wage rates are matched by growing profits. In the long run, however, it is possible that indigenous labour may also benefit from the dynamic expansion allowed by immigration.

Secondly, there are social effects. By coming in at the bottom of the labour market, the immigrants have allowed many indigenous workers to move out of unskilled jobs and to achieve real social promotion. The number of white-collar workers has grown, while the number of indigenous manual workers has shrunk. This promotion has had important effects on the consciousness of indigenous workers. Those who have obtained better jobs no longer feel that they belong to the lowest group of society and that improvements can only be achieved collectively. Their advancement is taken as a sign that individual merit can bring gains, while the real causes for the upward movement are not perceived.[27] At the same time, such workers tend to distance themselves from the immigrants, who might in the long run threaten their newly-won privileges if allowed equal opportunities. Moreover, even those indigenous workers who have remained in unskilled occupations do not feel solidarity with immigrant workers. This group fears competition from immigrants and is afraid – not without justification – that they may be used by employers to put pressure on wages and conditions. At the same time the attempt to stigmatize immigrants as intrinsically inferior is an effort by such unskilled workers to maintain a higher social status for themselves, even though no objective basis for this exists. Analogies may be found in the well-known 'poor white' mentality in the Southern states of the USA, and in the attempts of low-level clerks to maintain their higher status position against blue-collar workers who often have higher earnings. The main roots of working-class prejudice towards immigrants are to be found in these relationships of competition. The result is that class consciousness is weakened, and tends to be replaced by a 'sectional consciousness', based on real and apparent conflicts of interest between the two strata within the working class.

Thirdly, immigration has political effects. The change in consciousness among indigenous workers lessens the political unity and strength of the working class. André Gorz has drawn attention to an additional factor:

311

Recourse to foreign workers leads, in particular, to the exclusion of an important part of the proletariat from trade-union action; a considerable decrease in the political and electoral weight of the working class; a still more considerable weakening of its ideological force and cohesion. In a word, it achieves the 'denationalization' of decisive sectors of the working class, by replacing the indigenous proletariat with an imported proletariat, which leads a marginal and cultural existence deprived of political, trade union and civil rights.[28]

Except in Britain, the overwhelming majority of immigrant workers are foreigners, who lack civil rights in the countries where they work. This means that a considerable proportion of the working class in contemporary Western Europe is disenfranchised. Not only do such immigrants lack the right to vote: their trade union rights are also restricted in some countries. Even where immigrant workers do in theory enjoy certain political rights, these can be eroded by repressive use of labour market legislation. If an immigrant only has a residence permit for a specific job – and this is usually the case – he is liable to deportation if dismissed by his employer. This special means of pressure is used by employers and authorities to discipline immigrant workers who take industrial or political action. Immigrants form a particularly vulnerable section of the working class, and their weak position may be used to undermine the strength of working-class organizations in struggles for better wages and conditions.

Even where immigrant workers are not deprived of civil rights, as in Britain,[29] their presence may cause serious problems for the labour movement. Differences in language, culture and traditions make it difficult to bring immigrants into the unions, and the problem is worsened by the anti-immigrant feelings of many indigenous workers. The unions have not been altogether successful in overcoming these difficulties. There can be little doubt that they have been weakened by immigration, particularly in those branches where immigrant workers form a large proportion, or even the majority, of the labour force.

The economic, social and political effects of immigration

which we have outlined are not separate phenomena but rather aspects of the general impact of immigration on society. To sum up this impact: immigration has brought about a split in the working class of Western Europe. This split weakens the working class and hence increases the power of the ruling class.

A division of the working class based on the granting of privileges to one part of it is nothing new. In *Imperialism, the Highest Stage of Capitalism*, Lenin described how a section of the British working class had 'become bourgeois' and was willing to 'be led by men bought by, or at least paid by, the bourgeoisie'. Britain's monopolistic position on the world market made possible the imperialist domination of underdeveloped regions and the exploitation of cheap labour in such areas through capital export. This allowed the creation of privileged sections among the British workers. The results of this situation were the growth of opportunism and the 'temporary decay of the working-class movement'.[30]

If today some of the workers of the underdeveloped countries are brought to Western Europe because it is more convenient for the capitalists to exploit them here than at home, this alters nothing in the basic situation: the ruling class gains both through the possibility of utilizing cheap labour, and through giving privileges to indigenous workers in order to encourage the development of false consciousness. The immigration of manual workers to Western Europe has been described as colonization in reverse.[31] The immigrants are given the jobs which no one else will do. This encourages the indigenous population to take on a colonialist mentality, regarding it as the inevitable destiny of the newcomers to carry out all the menial tasks. Immigration helps to give large sections of the indigenous working class the consciousness of a 'labour aristocracy' which supports or acquiesces in the exploitation of another section of the working class. In this way immigration helps to stabilize the capitalist order, not only economically, but also politically.

The change in the class consciousness of indigenous workers has gone further than the changes in actual conditions would justify: it has affected the majority, while improvements in wages, conditions and status have only been experienced by a section. Indeed, many workers have actually lost through immigration. But by bringing in workers from outside and compelling them to accept social and economic conditions inferior to those of other workers, it has become possible for the ruling class to promote the feeling of being in a privileged position among the majority of the working class. Workers who think that they have gained something and that they are no longer the lowest group in society are less likely to take militant action which might endanger their privileges. The split in the working class allows one section to be played off against the other, weakening the whole.

Workers who regard immigrants as inferior to themselves and who tacitly support their exploitation are victims of a false consciousness. Their behaviour is seriously detrimental to their own interests because it weakens the labour movement and reduces the political strength of the working class. The fight to secure civil rights and equality in economic and social matters for immigrants is important for all workers. It is a struggle for their own future, because only a united working class will be able to achieve any basic changes in social conditions. But the false consciousness which gives rise to prejudice and discrimination will not be destroyed by humanitarian pleas. It can only disappear when it is supplanted not merely by a correct understanding of the position of immigrant workers, but by a class consciousness which reflects the true position of all workers in society.

Notes

1. Letter to S. Meyer and A. Vogt, 9 April 1870, in Karl Marx, Frederick Engels, *On Britain*, Moscow: Foreign Languages Publishing House, 1962, second edition, pp. 551–2, emphasis in original.
2. Albert Delpérée, 'Die Wanderung von Arbeitnehmern', *Deutsche Versicherungszeitschrift* (March 1965), p. 71.
3. Günther Bartsch, 'Das neue Proletariat', *Vorwärts* (27 November 1963).
4. H. Bartoli, *Liaisons sociales – documents* (No. 119/65, 17 November 1965), p. 2.

5. Cf. Iring Fetscher, *Der Marxismus*, vol. II, Munich: Piper, 1962, pp. 384–5; Georg Lukacs, *Geschichte und Klassenbewusstsein*, Amsterdam: Thomas de Munter, 1967 (photo-mechanical reprint of 1923 edition), pp. 66–7.

6. 'Manifesto of the Communist Party', in Karl Marx and Friedrich Engels, *Selected Works*, vol. I, Moscow: Foreign Languages Publishing House, 1962, p. 35.

7. *ibid.*, p. 41.

8. *ibid.*, p. 44.

9. In some places, Marx refers to landowners and capitalists as separate classes, forming together with the proletariat, the three great classes of modern, capitalist society. Cf. *Capital*, vol. III, Moscow: Foreign Languages Publishing House, 1962, p. 863. In other places they are referred to as the two great sections of the bourgeoisie. See *18th Brumaire of Louis Bonaparte*.

10. Ralf Dahrendorf, *Gesellschaft und Freiheit*, München: Piper, 1965, p. 150.

11. T. B. Bottomore, *Sociology – A Guide to Problems and Literature*, London: Unwin University Books, 1962, pp. 188–9.

12. Kingsley Davis and Wilbert E. Moore, 'Some Principles of Stratification', *American Sociological Review* (April 1945), quoted in Bottomore, *op. cit.*, p. 195.

13. T. B. Bottomore, *op. cit.*, p. 190.

14. Like any theory, that of *embourgeoisement* is a product of its time. Today, in 1972, when unemployment in Britain and the USA is at the highest level for many years, when real wages are declining at least in the latter country, and when large-scale strike movements have taken place in several countries, *embourgeoisement* seems far less plausible than it did a few years ago.

15. For a fuller discussion and references to representatives of the *embourgeoisement* theory see J. H. Goldthorpe, *et al.*, *The Affluent Worker in the Class Structure*, Cambridge University Press, 1969, Introduction.

16. Paul Jostock in Marianne Feuersenger (ed.), *Gibt es noch ein Proletariat?*, Frankfurt: Europaische Verlagsanstalt, 1962, p. 13.

17. Cf. Hans Paul Bahrdt, in Feuersenger, *op. cit.*, pp. 16–17.

18. Cf. Jostock, in *ibid.*, pp. 12–13.

19. J. H. Goldthorpe, *et al.*, *op. cit.*, p. 24.

20. Cf. André Gorz 'Work and Consumption', in Perry Anderson and Robin Blackburn (eds), *Towards Socialism*, London: Fontana, 1965. Also Herbert Marcuse, *One-Dimensional Man*, London: Sphere Books, 1968.

21. Cf. J. H. Goldthorpe, *et al.*, *op. cit.*, pp. 158–9.

22. F. Engels, letter to F. A. Sorge, in *On Britain*, p. 568.

23. F. Engels, 'The English Elections', in *ibid.*, p. 505.

24. Cf. H. P. Bahrdt, in M. Feuersenger, *op. cit.*, pp. 22–3.

25. Typical for the erosion of the privileged conditions of white-collar employees is the recent growth in temporary employment of office workers in several countries. The workers are engaged by agencies who supply them to employers on request. The workers are paid by the hour and have no security of employment whatsoever.

26. J. H. Goldthorpe, *et al.*, *op. cit.*, p. 163.

27. We do not mean to suggest that immigration has been the only factor causing changes in the conditions and consciousness of the working class. We wish merely to emphasize that it has been one important factor which has been generally neglected.

28. André Gorz, 'Immigrant Labour', *New Left Review*, 61 (May–June 1970).

29. Under the new immigration legislation introduced by the Conservative Government in 1971 the situation of immigrants in Britain will become similar to that prevailing in the other countries. Recruited for specific jobs, immigrant workers may be subject to deportation if dismissed.

30. V. I. Lenin, *Imperialism, the Highest Stage of Capitalism*, Moscow: Progress Publishers, 1966, 13th edition, pp. 96–101.

31. Cf. J. Neumann, *Die Kriminalität der italienischen Arbietskröfte im Kanton Zürich*, Zurich: Juris Verlag, 1963, p. 33; R. Girod, 'Foreign Workers and Social Mobility in Switzerland', in IILS *Symposium on Migration for Employment in Zurich*, Geneva: International Institute for Labour Studies, 1965 (mimeo), p. 1.

12. State and society under liberalism and after

Gianfranco Poggi

If we consider together the imposing institutional edifice [. . .] and the society that the advance of the capitalist mode of production generated in the West in the late-eighteenth and nineteenth centuries, we may be struck at first by the differences in the institutional principles and in the nature of the interests typically operating in each. The state is first and foremost a unitary entity. Externally, in its pursuit of advantage *vis-à-vis* other sovereign states, it obeys an imperious 'reason' of its own, inapplicable to any other social pursuit. Internally, it speaks the abstract and general language of law, making and enforcing decisions supposedly oriented to nondivisive, widely shared interests, assembling unto itself all faculties and facilities of rule, and recognizing no subject as its equal, except in its external relations.

The society, on the other hand, appears as a vast, though bounded, multitude of discrete, self-interested and self-activated individuals relating to one another primarily through private choice. Such relations may generate legally enforceable effects, but these are deemed to be the individual's responsibility, to rest on his autonomous ability to obligate himself in exchange for benefits sought. Furthermore, the actual enforcement of such effects, though initiated by individuals in their own interest (typically through court actions), is not the individual's business but the state's. For as we have seen, in the modern state individuals as such cannot exercise on one another powers of rule, and must recognize one another as juridically free and equal. Their mutual relations are unceasingly structured and destructured by the myriad impacts of their interested choices and expressions of prefer-

From G. Poggi, *The Development of the Modern State*, London: Hutchinson University Library, 1978, pp. 117-49.

ence through the neutral, automatic operations of the market and of the forums of opinion and taste.

For individuals so conceived, the activation of their public as against their private capacities – the shift from the concerns of *homo oeconomicus* to those of the citizen – constitutes a radical reorientation of the self, an arduous feat of self-transcendence. To make this possible, as we have seen, complex and sophisticated political arrangements both 'couple' and 'uncouple' society and the state. Tocqueville claimed to have seen the Americans perform that feat frequently and easily, especially by participating in voluntary civic associations.[1] And it could be argued that within the sphere of society itself increasing institutional differentiation required of most individuals role-shifts of nearly comparable magnitude on a day-to-day basis. The transition from acquisitive businessman to devoted father or husband, for example, was nearly as radical as that from businessman to member of a civic organization.

Marx, however, was not far wrong in his bloody-minded suspicion that the duty imposed on the members of the 'civil society' periodically to experience 'ecstasies'[2] – to sublimate away their mundane, egoistic interests in order to act as citizens – was at best a high-flown idealistic abstraction, at worst a deceitful cover for substantial continuities and congruities between the interests pursued in each sphere. Whether despite or because of the differences in their institutional principles, state and society in the liberal era were in fact intrinsically compatible, were indeed necessarily complementary realities. What is more, in the liberal design the state was to be an instrumentality of the society rather than vice versa – an instrumentality specialized in the exercise of rule *over* the society. If this conception involves an implicit contradiction (How can the state both serve the society and rule over it?), the explanation for it lies in the fact that the society was not a fused but a split reality.

Essentially, the liberal state was constructed to favor and sustain through its acts of rule the class domination of the bourgeoisie over the society as a whole. This was the end to which the institutional principles of the state were ultimately directed, as it was the reason for their apparent contrast with those of the society. For example, the state attached to all individuals abstractly equal faculties for freely disposing of their own resources; the reason for this was that the capitalist mode of production required labor power to be sold for wages through individual employment contracts. Again, the state was enjoined from interfering in the market, except in such generalized ways as by regulating the money system or the machinery for the enforcement of contracts; the reason for this was that the nineteenth-century market was capable of doing on its own terms nearly all the allocating that needed to be done, and in doing so automatically directed the processes of production and accumulation to the advantage of capital owners. The equality of all individuals before the law made sense as a constitutional principle because as a matter of course the legal protection of private property directed the order-keeping, law enforcement and repressive activities of police and courts to favor the interests of the propertied groups.[3] The distinctive features of modern law as a body of stated rules, Habermas argues, reflect the specific moral and cultural preferences of the bourgeoisie: such rules allow a free ambit to bourgeois 'inwardness' because they are external, to bourgeois individuality because they are general, to bourgeois subjectivity because they are objective, and to bourgeois concreteness because they are abstract.[4]

In sum, in Habermas's view, as in other Marx-inspired critical interpretations of the state/society distinction, the state's institutional principles are instrumental to bourgeois class dominance within the society; political structures are primarily responsive to the requirements of the capitalist mode of production, at the same time expressing and concealing the functional subordination of political to economic power.[5] Such arguments strike me as correct but somewhat partial. After all, the state/society distinction did not *originate* from the relationship between political and economic power. It had earlier found fundamental expression in the slow but inexorable disentanglement of the Western state from the Church(es) and Christianity through the tortuous story that leads from *cuius regio eius religio* through religious tolerance and freedom of conscience to the 'secular state'. In this story, it would seem, not economic interests but *raison d'état* and a momentous, autonomous development in religious awareness and in moral consciousness played a critical role. Matters of creed and cult, not of property and contract, had been the first to be claimed as 'private' with respect to the state, as proper for the state to ignore or to safeguard impartially.

Yet momentous as it had been, the religious dimension of the state/society distinction had set over against the state a social force – the militant Christianity of Protestant Reformation and Catholic Counter-Reformation – that despite its surface vigor was historically *recessive*. When that distinction was later institutionalized, the state's counterpart was on the contrary an *ascendant* force, inherently dynamic and powerfully expansive – whether one calls it Money, the Economy, the Market, or Capital. One can recognize that in the story of the 'separation' between state and society the religious aspect had operated early, independently, and significantly, and yet accept the Marxian view to the extent of recognizing that the economic aspect entailed for the state itself a much more serious challenge. Whereas religion, once separated from the state, was to confront it with progressively fewer and weaker claims, the capitalist economy was in a position largely to dictate the terms and determine the significance of its own separation from the state.

To put it another way, under capitalism the economy does not operate within the societal sphere simply as one 'factor' among and co-ordinate with others; rather, it imperiously *sub*ordinates or otherwise reduces the independent significance of all other factors, including religion, the family, the status system, education, technology, science, and the arts. The capitalist mode of production gains an ever wider and firmer hold on the social process at large; 'exchange values' progressively drive out 'use values'; all manner of human interests are processed through the market and subjected to its rules. To phrase the point with Marx, the 'political economy' constitutes not one aspect or phase but 'the anatomy' itself of the civil society.[6]

To see what challenge this entailed for the state, it is enough to point out that the state's social mission had often been seen (for instance, in the Hegelian tradition) as involving the homogenizing and hegemonizing, as it were, of a society conceived as inherently fragmented, atomized, and centerless. Yet with so much 'homogenizing and hegemonizing' in fact done by the capitalist economic system, what is left for the state to do? Will its institutional separation from the society allow it enough leverage to maintain its autonomy, or perhaps even to 'fight back' and gain a hold over the economic process itself?

These questions suggest two contestants struggling for superiority while each maintaining a separate identity and a firm base in its distinctive territory. However, the imagery I develop in this chapter chiefly envisages rather the progressive compenetration of the two territories, the displacement and erosion of the line separating state from society. I shall restate and synthesize familiar arguments according to which the institutional differentiation between socio-cultural and economic processes on the one hand and political processes on the other, which was characteristic of the West in the nineteenth century, has largely ceased to operate in our own. However, the state still functions in our time within and through political and juridical *forms* derived from the liberal-democratic nineteenth-century constitution; it does so to an extent sufficient partly to disguise and partly to limit the changes in the *substance* of the political process, but at the same time it modifies and distorts the forms themselves.[7]

In a later section I shall take as an example of this last point the inexorable but formally concealed displacement of elected legislatures from the center of the state. But before discussing this consequence of the compenetration of the political and societal realms, we must consider a range of phenomena that may be viewed as causes and/or manifestations of that development.

THE PRESSURE OF COLLECTIVE INTERESTS

I shall consider first, in this section and the two that follow, some pressures on the state/society line that have originated from the society side and have led to a greater involvement between state and society than the classical constitutional model allowed for. I shall focus on phenomena reflecting the evolving dynamic of the capitalist economic system.

Capitalism is a system of power. It entails the self-perpetuating dominance of the capital-owning class over those social groups whose livelihood and social standing depend on the sale of labor power; and to this extent it generates contrasting sets of typical interests in the two key classes. The safest way to uphold this central facet of modern Western society in the sphere of the state is to exclude from the constitutional political process the claims and demands of groups in whose interest it may lie to abolish capital ownership, to modify its distribution, or to interfere with its chances for profit or its control over accumulation.

In the nineteenth and early twentieth centuries, the chief means of excluding from the political arena groups whose interests might be incompatible with the maintenance and prosperity of the capitalist system was the restriction of suffrage.[8] Without the franchise, such groups were limited to the exercise of civil rights having no direct political significance, or to unconstitutional forms of political dissent containable through police and other repressive action. Once incompatible interests were 'filtered out' of the political process in this way, public institutions, and signally parliament, could attend to the resolution of such contrasting interests as were generated within the framework of capitalist-bourgeois institutions and values.[9] The rights to vote and to hold office were accordingly restricted to men possessing property and/or educational qualifications. The justification for this took the line that the ability to deliberate on distinctively public and political concerns (directly or through representatives) in an enlightened and critical manner could only be imputed to individuals possessing a stake in the market system – entrepreneurs, professionals, rentiers, at most the more established self-employed workers. We might say, to use again Marx's ironic image, that to experience 'ecstasies', to jump as it were out of one's own private skin into the lofty forum where an informed and public-spirited citizenry agitated issues of general significance, one needed a secure platform in a proper home, with a duly constituted and patriarchally run family, a respectable patrimony, a capital to risk, or sophisticated skills to put to independent use.[10]

It matters little whether or not we take seriously these arguments and their multiple variants in liberal thinking. The point is that the disfranchised themselves took them seriously. It was expressly in order to bring into the political arena interests in contrast to and not easily 'balanceable' with those of the capital-owning class that they sought the franchise, eventually gained it, and used it (with varying success) to bring the state's power to bear on their condition and to reduce or ameliorate their economic inferiority.[11] For various reasons, the subaltern strata could not long be prevented from obtaining the franchise and seeking to put it to their own use. The growing fiscal and military needs of the state were leading it to engage ever-larger numbers of the masses in an increasingly direct relation to itself; and some degree of legitimate participation in the country's political process suggested itself as a counterpart to burdens imposed.[12] Also, the possession by the masses of basic civil rights, which we have seen was required by the capitalist mode of production, gave the disfranchised a toehold in the larger society and a means of taking part in 'public activities' to the end of gaining political rights.[13] Similarly, an increasingly sophisticated industrial technology made at least minimum literacy a requisite of the work force; but the resulting establishment of public education systems constituted an encroachment on the state/society line and increased the workers' ability to organize and mobilize themselves. Finally, where even a rudimentary party system involving competition for votes existed, the 'outs' were often led to promote the enlargement of the electorate in order to be rewarded at the polls by the newly enfranchised.[14]

The existence of the liberal 'public realm', where issues could be debated and associations formed among individuals sharing interests and views, was used not only by the lower classes to agitate for electoral rights but by both privileged and underprivileged economic actors to organize coalitions to further their economic and status advantage. The operations of these coalitions – typically trade unions and employers' associations – introduce elements of coercion and 'bargaining' into the processes allocating the social product between labor and capital or between different sections of each. This in turn has the effect of modifying or suspending the classical rules according to which markets are supposed to operate (through unplanned, mechanical adjustments among myriad individual choices). The impact of this development on the state/society line can be seen in the fact that the rules on such matters as collective bargaining and union membership, together with much legislation dealing with 'welfare', form a corpus (labeled 'labor', 'industrial', or 'social' law) that straddles the divide between private and public law.

Furthermore, those same coalitions or organizations represent and mobilize interests of such magnitude that they become capable of engaging various state organs in a distinctive game of 'pressure' or 'interest' politics played outside the public realm and without the mediation of parliament. Thus interests that on the face of it are purely private – since the organizations in question are mostly formed and run under the empire of the common law, without public recognition and control – are found either activating or blocking public policies that directly affect them. They do so with such effectiveness that the state frequently finds it in its own interest to associate such organizations in its own operations,[15] co-opting their leaders into organs deliberating administrative policies, consulting them on legislation, using their facilities to monitor the interests they organize, and expecting them on occasion to discipline their members or curb their demands in order to ensure the success of certain state initiatives.[16] Moreover, in this fashion the allocation of the social products through acts of rule (formally still originating from the state's undivided sovereignty) becomes ostensibly the key issue of the political process. Accordingly, interests of a private nature are either openly given voice in that process, or covertly allowed to affect it, or sometimes offered opportunities to engage in *de facto* acts of rule themselves.

CAPITALIST DEVELOPMENTS: EFFECTS ON THE OCCUPATIONAL SYSTEM

Above, I linked some encroachments on the state/society line with the nature of capitalism in its conceptually minimal form – a productive system where profit is appropriated by a capital-owning class that purchases on the market the labor power of the propertyless. But both those encroachments and others can be seen as deriving from *developments* in the capitalist mode of production – in the structure of the dominant production units, the distribution of capital ownership, and so forth. In particular, the long-term trend toward higher levels of capitalization of industrial enterprises produces, more or less directly, several effects relevant to our argument. A number of these effects are mediated through a changing occupational structure. In particular, a more advanced industrial base requires an increasingly differentiated, literate, skilled and better-motivated work force. As a result, the composition of the work force changes, and its rising level of education increases its political awareness and leads it to make increasing claims on the action of the state.

Here I should like to focus briefly on occupational changes occurring within middle-class strata – those traditionally associated with the bourgeoise in terms of status, life-style, self-conception, cultural preferences, and political orientation. The key phenomenon is the development of a large employee middle class, whose position in the production system (though not in the consumption system) comes to resemble that of the manual working class. This development has two effects. First, it makes economic self-sufficiency untenable as a suffrage qualification, since increasingly sizeable groups would come to lose the franchise as a result; and we have seen that the trend is toward increasing rather than decreasing the franchise. Second, it leads the employee middle class to imitate and outdo the manual working class in pressing the state to safeguard its 'private' interests. It seeks to preserve through state action that economic security and social standing it can no longer ground either on the possession of a family patrimony (see Keynes's 'euthanasia of the rentier'), or on the ability to maintain its independence while placing on the market valued, sophisticated services.

Yet even when employee strata find sufficient demand for their services on the labor market, and even when their income allows them to maintain a middle-class standard of living, they still look outside the market system to the state to satisfy their aspirations for security. Habermas outlines the long-term results of these developments as follows in a discussion of their impact on the institutional configuration of the modern urban family:

> As the family property becomes reduced to the income from employment of the single breadwinner, the family loses its ability to look after itself in emergencies and to make its own provisions for old age . . . The risks of unemployment, accident, illness, old age, and death of the breadwinner must be covered largely through welfare provisions of the state . . . The individual family member relies on public guarantees of its basic requirements, whereas the bourgeois family used to bear the risk privately. Over and above such needs resulting from emergency situations, provisions are also publicly made for various other aspects of existence, from housing to employment services, occupational and educational counseling, the monitoring of health, etc. . . . The bourgeois family, no longer needed as the typical locus of capital formation through savings, increasingly loses also the functions of nurturance and education, protection, moral support and guidance, elementary tradition and orientation. It loses the ability to shape behavior even in the spheres that in the (classical) bourgeois family were considered as the most intimate seat of privacy. In a way, through such public guarantees of its status, the family, this private residuum, becomes itself deprivatized.[17]

As industrialization progresses and raises the standard of living and the expectations of the whole working population, the effects of the phenomena Habermas lists extend beyond the middle-class family to the contemporary Western family at large and have a correspondingly greater impact on the state/society line.

CAPITALIST DEVELOPMENTS: EFFECTS ON THE PRODUCTION SYSTEM

Qualitatively similar but even more massive effects than those discussed above can be traced to changes in the dimensions and structures of the dominant production units as the joint-stock company and the corporation become the protagonists of the expanding industrial economy. To begin with, the very concession of corporate status to the joint economic endeavors of individuals is of doubtful legitimacy in the face of liberal ideology, and has strong preliberal, as well as antiliberal, antecedents.[18] The facts that in American parlance corporations are often labeled 'public' (as in 'going public'), and that a complex and by no means automatic political-legal decision is required to confer on corporations a legal capacity distinct from that of the individual owners, suggest how awkward such artificial subjects are from the standpoint of the distinction between public and private law. The same point is implicit in the complex (though mostly ineffectual) provisions whereby various governmental or semi-governmental bodies – from courts to securities commissions – monitor the legality of some corporate operations. Furthermore, in the twentieth century there has been a strong trend in Western countries (with the partial exception of the United States) toward the formation of industrial corporations totally owned or at least controlled by the state, which may finance its investments from public funds. Parliament or the government may appoint such corporations' top executives, and may mandate and direct their industrial policies.[19]

Many large economic units, even when their formally 'private' capital base allows them to fend off any effective public control over their investments and industrial strategies, operate in fact as semipublic or quasipublic entities *vis-à-vis* their employees, and to a lesser extent their customers. This is particularly clear when such units engage (as they often do) in activities that are at best distantly related to their central industrial object. As Bahrdt phrases this point:

There are industrial firms that build houses and flats for their employees or make arrangements whereby they can purchase their own homes. They build public parks, schools, churches and libraries; they arrange concerts and theater outings; they run adult education courses; they look after the aged, widows and orphans. In other words, a range of functions originally carried out by institutions public not

327

only in the juridical but also in the sociological sense are undertaken by organizations whose activities are non-public . . . The 'private' sphere of operation of a large firm runs right through the existence of the town where it is located, and brings into being a phenomenon to which one may rightly attach the label of industrial feudalism.[20]

Even more significant effects of this kind derive from the fact that large firms constitute for their employees a 'quasi-polity' – a constitutional and legal system of their own, effectively preserved from interference and control by properly political, state organs.[21] The administrative and semijudicial decisions of such a system are sometimes negotiated between management and the employees' representatives. Yet their tremendous impact on the existence of the employees (and not merely the occupational aspects of that impact, as Bahrdt reminds us) is not mediated within and through the public realm proper, and takes little cognizance of the employees' rights as citizens. Furthermore, the individual employee normally has very little control even over those people or organizations who supposedly represent him to his employer. Finally, where the treatment of employees (pay, security, working conditions, pension rights, fringe benefits) is comparatively generous, the costs are chiefly borne by the larger public – as consumers or taxpayers.

This last remark points to another, all-important result of the dominance of large firms in advanced industrial economies. The operations of such firms deeply modify the working of the market, since they can establish with one another, with smaller firms, with suppliers, and with consumers relations incompatible with the competitive model. For instance, large corporations can usually finance themselves from profits and can thus escape the control of external capital markets; or if they go to such markets for financing, they find them controlled by a few large, corporate investors rather than by a multitude of small savers and investors. Further, large firms capable of generating demand through new products, advertising and price strategies effectively invert the 'classical sequence' whereby the sovereign consumer generated profit opportunities for firms competing for his preferences.

But the competitive market was not just the only proper market; it was also the economic environment presupposed by the liberal state/society distinction. There were two reasons for this. First, the competitive market was self-equilibrating, and could thus dispense with *ad hoc* regulation and intervention by the state. Second, the competitive market did not appear to countenance the emergence of power relations between economic actors, and thus seemed to leave the state as the only entity wielding power within and for a given national society. The increasing dominance of large firms maximizing not only their profits but also their control over markets, their own growth, and their power over one another and the larger society contradicts both the above assumptions and sharpens immeasurably that challenge I argued earlier the capitalist mode of production always poses to the state's power.

The control that the large firms exercise over the economic process and hence over the whole societal realm allows them to influence the state itself, to persuade the state at the very least not to 'interfere' with their activities, and at best to place some of its faculties of rule at their disposal. In the twentieth century, capitalist business has achieved massive (though not uniform) success with this strategy, and has thoroughly affected the state's activities by magnifying their scope, modifying their forms, and orienting them to interests that would not have been recognized as proper public concerns in the nineteenth century. For instance, with the intent of starting, strengthening or modernizing units operating in the advanced branches of industry, the state now assigns to firms colossal funds, raised from public revenues, to be deployed according to the logic of profit – still intrinsically a 'private' logic, whatever the terms under which the firms operate and the funds are assigned. Moreover, the state's costly effort to enlarge and modernize the public education system, whatever the stated aims behind it, serves the end (not always achieved) of supplying industry with the inputs of trained manpower and sophisticated scientific, technological and managerial know-how it needs to function and to advance. On the output side, too, the state's interest in 'stable growth', 'full employment' and so forth commits it to massive expenditures intended to support the demand for industrial products – arguably with inflationary side effects. Recent radical interpretations even view most of the so-called welfare expenditures of the contemporary Western state – expenditures we suggested previously were made as a result of the lower strata's newly acquired political effectiveness – as ways in which the state underwrites (largely at the expense of those lower strata as taxpayers) the tremendous costs of the operations of private corporations.[22]

The German constitutional lawyer Böckenförde argues that by engaging in such activities the Western state has subordinated itself to the economic process. (Note that, not being a Marxist, he does not specify the significance of this phenomenon for *class* relations.)

> The fact that the contemporary state has identified itself with the economy results in the fact that to a large degree it operates at the service of the industrial-economic process. The range of the state's economic tasks grows, but so does the feebleness of its capacity for self-determination. It carries out functions of regulation and control, but not in the capacity of a 'higher third party' that holds the reins; rather, it simply undertakes functions complementary to the industrial-economic process. It is not the state itself that sets what aspects of the economic process will be promoted and regulated; rather, the state reacts to givens and trends that automatically issue from that process itself. Overall control is not exercised by the state, but rather by the industrial-economic process itself.[23]

In my view it is an exaggeration (though not a wild one) to view the state as only a passive participant in the development we have discussed above. The state does not simply react to impulses originating in its counterpart, whether we call it 'the industrial-economic process', with Böckenförde, or Capital, or something else. Some encroachments on the state/society line result not from the state's being 'pulled' over the line, as it were, but from its 'pushing' itself over it. What makes the trend towards the obliteration of the state/society line so powerful is precisely the fact that several phenomena, distinctive and even otherwise mutually contradictory, are at one in causing it.

We have already seen, for instance, how the peculiarly political dynamic of 'ins' versus 'outs' favored the extension of the franchise and consequently the activation of state policy to the advantage of ever-lower societal strata. But other phenomena discussed in this chapter can be connected with the state's pursuit of its distinctive interests. Take the theme (quintessentially political, in Carl Schmitt's view) of each state's commitment to preserve and aggrandize its own power among states. Clearly under modern conditions this commitment requires a state to give itself an adequate industrial base. But in the advanced industrial era, creating and maintaining such a base requires financial, technological, entrepreneurial and organizational resources that only the biggest corporations *or* the state can command.[24] And since the biggest corporations are multinational, and as such very awkward customers for a given state,[25] it often falls to the state alone to take the lead in sponsoring the formation of adequately large and powerful productive undertakings. It is significant that Germany and Japan, which initiated two of the more successful non-liberal variants of capitalist industrialization, were also countries with strong military-political traditions and penchants for aggressiveness – very Schmitt-minded countries, as it were. And French *dirigisme* showed significant advances under de Gaulle – of the Western statesmen of his day probably the most single-mindedly committed to the specificity and the supremacy of 'the political'.

Böckenförde may be justified in arguing that the state (at any rate in the West) subordinates itself to the apolitical logic of 'the industrial-economic process' by becoming over-involved in economic tasks. But sometimes it gets itself into that predicament while pursuing interests of a non-economic nature. Indeed, it could avoid the problem only by leaving the country industrially underdeveloped or by surrendering its industrial development to one or more multinational corporation; and both solutions would threaten the country's independent political existence.

THE SEARCH FOR LEGITIMACY

[. . .] I have followed Max Weber in suggesting that the modern state's specific form of legitimacy is its appeal that its commands be recognized as binding because *legal*, that is, because issued in conformity with properly enacted, general rules. However, I have also followed Carl Schmitt to the extent of recognizing that the motivating force of such a notion is relatively weak because it does not evoke a strong substantive ideal, a universally shared standard of intrinsic validity, but instead refers to purely formal, contentless considerations of procedural correctness. This inherent weakness in its legitimacy becomes a progressively greater liability for the modern state in the post-liberal era – on two counts. First, as we shall see below, some institutional premises and expressions of legal rationality became eroded (e.g. the centrality of parliament, the supremacy and generality of law, the division of powers). Second, some developments displacing the state/ society line increase the political leverage of social forces (from the underprivileged strata to the new, corporate aggregations of socioeconomic power) that do not stand to gain from the strict observance of procedural rules, and that would prefer, given the chance, to take liberties with the rule of law.

Thus on the one hand, the legitimizing significance of legal rationality remains weak or becomes weaker, whereas on the other hand, industrial advances and the increasing complexity of society (to mention only two factors) make more and more extensive and burdensome that 'web of rules' either directly produced by the state or ultimately sanctioned by it, and enveloping social life in all its aspects.[26] Hence it becomes urgent for the state to find a means of renewing its lease on legitimacy, of generating a new legitimizing formula for itself.

Toward the end of the liberal era (late nineteenth and early twentieth centuries), when class contrasts were relatively strong and threatening, most Western states shored up their legitimacy by focusing on imperial and colonial gains and the related international conflicts. Since the Second World War, however, Western nations have ceased to play power politics with one another with the same urgency and visibility as before; they have formed a bloc under the military and diplomatic leadership of the United States, and they have created Atlantic and European alliances and supranational organizations. In an early phase, of course, this mutual accommodation was accompanied by 'Cold War' tensions with the Eastern bloc that to some extent replicated – with the addition of new ideological tones – former emphases on national interest. But in the long run, the state found a new and different response to the legitimacy problem: increasingly it treated industrial growth *per se* as possessing intrinsic and commanding political significance, as constituting a necessary and sufficient standard of each state's performance, and thus as justifying further displacements of the state/society line.

Particularly in the 1950s and 1960s, an ideal variously termed 'industrial development', 'economic growth' or 'affluence' gained an overwhelming grip on the public imagination. It was unanimously endorsed (at any rate in their rhetoric) by political leaders of all persuasions, who treated it on the one hand as utterly self-justifying, and on the other as validating whatever burdens the state might impose on society. It is probably correct to see in this phenomenon another expression of the tyrannical hold of the capitalist mode of production on contemporary social existence at large. (But since something very similar happened at about the same time in Eastern Europe, perhaps we should speak of the tyranny of industrialism.) Yet as I have suggested, one can also see this phenomenon as 'co-determined' by developments in the political sphere: for once the experience of two World Wars and the terrifying prospect of nuclear disaster made the pursuit of old-fashioned power politics among Western states an unacceptably disturbing proposition, the pursuit not of power abroad but of prosperity at home became the chief justification for the state's existence and the lodestar of its operations (at least outwardly).

Thus, Böckenförde may be right in arguing that by becoming overinvolved in the industrial-economic process the state subordinates itself to the logic of that process; yet the state's very involvement may be seen as an attempted response to specifically political problems concerning its legitimacy. In fact, it has been argued by A. Gehlen[27] that the developments under discussion add to Max Weber's three types of legitimacy a fourth, contemporary one labeled 'social eudaemonic' and characteristic of states seeking legitimacy through acts of rule that assist the economic system in producing an ever-increasing flow of goods and services for the consumer. Note how directly this understanding of legitimacy points to our main theme: as what were originally 'private' concerns of individual consumers become of direct and critical 'public' significance, the state/society line is obliterated.

INTERNAL PRESSURES TOWARD THE EXPANSION OF RULE

We must also consider how the very nature and internal constitution of the modern state 'push' it over into what in liberal terms was societal territory.

As with any other aspect of the social division of labor, the formation of a specialized political organization generates a set of distinctive, self-regarding interests competing with other parts of the division of labor to maximize its own returns from the working of the whole. In the liberal view, the formation of excessive imbalances in the resulting distribution of facilities and rewards is limited in three ways: by supply-and-demand mechanisms (essentially, by customers taking their demand elsewhere when threatened with exploitation by any one supplier); by diffuse feelings of solidarity overriding invidious interests; and by legal arrangements preventing the component parts of the division of labor from getting away with too much in their dealings with one another and with the whole.

But the very nature of the modern state undercuts the effectiveness of these restraints when applied to its *own* relations to the other parts of the social division of labor. The state monopolizes a crucial faculty – society-wide, generalized coercive power – and to that extent is exempt from supply-and-demand, market-like curbs. It operates as *itself* the chief referent of feelings of interindividual, intergroup solidarity,[28] and treats submission to itself as the standard expression of those feelings. Finally, the state itself produces and enforces law, the main institutional guarantee of solidarity. In sum, the state is constituted to exercise *rule over society* – whether on behalf of all or part of the society. Hence the state tends to increase its power by widening the scope of its activities, by extending the range of societal interests on which rule is brought to bear.[29]

Under liberalism, three overlapping constitutional arrangements were expected to safeguard the distinctiveness and autonomy of the societal realm in the face of the state: first, the division of powers, whereby the state's power was disaggregated into separate packages of interlocking but mutually limiting faculties of rule entrusted to different organs; second, the liberal 'public realm', through which the society itself was supposed to mandate and monitor the exercise of state power; and third, the state's submission to its own law. The erosion and breakdown of the liberal design has resulted mainly from inadequacies in the last two arrangements. As I pointed out [elsewhere], the state could not ultimately be bound by its own law precisely because it was its *own* law, positive law, and as such intrinsically changeable, with only procedural, formal constraints on its changeability. Furthermore, 'the' society was in fact inherently fissured by conflicts; and there would always be parties to such conflicts in whose immediate interest it lay to favor and invoke, rather than oppose, some extension of rule into new societal domains. Once these two factors made it juridically and politically possible for the state as a whole to transgress and push back its boundary with society, society could not be adequately safeguarded by the one remaining constitutional arrangement – the division of powers. For what is the use of carefully distributing powers of rule among state organs so that they may 'check and balance' one another if those organs can increase their prerogative at the expense of society rather than directly of one another?

Far from helping contain the state within its boundaries, the division of powers in fact led the state as a whole to increase its prerogative through the competition engendered among all its units and subunits over *their* respective prerogatives. For however much the articulation of the system of rule into organs, branches, departments, sections, and so forth may have been conceived as part of a unitary, harmonious organizational design, the component elements in that design became fairly quickly the seats of invidious interests all struggling to increase their autonomy, their reciprocal standing, and their command over resources. And this struggle placed a premium on a unit's ability to define a new societal interest as the legitimate target of its activity, and thus as the justification for its existence and for its standing relative to other units. Furthermore, the individuals elected or appointed to state office cannot be expected to act exclusively on behalf of the interests constitutionally assigned to each office; nor, for that matter, can they be expected to act exclusively on behalf of the constitutionally doubtful but compelling micropolitical interests they acquire in the autonomy and standing of the unit of which their office is part. Instead, all individuals orient at least part of their conduct to strictly private interests, particularly to increasing income and status from officeholding, to making a career of it.

Now these individual interests do not so much exercise a direct pressure on the state/society line as add urgency to those interests that do. For instance, a claim that a new phase or aspect of societal business ought to be 'administered' by a unit of the civil service can often be used to argue for an increase in the unit's staff. In turn, such an increase may generate new openings at supervisory levels, and thus favor the career interests of the civil servants making up the unit. Under such conditions the force of private interests may be expected to help propel a claim toward realization.

One need not subscribe to popular demonology about 'power-grasping bureaucrats' or share the related 'metaphysical pathos' to recognize that pressures on the state/society line do originate in these ways (often, of course, in association with pressures from the societal side) and are particularly intense within the state's administrative apparatus.[30] Let us consider soberly the following five statements:

1. Examination of the workings of state organs in the light of economic theory indicates that such organs tend to maximize their budgets rather than the ratio of units of service

to units of expended resources.[31] Ultimately, this means that they seek to command ever-increasing amounts of societal resources.

2. The very size and complexity of the administrative apparatus of a contemporary state tend to isolate it (or individual parts of it) from direct societal counterpressures, thus breaking the cybernetic cycle between the administration and the societal environment.[32]

3. Public agencies often reach out into the society and either incorporate sections of it into themselves or make sections of it into the objects of acts of rule; they do this in order to reduce the complexity and turbulence of the societal environment, to stabilize it and their relations to it. It is more comfortable and 'natural' for an agency to adopt a posture of administrative control over a given societal interest than to treat it as an autonomous entity or as a party in bargaining relations.

4. Within highly professionalized public agencies, selective recruitment, intense socialization of entrants, strong *esprit de corps*, and a shared and valued administrative philosophy of long standing and great prestige can preserve institutional traditions from outside influences. But some such traditions may be preliberal in origin and antiliberal in inspiration; if so, they necessarily impart to the agency's policies a bias against respecting the state/society line. If the 'despotic' traditions of some senior sections of the French bureaucracy survived the Revolution itself (as Tocqueville held), they are likely to be still active, in however muted a fashion, under the Fifth Republic. And the Prussian administrative legacy inherited by the Wilhelmine *Obrigkeitsstaat* – and whose hold on the German civil service Weimar could not break and Hitler put to good use – is probably still alive and well in Bonn (and East Berlin!).[33] Finally, Bourbon tendencies – in truth, more favorable to bureaucratic parasitism and corruption than to aggressive encroachment on the autonomy of society – are still powerfully at work within the Italian bureaucracy.

5. Finally, two critical, novel experiences of the twentieth-century state – total war and total dictatorship – have left upon the official mind the world over an indelible and possibly

tempting memory of how rapidly, ruthlessly and efficiently (and with what good conscience) the state can increase its grip on society.

CONSEQUENCES OF THE PRESSURES FROM STATE AND SOCIETY

So far I have suggested some major causes and manifestations – on both sides – of the progressive displacement of the state/society divide in the twentieth century. In this section I shall consider some of the consequences for the structure of the contemporary Western state. The most visible ones are probably the quantitative ones: for example, large increases in the number of public employees and in the share of the social product the state controls through acts of rule and absorbs in its operations; or the proliferation of administrative agencies. I prefer to deal briefly with some qualitative changes, affecting in particular parliamentary institutions and the electoral and legislative processes. Considerable as they are, such changes frequently are not clearly registered in the state's *formal* constitutional structures, which remain those designed between the late eighteenth and the early twentieth centuries.

As we saw in the last chapter, parliament necessarily held a key position in the nineteenth-century state, under whatever name and organizational form it took. Whether or not it was formally the seat of sovereignty, and whatever its relations to the executive, parliament bore the responsibility for processing the political demands expressed through the electoral system into laws – that is, into the essential language and medium of all state operations. Now practically all phenomena displacing the state/society line impinge on this unique position of parliament. In particular, the progressive extension of the franchise not only allows interests not easily 'balanceable' with those of the capital-owning class to set the themes of the electoral and legislative processes but also modifies the modalities of those processes.

Previously, contrasts between 'balanceable' interests could be settled by open-ended debate between currents of parliamentary opinion,[34] each seeking to increase its support from among a majority of relatively uncommitted parliament members. According to liberal theory (and to a lesser extent practice) each member was accountable to the nation as a whole, not to his own immediate electorate. The latter, being anonymous and unincorporated, could not closely mandate and monitor the members' parliamentary activity (at any rate between elections); it was supposed to trust his judgement, as formed and expressed in parliamentary debate, rather than expect him to abide by a pre-established, narrow program. This diminished the elected member's accountability to and dependence on specific societal interests, and correspondingly increased the leeway for controversy and compromise in the legislative chamber(s). Thus parliament functioned 'creatively' (because open-endedly) and produced political and legislative decisions that were not preprogrammed. Of course, extensive and fairly stable alignments among members of parliament existed on both sides of the government/opposition divide. But these alignments were largely internal to parliament itself and were focused not on narrow, contrasting societal interests but on specifically political themes and broad philosophies of state action.

However, as ever-broader masses of the population became enfranchised, only organized parties could effectively mobilize this new, vast, and untrained electorate. But the membership and electoral following of such parties matched the map of societal cleavages more closely than liberal theory deemed decent; and the specific interests those parties represented were not so easily 'balanced' against the established ones. Furthermore, because they were organized, parties were able to direct and monitor the conduct of their parliament members fairly closely. In the chamber(s), the party members formed themselves into the 'party-in-parliament', with a division of labor and a hierarchical structure, thereby stabilizing majority and minority alignments to an extent previously unknown.

Since the organized parties select the candidates they place on the ballot, and mandate and control their actions when elected, it might seem at first sight that this gives the rank-and-file party members considerable political leverage, thus diffusing political awareness and effectiveness within the population (at whatever cost to the liberal theory of representation). However, whatever the internal constitutions of the parties themselves, their organizational dynamics progressively curb the effective leverage of the rank and file and magnify that of the party leadership.[35] The latter, since the parties themselves are mostly 'private' associations, are not accountable to the broad public; and their organizational control over the party makes them increasingly independent even of its membership and electorate.

It is true that most party leaders are also among the party's members of parliament, and in this capacity receive a public investiture. But increasingly the conferral of a public position can be manipulated through internal party arrangements, for the electorate of any given party is largely a 'captive' one. Furthermore, since conflicts frequently arise between the party organization and the party-in-parliament, the former elaborates relatively specific ideological guidelines and legislative platforms that it seeks to make binding on the latter.

The open-endedness and creativity of the parliamentary process is thus diminished. Increasingly, parliament is reduced to a highly visible stage on which are enacted vocal, ritualized confrontations between preformed, hierarchically controlled, ideologically characterized alignments. Each party-in-parliament may well be rent by internal controversy and engaged in a tug-of-war with its party organization, but in parliament it generally presents a united front, supporting unanimously whatever position is laid down by the leadership as party policy on a given issue. Under such conditions, parliament no longer performs a critical, autonomous role as a mediator between societal interests; instead, its composition and operations simply register the distribution of preferences within the electorate and determine in turn which party will lead the executive. How a party's parliament members will vote on a given issue is decided by the issue's ideological color and by its bearing on the all-important question of whether the party will remain in power or in the opposition. In comparison with these two determinants, the *merits* of the issue are relatively insignificant and are not effectively weighed in debate.

Around the middle of the twentieth century, as we have seen, the political process in Western countries begins to revolve around the question of how to promote 'industrial development', 'affluence', and so forth – this being seen as the only large issue (other than war, hot or cold) that might provide the basis for a reconciliation of societal interests long perceived as 'unbalanceable'. This development (besides having direct effects on the state/society line, as already indicated) diminishes the relevance of the parties' ideological heritage, since the issue in question – how to increase the national product – is said to be ultimately a 'technical' rather than a political one. The consequent loosening of the party's ideological moorings further increases the autonomy of its leadership with respect to its organizational and electoral base; but it does nothing at all to restore the significance of the electoral process and of parliament.

Elections, fought between increasingly catchall parties, are basically intended to produce a plebiscitary mandate for one party; once secure in its parliamentary majority, that party can then pragmatically develop its policies while obeying a dwindling minimum of doctrinal commitments.[36] Campaigns thus become largely investiture rituals, and are increasingly characterized by marketing techniques, with a great deal of image-mongering and pseudopersonalization of issues through a focus on candidate 'charisma'. In elaborating or justifying their policies between elections, both the party (or coalition of parties) in power and its opponents appeal less and less to ideological criteria (often sneeringly characterized as 'party-political') and more and more to the reasonings of 'experts' in macroeconomic and administrative management. This is only appropriate, because the whole society is increasingly conceived of as a firm intent on maximizing or optimizing the ratio of its outputs to its inputs. Accordingly, the state's task is seen as that of managing that firm after the fashion of the contemporary large corporation – with a 'technostructure' erecting and operating multiple overlapping 'sociotechnical' systems.

Once the political process is so (mis)conceived, parliament has little of distinctive significance to contribute to it. The vacuum left by the devaluation of ideology (or at any rate of certain ideologies) is filled not by a renewal of open-ended discourse but by an appeal to economic, technological and

341

managerial 'expertise'. And to supply that expertise or to control its employment in the conduct of rule does not seem a job parliament can adequately do. Instead, the job falls mainly to the professional civil service, which enlists the support of research institutes, planning units, and consultative bodies manned chiefly by the 'scientific estate' and by spokesmen for the larger corporations and other interest groups. As a result, administrative decisions are increasingly articulated in a language that effectively screens them from parliamentary criticism and public debate, and that frequently provides a convenient cover for the interests actually dictating those decisions. The classical parliamentary means for monitoring and auditing the operations of the executive (from the vote on the budget to parliamentary questions) lose effectiveness in the face of this phenomenon and related ones. For instance, many new administrative agencies arise outside the framework of ministerial organization and even in formal terms are not easily held accountable to parliament through its right to question ministers. Paradoxically, the gigantic growth of public revenues and expenditures makes parliamentary control more necessary than ever but also increasingly impossible; the bewildering size and complexity of budgets and other accounting instruments both demand and prohibit parliamentary oversight. Moreover, the legislative overload straining the working capacity of most parliaments reduces the amount of time available for monitoring activities.

These last points should not suggest that parliaments can effectively defend their much-threatened supremacy over the executive and the administration through their legislative prerogative. Executive and administration in fact largely control the volume and the content of the legislation they themselves process through parliament. In the eyes of ministers and top civil servants, legislation has become too important to be left to legislators. Laws are drafted almost exclusively outside parliament; they deal largely with matters of primarily administrative significance; and they mostly serve to validate in formal terms decisions reached by civil servants in their technocratic wisdom (much assisted by interested pressure groups). Furthermore, contemporary legislation has largely lost those features of generality and abstractness that made 'classical' legislation into the instrument *par excellence* of parliamentary supremacy. Many laws are effectively *ad hoc* measures of an intrinsically administrative nature given the form of law in order to legalize the expenditures they involve and shield ministers and civil servants from having to take political or personal responsibility for them. In view of the enormous tasks of 'societal management' borne by contemporary governments, administrative action cannot be meaningfully programmed in the classical manner – that is, by means of a law stating general conditions under which a given administrative action is to be taken. Instead, programs directing an agency, say, to increase the country's steel-making capacity by x per cent, or to reduce industrial pollution in a given river by y per cent over z years, must leave the measures to be taken towards the target in question to administrative discretion, supposedly informed by the appropriate nonlegal expertise.[37] It then becomes impossible for parliament (or a judicial organ, or for that matter a higher agency)[38] to control the agency's conduct by checking whether it corresponds with abstractly stated rules, since no such rules do or can exist.

The cumulative impact of all these phenomena – to which one might add such others as the operations of multinational firms and supranational organizations – is to shunt parliament away from the effective center of a country's political life, leaving in control the state's executive organs, and especially its administrative apparatus, now thoroughly 'interlaced' with those various controlling nonstate forces. Yet parliament remains the chief institutional link between the citizenry and the state. If it ceases to operate as an *effective* link, what or who can politically direct, control and moderate the ever-growing mutual involvement between state and society?

The parties demand from the electorate a more and more generic, less and less binding mandate; yet they cannot effectively be held accountable for its execution, since whatever their differences on other issues they all cherish their shared monopoly of institutionalized political representation. The very size and complexity of the administrative apparatus insulates it from political control. The so-called media are no longer relatively open channels for political expression and forums for public debate (as newspapers originally were). In several Western countries in the 1960s and 1970s the courts have enjoyed occasional successes in reasserting much-battered ideas of legality in the conduct of public business; but theirs is a rearguard action, limited in its scope by its primary reference to criminal laws. Nor is it plausible to expect an effective defense of the distinctiveness and autonomy of the societal realm to be mounted by economic and other organizations; on the contrary, most of them appear only too eager to 'colonize' the political realm, overtly or covertly appropriating public resources and usurping faculties of rule in order to place them at the service of sectional social interests (at best) or of the narrow oligarchies that run them (at worst).

These considerations, purposely overstated, point to what seem to have become structural givens of the political process and its relations to the wider society in the contemporary West. Their implications become even more ominous when one considers also a few conjunctural facts concerning the countries in question in the period between the mid-1960s and the mid-1970s. The general import of these facts is that the institutional apparatus of the state, even apart from the question of whether it does or does not respect its original constitutional design and thus its boundary with society, has serious difficulties with a number of threatening problems. These problems are interconnected, and they are also linked with the phenomena discussed in the previous sections. Here, however, I shall disregard the connections and simply list the problems alone.

1. Political dissent over the period mentioned manifests itself frequently in unconstitutional and sometimes in criminal forms; and its aims are sometimes the total rejection and subversion of, or secession from, the established political system. At least in some cases, these developments are the result of the closing off of constitutional means of political expression to the broad public, which makes the system impenetrable by and unresponsive to legitimate demands. Furthermore, the reactions of established authorities often violate constitutional principles in turn, thereby increasing the political alienation of certain social groups.

2. The so-called 'welfare system' of various states appears both unable to remedy any but the most extreme forms of

economic and social deprivation and incapable of effectively reducing the range of wider socioeconomic inequalities; moreover, its direct and administrative costs place an increasingly burdensome fiscal strain on the population and the productive system.

3. Drastic and repeated failures of statesmanship and of political judgement, as well as glaring 'scandals' and 'affairs', reveal that at the very top of some states the intellectual and moral qualities of political leadership are demoralizingly low.

4. The state's law-enforcement apparatus proves increasingly incapable of guaranteeing the citizens' security in public places and in their homes, the wholesomeness and amenity of their physical environment, and the prevention and repression of large-scale depredations of the public (both as consumers and as taxpayers) by business firms.

5. Generally, the administrative apparatus of most states, though absorbing an increasing share of the national product, displays a decreasing capacity for effective societal management.

6. Most importantly, the state machinery for monitoring, supporting and steering the national economy proves inadequate to its tasks time and again. By the mid-1970s in most Western countries, the Keynesian and post-Keynesian apparatus of economic policy is in disarray in the face of a baffling combination of stubborn inflationary and recessionary trends.

This last phenomenon (whatever its causes) is politically significant especially insofar as it affects the state's legitimacy. I have previously suggested that legal-rational legitimacy is inherently weak as a source of moral motivations for compliance, that it has been further weakened by developments discussed in this chapter, that in the 1950s and 1960s all Western states sought to counter the resulting legitimacy deficit by claiming that rule was exercised chiefly in order to sustain industrial development, and so forth. But in the 1960s some sizable minorities began to question the moral significance of what seemed to be the continuous advance of Western populations toward a better standard of living and the moral validity of the claim for loyal compliance the state was basing on that advance. In the 1970s, as we have seen, that advance has become more laborious and uncertain; its benefits have been revealed to be much more unequally distributed than had seemed to be the case; and in some states, at least, it appears to have been interrupted altogether, perhaps for good. Thus the legitimacy formula in question (like any other such formula in a comparable situation) threatens to 'go into reverse', to increase rather than fill the legitimacy vacuum.

Viewed from the standpoint of the state, this phenomenon opens three main possibilities. First, the state can try to do without a legitimizing formula and rely on intimidating and repressing the disaffected sections of the citizenry and on favoring the rest in order to maintain control over society. Second, it can fall back on the earlier legitimizing formula of power politics, seeking to generate a wider consensus by pointing to the real or imaginary military threat posed to one state or coalition of states by other states or coalitions. Or, third, it can try to 'sell' the society on a new formula – preferably one superficially attractive enough to evoke wide acclaim (with the help of the media), and general enough not to commit the state to anything in particular. (In the early 1970s 'The Quality of Life' appeared to be a plausible candidate for such a formula.)

Whatever their respective probabilities of success, none of these outcomes (or even possible combinations of them) appears attractive. All seek to carry forward the basic trend in the institutional development of the modern state – the gathering unto it of ever more extensive and formidable faculties and facilities of rule – despite awareness that, paradoxically, that trend is making the state increasingly incapable of effectively exercising rule, of establishing rational control over the social process. Furthermore, all these outcomes more or less openly forsake two political ideas that, though they have sustained the basic trend in the state's development over the last two centuries, have at the same time afforded it a justification and a corrective: the liberal idea of the rule of law, and the democratic idea of the participation of the ruled in the process of rule. Only these two ideas connect the past evolution of the modern state with the moral heritage of the West, and thus with a wider ethical vision of humanity as the collective protagonist of a universal moral venture.[39]

Personally, I think that in seeking both moral inspiration and strategic guidance, Western opposition to the present disturbing tendencies in state/society relations must turn once more to those (and perhaps to some other) liberal and democratic ideas.[40] I am aware that on a number of grounds this sounds like a counsel of despair. Both liberalism and democracy have been tried and found wanting, it might be argued, or indeed have been so much a part of the problem in the past that we cannot seriously consider them now a part of the solution. One may also point to inherent and possibly insoluble contrasts between liberalism and democracy, and doubt the possibility of institutionally embodying both except at the cost of compromises that would weaken and disfigure each. Or one may suggest, more hopefully, that socialism is an alternative that transcends both liberalism and democracy by forcefully raising the problems set by the economic structure of society.

Yet in my view socialism is less relevant than liberalism and democracy to the dilemmas that face contemporary Western society as a result of trends in the state's structure and functioning. Liberalism and democracy have the advantage over socialism of directly addressing some key problems arising from the necessity of rule instead of downgrading such problems to the status of technical matters to be settled unproblematically after a revolution in the control over the means of production.[41] To those problems liberalism and democracy may perhaps (on the present record) offer wrong solutions; but wrong solutions to the right problems may be more valuable, theoretically and pragmatically, than a misguided attempt to ignore or bypass those problems.

Thus, insofar as the range of sources of inspiration available in Western societies today is still bounded by liberalism, democracy, and socialism (with their several variants) – and I for one cannot look beyond those bounds[42] – an imaginative and innovative reconsideration of the traditions of liberalism and democracy appears as a necessary, though of course not sufficient, condition for positive action.

Notes

1. See, for example, *Democracy in America*, London, 1969, vol. 2, p. 698.

2. K. Marx, *Early Writings*, Harmondsworth, 1970, p. 181.

3. A. Gouldner, *The Coming Crisis of Western Sociology*, New York, 1970, pp. 304–13, gives an excellent statement of this point.

4. J. Habermas, *Strukturwandel der Offentlichkeit*, 5th ed., Neuwied, 1971, pp. 74–5. My debt to this book (and to others of Habermas's writings) is particularly considerable in the first few sections of this chapter. The reader might note, however, that some of Habermas's arguments have been controverted; see, for instance, W. Jäger, *Offentlichkeit und Parlamentarismus: Eine Kritik an Jürgen Habermas*, Stuttgart, 1973.

5. 'Though politics ideally stands above the power of money, it has in fact become money's bondsman.' K. Marx, *Frühe Schriften*, Stuttgart, 1962, vol. 1, p. 483. For a general statement of this position, yet one emphasizing the extent to which the nature of the capitalist mode of production prohibits the direct conferral of public power on the capitalist class as such, see U. K. Preuss, *Bildung und Herrschaft*, Frankfurt, 1975, pp. 7–44.

6. For two differently derived statements of the societal supremacy of the economy and its distinctive interests, see the section on the 'civil society' in G. W. F. Hegel, *Philosophy of Right*, Oxford, 1942, pp. 122ff.; and E. Troeltsch, *The Social Teachings of the Christian Churches*, New York, 1960, p. 28.

7. J. Habermas *et al.*, *Student und Politik*, Neuwied, 1961, p. 23.

8. On the significance of this principle for the bourgeois-liberal polity, see L. Kofler, *Staat Gesellschaft und Elite Zwischen Humanismus und Nihilismus*, Ulm, 1960, pp. 126ff.

9. T. Geiger, *Saggi sulla società industriale*, Turin, 1970, pp. 613, 617f. This is the Italian translation of Geiger's *Demokratie ohne Dogma*, 1964.

10. See A. Gouldner, *Dialectics of Ideology and Technology*, London, 1976, pp. 101f.

11. The argument here and below about 'balanceable' versus 'unbalanceable' interests, and about the impact of the latter's entry into politics, is based on W. Hoffman, 'Staat und Politisches Handeln Heute', in his *Abschied vom Bürgertum*, Frankfurt, 1970, pp. 179ff. On the varying success of the subaltern strata, see

R. Bendix, *Nation-Building and Citizenship*, New York, 1964, pp. 74ff.

12. See, for example, L. Charnay, *Société militaire et suffrage politique en France depuis 1789*, Paris, 1964.

13. See C. B. Macpherson, *The Real World of Democracy*, Oxford, 1966, pp. 8f.

14. For a sophisticated treatment of this and other aspects of the lower classes' entry into politics focused on a historically significant variant of this phenomenon, see G. Roth, *The Social Democrats in Imperial Germany*, Totowa, NJ, 1962.

15. See T. Lowi, *The End of Liberalism*, New York, 1969, chapter 4, for some American examples of this phenomenon and a critique of its consequences.

16. C. Offe, *Leistungsprinzip und industrielle Arbeit*, Frankfurt, 1970, p. 13.

17. Habermas, *Strukturwandel der Offentlichkeit*, pp. 187f.

18. Lowi, *End of Liberalism*, p. 6. For a more technical statement of the 'privileging' nature of such legal operations, see F. Galgano, *Storia del diritto commerciale*, Bologna, 1976, chapters 3 and 6.

19. On some of these arrangements, see A. Schofield, *Modern Capitalism*, Oxford, 1966.

20. H. P. Bahrdt, *Die moderne Grosstadt*, Rowohlt, 1962, pp. 43f.

21. For a discussion of this phenomenon from the perspective of the sociology of law, see P. Selznick, *Law, Society and Industrial Justice*, New York, 1969.

22. See, for instance, J. O'Connor, *The Fiscal Crisis of the State*, New York, 1973.

23. E.-W. Böckenförde, 'Die Bedeutung der Unterscheidung von Staat und Gesellschaft im demokratischen Sozialstaat der Gegenwart', in *Rechtsfragen der Gegenwart*, Stuttgart, 1972, pp. 11ff. (this passage at p. 28). V. Ronge and G. Schmieg, *Restriktionen politischer Planung*, Frankfurt, n.d., can be seen as supporting Böckenförde's main argument from a different perspective while at the same time applying it to the uses of 'planning' as a technique of political-administrative management.

24. See P. Saraceno, 'Le radici della crisi economica', *Il Mulino* 25, no. 243, January-February 1976, p. 3ff.

25. In this chapter, as elsewhere, I have purposely avoided any discussion of the considerable but currently somewhat over-fashionable problem of the relation between national states, on the one hand, and multinational corporations and supranational organizations, on the other.

26. I borrow the expression 'the web of rules' from C. Kerr *et al.*, *Industrialism and Industrial Man*, London, 1962, p. 76.

27. A. Gehlen, *Studien zur Anthropologie und Soziologie*, Neuwied, 1963, p. 255.

28. See the significance attributed to political ceremonies and symbols in discussions of the role of communal rituals in contemporary society in R. Bellah, 'Civil Religion in America', in his *Beyond Belief*, New York, 1970, pp. 168ff.

29. This follows from the very notion of 'scope' as a component of influence or power. See, for instance, H. Lasswell and A. Kaplan, *Power and Society*, New Haven, Conn., 1950, pp. 73, 77.

30. See A. Gouldner, 'Metaphysical Pathos and the Theory of Democracy', in S. M. Lipset and N. Smelser (eds), *Sociology: The Progress of a Decade*, Englewood Cliffs, NJ, 1961, pp. 80ff.

31. W. Niskanen, *Bureaucracy: Servant or Master?*, London, 1973, pp. 20ff.

32. M. Crozier, *The Bureaucratic Phenomenon*, Chicago, 1964.

33. A. Görlitz, *Demokratie im Wandel*, Cologne, 1969, p. 84.

34. The significance of discussion for classical parliamentarism is much emphasized in C. Schmitt, 'Die Prinzipien des Parlamentarismus', in K. Kluxen (ed.), *Parlamentarismus*, Cologne, 1967, pp. 41ff.

35. On this point, the statement by R. Michels in *Political Parties*, London, 1915, remains fundamental.

36. See O. Kirchheimer, *Politics, Law and Social Change*, New York, 1969, pp. 245–371.

37. For the distinction between 'conditional' and 'target' programming of administrative action, rephrased here, see N. Luhmann, 'Opportunismus und Programmatik in der öffentlichen Verwaltung', in his *Politische Planung*, Opladen, 1971, pp. 165ff.

38. See R. Mayntz and F. Scharpf (eds), *Planungsorganisation*, Munich, 1973, chapter 4.

39. The thesis that it is the paradoxical particularity of the West to have its distinctive cultural achievements acquire universal significance is stated in the opening sentences of the 'Einleitung' to M. Weber, *Gesammelte Aufsätze zur Religionssoziologie*, Tübingen, 1920, vol. 1, pp. 1–5.

40. See for instance N. Matteucci, *Il liberalismo in un mondo in transformazione*, Bologna, 1972; and K. O. Hondrich, *Theorie der Herrschaft*, Frankfurt, 1975.

41. For a vigorous contemporary restatement of the political inadequacies of the socialist, and particularly the Marxist, traditions, see N. Bobbio, *Quale socialismo?*, Turin, 1976. On the troubled relations between the socialist and the democratic traditions, see A. Rosenberg, *Demokratie und Sozialismus*, Frankfurt, 1964.

42. R. M. Unger's *Knowledge and Politics*, New York, 1975, is distinguished among other things by the combination of learning, lucidity and passion with which it criticizes the liberal tradition and seeks to project a radically new understanding of the present political predicament of the West that will also transcend some of the assumptions and limitations of democratic theory.

Section III
Change, History and Society

Section III deals with two issues of continuing importance
for sociological thought – those of comparison and historical
development – and each reading has been selected for the light
it throws upon these concerns.

In 'Evolution of the family' (Reading 13), Jack Goody
questions the widespread assumption that there is a general
development in human societies from patterns of extended
kinship to conjugal family units, a movement often associated
with other wider trends – from kinship to territoriality, status
to contract, mechanical to organic solidarity, *Gemeinschaft*
to *Gesellschaft*, and ascription to achievement. Through a
careful comparative analysis of the relationship between the
family and the 'domestic group' in a large number of societies,
Goody demonstrates that the issues raised are more
complicated than had been previously thought. As such, his
discussion provides an excellent example of the way in which
careful sociological analysis corrects previous assumptions
and provides a more sophisticated basis on which further
investigations can build.

André Gorz similarly challenges common assumptions
about the ameliorative effects of the development of
technology in 'Technical intelligence and the capitalist division
of labour' (Reading 14). Technological growth, he suggests, is
commonly seen by both left- and right-wing observers as
reducing the necessity for physically arduous but mentally
undemanding work, and as increasing the possibilities of
liberation in work and leisure. Where such innovation has
taken place under conditions of Western capitalist exploitation,
however, Gorz claims that these improvements have not been
forthcoming. Production is still primarily geared to profit and
the labour of the worker remains alienated, though now
subject also to an increasingly complex technical 'logic' and

353

hierarchy, from which it is more difficult to escape.

Herbert Gans's modern classic 'Urbanism and suburbanism as ways of life' (Reading 15) takes up another set of widely held but unrealistic beliefs, this time concerning the relationship between patterns of residence, social relationships and the character structure of the individual. Many theorists had argued that a straightforward contrast could be drawn between the town and the country as ways of life, and that each represented a typical system of social relations and patterns of behaviour. Rural life was seen as consisting in primary, face-to-face relations, associated with 'community'. whilst urban life was marked by secondary, segmental and transitory contacts. Personal characteristics were determined by these contrasting locations, and modern society was seen as in transition from a primarily rural to an urban existence, with predictable consequences, often deplored, for the individual and social relationships. It was Gans's achievement, as Goody's and Gorz's, to show that the rich texture of social relationships cannot be forced into such an over-simplified strait-jacket.

Each of the foregoing examines societies in the midst of change, and each argues that the process of change is more complex than is popularly supposed. Paradoxically, however, society, constantly changing, constantly has order imposed upon it. A key aspect of this ordering is the acceptance of the social structure as legitimate by the vast majority of people for most of the time. Where such legitimacy is intact, the structure of society and the outcome of social and political change are unquestioned. When such legitimacy is challenged, however, questions of social order and social change are raised directly, and the structure of society itself is open to negotiation. In 'Theorems of motivation crisis' (Reading 16), Jurgen Habermas, combining perspectives drawn from Marxism, Systems Theory and Phenomenological Sociology, notes that the continued existence of particular social systems depends upon the formation of individuals who will behave in an appropriate fashion. He observes, however, that, since the formation of character structure and patterns of motivation are dependent upon diverse aspects of the wider social structure, they can never be taken for granted.

The body of his analysis is concerned to identify recent changes within Western societies which can be seen to contribute to the interruption of the production of individuals appropriate to them. Society itself, Habermas argues, produces, and in ever greater numbers, those groups which challenge its legitimacy.

Habermas's contribution is unrepentantly theoretical and, as he himself admits, must be tested against empirical reality. In 'Social conflict, legitimacy and democracy' (Reading 17), Seymour Martin Lipset presents us with a different approach and conclusions. Through a detailed comparative historical analysis, Lipset argues for the overriding superiority of the democratic form of polity traditionally associated with Western Europe and the USA. He suggests, however, the fragility of this democracy and identifies the numerous factors, external and internal, to any nation, which constantly threaten it. The preservation of democracy, a value Lipset explicitly espouses, can only be ensured through political action which constantly re-emphasizes its legitimacy. If Habermas's approach is systemic, Lipset provides us with a classical form of voluntaristic analysis.

In 'The student movement: crisis and conflict' (Reading 18), Alain Touraine advances a detailed interpretation of a situation in which the legitimacy of a social structure was questioned. Examining the student movement which, in France in May 1968, precipitated a crisis that nearly brought down a government and transformed a society, he argues the inadequacy of interpretations which see this event as a mere triumph of will and ideas, the assault of one system of thought upon another, and of those which stress structural factors and changes. The student movement must be seen both in terms of the social system, and its parts, which gave it birth, and of the political actions available to it, its allies and opponents over time. Only by integrating these approaches in an analysis truthful to the actual events can we account for the successes and failures of this social movement and begin a coherent theoretical and historical explanation.

13. Evolution of the family

Jack Goody

FAMILY, HOUSEHOLD AND DOMESTIC GROUP

Text books in the social sciences are full of statements about the general trend in human societies from patterns of extended kinship to conjugal families. On a more general level the change has been seen as one connected with the general move from kinship to territoriality, from status to contract, from mechanical to organic solidarity, from *gemeinschaft* to *gesellschaft*, from ascription to achievement. There is no need to lengthen the list of vague polarities.

With the general trend that this list implies few would disagree. But when we come to deal more specifically with the movements in family structure, difficulties arise. The main problem for the evolution of the family is to understand just what is evolving. The English term 'family' is a polysemic word used to describe a conjugal pair and their young ('starting a family'), the members of a household ('one of the family'), a range of bilateral kin ('relatives') or a patronymic group, usually associated with a title ('the Churchill family'). And there are wider semantic usages, extending to the human ('the family of man') and non-human ('the family of sweet peas') species.

Discussions of the evolution of the family and changes in household composition centre upon the emergence of the kind of family (referred to as elementary, nuclear or conjugal) that is supposed to be a concomitant of industrialisation, either as cause or effect. The implication here is that the 'nuclear family' has become more independent in economic, residential and other terms. Given that separate residence appears to be related to such independence, attention has been concentrated upon the mean size of households in order to obtain some

From P. Laslett and R. Wall (eds), *Household and Family in Past Time*, Cambridge: at the University Press, 1972, pp. 103–24.

measure of a change from the dominance of extended networks of 'kin' to smaller 'family' units.

An examination of the figures for England reveals, however, as Laslett points out, that mean household size (MHS) has been relatively constant from the sixteenth century to the beginning of the present century.[1] Does this mean that special conditions obtained in Western Europe which assisted the emergence of industrial (i.e. non-familial) productive systems?

The hypothesis is tempting, especially as interesting suggestions have been made as to the possible relationships between delayed marriage and capital accumulation.[2] Certainly basic changes in kinship systems turn around the processes associated with industrialisation, urbanisation and 'modernisation'. But in my view the household is not a very sensitive indicator of such change. Indeed the whole problem has been clouded by analytic problems which have obscured the relationship of household composition to kinship structure in general, and more specifically to the elementary family.

The discussion concerning 'family' or 'household' size has got somewhat confused, largely because of miscommunication. Reacting against the myth of primitive promiscuity, Malinowski first established the existence of an elementary type of family among the Australian aborigines, and despite having worked among a society that emphasised social matriliny and rejected biological paternity, later insisted on the critical role of the family in social life. Using cross-cultural data, Murdock went on to argue that the elementary (or nuclear) family was universal, even as a residential unit. The theme was taken up by Talcott Parsons. Basing himself upon socialisation studies, cross-cultural research and the results of experiments in small groups, he claimed that the small family provided the most satisfactory framework for the bringing up of children; hence its universality.

Other writers, particularly comparative sociologists, have been critical of these ideas, partly because claims for the nuclear family often neglect theoretically important cases which, while they do not contradict the claim that some kind of small domestic unit is universal, do modify certain structural implications derived from the nuclear family model. More importantly, they have seen the core of the problem to lie not at the level of small family units but in the kind and degree of articulation of such units into larger kin-based structures. To put it another way, the opposition between 'family' and 'kinship' (or small and large family systems) is quite inadequate unless it recognises explicitly that all societies with more inclusive patterns of kinship also have, at the turning centre of their world, smaller domestic groups that are involved in the processes of production, reproduction, consumption and socialisation.

I want to clarify some of the issues involved in discussing 'family change' and to place these in a broad comparative framework. Both clarification and comparison are essential, since the problems that are being discussed, implicitly or explicitly, concern the relationships of family composition to economic and other variables: these can be confirmed by two procedures, by examining the same society over time or by examining different societies at different stages of development. To do this we need a set of analytic constructs. But even the referent of the phrase 'elementary family' is not at all clear. When Malinowski and Murdock claim that the elementary family is universal,[3] the statement can be profitably discussed only when certain parameters are established. If co-residence is a defining characteristic of the 'family' in question, then this contention holds neither for groups like the Nayar and Ashanti nor for Caribbean societies (at least in the behavioural sense – the normative position is less clear). Nevertheless it is clear that in the vast majority of societies, it is possible to isolate a significant unit that approximates to one of the various models of the elementary family.

Put in this way, the proposition is unlikely to arouse much objection. Put in a different way, with implications of extension[4] or of opposition between family and kinship, and many a hackle will be raised. In sum, the situation has been thoroughly confused by the concepts we have failed to develop. [. . .]

It seems more useful to approach the question from another direction. In discussing the way in which the developmental cycle influenced family and household,[5] we used the phrase 'domestic group' in order to circumvent some of the definitional problems and introduce an element of flexibility. This phrase is an overall term for three main kinds of unit, namely, the *dwelling unit*, the *reproductive unit*, the *economic unit*.[6] The economic unit is again a generic term which covers the persons jointly engaged in the process of production and consumption.[7] In agricultural societies (as well as in craft production) these units tend to be closely linked together; in industrial societies they are usually quite distinct.

THE HOUSEHOLD AS A DWELLING GROUP

It is frequently the first of these units, the dwelling group, that we refer to as a family ('living as one of the family'), though more usually we apply the almost equally ambiguous word 'household'.[8] Ambiguous because it carries both the meaning of consumption unit (Mrs Beeton's *Household Management*) as well as of dwelling group. In Western societies these ambiguities may present no great problem, at least if we think of an apartment house as a series of separate 'households'. But in many other societies, the situation is much less clear cut. To bring out the nature of the problem involved, let me refer to the societies from a part of the world with which I am personally familiar. Figures 1 and 2 are diagrams of LoDagaba compounds (houses) from northern Ghana. The dwelling group is a large one, an average of 16·3 in 1960. The production unit is often smaller in size; in the instance shown here there were three such groups, though in the largest of these, where the compound head farmed with the help of his sons, the young men planted certain crops on their own behalf, to sell for cash or to consume themselves. As far as consumption was concerned, the productive units were yet further divided; each wife was allotted her own share of grain out of the common granary and this she used to cook for her husband and her children.

When such a dwelling group divides, as the larger one later did on the death of the compound head, smaller dwelling units emerge, of the kind illustrated in Figure 1. Two brothers (or a man and his growing son) decide to build a house of their own in the vicinity. With them will go the members of their respective units of production. From the standpoint of the reproductive unit, nothing changes except the location. There is little change too for the productive unit since in most cases the migrating group will already have been working on its own, so both production and consumption are distinct by the time the 'household' (the dwelling group) splits up. Only residential unity is broken.

Though residential fission has great significance for the LoDagaba, the reason and the occasion vary among different sub-groups. Where in Birifu (LoWiili) the average compound

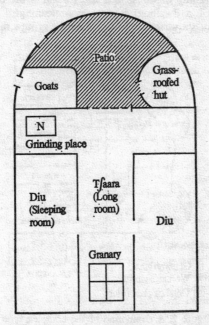

Figure 1. A dwelling of the simplest type, occupied by an elementary family (LoDagaba, northern Ghana)

Diagonal lines indicate unroofed walled area. Broken line indicates line of posts supporting roof.

After Goody, *The Fission of Domestic Groups among the LoDagaba* (1958).

size was 16·3, only a few miles away around Lawra (among the LoSaala) the compounds number about 100 members.[9] Some hundred miles south, in western Gonja, the 'compounds' are as large or even larger. Half a village may be under one roof, each sector being built up (quite literally) of small units very similar to the basic apartment among the LoDagaba. Figure 3 shows one such unit at Seripe. According to the 1960 census Seripe has six 'houses' and a population of 356.

My point here is that for these groups an extensive comparison of family or household size (meaning the number of occupants of a dwelling) is not very meaningful from the standpoint of the structure of the domestic groups that occupy

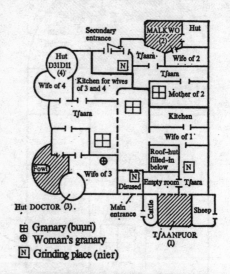

Figure 2. A compound of the complex type
(LoDagaba, northern Ghana)

Diagonal lines indicate unroofed walled area. Broken lines indicate line of posts supporting roof. Thick line indicates boundary of enclosed apartment with separate entrance. Quarters of the four adult married males are given in capitals.

After Goody (1958).

them;[10] 'household size' is relatively unimportant from the domestic standpoint, since the basic reproductive and economic units remain much the same in each case. It is true that the occupants of one of these sections may form a sort of kinship group, as indeed is almost bound to happen in communities

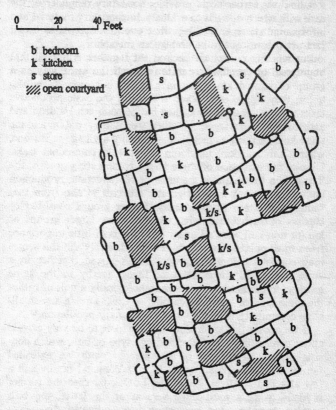

Figure 3. Plan of section of Seripe, Gonja, northern Ghana

After Wakely and Mumtaz, *Bui Resettlement Survey* (1965).

where spatial mobility is low. But there is more to it than this, for each 'compound' (or ward) had a large central granary which supported the elders, and the occupants themselves speak of 'eating together'. In 1965 we lived in the town of Bole for several months and had a room in just such a section. We never saw a communal meal actually taking place. Reading our earlier notes provides a salutary reminder of the care with which one has to evaluate documentary material and informants' statements alike; what one first accepts as literal fact often turns out to be ambiguous metaphor.

But whether or not the section eat together is not all that important. In fact they operate in much the same way as a group of related kin living in adjacent but separate households; they helped each other in some of the basic productive tasks such as clearing land, they buried each other's dead and assisted with marriages; in other words they did much the same kind of thing as neighbours in many a village in Europe, where 'kith and kin' may join together in communal tasks. Despite the existence of these larger co-operating groups, the 'family' (in the shape of the units of reproduction, production and consumption) was not greatly different in size from that found in Western Europe today. Larger groups consisted of clusters of such basic units; whether these larger groups of kin (or non-kin) were all under one roof is of little importance from most points of view. An 'extended family' (in this sense) may consist of domestic groups either linked together in a large compound (household) or living nearby in the same locality; in the latter case it is morphologically a unit of rather the same kind of 'extended family' as exists among any small-scale community with a relatively stationary population.[11]

If we accept this argument, then we have to be very careful about contrasting a so-called zadruga type of unit, which consists of, say, a fortress of 100 persons, with 'an extended family' that comprises a small farm, a conjugal family and a few attached relatives. As in the LoDagaba case the former is likely to be a multicelled version of the latter, the cells coming together for protection, for administrative convenience, or simply because that was the way the house had been built in the first place; permanent stone dwellings structure family composition in much more radical ways than mud huts and bamboo shelters, for the latter constantly change their shape according to the number and nature of those who live there.[12]

THE UNITS OF PRODUCTION,
REPRODUCTION AND CONSUMPTION

Certainly there are basic differences in the range of a man's kin and in their role that are effected by long-term evolutionary changes. But except in rather exceptional cases, the average size of the basic units of reproduction, production and consumption vary within fairly narrow limits from society to society, whatever the economy. One could substantiate this in terms of units of reproduction, by pointing to the fact that in polygynous systems most men have only one wife for most of the time; or that numbers of live births have usually tended to go down as the prospects of survival go up; in any case there is a physiological limit to the number of children a woman can produce. All this keeps the numbers of offspring of a mating pair within certain limits. These limits also apply to consumption groups, which usually centre upon an adult woman. But I want to make the same point with regard to another kind of group, the basic unit of production in agricultural societies, 'the farm family'.

Concentrating upon units of production rather than consumption means taking men rather than women as the focus of one's analysis, a procedure which tends in many cases to produce larger 'households'.[13] While the selection of this focus clearly presents difficulties when we are dealing with industrial societies, in which the units of production and consumption are inevitably distinct, the alternatives seem to me less realistic and less theoretically significant for agricultural communities. It is true that large groups of varying size often assemble to carry out certain major agricultural tasks, such as the clearing of new land, farming for affines, harvesting crops. But the usufructory rights over land and its produce are normally vested in a small group of persons who jointly carry out the day-to-day tasks of supplying and running a household in the economic sense.

Table 1. A comparison of units of agricultural production ('farm families') derived from intensive studies

Continent	People	Productive system	Mean size of 'household'[a]	Units in sample	Acreage per head	Source
Africa: West	LoWiili (1950)	Traditional, savannah	11.1	50	0.9	Goody (1958), p. 65
	LoDagaba (1950)	Traditional, savannah	7.0	50	1.8	Goody (1958), p. 65
	Tallensi (1933)	Traditional, savannah	7.86	81	—	Fortes (1949), p. 64
	Hausa: Zaria (1950)	Savannah	6.7	90	—	M. G. Smith (1955), p. 177
	Katsina (1967)	Savannah (plough)	11.9	30	—	Anthony and Johnston (1968), p. 48a
	Katsina (1967)	Savannah (no plough)	6.4	30	—	
	Yoruba: Abeokuta and Ijebu	Cocoa	6.5	—	—	Galletti, Baldwin and Dina (1956), p. 133
	Ibadan	Cocoa	8.8	—	—	"
	Oyo	Cocoa	9.7	—	—	"
	Ondo	Cocoa	9.8	—	—	"
	Akan: Oda	Cocoa	4.41	—	—	Tetteh (1967), p. 214
	Ibo: Uboma	Traditional, forest	5.97	—	—	Upton (1966), p. 104
	Fulani: Wodaabe	Pastoral	5.1	39	—	Stenning (1959), p. 160
Africa: East	Sukuma	Traditional, savannah	7.11	—	—	Allan (1967)
	Mambwe	Traditional, savannah	5.18	—	—	"
	Lala	Traditional, savannah	4.81	—	—	"
	Lala	Traditional, savannah	4.22	—	—	"
	Lamba	Traditional, savannah	5.52	23	—	"
	Buganda: Kamira (1965) old	—	5.9	83	—	Robertson (1967)
	Budada (1965) new	—	4.45	43	—	Robertson (1967)
	Bunyoro: Buchunga (June 1961)	Savannah, with cash crops	3.75	102	—	Low (1961), app. 2

Region	Location					Source
Asia: China	Yunnan[b] (Spring 1938)	—	5·4	—	—	Fei and Chang (1948), p. 64
	(Autumn 1939)	—	4·9	—	—	Fei and Chang (1948), p. 64
Asia: Tibet	dKang-mdzes village	—				
	Taxpayers		3·40	410	1·00	Carrasco (1959), p. 67–9
	Servants		2·80	38	0·2	,,
	Subjects of monasteries		2·77	44	0·5	,,
	'Side-dwellers'		1·88	56	0·9	,,
Asia: India	North, Rampur[c] (1953)					
	Jat		8·3	78	—	Lewis (1958), pp. 118, 137
	Brahman		7·33	15	—	,,
	Camar		5·1	21	—	,,
	Bhangi		5·2	10	—	,,
	Kumhar		5·57	7	—	,,
	Mysore (1954)					
	Wangala		4·98	192	—	Epstein (1962), pp. 21–4
	Dalena		4·62	153	1·04	Epstein (1962), pp. 196–7
	Uttar Pradesh (1954–7)					
	Meerut and Musaffarnagar		7·6	—	1·4	Indian Agriculture (1967)
	Punjab (1954–7)					
	Amritsar and Ferozepur		8·1	—	2·2	,,
	West Bengal (1954–7)					
	Hooghly and Parganas		6·4	—	0·5	,,
	Madras (1954–7)					
	Coimbatore and Salem		5·4	—	1·4	,,
	Maharashtra (1955–7)					
	Ahmednagar		7·0	—	3·0	,,
	Nasik		6·5	—	2·8	,,
	Akota and Amraoti		5·9	—	3·7	,,
	Andhra Pradesh (1957–60)					
	West Godavari		5·5	—	1·5	,,

Table 1. continued

Continent	People	Productive system	Mean size of 'house-hold'[a]	Units in sample	Acreage per head	Source
	Orissa (1957–60)					
	Sambalpur	—	5·1	—	1·0	,,
	Bihar (1959–60)					
	Monghyr North Zone	—	5·5	—	0·8	,,
	Monghyr Central Zone	—	7·8	—	0·6	,,
	Monghyr South Zone	—	7·1	—	1·5	,,
	Haryana (1961–3)					
	Karnal, Rohtak, Jind	—	8·4	—	0·3	,,
Asia: Ceylon	Pul Eliya[c] (1871)	Padi	3·57	14	—	Leach (1961), p. 332
	Pul Eliya (1954)	Padi	3·74	39	—	Leach (1961), p. 332
Asia: Sarawak	Land Dayak[d] (1950)	Padi	8·00	16	—	Geddes (1954), p. 36
America: W. Indies	Belaire	—	5·6[e]	74	—	Spens (1970), p. 328

[a] Average size of unit of agricultural production.

[b] The figures are qualified by the remark, 'excluding the single adults'. I am not sure whether these figures apply to the whole community, including the landless labourers.

[c] I have assumed that the figures for families are also those for farm families.

[d] The Land Dayak figures are all from one longhouse; the ethnography suggests that there may well be some selection of longhouse occupants in favour of larger families.

[e] This figure refers to occupants of houses; excluding solitary persons, it rises to 6·1. Some individuals in large households have separate holdings and some households are divided economically; hence the number for the unit of production could be somewhat lower.

How large is this 'farm family'? Figures are not easy to come by; the most reliable data are generally given in reports of small intensive surveys, and even here essential information on the size and organisation of the basic unit of production is often lacking. The figures that I have managed to collect together are given in Table 1. These figures on farm families, work units or garden families, as they are variously called, display only limited differences in widely separated parts of the world. The range of average size is roughly the same in Africa and Eurasia. In Asia, the Jat of North India have farm units of 8·3 strong;[14] in another Indian area, Haryana, the figure is 8·4; the numbers for the Land Dyak of Sarawak, who are padi cultivators, are roughly the same.[15] In Africa, the figure for the Tallensi of northern Ghana is 7·86; and that for the LoWiili 11·1.[16] If we turn to the other end of the scale, we find the lower castes in the Jat village of Rampur having a household strength of 5·3, nearly the same as Fei and Chang give for a village in the Yunnan province of China in spring 1938 (5·4);[17] in Ceylon, the productive unit in Pul Eliya numbers 3·74;[18] in Tibet the units are smaller still. These lower figures are again very close to the size of the farm family in a number of East African peoples, where the lowest figure (3·75) occurs among the Bunyoro.[19]

The same thing is true if we look at the figures marshalled by demographers and discussed by Burch (1967). The most recent statistical information issued by the United Nations (1967) shows relatively little differences in 'household' size, that is, in the size of units of consumption (Table 2). In India the MHS is 5·2; in Africa the figures range from 3·5 to 5·2; only in rural South America do we reach numbers of six persons in a household. These small figures are recorded despite the widespread tendency to identify dwelling with units of production and consumption. While demographic factors are directly relevant to the size of the units of reproduction, they are clearly not the only ones tending to keep other domestic units so restricted in size; we have to introduce further variables such as the system of marriage, adoption, production and inheritance; a 'stem family' is in effect defined by the mode of transmission. It is in spite of, not because of, variations in fertility and mortality that such groups remain

Table 2. *Mean household size from census material*[a]

Country and year T Total U Urban R Rural			Mean size of household[b]	No. of households
Africa				
Congo (Brazzaville) 1958	U		4·0	13,428
Ethiopia	1961	U	3·5	123,755
Mauritius	1962	T	4·9	138,368
		U	5·2	46,227
		R	4·8	92,141
Morocco	1960	T	4·8	2,409,750
		U	4·3	787,450
		R	5·1	1,622,300
St Helena 1956		T	4·7	998
Tanzania	1958	R	3·9	20,349
United Arab Republic 1960	U		4·8	1,992,491
Elsewhere				
Canada	1961	T	3·9	4,554,493
		U	3·7	3,280,468
		R	4·2	1,274,025
Dominica 1960		T	4·2	14,218
Jamaica	1960	T	4·0	401,743
		U	2·7	142,298
		R	4·8	259,445
India	1960	T	5·2	83,523,895
		U	5·2	—
		R	5·2	—
Israel	1963	T	3·8	594,800
		U	3·9	—
		R	3·4	—
U.K.	1961	T	3·0	14,640,897
		U	3·0	—
		R	3·1	—

[a] Selected from United Nations Statistical Office, Department of Economic and Social Affairs, *Statistical Year Book* (1967).

[b] The highest figures in Asia are Kuwait (1961), 6·1 ($n = 52{,}851$); in Europe, San Marino (1965), rural, 4·8 ($n = 678$); in South America, rural figures reach 6·0.

relatively limited in size.[20] The reasons why they do so, interesting as they are, cannot be enlarged upon here.

The figures from intensive studies are more reliable and less averaging than the aggregate figures for nations that are differentiated by strata, ethnicity and by region. In Ghana, for example, there can be only a limited value in averaging material on northern (patrilineal) and southern (matrilineal) peoples, especially since, in the matrilineal groups, members of the reproductive unit, the productive unit and even the unit of consumption often live in separate dwellings.[21] Another factor to be reckoned with in interpreting these figures is the difficulty of defining a 'household' in such societies. While large compounds form a household in the residential sense, they break up into smaller units for the major socio-economic tasks of reproduction, production and consumption. But even the polygynous family divides into its constituent elements for reproduction and consumption; for some purposes this element consists of the core mother–child unit. In many parts of Ghana it is a common sight to see a young girl taking an evening meal from the compound where her mother lives to her father's house; later that night the meal may be followed by the cook. Which is the household? Any polygynous society will present yet further problems if the criterion is 'one hearth', 'one cooking group'. In order to avoid these difficulties I shall concentrate upon the figures presented in Table 2. Here we see that the continental distribution shows no great difference in the *range* of average size. Difference in continent also means a difference in agricultural economy. Many African societies still practise shifting agriculture with the hoe; many Asian societies farm more intensively, using more advanced techniques (irrigation and the plough) and more productive crops (e.g. rice); while in Western Europe, the economic situation was yet more developed even before the onset of the industrial and agricultural changes of the eighteenth century. Yet this long-term, evolutionary type of change in the economy has no direct counterpart in unidirectional changes in the size of the farm family, that is in the unit of production and consumption. Indeed, from the standpoint of size, we find smaller average households in agricultural societies in Africa and in Asia than we do in England. Laslett notes that 'mean

371

household size remained fairly constant at 4·75 or a little under, from the earliest point for which we have found figures [sixteenth century] until as late as 1901. There is no sign of the large extended coresidential family group of the traditional peasant world giving way to the small, nuclear, conjugal household of modern industrial society.'[22] The same words could be used about household size in most parts of the traditional peasant world of Asia and Africa, if we are referring to the size of the basic units of production. This similarity exists despite the effects of (i) polygyny, (ii) what Hajnal calls the 'European marriage pattern', with its late marriage age and its high proportion of people who never marry at all, (iii) the possibly associated differences in birth and death rates.[23]

But while the overall *range* of the mean size of the farm family is roughly the same, the tentative figures we have assembled do display some differences. The farm family in Africa tends to be slightly larger than in Asia; and that in West Africa larger than in East. Such differences in size can clearly be related to differences in the generation structure, or in the number of children, of adult women (wives or sisters), of adult men (husbands or brothers), of attached personnel, i.e. those in servile statuses (slave, servant, client) or of more distant kin. The demographic factors making for an increase or decrease in the number of children cannot be considered here; obviously the greater expectancy of life that characterises 'advanced societies' makes for a potential increase in the size of the farm family, while the commitment to monogamy makes for a decrease. Setting on one side these very important factors, I want to concentrate upon adult males and their relationship to the productive processes.

One major factor determining the size of farm families is the point in the developmental cycle of domestic groups where a split occurs in the units of production and consumption. In his discussion of the Tallensi material, Fortes notes that 'economic needs and structural cleavages are chiefly responsible for fission in the joint family . . .'[24] In an agricultural society the economic factors have mainly to do with rights in the means of production, namely land, and especially in plough farming and livestock. When the land is split, the group that farms it inevitably divides; and the opposite process also occurs. The land is likely to split, to be reallocated, at the death of the holder, where more than one member of the inheriting group survives. Alternatively, where members of the sibling group continue to farm together after their father's death (and in polygynous societies this is especially likely to occur with full brothers), then the farm unit will be correspondingly larger. Such a practice accounts for the relatively large size of the farming group among the LoWiili of northern Ghana (11·1); earlier fission of the group accounts for the smaller size of the farming unit among the LoDagaba and the Tallensi of the same region.[25] In a previous publication I have tried to relate this difference between the LoWiili and the LoDagaba to differences in the system of inheritance. Among the LoWiili 83 per cent of men farmed with another adult kinsman; in two-thirds of the cases this male was a brother. Among the LoDagaba the proportion was less. The 'unit of production' consisted of 11·1 members among the LoWiili and 7·0 among the LoDagaba; in the former case the average farm was 0·9 acres per person, in the latter 1·8. Neither of these differences had any direct bearing on the size of the compound, that is of the household in the sense of houseful.[26]

Hence while the basic work groups generally remain small, their size varies with the timing of family fission. The rhythm of the domestic cycle differs from society to society. In some cases sons set up their own economic and residential units before the father dies; in others they separate at his death, and in others they continue to farm together until their own children reach adulthood. The structure of the farm family thus depends on a variety of factors, such as the nature of inheritance, the type of economy (mixed economies may require more hands), etc. But the important point to notice is that, excluding servants, the variations in size all fall within the group of close siblings or affines, so that the range is not great. Looking at the problem of 'family evolution' in terms of the three types of unit mentioned above, we can conclude that the domestic 'family' never was extended to any degree; so that the changes in size wrought by the industrial revolution, urbanisation, modernisation, etc., though significant, are small. The extended family did not break up with the industrial revolution; it was already segmented for most social purposes, including the basic ones of reproduction, production and consumption. On the average households and housefuls became somewhat smaller.

I have concentrated here on the comparison of the size rather than of the composition of critical domestic groups and in doing so have perhaps placed too great an emphasis on the similarity in the structure of industrial and pre-industrial societies in order to dispose of the myth of the extended 'family' as some sort of undifferentiated commune. The main changes that have occurred do not centre upon the emergence of the 'elementary family' out of 'extended kin groups', for small domestic groups are virtually universal. They concern the disappearance of many functions of the wider ties of kinship, especially those centring on kin groups such as clans, lineages and kindreds. The ties may continue (as in the case of a Scottish clan) but the functions radically alter with the proliferation of other institutional structures that take over many of their jobs. It is the process whereby kinship relations shrink, largely but not entirely, to the compass of a man's family of birth and family of marriage, a change which has been so well discussed in Goode's comparative study.[27] Changes of this kind cannot be derived from the study of the household alone, since they have to do with the relationships between members of separate households, and especially adjacent ones. Specific steps have to be taken to obtain the information required to document changes in the morphology or function of such a network and it is rarely possible to do this from the usual type of census based upon domestic groups. While numerical statements about these changes can be made, the problem of doing so is far from easy.

If one employs 'family' for domestic units of this kind and uses 'kin' (or 'relatives') to describe wider ties, then it is clear that the term 'extended family' is almost invariably misleading unless one is thinking of a certain frequency of say, three-generational or fraternal households in the total population.

The variations in size among domestic groups are inevitably small, but the fact that they are so should not obscure the importance of 'extended family' ties in another sense, especially when these more distant kin form the basis of local groupings. In this respect there is certainly a major difference between more and less industrialised societies, though at what point the change occurs is difficult to ascertain; the kind of information to answer this question cannot be derived from census data as presently collected. To put it another way, the fact that the 'family' or 'household' is always small does not say anything about the importance attached to kinship ties in a more general sense. Indeed, even the kind of 'stem family' sometimes found among Scandinavian farmers or among Irish countrymen, where the parents have retired to a special house on the farm, might well get classified as distinct 'households' if the main focus of attention was separate hearths, or even separate houses. But such households are maintained out of the same productive estate and hence constitute one 'farm family'. It is a realisation of this fact that makes many anthropologists suspicious of the distinction between 'family' and 'kinship' and hence of conclusions that turn on this distinction.[28] [. . .]

There is, however, one aspect of the figures given in Table 1 I have not touched upon. While the range in the size of the farm family is roughly comparable in Africa and Asia, there is a trend towards larger units in Africa, particularly in the West. This difference seems to reflect long-term changes. When we compare the systems of inheritance and succession in these two major continental areas of the Old World, we find that Eurasia is characterised by lineal modes of transmitting relatively exclusive rights while Africa is much more mixed. Certain areas of East and southern Africa are marked by a lineal form of inheritance whereby property is divided among a man's children according to their maternal origin. The system, where each matri-segment gets an equal (*per stirpes*) share, has been called by Gluckman 'the house-property complex'.[29] But in West Africa, where the units of production are larger, lateral inheritance prevails (especially in matrilineal systems).[30] When brothers stand in expectation of inheriting

375

goods or movables from one another, it seems reasonable to suggest that they will farm together for a longer period than when their property goes direct to their sons. In other words, the lineal inheritance of productive resources means, all else being equal, the earlier fission of the unit of production, since brothers are unlikely to farm together unless they also inherit from each other. From this standpoint, primogeniture is simply an aggravated form of lineal transmission.[31]

In Eurasia the transmission of property to offspring is also marked by a feature which is rarely if ever found in non-Muslim Africa, namely the passing down of male property to both sons and daughters, either by the dowry or *causa mortis*. I have argued elsewhere that 'downward' or lineal transmission is a means of preserving socio-economic differences and is related to advanced agriculture, where status depends to a greater extent upon the holding of land and property. In African societies, on the other hand, agriculture is generally shifting, extensive, and rights to land can be acquired through membership of a kin group as well as by inheritance from close kin. The system, in other words, is more corporate and less particularistic than in Eurasia; inheritance is therefore more likely to be lateral. The Eurasian system is one in which, since women are bearers of (male) property, marriage involves the conjunction of two property holders and the establishment of some kind of conjugal fund, which again tends to differentiate brother from brother. The effect of these differences on the structure of the unit of production (especially important when women control land) is to lead to earlier fission between parents and children as well as between members of the sibling group.

The figures in Table 1 raise a further question. Why is there a greater tendency to lineal inheritance and smaller productive units in East Africa? The answer is far from clear but it is possibly related to the greater importance of cattle and other livestock on that side of the continent. Cattle create a possible focus for differentiation and hence may tend to a pressure on downwards transmission, on providing for one's lineal descendants before one's collaterals. Where parcels of property are of roughly equal value, the direction in which they move is of little importance. Their distribution becomes of critical importance where the parcels are of different value.

There is a final problem which arises from differences within rather than between societies. In looking at the size of units of production, it is clear that the richer (or more progressive) farmers live and work in larger groups than the average for that community. The difference emerges in all the African studies done by the Stanford group (Table 3) and it is equally the case in India and Tibet that the economically higher castes have larger 'farm families' than the lower ones. At first sight this fact might appear to contradict the hypothesis that the more advanced the agricultural or industrial economy, the smaller the mean size of households (within small limits and an unsteady trend). However, in differentiated societies larger households (consisting of kin plus non-kin) generally occur among the richer individuals, whether peasants or nobility.[32] Even where the dwelling and reproductive units are actually smaller, the network of relationships between kin may be stronger. As Goode notes, 'even in the modern Western world, upper-strata families maintain a far larger extension of kin and far greater control over their own young than do lower-strata families'.[33] In Northern Nigeria plough farmers have larger 'farm families' than hoe farmers.

CONCLUSION

A consideration of the problems arising out of the comparative analysis of the 'family' and 'household' suggests that, especially in pre-industrial societies, particular importance should be given to the study of the unit of production, the farm family. Figures on the size of this group in some African and Asian societies (see Table 1) show that although the range of variation is relatively small, there were some important differences.

First, unless factors of house construction interfere (e.g. where a shortage of housing forces young couples to live with in-laws, against the trend of current norms and individual preference), there is inevitably an internal variation in the *size of individual households* in both senses of the word, dwelling groups and units of consumption. Demographic factors apart, a major factor in the variation is the stage in

Table 3. *Mean size of farming unit, comparing 'progressive' farmers and their neighbours*[a]

People	Mean size of unit			N	Average acreage			Source
	Progressive farmers[b]	Neighbours[b]	Subsample[b]		Progressive farmers	Neighbours	Subsample	
Gusii (Kenya)	10·0 (2·6)	9·1 (2·6)	9·1 (2·6)	120	11·9	7·0	8·2	Field Survey, 2; 58a, 59b
Teso (Uganda)	10·8 (5·5)	8·3 (3·8)	8·9 (4·2)	60	34·3	12·7	18·1	Field Survey, 3; 63a, 64b
Geita district (Tanzania)	—	—	7·06 (2·9)	60	—	—	20·5	Field Survey, 4; 52a, 53a
Mazabuka district (Tonga, Zambia)	16·3 (4·9)	8·0 (3·0)	n.d.	60	56	21	n.d.	Field Survey, 5; 55a, 57a
Northern Katsina (Nigeria)	Plough 11·9 (6·7)	No plough 6·4 (4·1)	—	60	Plough 20·2	No plough 6·7	—	Field survey, 6; 48a, 48b
Bawku (Ghana)	—	—	9·4 (5·2)	60	—	—	10·7	Field survey, 7; 43a, 45a
Akim Abuakwa (Ghana)	—	—	8·5 (3·2)	60	—	—	Cocoa groves: acreage 45·2	Field survey, 8; 51a, 52a

[a] Based on Stanford Food Research Institute, Field study of agricultural research, *Reports*.

[b] The number of adults per farming group is given in parentheses.

Note: 'Progressive farmers' were those farmers considered to be so by the local departments of agriculture.

the developmental cycle of domestic groups; most societies will have nuclear, extended (lineally) and expanded (laterally) families in different proportions; the terms characterise domestic groups, which rarely have one unchanging form.

Secondly, variation in the *mean size of household* often exists among the sub-groups of a 'society', defined either by territory (e.g. the Yoruba) or by status (e.g. Rampur, North India).[84] In stratified societies the upper status groups tend to have larger domestic units (as well as more land and capital).

Thirdly, there is much variation between societies, even when we hold continent and economy constant; these variations depend upon factors such as mating pattern, phasing of family dispersal, system of inheritance, type of economy and nature of migration.[85]

Fourthly, there appears to be a trend towards larger productive units in certain parts of Africa, which is related to the greater stress on lateral modes of inheritance and ultimately to the simpler system of agricultural production.

I have tried to establish that it is not only for England that we need to abandon the myth of the 'extended family' – as the term is often understood. In one form or another this myth has haunted historical and comparative studies since the time of Maine and Fustel de Coulanges, whether the work has been undertaken by historians, sociologists or anthropologists. Whatever the shape of the kin groups of earlier societies, none were undifferentiated communes of the kind beloved by nineteenth-century theorists, Marxist and non-Marxist alike. Units of production were everywhere relatively small, kin-based units; differences in size and context are important in the comparative study of the family, but they should never obscure the basic similarities in the way that domestic groups are organized throughout the whole range of human societies.[86]

Notes

1. P. Laslett and R. Wall, *Household and Family in Past Time*, Cambridge: Cambridge University Press, 1972, pp. 137–9.
2. Hajnal, *European Marriage Patterns in Perspective* (1965).
3. Malinowski, *Kinship* (1930), p. 23; Murdock, *Social Structure* (1949), p. 3.
4. Malinowski (1930).
5. Fortes, 'Introduction', in Goody, *The Developmental Cycle in Domestic Groups* (1958).
6. For an attempt to clarify the words used in the analysis of domestic groups, see Castillo *et al.*, *The Concept of the Nuclear and Extended Family* (1968).
7. In certain contexts each of these units has to be broken down a stage further for analytic purposes (e.g. into units of socialisation), but this necessary task cannot be undertaken here.
8. A failure to distinguish between the household as a dwelling group and unit of consumption and the family as a reproductive unit has been the subject of a considerable discussion of the West Indian domestic institutions. See especially Raymond T. Smith, *The Negro Family in British Guiana* (1956); M. G. Smith, *West Indian Family Structure* (1962); Adams, *An Inquiry into the Nature of the Family* (1960); Mintz and Davenport (eds), *Working Papers in Caribbean Social Organisation* (1961); Goode, *Illegitimacy, Anomie and Cultural Penetration* (1961); Raymond T. Smith, *Culture and Social Structure in the Caribbean* (1963); Otterbein, *Caribbean Family Organisation* (1965); Goode, *Note on Problems in Theory and Method* (1966); Bender, *A Refinement of the Concept of Household* (1967). Much of this discussion is anticipated in Fortes's analysis of domestic groups among the Tallensi and the Ashanti of Ghana; in the former the units of consumption and reproduction are contained within larger dwelling units; among the latter, the reproductive and economic units are usually distinct from the dwelling group at any one time; the latter is more often based upon the sibling rather than the conjugal bond. See Fortes, *Web of Kinship among the Tallensi* (1949) and *Kinship and Marriage among the Ashanti* (1950). Adams's separation of the 'elementary family' into dyadic relationships is useful for a range of analytic problems.
9. Bohannan, *Tiv Farm and Settlement* (1954), p. 4, records a

similar variation in compound size among the Tiv of Northern Nigeria; in the south the largest contained 80 persons, while the average was 17.

10. There are differences, but these are not associated with the variables we are considering.

11. The dangers of concentrating an analysis of kinship and the family upon the household have been discussed by Solien, *Household and Family in the Caribbean* (1960). See also Raymond T. Smith (1963), p. 33. 'The concentration of attention upon the household as a functioning unit of child-care and economic organisation has tended to divert attention from the networks of relationship linking households to each other.'

12. In studying the household comparatively, it is worth reminding ourselves that the sheltering functions of a dwelling are of considerably less importance in tropical regions than they are in cooler climates. Shelter is not a basic problem in the tropical or semi-tropical environment, partly because of climate and partly because the land and materials for the construction of a dwelling are more freely available. This fact has implications not only for the comparative study of family structure but also for the planning of development. In Africa, recently, architects and engineers of the European tradition have been responsible for spending millions of pounds of public money in the construction of standardised permanent dwellings in rural areas affected by dams and similar schemes, using large quantities of imported goods. Given the availability of land and materials, there would have been an enormous saving had individuals been encouraged to build improved dwellings of the traditional type, which would have given greater flexibility in accommodating population movements as well as the usual growth and decline of domestic groups. The standardisation of units has led to an overall lowering of standards of living in larger polygynous households. In the resettlement areas along the Volta lake in Ghana I have come across a man's wives having to share the same sleeping quarters in a manner unheard of in traditional society. Almost everywhere in West Africa the process of urbanisation involves living under more crowded and insanitary conditions than obtain in the country, even though water may come from a tap and light from an electric lamp.

13. For an estimate of mean household size based on the male population, see Hammel in *Household and Family in Past Time*, *op. cit.*, pp. 361–2.

14. Lewis, *Village Life in Northern India* (1958).

15. 8.00. Geddes, *The Land Dyaks of Sarawak* (1954).

16. This is the highest figure I have for traditional agriculture,

though the farming unit of the Tiv (northern Nigeria) appears to be much larger. Bohannan (1954) treats the compound as the labour unit for certain purposes; the average size is much like that of the LoDagaba, namely, 17. But he goes on to say that, 'a large compound breaks up into smaller groups in performing many agricultural tasks ... full siblings tend to work together ... When full brothers become older, with adult sons of their own, they are likely to farm separately.' See Bohannan (1954), pp. 23–5. Since this developmental process is very much like that of the LoWiili, the unit of production will presumably be roughly the same.

17. Fei and Chang, *Earthbound China* (1948).

18. Or 4·56 if we work on the basis of 32 'families'; the boundaries vary. Leach, *Pul Eliya* (1961).

19. Low, *Mutala Survey of Buchanga* (1961).

20. Burch, see *Household and Family in Past Time, op. cit.*, pp. 97–100, takes a different view.

21. Fortes (1949); (1950).

22. See Laslett in *Household and Family in Past Time, op. cit.*, p. 126.

23. Hajnal (1965), p. 131.

24. I should finish the rest of the quotation which is at least equally relevant: 'and religious and jural sanctions for the re-integration of an expanded family'. Fortes (1949), 77. Many formal models of the family processes direct their attention almost exclusively to the dominant process of fission, forgetting the subordinate process of fusion.

25. Fortes (1949); Goody (1958).

26. Compare Laslett in *Household and Family in Past Time, op. cit.*, pp. 34–9.

27. Goode, *World Revolution and Family Patterns* (1963).

28. E.g. Fallers, *The Range of Variation in Family Size* (1965); Schneider, *Kinship and Biology* (1965).

29. Gluckman, *Kinship and Marriage among the Lozi and Zulu* (1950).

30. I have discussed this point in more detail in *Sideways or Downwards* (1970) and in *Inheritance and Women's Labour in Africa* (1972).

31. Gavelkind was equally lineal, but more sons participated.

32. In particular see the studies of pre-industrial England: Laslett in *Household and Family in Past Time, op. cit.*, pp. 153–4; Anderson's analysis of rural Lancashire in 1851, *ibid.*, pp. 220–1; and the study by Klapisch of fifteenth-century Tuscany, *ibid.*, pp. 275–7. Even in twentieth-century America kin are more prevalent in the wealthier households, see Pryor, *ibid.*, pp. 577–8.

33. Goode (1963), p. 372.

34. On the absence of 'joint families' among Untouchables, see Epstein, *Economic Development and Social Change in South India* (1962), p. 176.

35. Though we often think of urban migration mainly in terms of men (hence the suggested link with the increased proportion of female-headed household), the movement of women is more pronounced than that of men under certain conditions. By and large this is true of Europe in the past as well as the present; in Zurich between the fourteenth and seventeenth centuries, the proportion of women, especially of single women, was high (i.e. 2974 to 2185 in 1637), Hajnal (1965), p. 117.

36. See in particular Hammel's study of the evolution of the Zadruga, *op. cit.*, pp. 335–40, 370–3.

14. Technical intelligence and the capitalist division of labor

André Gorz

I

Up to recent years, it was traditionally assumed by most Marxists that the development of productive forces was something intrinsic and intrinsically positive. Most Marxists held the view that capitalism, as it matured, was producing a material base which could be taken over by a socialist society and upon which socialism could be built. It was widely held that *the higher* the development of productive forces, *the easier* the building of socialism would be. Such productive forces as technology, science, human skills and knowledge, and abundant dead labor were considered assets that would greatly facilitate the transition to socialism.

These views were based somewhat mechanically upon the Marxian thesis regarding the deepening contradiction between productive forces on the one hand and social relations of production on the other hand. Most orthodox communist parties clung to the view that capitalist relations of production were stifling the development of productive forces and that socialism, by tearing down the so-called superstructure of the capitalist state and of capitalist social relations, could set free at one blow a tremendous potential for socio-economic development and growth.

This view still pervades the political attitude of the Western European communist parties. They usually consider all available productive capacity, all available manual, technical, professional and intellectual skills as forces that will be valuable and useful during the transition period: socialism, so the story goes, will be capable of putting them to *good* social uses and of rewarding their labor, whereas capitalism either misuses

From *Telos*, 12 (1972), pp. 27–35.

them or puts them to no use at all.

I shall try to illustrate that these simplistic views no longer hold true. We can no longer assume that it is the productive forces which shape the relations of production. Nor can we any longer assume that the autonomy of productive forces is sufficient for them to enter *spontaneously* into contradiction with the capitalist relations of production. On the contrary, developments during the last two decades rather lead to the conclusion that the productive forces *are shaped* by the capitalist relations of production and that the imprint of the latter upon the first is so deep that any attempt to change the relations of production will be doomed unless a radical change is made in the very nature of the productive forces, and not only in the way in which and in the purpose for which they are used.

This aspect is by no means irrelevant to the topic of 'technical intelligence' dealt with here. It is, on the contrary, a central aspect. In my view, we shall not succeed in locating technical and scientific labor within the class structure of advanced capitalist society unless we start by analyzing *what functions* technical and scientific labor perform in the process of capital accumulation and in the process of reproducing capitalist social relations. The question as to whether technicians, engineers, research workers and the like belong to the middle class or to the working class must be made to depend upon the following questions: 1. (a) Is their function required by the process of material production *as such*, or (b) by capital's concern for ruling and for controlling the productive process and the work process from above? 2. (a) Is their function required by the concern for the greatest possible efficiency in production technology, or (b) does the concern for efficient production technology come second only to the concern for 'social technology', i.e. for keeping the labor force disciplined, hierarchically regimented and divided? 3. (a) Is the present definition of technical skill and knowledge primarily required by the technical division of labor and thereby based upon scientific and ideologically neutral data, or (b) is the definition of technical skill and knowledge primarily social and ideological, as an outgrowth of the social division of labor?

Let us try to examine these questions. And to begin with,

let us focus attention on the supposedly most creative and most sought after area of employment by asking ourselves: what is the economic purpose of the quickening pace of technological innovation which, in turn, calls for an increasing proportion of technical and scientific labor in the fields of research and development?

We may consider that up to the early 1930s the main purpose of technological innovation was to reduce production costs. Innovation aimed at saving labor, at substituting dead labor for living labor, at producing the same volume of goods with a decreasing quantity of social labor. This priority of labor-saving innovation was an intrinsic and classical consequence of competitive capitalism. As a result, most innovation was concentrated in the capital goods sector.

But this type of innovation, while keeping a decisive importance, has been overshadowed from the early fifties onwards by innovation in the consumer goods sector. The reason for this shift is quite clear: sooner or later, increasing productivity will meet an external limit, which is the limit of the market. If the market demand becomes saturated for a given mix of consumer goods, the wider reproduction of capital tends to grind to a halt and the rate of profit to fall. If innovation were to remain concentrated mainly on capital goods, the outlets for consumer goods production could be made to grow only by lowering prices. But falling prices would slow down the cycle of capital reproduction and rob monopolies of new and profitable opportunities for capital investment.

The main problem for monopolies in a virtually saturated market is therefore no longer to expand their production capacities and to increase productivity; their main problem is to prevent the saturation of the market and to engineer an on-going or, if possible, an expanding demand for the very type of commodities which they can manufacture at maximum profit. There is only one way to reach this result: constant innovation in the field of consumer goods, whereby commodities for which the market is near the saturation point are constantly made obsolete and replaced by new, different, more sophisticated products serving the same use. The main function of research is therefore to accelerate the obsolescence and replacement of commodities, i.e. of consumer as well as capital goods, so as to accelerate the cycle of reproduction of capital and to create profitable investment opportunities for a growing mass of profits. In one word: *the main purpose of research and innovation is to create new opportunities for profitable capital investment.*

As a consequence, monopolist growth and the growth of the GNP no longer aim at or result in improved living conditions for the masses. In North America and tendentially in Western Europe, growth no longer rests on increasing physical quantities of available goods, but, to an ever larger extent, on substitution of simpler goods by more elaborate and costly goods whose use value is no greater – it may well be smaller.

This type of growth is obviously incapable of eliminating poverty and of securing the satisfaction of social and cultural needs; it rather produces new types of poverty due to environmental and urban degradation and to increasingly acute shortages in the fields of health, hygiene and sanitation, to overcrowding, etc.

The point I am driving at is that the type of productive forms which we have at hand, and more specifically the type of technical and scientific knowledge, competence, and personnel, *is to a large extent functional only to the particular orientation and priorities of monopolist growth.* To a large extent, *this type* of technical and scientific personnel would be of little use in a society bent on meeting the more basic social and cultural needs of the masses. They would be of little use because their type of knowledge is hardly relevant to what would be needed to improve the quality of life and to help the masses to take their destiny in their own hands. E.g. technical and scientific workers, though they may know a lot about the technicalities of their specialized fields, know very little nowadays about the ways to make the work process more pleasant and self-fulfilling for the workers; they know very little about what is called 'ergonomy' – the science of saving effort and avoiding fatigue – and they are not prepared to help workers into self-organizing the work process and into adjusting production technology to their physical and psychic needs. (Moreover, they are not generally capable of conveying their specialized knowledge to workers holding less or different training and of sharing it with them.) In other words, technical and scientific knowledge is not only to a large extent disconnected from the needs and the life of the masses; it is also culturally and semantically disconnected from general comprehensive culture and common language. Each field of technology and science is a typical sub-culture, narrowly specialized in its relevance, generally esoteric in its language and thereby divorced from any comprehensive cultural concept. It is quite striking that though a large majority of intellectual workers are engaged in technical and scientific work, we do not have *one* scientific and technical culture, but a great number of fragmentary sub-cultures, each of which is bent on devising technical solutions to technical problems, and none of which is qualified to put its specialized concern into a broader perspective and to consider its general human, social and civilizational consequences. Hence this paradox that the main intellectual activity of advanced industrial societies should remain sterile as regards the development of comprehensive popular culture. The professionals of science and technology, and more specifically of research and development, must be seen as a kind of new mandarins whose professional pride and involvement in the particular fields of their activity is of little relevance to the welfare and the needs of the community and of humanity generally: most of their work is being done on problems that are neither the most vital nor the most interesting as regards the well-being and happiness of the people. Whether in architecture, medicine, biology, or physics, chemistry, technology, etc., you can't make a successful career unless you put the interest of capital (of the company or corporation or the State) before the interest of the people and are not too concerned about the purposes which the 'advancement of Science and Technology' is to serve. The so-called concern about Science and Technology *per se* – the belief that they are value free and politically neutral, and that their 'advancement' is a good and desirable thing because knowledge *can* always be put to good uses, even if it is not, presumably – is nothing but an *ideology* of self-justification which tries to hide the subservience of science and technology – in their priorities, their language, and their utilization – to the demands of capitalist institutions and domination. This fact, of course, should not surprise us:

technical and scientific culture remains fragmented and divorced from the life and the overall culture of the people because the object to which it relates, that is, the means and processes of production, is itself alienated from the people. In a society where the means and processes of production are estranged from the people and erected to the status of *die Sache selbst*, in such a society it is not astonishing that the knowledge about the means and processes of production should be an estranged knowledge, a knowledge as reified (*versachlidet*) as its object itself, a knowledge that forbids, through its narrow concern for a particular aspect of *die Sache*, a comprehensive understanding of what everything is about (*warum es im Gesamten geht*).

Technical and scientific culture and competence thus clearly bear the mark of a social division of labor which denies to all workers, including the intellectual ones, the insight into the system's functioning and overall purposes, so as to keep decision-making divorced from productive work, conception divorced from execution, and responsibility for producing knowledge divorced from responsibility for the uses knowledge will be put to.

But however estranged technical and scientific workers may be from the process of production, and however significant their role in producing surplus value or, at least, the conditions and opportunities for profitable investment, this stratum of workers *cannot* be immediately assimilated to the working class, that is, to the class of productive workers. Before making such an assimilation – and before speaking à propos the technical worker of a 'new working class' – we have to distinguish:

(a) situations where plants are run by an overwhelming majority of technicians doing repetitive or routine work and holding no authority or hierarchical privilege over production workers; and

(b) situations where technical workers supervise, organize, control and command groups of production workers who, whatever their skills, are credited with inferior knowledge, competence and status within the industrial hierarchy.

A great number of misunderstandings have arisen owing to the fact that sociologists like Serge Mallet have focused attention on situation (a), whereas situation (b) is, for the moment and for the near future, still much more widespread and sociologically relevant, at least in Europe. I shall therefore start by examining situation (b) and comment later on the ambiguity of the technical workers' protest movement, a movement which can hardly be understood unless it is related to the ongoing transition from situation (b) to situation (a).

II

To understand the function of technical workers in manufacturing industries, we have to see that their role is both technical and ideological. They are entrusted not only with keeping production to certain pre-determined technical standards; they are also and mainly entrusted with maintaining the hierarchical structure of the labor force and with perpetuating capitalist social relations, that is, with keeping the producers estranged from the product and from the process of production.

There is ample documentary evidence for the fact that this second aspect of their role takes precedence over the first. But this fact has usually escaped the attention of capitalist societies, and only the Chinese cultural revolution has led Western observers to pay attention to it. Until recently, it was most commonly assumed that since industrial production in factories or large mechanical plants requires the division, specialization and separation of tasks, it was quite natural that minutely divided repetitive and unskilled tasks needed to be co-ordinated, supervised, planned and timed by people responsible either for part or for all of the complex final product, or for part or all of the work process: these people had to have both superior technical skills and intellectual and hierarchical authority.

But if we look into it more closely, we must ask: why must labor be minutely divided? Why must the narrowly specialized tasks be performed separately by different workers? The reasons given are: 1. narrow specialization requires less skill and training; 2. repetitive tasks enable the workers to work faster and more efficiently.

In truth, neither of these reasons holds true.[1] Experiments conducted mainly in the US have demonstrated that productivity can be greatly enhanced by enlarging the jobs and replacing repetitive assembly-line work by team work, i.e. by giving teams responsibility for a complex product and allowing each team to organize production as it deems most convenient. In this system, the repetitiveness and separation of tasks are abolished and workers are incited to achieve and to display a spectrum of skills, and to take over the coordination, planning, timing, and even the testing of their production. Of course, the coordination of the different work teams and technicians or engineers undergoes a fundamental change: it ceases to be hierarchical and authoritarian. It cannot remain such. The system, in order to work, must rest on the workers' consent, initiative and sense of responsibility; relations of cooperation and mutual trust between work teams and technicians or engineers become indispensable: the latter can no longer give orders and demand obedience; they must seek the workers' consent and therefore have to explain and discuss each of their concerns. Moreover, they must be at the workers' disposal, ready to help them solve problems they meet and to achieve improvements, modifications and innovations of the work process, the tools and the products.[2]

In this type of organization, as enacted in China and envisioned in Europe (mainly in Italy) by political and labor activists, sharp differences between workers on the one hand and technicians and engineers on the other hand tend to disappear. Production work and the acquisition of new skills and knowledge proceed together; working and learning or studying cease to be separated. From his early adolescence onward, everyone is at the same time both a producer and a student. No one is meant to remain blocked in unskilled, stupid and 'inferior' jobs: an 'evolutive profile' (or 'career') is sketched out in each industry whereby each worker's work is to be progressively enriched, the reduction of working time being designed to allow free time for studying. The work process and production technology of course must be radically reshaped so as to allow for the maximum display of the producers' capabilities and creativity.[3]

That such a reshaping of production technology should be possible without increasing the *social* costs of production to the *whole* economy is a demonstrable fact; experiments in the US even demonstrate the superior micro-economic efficiency of the type of work organization that abolishes hierarchical authority and control and appeals to team spirit and creativity. The question to which we have to revert then is: why is such a type of technology not generally available? Why has capitalism consistently promoted a technology that rests on the minute and stupefying fragmentation of tasks: a technology that requires the hierarchic structure of the work force and the hierarchic separation of manual and technical and intellectual labor? Why does 'rationalization' and 'modernization' keep replacing skilled work and work teams with unskilled repetitive work that leaves most workers' capabilities unemployed, that denies them the possibility of thinking and developing into complete human beings? Why does the capitalist system instead transfer most of the intellectual, creative and skilled dimensions of production work on to a pyramidally structured personnel of supervisors, technicians and engineers who receive an essentially abstract training and are instrumental in making and keeping the workers stupid?

There is one main, fundamental reason: the hierarchical division of labor destroys the power of the workers over the work process and maximizes the bosses' (or their representatives') power of control over the work force. The minute division of labor renders the process of production totally extraneous to the workers; it robs them of the possibility of determining how much work they want to do, it prevents them from tampering with work speeds. It makes them work to the limits of their physical and nervous capabilities – a thing no one would do unless personally committed to the purpose of his work, and even then not permanently. In a word, the capitalist division of labor is functional to a system that rests on *forced labor* and that therefore can rely only on regimentation and hierarchical control, not on the workers' consent and cooperation. To sum it all up, we have the following vicious circle:

1. Since the purpose of production is not the satisfaction of the producers' needs, but the extortion of surplus labor, capitalist production cannot rely upon the workers' willingness to work;

2. the less capitalist management wishes to rely upon the willingness of the workers, the more extraneous, regimented and idiotic work has to become;

3. the more extraneous, regimented and idiotic work becomes, the less capitalist management *can* rely upon the workers' willingness.

Hierarchical regimentation thus *appears* to be a necessity that flows from production technology; but in truth it is built into production technology insofar as the latter is itself a reflection of the social division of labor.

Whether we like it or not, we must see technicians in the manufacturing industries as key instruments of the hierarchical regimentation required by the capitalist division of labor. Their role is to oversee the domination of mechanical processes over living labor; their role is to make sure thereby that the maximum labor and surplus value is extracted from each worker. Their role is to dequalify workers by monopolizing the technical and intellectual skills required by the work process. They embody the dichotomy between manual and intellectual work, thought and execution. They hold significant financial, social and cultural privileges. They are the workers' most immediate enemy: they represent the skill, knowledge and virtual power of which workers have been robbed. In a machine tool shop, every one technician that is hired will turn five, ten or twenty hitherto skilled workers into unskilled underdogs, thereby enabling the boss to pay them unskilled wage rates. [. . .]

From a political viewpoint, we must therefore consider that there is an unbridgeable *objective* class distinction between technical supervisory staff and production workers. This class barrier can be overcome only by a powerful ideological thrust enhancing class consciousness. Mainly in situations of acute crisis and upheaval, technical supervisory personnel can be brought to side with the working class and to feel one with it. This possibility rests on the fact that technical and engineering personnel, though they hierarchically oppress the workers, are themselves frustrated, estranged and oppressed from above. *Vis-à-vis* their superiors, they are in the same situation as are their inferiors *vis-à-vis* themselves. [. . .]

Notes

1. The point I am trying to make here, and which has been very convincingly documented by Professor Stephen Marglin of Harvard University in a forthcoming essay, is that technology has been shaped by capitalism so as to secure maximum control over and exploitation of labor, not to secure maximum *production* of goods.

Control and exploitation are obviously inseparable, but the distinction between maximum exploitation and maximum production is a crucial one: it implies that *capitalism uses the most efficient production technology only so far as the latter is compatible with maximum control and exploitation.* Capital's goal is maximum profit, and since the latter requires total power to dispose over the work force's labor, it may well be attained – and actually has been attained – to the detriment of the greatest possible technological efficiency and productivity.

The point Professor Marglin has documented is that – contrary to most historians' belief and contrary to Marx's assumption – industry did not develop from a new and more efficient technological base, but, on the contrary, new technologies developed *after* the concentration of artisanal production in large factories. The motive of this concentration was *not* the factories' superior technology – they used the same technology as the artisans – but the capitalist bosses' (the outputters') desire to 1. control and market the weavers' total production which, if not physically controlled in the factories, would have been partly embezzled; 2. maximize the input of work, i.e. compel the weavers to work longer hours at greater speed than they would have done had they remained the owners of their tools; 3. take control of all technological innovation so as to use it for the sake of capital accumulation and not for purposes of more immediate interest; 4. organize production in such a way that the cycle of production could not dispense with the capitalist's function.

It is undeniable, of course, that capitalist industry did result in more efficient and more productive technology. But the point that must be stressed is that production technology has borne from the beginning the imprint of capitalist relations of production and was shaped by them. And that, therefore, it is by no means absurd to infer that a quite different production technology may have developed – and may develop – if not maximum control over and exploitation of the work force, but – as seems to be the case in China – maximum collective initiative and responsibility in the maximization of social production is the main goal.

Fragmented and repetitive assembly-line work must be re-examined from this angle. It is quite certain that assembly-line production contained some significant technological advancements and the mechanization of hitherto manual tasks. But it must also be seen that increased mechanization has always served a double purpose: the introduction of more efficient machinery has usually gone hand in hand with increased *intensity* (or input) of work by *each* laborer. It is not at all certain that the increased productivity achieved through repetitive assembly-line technology could not have been achieved *without* the fragmentation of work into repetitive jobs. The latter served the obvious purpose of eliminating the quite significant control which the *skilled* worker had over his working speed and working time, a control which enabled him to withhold a good part of his labor force from the capitalist employer. (On the very dubious effectiveness of monetary incentives on piece-work productivity and the practical impossibility of extracting maximum production effort from piece workers, see William F. Whyte, *Money and Motivation*, New York: Harper and Row, 1955; Harper Torchbooks, 1970.)

The minimization of skill has been a consistent policy of capitalist management, since it maximized the workers' dependence and manageability and reflected the *social* division of labor in its *technical* division. It is therefore no accident that bourgeois social relations should have re-emerged in all those so-called 'socialist' countries where the capitalist technical division of labor was used as a standard method. (On the originality of the Chinese revolution in this respect, see Marco Macciò, 'Parti, Techniciens et Classe Ouvrière dans la Révolution Chinoise', *Les Temps Modernes*, August–September 1970; and Jean Daubier, *Histoire de la Révolution Culturelle*, Maspero, 1970.)

2. These experiments are known in the US as 'job enlargement' and Scanlon Plan Y. They do *not* imply far-reaching technological changes and rest mainly on a different work organization using traditional technologies, e.g. assembly-line work. But they give the workers control and responsibility over the work process and the product and allow them to display their inventiveness.

Among the more accessible writings on the subject see: Judson Goodlin's articles in *Fortune*, July 1970 and September 1970; 'Getting at the Root of a Labor Crisis', *Business Week*, 17 October 1970, pp. 56–7; William F. Whyte, *Money and Motivation*, *op. cit.*, chapters 10 and 14; Charles Hampden Turner, *Radical Man*, Cambridge, Mass.: Schenkman, 1970, chapter VIII.

3. See Antonio Lettieri, 'Qualifiche, Scuola e Orari di Lavoro', *Problemi del Socialismo*, 49, November–December 1970.

15. Urbanism and suburbanism as ways of life

Herbert J. Gans

The contemporary sociological conception of cities and of urban life is based largely on the work of the Chicago School, and its summary statement in Louis Wirth's essay 'Urbanism as a Way of Life' [40]. In that paper, Wirth developed a 'minimum sociological definition of the city' as 'a relatively large, dense and permanent settlement of socially heterogeneous individuals' [40, p. 50]. From these prerequisites, he then deduced the major outlines of the urban way of life. As he saw it, number, density and heterogeneity created a social structure in which primary-group relationships were inevitably replaced by secondary contacts that were impersonal, segmental, superficial, transitory and often predatory in nature. As a result, the city dweller became anonymous, isolated, secular, relativistic, rational and sophisticated. In order to function in the urban society, he was forced to combine with others to organize corporations, voluntary associations, representative forms of government, and the impersonal mass media of communications [40, pp. 54–60]. These replaced the primary groups and the integrated way of life found in rural and other pre-industrial settlements.

Wirth's paper has become a classic in urban sociology, and most texts have followed his definition and description faithfully [5]. In recent years, however, a considerable number of studies and essays have questioned his formulations [1, 5, 13, 15, 17, 19, 20, 23, 24, 27, 28, 30, 35, 38, 41].[1] In addition, a number of changes have taken place in cities since the article was published in 1938, notably the exodus of white residents to low- and medium-priced houses in the suburbs, and the decentralization of industry. The evidence from these studies

From R. L. Pahl (ed.), *Readings in Urban Sociology*, Oxford: Pergamon Press, 1968, pp. 95–118.

and the changes in American cities suggest that Wirth's statement must be revised.

There is yet another, and more important reason for such a revision. Despite its title and intent, Wirth's paper deals with urban-industrial society, rather than with the city. This is evident from his approach. Like other urban sociologists, Wirth based his analysis on a comparison of settlement types, but unlike his colleagues, who pursued urban–rural comparisons, Wirth contrasted the city to the folk society. Thus, he compared settlement types of pre-industrial and industrial society. This allowed him to include in his theory of urbanism the entire range of modern institutions which are not found in the folk society, even though many such groups (e.g. voluntary associations) are by no means exclusively urban. Moreover, Wirth's conception of the city dweller as depersonalized, atomized and susceptible to mass movements suggests that his paper is based on, and contributes to, the theory of the mass society.

Many of Wirth's conclusions may be relevant to the understanding of ways of life in modern society. However, since the theory argues that all of society is now urban, *his analysis does not distinguish ways of life in the city from those in other settlements within modern society.* In Wirth's time, the comparison of urban and pre-urban settlement types was still fruitful, but today, the primary task for urban (or community) sociology seems to me to be the analysis of the similarities and differences between contemporary settlement types.

This paper is an attempt at such an analysis; it limits itself to distinguishing ways of life in the modern city and the modern suburb. A re-analysis of Wirth's conclusions from this perspective suggests that his characterization of the urban way of life applies only – and not too accurately – to the residents of the inner city. The remaining city dwellers, as well as most suburbanites, pursue a different way of life, which I shall call 'quasi-primary'. This proposition raises some doubt about the mutual exclusiveness of the concepts of city and suburb and leads to a yet broader question: whether settlement concepts and other ecological concepts are useful for explaining ways of life.

THE INNER CITY

Wirth argued that number, density and heterogeneity had two social consequences which explain the major features of urban life. On the one hand, the crowding of diverse types of people into a small area led to the segregation of homogeneous types of people into separate neighbourhoods [40, p. 56]. On the other hand, the lack of physical distance between city dwellers resulted in social contact between them, which broke down existing social and cultural patterns and encouraged assimilation as well as acculturation – the melting pot effect [40, p. 52]. Wirth implied that the melting pot effect was far more powerful than the tendency towards segregation and concluded that, sooner or later, the pressures engendered by the dominant social, economic and political institutions of the city would destroy the remaining pockets of primary-group relationships [40, pp. 60–2]. Eventually, the social system of the city would resemble Tönnies's *Gesellschaft* – a way of life which Wirth considered undesirable.

Because Wirth had come to see the city as the prototype of mass society, and because he examined the city from the distant vantage point of the folk society – from the wrong end of the telescope, so to speak – his view of urban life is not surprising. In addition, Wirth found support for his theory in the empirical work of his Chicago colleagues. As Greer and Kube [19, p. 112] and Wilensky [38, p. 121] have pointed out, the Chicago sociologists conducted their most intensive studies in the inner city.[2] At that time, these were slums recently invaded by new waves of European immigrants and rooming house and skid row districts, as well as the habitat of Bohemians and well-to-do Gold Coast apartment dwellers. Wirth himself studied the Maxwell Street Ghetto, an inner-city Jewish neighborhood then being dispersed by the acculturation and mobility of its inhabitants [39]. Some of the characteristics of urbanism which Wirth stressed in his essay abounded in these areas.

Wirth's diagnoses of the city as *Gesellschaft* must be questioned on three counts. First, the conclusions derived from a study of the inner city cannot be generalized to the entire urban area. Second, there is as yet not enough evidence to prove – nor, admittedly, to deny – that number, density and heterogeneity result in the social consequences which Wirth proposed. Finally, even if the causal relationship could be verified, it can be shown that a significant proportion of the city's inhabitants were, and are, isolated from these consequences by social structures and cultural patterns which they either brought to the city or developed by living in it. Wirth conceived the urban population as consisting of heterogeneous individuals, torn from past social systems, unable to develop new ones, and therefore prey to social anarchy in the city. While it is true that a not insignificant proportion of the inner city population was, and still is, made up of unattached individuals [26], Wirth's formulation ignores the fact that this population consists mainly of relatively homogeneous groups, with social and cultural moorings that shield it fairly effectively from the suggested consequences of number, density and heterogeneity. This applies even more to the residents of the outer city, who constitute a majority of the total city population.

The social and cultural moorings of the inner city population are best described by a brief analysis of the five types of inner city residents. These are:

1. the 'cosmopolites';
2. the unmarried or childless;
3. the 'ethnic villagers';
4. the 'deprived'; and
5. the 'trapped' and downward mobile.

The 'cosmopolites' include students, artists, writers, musicians and entertainers, as well as other intellectuals and professionals. They live in the city in order to be near the special 'cultural' facilities that can only be located near the center of the city. Many cosmopolites are unmarried or childless. Others rear children in the city, especially if they have the income to afford the aid of servants and governesses. The less affluent ones may move to the suburbs to raise their children, continuing to live as cosmopolites under considerable handicaps, especially in the lower-middle-class suburbs. Many of the very rich and powerful are also cosmopolites, although they are likely to have at least two residences, one of which is suburban or exurban.

The unmarried or childless must be divided into two subtypes, depending on the permanence or transience of their status. The temporarily unmarried or childless live in the inner city for only a limited time. Young adults may team up to rent an apartment away from their parents and close to job or entertainment opportunities. When they marry, they may move first to an apartment in a transient neighbourhood, but if they can afford to do so, they leave for the outer city or the suburbs with the arrival of the first or second child. The permanently unmarried may stay in the inner city for the remainder of their lives, their housing depending on their income.

The 'ethnic villagers' are ethnic groups which are found in such inner city neighborhoods as New York's Lower East Side, living in some ways as they did when they were peasants in European or Puerto Rican villages [15]. Although they reside in the city, they isolate themselves from significant contact with most city facilities, aside from workplaces. Their way of life differs sharply from Wirth's urbanism in its emphasis on kinship and the primary group, the lack of anonymity and secondary-group contacts, the weakness of formal organizations, and the suspicion of anything and anyone outside their neighborhood.

The first two types live in the inner city by choice; the third is there partly because of necessity, partly because of tradition. The final two types are in the inner city because they have no other choice. One is the 'deprived' population: the very poor; the emotionally disturbed or otherwise handicapped; broken families; and, most important, the non-white population. These urban dwellers must take the dilapidated housing and blighted neighborhoods to which the housing market relegates them, although among them are some for whom the slum is a hiding place, or a temporary stop-over to save money for a house in the outer city or the suburbs [27].

The 'trapped' are the people who stay behind when a neighborhood is invaded by non-residential land uses or lower-status immigrants, because they cannot afford to move, or are otherwise bound to their present location [27][3] The 'downward mobiles' are a related type; they may have started life in a higher class position, but have been forced down in the socio-economic hierarchy and in the quality of their accommodations. Many of them are old people, living out their existence on small pensions.

These five types all live in dense and heterogeneous surroundings, yet they have such diverse ways of life that it is hard to see how density and heterogeneity could exert a common influence. Moreover, all but the last two types are isolated or detached from their neighborhood and thus from the social consequences which Wirth described.

When people who live together have social ties based on criteria other than mere common occupancy, they can set up social barriers regardless of the physical closeness or the heterogeneity of their neighbors. The ethnic villagers are the best illustration. While a number of ethnic groups are usually found living together in the same neighborhood, they are able to *isolate* themselves from each other through a variety of social devices. Wirth himself recognized this when he wrote that 'two groups can occupy a given area without losing their separate identity because each side is permitted to live its own inner life and each somehow fears or idealizes the other' [39, p. 283]. Although it is true that the children in these areas were often oblivious to the social barriers set up by their parents, at least until adolescence, it is doubtful whether their acculturation can be traced to the melting-pot effect as much as to the pervasive influence of the American culture that flowed into these areas from the outside.[4]

The cosmopolites, the unmarried and the childless are detached from neighborhood life. The cosmopolites possess a distinct sub-culture which causes them to be disinterested in all but the most superficial contacts with their neighbors, somewhat like the ethnic villagers. The unmarried and childless are detached from neighborhood because of their life-cycle stage, which frees them from the routine family responsibilities that entail some relationship to the local area. In their choice of residence, the two types are therefore not concerned about their neighbors, or the availability and quality of local community facilities. Even the well-to-do can choose expensive apartments in or near poor neighborhoods, because if they have children, these are sent to special schools and summer camps which effectively isolate them from neighbors. In addition, both types, but especially the childless and unmarried, are transient. Therefore, they tend to live in areas marked by high population turnover, where their own mobility and that of their neighbors creates a universal detachment from the neighborhood.[5]

The deprived and the trapped do seem to be affected by some of the consequences of number, density and heterogeneity. The deprived population suffers considerably from overcrowding, but this is a consequence of low income, racial discrimination and other handicaps, and cannot be considered an inevitable result of the ecological make-up of the city.[6] Because the deprived have no residential choice, they are also forced to live amid neighbors not of their own choosing, with ways of life different and even contradictory to their own. If familial defenses against the neighborhood climate are weak, as is the case among broken families and downward mobile people, parents may lose their children to the culture of 'the street'. The trapped are the unhappy people who remain behind when their more advantaged neighbors move on; they must endure the heterogeneity which results from neighborhood change.

Wirth's description of the urban way of life fits best the transient areas of the inner city. Such areas are typically heterogeneous in population, partly because they are inhabited by transient types who do not require homogeneous neighbors or by deprived people who have no choice, or may themselves be quite mobile. Under conditions of transience and heterogeneity, people interact only in terms of the segmental roles necessary for obtaining local services. Their social relationships thus display anonymity, impersonality and superficiality.[7]

The social features of Wirth's concept of urbanism seem therefore to be a result of residential instability, rather than of number, density, or heterogeneity. In fact, heterogeneity is itself an effect of residential instability, resulting when the influx of transients causes landlords and realtors to stop acting as gatekeepers – that is, wardens of neighborhood homogeneity.[8] Residential instability is found in all types of settlements and, presumably, its social consequences are everywhere similar. These consequences cannot therefore be identified with the ways of life of the city.

THE OUTER CITY AND THE SUBURBS

The second effect which Wirth ascribed to number, density and heterogeneity was the segregation of homogeneous people into distinct neighborhoods,[9] on the basis of 'place and nature of work, income, racial and ethnic characteristics, social status, custom, habit, taste, preference and prejudice' [40, p. 56]. This description fits the residential districts of the *outer city*.[10] Although these districts contain the majority of the city's inhabitants, Wirth went into little detail about them. He made it clear, however, that the socio-psychological aspects of urbanism were prevalent there as well [40, p. 56].

Because existing neighborhood studies deal primarily with the exotic sections of the inner city, very little is known about the more typical residential neighborhoods of the outer city. However, it is evident that the way of life in these areas bears little resemblance to Wirth's urbanism. Both the studies which question Wirth's formulation and my own observations suggest that the common element in the ways of life of these neighborhoods is best described as *quasi-primary*. I use this term to characterize relationships between neighbors. Whatever the intensity or frequency of these relationships, the interaction is more intimate than a secondary contact, but more guarded than a primary one.[11]

There are actually few secondary relationships, because of the isolation of residential neighborhoods from economic institutions and workplaces. Even shopkeepers, store managers and other local functionaries who live in the area are treated as acquaintances or friends, unless they are of a vastly different social status or are forced by their corporate employers to treat their customers as economic units [30]. Voluntary associations attract only a minority of the population. Moreover, much of the organizational activity is of a sociable nature, and it is often difficult to accomplish the association's 'business' because of the members' preference for sociability. Thus, it would appear that interactions in organizations, or between neighbors generally, do not fit the secondary-relationship model of urban life. As anyone who has lived in these neighborhoods knows, there is little anonymity, impersonality or privacy.[12] In fact, American cities have sometimes been described as collections of small towns.[13] There is some truth to this description, especially if the city is compared to the actual small town, rather than to the romantic construct of anti-urban critics [33].

Postwar suburbia represents the most contemporary version of the quasi-primary way of life. Owing to increases in real income and the encouragement of home ownership provided by the FHA, families in the lower-middle class and upper working class can now live in modern single-family homes in low-density subdivisions, an opportunity previously available only to the upper and upper-middle classes [34].

The popular literature describes the new suburbs as communities in which conformity, homogeneity and other-direction are unusually rampant [4, 32]. The implication is that the move from city to suburb initiates a new way of life which causes considerable behavior and personality change in previous urbanites. A preliminary analysis of data which I am now collecting in Levittown, New Jersey, suggests, however, that the move from the city to this predominantly lower-middle-class suburb does not result in any major behavioral changes for most people. Moreover, the changes which do occur reflect the move from the social isolation of a transient city or suburban apartment building to the quasi-primary life of a neighborhood of single-family homes. Also, many of the people whose life has changed reported that the changes were intended. They existed as aspirations before the move, or as reasons for it. In other words, the suburb itself creates few changes in ways of life. Similar conclusions have been reported by Berger in his excellent study of a working-class population newly moved to a suburban subdivision [4].

A COMPARISON OF CITY AND SUBURB

If urban and suburban areas are similar in that the way of life in both is quasi-primary, and if urban residents who move out to the suburbs do not undergo any significant changes in behavior, it would be fair to argue that the differences in ways of life between the two types of settlements have been overestimated. Yet the fact remains that a variety of physical and demographic differences exist between the city and the suburb. However, upon closer examination, many of these differences turn out to be either spurious or of little significance for the way of life of the inhabitants [34].[14]

The differences between the residential areas of cities and suburbs which have been cited most frequently are:

1. Suburbs are more likely to be dormitories.
2. They are further away from the work and play facilities of the central business districts.
3. They are newer and more modern than city residential areas and are designed for the automobile rather than for pedestrian and mass-transit forms of movement.
4. They are built up with single-family rather than multi-family structures and are therefore less dense.
5. Their populations are more homogeneous.
6. Their populations differ demographically: they are younger; more of them are married; they have higher incomes; and they hold proportionately more white-collar jobs [8, p. 131].

Most urban neighborhoods are as much dormitories as the suburbs. Only in a few older inner city areas are factories and offices still located in the middle of residential blocks, and even here many of the employees do not live in the neighborhood.

The fact that the suburbs are farther from the central business district is often true only in terms of distance, not travel time. Moreover, most people make relatively little use of downtown facilities, other than workplaces [12, 21]. The downtown stores seem to hold their greatest attraction for the upper-middle class [21, pp. 91–2]; the same is probably true of typically urban entertainment facilities. Teenagers and young adults may take their dates to first-run movie theaters, but the museums, concert halls and lecture rooms attract mainly upper-middle-class ticket-buyers, many of them suburban.[15]

The suburban reliance on the train and the automobile has given rise to an imaginative folklore about the consequences of commuting on alcohol consumption, sex life, and parental duties. Many of these conclusions are, however, drawn from selected high-income suburbs and exurbs, and reflect job tensions in such hectic occupations as advertising and show business more than the effects of residence [29]. It is true that the upper-middle-class housewife must become a chauffeur in order to expose her children to the proper educational facilities, but such differences as walking to the corner drug store and driving to its suburban equivalent seem to me of little emotional, social or cultural import.[16] In addition, the continuing shrinkage in the number of mass-transit users suggests that even in the city many younger people are now living a wholly auto-based way of life.

The fact that suburbs are smaller is primarily a function of political boundaries drawn long before the communities were suburban. This affects the kinds of political issues which develop and provides somewhat greater opportunity for citizen participation. Even so, in the suburbs as in the city, the minority who participate are the professional politicians, the economically concerned businessmen, lawyers and salesmen, and the ideologically motivated middle- and upper-middle-class people with better than average education.

The social consequences of differences in density and house type also seem overrated. Single-family houses on quiet streets facilitate the supervision of children; this is one reason why middle-class women who want to keep an eye on their children move to the suburbs. House type also has some effects on relationships between neighbors, insofar as there are more opportunities for visual contact between adjacent homeowners than between people on different floors of an apartment house. However, if occupants' characteristics are also held constant, the differences in actual social contact are less marked. Homogeneity of residents turns out to be more important as a determinant of sociability than proximity. If the population is heterogeneous, there is little social contact between neighbors, either on apartment-house floors or in single-family-house blocks; if people are homogeneous, there is likely to be considerable social contact in both house types. One need only contrast the apartment house located in a transient, heterogeneous neighborhood and exactly the same structure in a neighborhood occupied by a single ethnic group. The former is a lonely, anonymous building; the latter, a bustling microsociety. I have observed similar patterns in suburban areas: on blocks where people are homogeneous, they socialize; where they are heterogeneous, they do little more than exchange polite greetings [16].

Suburbs are usually described as being more homogeneous in house type than the city, but if they are compared to the outer city, the differences are small. Most inhabitants of the outer city, other than well-to-do homeowners, live on blocks of uniform structure as well – for example, the endless streets of rowhouses in Philadelphia and Baltimore or of two-story duplexes and six-flat apartment houses in Chicago. They differ from the new suburbs only in that they were erected through more primitive methods of mass production. Suburbs are of course more predominantly areas of owner-occupied single homes, though in the outer districts of most American cities homeownership is also extremely high.

Demographically, suburbs as a whole are clearly more homogeneous than cities as a whole, though probably not more so than outer cities. However, people do not live in cities or suburbs as a whole, but in specific neighborhoods. An analysis of ways of life would require a determination of the degree of population homogeneity within the boundaries of areas defined as neighborhoods by residents' social contacts. Such an analysis would no doubt indicate that many neighborhoods in the city as well as the suburbs are homogeneous. Neighborhood homogeneity is actually a result of factors having little or nothing to do with the house type, density or location of the area relative to the city limits. Brand new neighborhoods are more homogeneous than older ones, because they have not yet experienced resident turnover, which frequently results in population heterogeneity. Neighborhoods of low- and medium-priced housing are usually less homogeneous than those with expensive dwellings because they attract families who have reached the peak of occupational and residential mobility, as well as young families who are just starting their climb and will eventually move to neighborhoods of higher status. The latter, being accessible only to high-income people, are therefore more homogeneous with respect to other resident characteristics as well. Moreover, such areas have the economic and political power to slow down or prevent invasion. Finally, neighborhoods located in the path of ethnic or religious group movement are likely to be extremely homogeneous.

The demographic differences between cities and suburbs cannot be questioned, especially since the suburbs have attracted a large number of middle-class child-rearing families. The differences are, however, much reduced if suburbs are compared only to the outer city. In addition, a detailed comparison of suburban and outer city residential areas would show that neighborhoods with the same kinds of people can be found in the city as well as the suburbs. Once again, the age of the area and the cost of housing are more important determinants of demographic characteristics than the location of the area with respect to the city limits.

CHARACTERISTICS, SOCIAL ORGANIZATION, AND ECOLOGY

The preceding sections of the paper may be summarized in three propositions:

1. As concerns ways of life, the inner city must be distinguished from the outer city and the suburbs; and the

latter two exhibit a way of life bearing little resemblance to Wirth's urbanism.

2. Even in the inner city, ways of life resemble Wirth's description only to a limited extent. Moreover, economic condition, cultural characteristics, life-cycle stage and residential instability explain ways of life more satisfactorily than number, density or heterogeneity.

3. Physical and other differences between city and suburb are often spurious or without much meaning for ways of life.

These propositions suggest that the concepts urban and suburban are neither mutually exclusive nor especially relevant for understanding ways of life. They – and number, density and heterogeneity as well – are ecological concepts which describe human adaptation to the environment. However, they are not sufficient to explain social phenomena, because these phenomena cannot be understood solely as the consequences of ecological processes. Therefore, other explanations must be considered.

Ecological explanations of social life are most applicable if the subjects under study lack the ability to *make choices*, be they plants, animals or human beings, Thus, if there is a housing shortage, people will live almost anywhere, and under extreme conditions of no choice, as in a disaster, married and single, old and young, middle and working class, stable and transient will be found side by side in whatever accommodations are available. At that time, their ways of life represent an almost direct adaptation to the environment. If the supply of housing and of neighborhoods is such that alternatives are available, however, people will make choices, and if the housing market is responsive, they can even make and satisfy explicit *demands*.

Choices and demands do not develop independently or at random; they are functions of the roles people play in the social system. These can best be understood in terms of the *characteristics* of the people involved; that is, characteristics can be used as indices to choices and demands made in the roles that constitute ways of life. Although many characteristics affect the choices and demands people make with respect to housing and neighborhoods, the most important ones seem to be class – in all its economic, social and cultural ramifications – and *life-cycle stage.*[17] If people have an opportunity to choose, these two characteristics will go far in explaining the kinds of housing and neighborhoods they will occupy and the ways of life they will try to establish within them.

Many of the previous assertions about ways of life in cities and suburbs can be analyzed in terms of class and life-cycle characteristics. Thus, in the inner city, the unmarried and childless live as they do, detached from neighborhood, because of their life-cycle stage; the cosmopolites, because of a combinations of life-cycle stage and a distinctive but class-based subculture. The way of life of the deprived and trapped can be explained by low socio-economic level and related handicaps. The quasi-primary way of life is associated with the family stage of the life-cycle, and the norms of child-rearing and parental role found in the upper working class, the lower-middle class, and the non-cosmopolite portions of the upper-middle and upper classes.

The attributes of the so-called suburban way of life can also be understood largely in terms of these characteristics. The new suburbia is nothing more than a highly visible showcase for the ways of life of young, upper-working-class and lower-middle-class people. Ktsanes and Reissman have aptly described it as 'new homes for old values' [22]. Much of the descriptive and critical writing about suburbia assumes that as long as the new suburbanites lived in the city, they behaved like upper-middle-class cosmopolites and that suburban living has mysteriously transformed them [7; 14, pp. 154–62; 25; 36]. The critics fail to see that the behavior and personality patterns ascribed to suburbia are in reality those of class and age [6]. These patterns could have been found among the new suburbanites when they still lived in the city and could now be observed among their peers who still reside there – if the latter were as visible to critics and researchers as are the suburbanites.

Needless to say, the concept of 'characteristics' cannot

explain all aspects of ways of life, either among urban or suburban residents. Some aspects must be explained by concepts of social organization that are independent of characteristics. For example, some features of the quasi-primary way of life are independent of class and age, because they evolve from the roles and situations created by joint and adjacent occupancy of land and dwellings. Likewise, residential instability is a universal process which has a number of invariate consequences. In each case, however, the way in which people react varies with their characteristics. So it is with ecological processes. Thus, there are undoubtedly differences between ways of life in urban and suburban settlements which remain after behavior patterns based on residents' characteristics have been analyzed, and which must therefore be attributed to features of the settlement [11].

Characteristics do not explain the causes of behavior; rather, they are clues to socially created and culturally defined roles, choices and demands. A causal analysis must trace them back to the larger social, economic and political systems which determine the situations in which roles are played and the cultural content of choices and demands, as well as the opportunities for their achievement.[18] These systems determine income distributions, educational and occupational opportunities, and in turn, fertility patterns, child-rearing methods, as well as the entire range of consumer behavior. Thus, a complete analysis of the way of life of the deprived residents of the inner city cannot stop by indicating the influence of low income, lack of education, or family instability. These must be related to such conditions as the urban economy's 'need' for low-wage workers, and the housing market practices which restrict residential choice. The urban economy is in turn shaped by national economic and social systems, as well as by local and regional ecological processes. Some phenomena can be explained exclusively by reference to these ecological processes. However, it must also be recognized that as man gains greater control over the natural environment, he has been able to free himself from many of the determining and limiting effects of that environment. Thus, changes in local transportation technology, the ability of industries to be footloose, and the relative affluence of American society have given ever larger numbers of people increasing amounts of residential choice. The greater the amount of choice available, the more important does the concept of characteristics become in understanding behavior.

Consequently, the study of ways of life in communities must begin with an analysis of characteristics. If characteristics are dealt with first and held constant, we may be able to discover which behavior patterns can be attributed to features of the settlement and its natural environment.[19] Only then will it be possible to discover to what extent city and suburb are independent – rather than dependent or intervening – variables in the explanation of ways of life.

This kind of analysis might help to reconcile the ecological point of view with the behavioral and cultural one, and possibly put an end to the conflict between conceptual positions which insist on one explanation or the other [9]. Both explanations have some relevance, and future research and theory must clarify the role of each in the analysis of ways of life in various types of settlement [6, p. xxii]. Another important rationale for this approach is its usefulness for applied sociology – for example, city planning. The planner can recommend changes in the spatial and physical arrangements of the city. Frequently, he seeks to achieve social goals or to change social conditions through physical solutions. He has been attracted to ecological explanations because these relate behavior to phenomena which he can affect. For example, most planners tend to agree with Wirth's formulations, because they stress number and density, over which the planner has some control. If the undesirable social conditions of the inner city could be traced to these two factors, the planner could propose large-scale clearance projects which would reduce the size of the urban population, and lower residential densities. Experience with public housing projects has, however, made it apparent that low densities, new buildings, or modern site plans do not eliminate anti-social or self-destructive behavior. The analysis of characteristics will call attention to the fact that this behavior is lodged in the deprivations of low socio-economic status and racial discrimination, and that it can be changed only through the removal of these deprivations. Conversely, if such an analysis suggests residues of behavior that can be attributed to ecological processes or physical aspects of housing and neighborhoods, the planner can recommend physical changes that can really affect behavior.

A RE-EVALUATION OF DEFINITIONS

The argument presented here has implications for the socio-logical definition of the city. Such a definition relates ways of life to environmental features of the city qua settlement type. But if ways of life do not coincide with settlement types, and if these ways are functions of class and life-cycle stage rather than of the ecological attributes of the settlement, a socio-logical definition of the city cannot be formulated.[20] Concepts such as city and suburb allow us to distinguish settlement types from each other physically and demographically, but the eco-logical processes and conditions which they synthesize have no direct or invariate consequences for ways of life. The sociologist cannot, therefore, speak of an urban or suburban way of life.

CONCLUSION

Many of the descriptive statements made here are as time-bound as Wirth's.[21] Twenty years ago, Wirth concluded that some form of urbanism would eventually predominate in all settlement types. He was, however, writing during a time of immigrant acculturation and at the end of a serious depression, an era of minimal choice. Today, it is apparent that high-density, heterogeneous surroundings are for most people a temporary place of residence; other than for the Park Avenue or Greenwich Village cosmopolites, they are a result of neces-sity rather than choice. As soon as they can afford to do so, most Americans head for the single-family house and the quasi-primary array of life of the low-density neighborhood, in the outer city or the suburbs.[22]

Changes in the national economy and in government housing policy can affect many of the variables that make up housing supply and demand. For example, urban sprawl may eventually outdistance the ability of present and proposed transportation systems to move workers into the city; further industrial decentralization can forestall it and alter the entire relationship between work and residence. The expansion of present urban renewal activities can perhaps lure a significant number of cosmopolites back from the suburbs, while a drastic change in renewal policy might begin to ameliorate the housing conditions of the deprived population. A serious depression could once again make America a nation of doubled-up tenants.

These events will affect housing supply and residential choice; they will frustrate but not suppress demands for the quasi-primary way of life. However, changes in the national economy, society and culture can affect people's characteristics – family size, educational level, and various other concomitants of life-cycle stage and class. These in turn will stimulate changes in demands and choices. The rising number of college graduates, for example, is likely to increase the cosmopolite ranks. This might in turn create a new set of city dwellers, although it will probably do no more than encourage the development of cosmopolite facilities in some suburban areas.

The current revival of interest in urban sociology and in community studies, as well as the sociologist's increasing curiosity about city planning, suggest that data may soon be available to formulate a more adequate theory of the relationship between settlements and the ways of life within them. The speculations presented in this paper are intended to raise questions; they can only be answered by more systematic data collection and theorizing.

Notes

1. I shall not attempt to summarize these studies, for this task has already been performed by Dewey [5], Reiss [23], Wilensky [38], and others.
2. By the *inner city*, I mean the transient residential areas, the Gold Coasts and the slums that generally surround the central business district, although in some communities they may continue

415

for miles beyond that district. The *outer city* includes the stable residential areas that house the working- and middle-class tenant and owner. The *suburbs* I conceive as the latest and most modern ring of the outer city, distinguished from it only by yet lower densities, and by the often irrelevant fact of the ring's location outside the city limits.

3. The trapped are not very visible, but I suspect that they are a significant element in what Raymond Vernon has described as the 'gray areas' of the city [32].

4. If the melting pot has resulted from propinquity and high density, one would have expected second-generation Italians, Irish, Jews, Greeks, Slavs, etc. to have developed a single 'pan-ethnic culture', consisting of a synthesis of the cultural patterns of the propinquitous national groups.

5. The corporation transients [36, 38], who provide a new source of residential instability to the suburb, differ from city transients. Since they are raising families, they want to integrate themselves into neighborhood life, and are usually able to do so, mainly because they tend to move into similar types of communities wherever they go.

6. The negative social consequences of overcrowding are a result of high room and floor density, not of the land coverage of population density which Wirth discussed. Park Avenue residents live under conditions of high land density, but do not seem to suffer visibly from overcrowding.

7. Whether or not these social phenomena have the psychological consequences Wirth suggested depends on the people who live in the area. Those who are detached from the neighborhood by choice are probably immune, but those who depend on the neighborhood for their social relationships – the unattached individuals, for example – may suffer greatly from loneliness.

8. Needless to say, residential instability must ultimately be traced back to the fact that, as Wirth pointed out, the city and its economy attract transient – and, depending on the sources of out-migration, heterogeneous – people. However, this is a characteristic of urban-industrial society, not of the city specifically.

9. By neighborhoods or residential districts I mean areas demarcated from others by distinctive physical boundaries or by social characteristics, some of which may be perceived only by the residents. However, these areas are not necessarily socially self-sufficient or culturally distinctive.

10. For the definition of *outer city*, see note 2.

11. Because neighborly relations are not quite primary, and not

quite secondary, they can also become *pseudo-primary*; that is, secondary ones disguised with false effect to make them appear primary. Critics have often described suburban life in this fashion, although the actual prevalence of pseudo-primary relationships has not been studied systematically in cities or suburbs.

12. These neighborhoods cannot, however, be considered as urban folk societies. People go out of the area for many of their friendships, and their allegiance to neighborhood is neither intense nor all-encompassing. Janowitz has aptly described the relationship between resident and neighborhood as one of 'limited liability' [20, chapter 7].

13. Were I not arguing that ecological concepts cannot double as sociological ones, this way of life might best be described as small-townish.

14. They may, of course, be significant for the welfare of the total metropolitan area.

15. A 1958 study of New York theater goers showed a median income of close to $10,000 and 35 per cent were reported as living in the suburbs [10].

16. I am thinking here of adults; teenagers do suffer from the lack of informal meeting places within walking or bicycling distance.

17. These must be defined in dynamic terms. Thus, class includes also the process of social mobility, stage in the life-cycle, and the processes of socialization and aging.

18. This formulation may answer some of Duncan and Schnore's objections to socio-psychological and cultural explanations of community ways of life [9].

19. The ecologically oriented researchers who developed the Shevsky-Bell social area analysis scale have worked on the assumption that 'social differences between the populations of urban neighborhoods can conveniently be summarized into differences of economic level, family characteristics and ethnicity' [3, p. 26]. However, they have equated 'urbanization' with a concept of life-cycle stage by using family characteristics to define the index of urbanization [3, 18, 19]. In fact, Bell has identified suburbanism with familism [2].

20. Because of the distinctiveness of the ways of life found in the inner city, some writers propose definitions that refer only to these ways, ignoring those found in the outer city. For example, popular writers sometimes identify 'urban' with 'urbanity', i.e. 'cosmopolitanism'. However, such a definition ignores the other ways of life found in the inner city. Moreover, I have tried to show that these ways have few common elements, and that the ecological features

417

of the inner city have little or no influence in shaping them.

21. Even more than Wirth's they are based on data and impressions gathered in the large eastern and midwestern cities of the United States.

22. Personal discussions with European planners and sociologists suggest that many European apartment dwellers have similar preferences, although economic conditions, high building costs, and the scarcity of land make it impossible for them to achieve their desires.

References

1. Axelrod, Morris. 'Urban Structure and Social Participation', *American Sociological Review*, 21 (February 1956), pp. 13–18.
2. Bell, Wendell. 'Social Choice, Life Styles and Suburban Residence', in William M. Dobriner (ed.), *The Suburban Community*, New York: G. P. Putnam's Sons, 1958, pp. 225–47.
3. Bell, Wendell, and Maryanne T. Force. 'Urban Neighborhood Types and Participation in Formal Associations', *American Sociological Review*, 21 (February 1956), pp. 25–34.
4. Berger, Bennett. *Working Class Suburb: A Study of Auto Workers in Suburbia*, Berkeley, Calif.: University of California Press, 1960.
5. Dewey, Richard. 'The Rural–Urban Continuum: Real but Relatively Unimportant', *American Journal of Sociology*, 66 (July 1960), pp. 60–6.
6. Dobriner, William M. 'Introduction: Theory and Research in the Sociology of the Suburbs', in William M. Dobriner (ed.), *The Suburban Community*, New York: G. P. Putnam's Sons, 1958, pp. xiii–xxviii.
7. Duhl, Leonard J. 'Mental Health and Community Planning', in *Planning 1955*, Chicago: American Society of Planning Officials, 1956, pp. 31–9.
8. Duncan, Otis Dudley, and Albert J. Reiss, Jr. *Social Characteristics of Rural and Urban Communities, 1950*, New York: John Wiley & Sons, 1956.
9. Duncan, Otis Dudley, and Leo F. Schnore. 'Cultural, Behavioral and Ecological Perspectives in the Study of Social Organization', *American Journal of Sociology*, 65 (September 1959), pp. 132–55.
10. Enders, John. *Profile of the Theater Market*, New York: Play-

bill, undated and unpaged.

11. Fava, Sylvia Fleis. 'Contrasts in Neighboring: New York City and a Suburban Community', in William M. Dobriner (ed.), *The Suburban Community*, New York: G. P. Putnam's Sons, 1958, pp. 122–31.

12. Foley, Donald L. 'The Use of Local Facilities in a Metropolis', in Paul Hatt and Albert J. Reiss, Jr (eds), *Cities and Society*, Glencoe, Ill.: The Free Press, 1957, pp. 237–47.

13. Form, William H., *et al.* 'The Compatibility of Alternative Approaches to the Delimitation of Urban Sub-areas', *American Sociological Review*, 19 (August 1954), pp. 434–40.

14. Fromm, Erich. *The Sane Society*, New York: Rinehart & Co., Inc., 1955.

15. Gans, Herbert J. *The Urban Villagers: A Study of the Second Generation Italians in the West End of Boston*, Boston: Center for Community Studies, December 1959 (mimeographed).

16. Gans, Herbert J. 'Planning and Social Life: An Evaluation of Friendship and Neighbor Relations in Suburban Communities', *Journal of the American Institute of Planners*, 27 (May 1961), pp. 134–40.

17. Greer, Scott. 'Urbanism Reconsidered: A Comparative Study of Local Areas in a Metropolis', *American Sociological Review*, 21 (February 1956), pp. 19–25.

18. Greer, Scott. 'The Social Structure and Political Process of Suburbia', *American Sociological Review*, 25 (August 1960), pp. 514–26.

19. Greer, Scott, and Ella Kube. 'Urbanism and Social Structure: A Los Angeles Study', in Marvin B. Sussman (ed.), *Community Structure and Analysis*, New York: Thomas Y. Crowell Co., 1959, pp. 93–112.

20. Janowitz, Morris. *The Community Press in an Urban Setting*, Glencoe, Ill.: The Free Press, 1952.

21. Jonassen, Christen T. *The Shopping Center Versus Downtown*, Columbus, Ohio: Bureau of Business Research, Ohio State University, 1955.

22. Ktsanes, Thomas, and Leonard Reissman. 'Suburbia: New Homes for Old Values', *Social Problems*, 7 (Winter 1959–60), pp. 187–94.

23. Reiss, Albert J., Jr. 'An Analysis of Urban Phenomena', in Robert M. Fisher (ed.), *The Metropolis in Modern Life*, Garden City, NY: Doubleday & Co., Inc., 1955, pp. 41–9.

24. Reiss, Albert J., Jr. 'Rural–Urban and Status Differences in Interpersonal Contacts', *American Journal of Sociology*, 65 (September 1959), pp. 182–95.

25. Riesman, David. 'The Suburban Sadness', in William M. Dobriner (ed.), *The Suburban Community*, New York: G. P. Putnam's Sons, 1958, pp. 375–408.
26. Rose, Arnold M. 'Living Arrangements of Unattached Persons', *American Sociological Review*, 12 (August 1947), pp. 429–35.
27. Seeley, John R. 'The Slum: Its Nature, Use and Users', *Journal of the American Institute of Planners*, 25 (February 1959), pp. 7–14.
28. Smith, Joel, William Form and Gregory Stone. 'Local Intimacy in a Middle-Sized City', *American Journal of Sociology*, 60 (November 1954), pp. 276–84.
29. Spectorsky, A. C. *The Exurbanites*, Philadelphia: J. B. Lippincott Co., 1955.
30. Stone, Gregory P. 'City Shoppers and Urban Identification: Observations on the Social Psychology of City Life', *American Journal of Sociology*, 60 (July 1954), pp. 36–45.
31. Strauss, Anselm. 'The Changing Imagery of American City and Suburb', *Sociological Quarterly*, 1 (January 1960), pp. 15–24.
32. Vernon, Raymond. *The Changing Economic Function of the Central City*, New York: Committee on Economic Development, Supplementary Paper No. 1, January 1959.
33. Vidich, Arthur J., and Joseph Bensman. *Small Town in Mass Society: Class, Power and Religion in a Rural Community*, Princeton, NJ: Princeton University Press, 1958.
34. Wattell, Harold. 'Levittown: A Suburban Community', in William M. Dobriner (ed.), *The Suburban Community*, New York: G. P. Putnam's Sons, 1958, pp. 287–313.
35. Whyte, William F., Jr. *Street Corner Society*, Chicago: The University of Chicago Press, 1955.
36. Whyte, William F., Jr. *The Organization Man*, New York: Simon & Schuster, 1956.
37. Wilensky, Harold L. 'Life Cycle, Work, Situation and Participation in Formal Associations', in Robert W. Kleemeier, *et al* (eds.), *Aging and Leisure: Research Perspectives on the Meaningful Use of Time*, New York: Oxford University Press, 1961, chapter 8.
38. Wilensky, Harold L. and Charles Lebeaux. *Industrial Society and Social Welfare*, New York: Russell Sage Foundation, 1958.
39. Wirth, Louis. *The Ghetto*, Chicago: The University of Chicago Press, 1928.
40. Wirth, Louis. 'Urbanism as a Way of Life', *American Journal of Sociology*, 44 (July 1938), pp. 1–24. Reprinted in Paul Hatt

and Albert J. Reiss, Jr (eds), *Cities and Society*, Glencoe, Ill.: The Free Press, 1957, pp. 46–64. [All page references are to this reprinting of the article.]
41. Young, Michael, and Peter Willmott. *Family and Kinship in East London*, London: Routledge & Kegan Paul, Ltd, 1957.

16. Theorems of motivation crisis

Jürgen Habermas

I speak of a motivation crisis when the socio-cultural system changes in such a way that its output becomes dysfunctional for the state and for the system of social labor. The most important motivation contributed by the socio-cultural system in advanced-capitalist societies consists of syndromes of civil and familial-vocational privatism. Civil privatism here denotes an interest in the steering and maintenance [*Versorgung*] performances of the administrative system but little participation in the legitimizing process, albeit participation appropriate to institutionally provided opportunities (high-output orientation versus low-input orientation). Civil privatism thus corresponds to the structures of a depoliticized public realm. Familial-vocational privatism complements civil privatism. It consists in a family orientation with developed interests in consumption and leisure on the one hand, and in a career orientation suitable to status competition on the other. This privatism thus corresponds to the structures of educational and occupational systems that are regulated by competition through achievement.

Both patterns of motivation are important to the continued existence of the political and economic systems. To defend the statement that these patterns of orientation are being systematically destroyed, we must assume the burden of proof for two independent theses. First, we must demonstrate the erosion of traditions in the context of which these attitudes were previously produced. Second, we must show that there are no functional equivalents for the spent traditions, for they are precluded by the logic of development of normative structures. In coordinating motivational patterns with stable traditional cultural patterns, I start with the oversimplified assumption

From J. Habermas, *Legitimation Crisis*, London: Heinemann Educational Books, 1976, pp. 75–92.

that attitudinal syndromes typical of a society must somehow be represented at the level of socially effective cultural value systems. I also rely on a correspondence of meaning structures at the levels of interpreted needs and cultural tradition.[1] In doing so, I neglect not only subcultural differences, but also the important sociological question, whether – and if so how – cultural patterns are reflected in personality structures through agencies of socialization and practices of childrearing.[2] Above all, I neglect the psychological question: of what components do very complex motivational patterns, introduced only from the point of view of functional imperatives, consist? For the rest, familial-vocational privatism, which crystallizes around the well delimited achievement motive, is positively determined; while civil privatism delimits attitudes only negatively, namely, on the basis of deficient contribution to will-formation.[3]

Privatistic motivational patterns can be coordinated with cultural patterns that represent a peculiar mixture of pre-capitalist and bourgeois elements of tradition. Motivational structures necessary for bourgeois society are only incompletely reflected in bourgeois ideologies. Capitalist societies were always dependent on cultural boundary conditions that they could not themselves reproduce; they fed parasitically on the remains of tradition. This is true above all of the syndrome of civil privatism. On the one hand, as far as expectations *vis-à-vis* the administrative system are concerned, civil privatism is determined by traditions of bourgeois formal law. On the other hand, with regard to a rather passive attitude *vis-à-vis* processes of will-formation, it remains tied to the traditionalistic civic ethic or, even, to familial orientations. Almond and Verba have shown that the conditions of stability in formal democracies can be met only through a 'mixed' political culture. The political theories of the bourgeois revolutions demanded active civil participation in a democratically organized will-formation.[4] However, bourgeois democracies, the old as well as the new type, require supplementation by a political culture that screens participatory behavioral expectations out of bourgeois ideologies and replaces them with authoritarian patterns remaining from pre-bourgeois traditions. Almond and Verba speak of a fusion of bourgeois with traditional and familiar forms of political culture. Engage ment and rationality find therein a counterbalance in particularism and a subordinate mentality.

> If elites are to be powerful and make authoritative decisions, then the involvement, activity, and influence of the ordinary man must be limited. The ordinary citizen must turn power over to elites and let them rule. The need for elite power requires that the ordinary citizen be relatively passive, uninvolved, and deferential to elites. Thus the democratic citizen is called on to pursue contradictory goals; he must be active, yet passive; involved, yet not too involved, influential, yet deferential.[5]

The other motivational syndrome, familial-vocational privatism, can be analyzed from analogous points of view. On the one hand, it is determined by the specifically bourgeois value orientations of possessive individualism and Benthamite utilitarianism.[6] On the other hand, the achievement-oriented vocational ethos of the middle class, as well as the fatalism of the lower class, need to be secured by religious traditions. These traditions are transposed into educational processes through corresponding family structures and techniques of childrearing. The educational processes lead to motivational structures that are class specific, that is, to the repressive authority of conscience and an individualistic achievement orientation among the bourgeoisie, and to external superego structures and a conventional work morality in the lower class. The 'Protestant ethic', with its emphasis on self-discipline, secularized vocational ethos, and renunciation of immediate gratification, is no less based on tradition than its traditionalistic counterpart of uncoerced obedience, fatalism, and orientation to immediate gratification. These traditions cannot be renewed on the basis of bourgeois society alone.

Bourgeois culture as a whole was never able to reproduce itself from itself. It was always dependent on motivationally effective supplementation by traditional world-views. Religion, having retreated into the regions of subjective belief, can no longer satisfy neglected communicative needs, even in conjunction with the secular components of bourgeois ideology (that is, an empiricist or rationalist theory of knowledge, the new physics, and the universalistic value systems of modern natural law and utilitarianism). Genuinely bourgeois ideologies, which live only from their own substance,

- offer no support, in the face of the basic risks of existence (guilt, sickness, death) to interpretations that overcome contingency; in the face of individual needs for wholeness [*Heilsbedürfnisse*], they are disconsolate;
- do not make possible human relations with a fundamentally objectivated nature (with either outer nature or one's own body);
- permit no intuitive access to relations of solidarity within groups or between individuals;
- allow no real political ethic; in any case, in political and social life, they accommodate an objectivistic self-interpretation of acting subjects.

Only bourgeois art, which has become autonomous in the face of demands for employment extrinsic to art,[7] has taken up positions on behalf of the victims of bourgeois rationalization. Bourgeois art has become the refuge for a satisfaction, even if only virtual, of those needs that have become, as it were, illegal in the material life-process of bourgeois society. I refer here to the desire for a mimetic relation with nature; the need for living together in solidarity outside the group egoism of the immediate family; the longing for the happiness of a communicative experience exempt from imperatives of purposive rationality and giving scope to imagination as well as spontaneity. Bourgeois art, unlike privatized religion, scientistic philosophy, and strategic-utilitarian morality, did not take on tasks in the economic and political systems. Instead it collected residual needs that could find no satisfaction within the 'system of needs'. Thus, along with moral universalism, art and aesthetics (from Schiller to Marcuse) are explosive ingredients built into the bourgeois ideology.[8]

I would like to divide into four steps the proof for the assertion that the socio-cultural system will not be able, in the long run, to reproduce the privatistic syndrome necessary for the continued existence of the system. I would like to make plausible (*a*) that the remains of pre-bourgeois traditions, in which civil and familial-vocational privatism are embedded, are being non-renewably dismantled; and (*b*) that core components of bourgeois ideology, such as possessive individualism and achievement orientation, are being undermined by changes in the social structure. I would then like to show (*c*) that the, as it were, denuded normative structures, that is, residues of world-views in bourgeois culture – which I find in communicative morality on the one hand and in the tendencies to a post-auratic art on the other – allow no functional equivalents for the destroyed motivational patterns of privatism. Finally, it must be shown (*d*) that the structures of bourgeois culture, stripped of their traditionalist padding and deprived of their privatistic core, are nonetheless still relevant for motive-formation, and are not simply being pushed to one side as a façade. Motivations important for continued existence can in no way be produced entirely independently of these enfeebled, or only limitedly effective, cultural traditions. Naturally, my goal in this connection too is merely to collect arguments and indicators for future empirical testing. I shall restrict myself to a few very general catchwords.

(*a*) The components of traditional world-views, which represented the context of and the supplement to bourgeois ideologies, were softened and increasingly dissolved in the course of capitalist development. This was due to their incompatibility with generalized social-structure forces of the economic and administrative systems, on the one hand, and with the cognitive attitudes proceeding from the system of science on the other. *Social-structural discrepancies* are a matter of problematic consequences of the expansion of areas of strategic-utilitarian action. Since Max Weber these tendencies have been examined from the point of view of the rationalization of areas of life once regulated by tradition.[9] The advanced-capitalist development of subsystems of purposive-rational action (and the corresponding drying-up of communicative zones of action) is, among other things, the consequence of first, a scientization of professional practice; second, expansion of the service sector through which more and more interactions were subsumed under the commodity form; third, administrative regulation and legalization of areas of political and social intercourse previously regulated informally; fourth, commercialization of culture and politics; and, finally, scientizing and psychologizing processes of child-rearing.

On the other hand, there exist *cognitive dissonances* between traditional world-views in the process of dissolution and the imperatives of the scientific system made binding through generalized formal schooling and congealed to a behaviorally effective syndrome in a kind of positivistic common consciousness. Three trends seem to me (with the necessary over-generalization) to be characteristic today of the structural alterations in world-views. *First*, dominant elements of the cultural tradition are losing the character of world-views, that is, of interpretations of the world, nature, and history as a whole. The cognitive claim to reproduce a totality is surrendered to changing popular syntheses of isolated items of scientific information on the one hand, and, on the other, to an art that retreats esoterically or passes over into life in a desublimated manner. *Further*, attitudes of belief, which since Protestantism have been extensively detached from cult practice, have once again been subjectivistically broken. The liberal disposition of taking-for-true [*Fürwahrhalten*], which is relativized from the start by the taking-for-true of another persuasion, corresponds to the recognition of a pluralism of competing beliefs that is undecided as to truth. Practical questions no longer admit of truth; values are irrational. *Finally*, moral conceptions have been detached from theoretical systems of interpretation. Bourgeois egoism, which became general as a utilitarian secular ethic, has detached itself from foundations in natural law and become unproblematic as 'common sense'. Since the middle of the nineteenth century, this process has become conscious as the 'sublation' [*Aufhebung*] of religion and philosophy, a highly ambivalent process. Religion today is no longer even a personal matter; but in the atheism of the masses, the utopian contents of tradition are also threatened. Philosophy has been stripped of its metaphysical pretension; but in the ruling scientism, those constructions before which a wretched reality must justify itself have also fallen apart.

(*b*) The components of bourgeois ideologies directly relevant to privatistic orientations are also losing their basis through social change.

Achievement ideology [*Leistungsideologie*]. According to bourgeois conceptions that have remained constant from the beginnings of modern natural law to contemporary election speeches, social rewards should be distributed on the basis of individual achievement. The distribution of gratifications should be an isomorphic image of the achievement differentials of all individuals.[10] The precondition for this is equal opportunity to participate in a competition that is regulated so as to neutralize external influences. The market was such an allocation mechanism. Since it has been recognized, even among the population at large, that social force is exercised in the forms of economic exchange, the market has lost its credibility as a fair (from the perspective of achievement) mechanism for the distribution of life opportunities conforming to the system. Thus, in more recent versions of the achievement ideology, occupational success mediated through formal schooling takes the place of success in the market. This version, however, can claim credibility for itself only if the following conditions are met:

- equal opportunity for admission to higher education;
- non-discriminatory standards of evaluation for performance in school;
- synchronous developments of the educational and occupational systems;
- labor processes whose material structure permits evaluation according to individually accountable achievements.

While educational justice, in terms of opportunities for admission and standards of evaluation, may have increased in all advanced-capitalist countries since World War II,[11] a countertendency can be observed in the other two dimensions. The expansion of the educational system is becoming increasingly independent of changes in the occupational system. Consequently, the connection between formal schooling and occupational success may become looser in the long run.[12] At the same time, there are more and more areas in which production structures and labor processes make evaluation according to individually accountable achievement increasingly improbable; instead, the extrafunctional elements of professional roles are becoming more and more important for conferring occupational status.[13]

Furthermore, fragmented and monotonous labor processes are increasingly penetrating even those sectors in which an identity could previously be formed through the occupational role. Intrinsic motivation to achieve is less and less supported by the structure of labor processes in spheres of labor dependent on the market. An instrumentalist attitude to labor is spreading even in traditional bourgeois vocations (middle- and higher-level employees, professionals). An extrinsic motivation to achieve can, however, be adequately stimulated by wage income only

- if the reserve army exercises an effective competitive pressure on the labor market;
- if there exist sufficient income differentials between the lower-paid groups and the inactive labor population.

Neither condition is automatically fulfilled today. Even in capitalist countries with chronic unemployment (USA), the division of the labor market (into organized sectors and competitive sectors) interferes with the nature-like competitive mechanism. In the subproletarian strata (O'Connor's 'surplus labor force') a rising 'poverty line' (recognized by the welfare state) has tended to equalize the standards of living of the lower-income groups and groups temporarily released from the labor process. In this way (as well as through resocialization performances for the sick and the criminal), the spurs to competition for status are weakened in the lower strata.

Possessive individualism. Historically, bourgeois society understood itself as an instrumental group that accumulated social wealth only by way of private wealth, that is, which secured economic growth and general welfare through competition between strategically acting private persons. Under these conditions, collective goals could be realized only through possessive-individualistic orientations to gain. This preference

429

system presupposed, naturally,

- that the private economic subjects could, in a subjectively unambiguous way, recognize and calculate needs that remained constant for a given time;
- that these needs could be satisfied with individually demandable goods (as a rule, with monetary rewards conforming to the system).

In developed capitalist societies, neither presupposition is any longer fulfilled as a matter of course. These societies have attained a level of social wealth at which it is no longer a question of averting a few fundamental risks to life and satisfying basic needs. Hence the individualistic preference system is unclear. In the expanded horizon of possible satisfying alternatives, prejudgments that can be monologically ascertained no longer suffice. Socialized upper-class culture, which once provided self-evident orientations for new consumption opportunities, no longer sets the standards (notwithstanding national differences). The constant interpretation and reinterpretation of needs has become a matter of collective will-formation. In this process, free communication can be replaced only by massive manipulation, that is, by strong, indirect control. The more freedom the preference system has, the more pressing become the problems of market policy for the suppliers. This is true, at least, if the appearance that consumers can decide privately and autonomously – that is, according to monologically certain preferences – is to be preserved. Opportunistic adaptation of consumers to market strategies of monopolistic competition is the ironic form of the consumer autonomy that is supposed to be maintained as the façade of possessive individualism. Moreover, collective commodities represent a growing proportion of consumable goods as production is increasingly socialized. Conditions of urban life in complex societies are becoming more and more dependent on an infrastructure (transportation, leisure, health care, education, etc.) that increasingly discards the forms of differential demand and private appropriation.

Orientation to exchange value. Finally, we shall draw attention here to tendencies that are weakening the socialization effects of the market, especially, on the one hand, the growth of those segments of the population who do not reproduce their lives through income for labor (schoolchildren and students, welfare recipients, those living on annuities, the sick, the criminal, the armed forces, etc.) and, on the other hand, the spread of areas of activity in which abstract labor is replaced by concrete labor.[14] In addition, with reduced working hours (and increased real income), the relevance leisure pursuits acquire as compared with occupational concerns does not directly privilege those needs that can be satisfied monetarily.

(c) The erosion of pre-bourgeois, as of bourgeois, residues of tradition permits normative structures to appear that are unsuited to reproduce civil and familial-vocational privatism. The components of cultural tradition dominant today are crystalized around scientism, post-auratic art, and universalistic morality. In each of these areas, irreversible developments, which have followed an internal logic, have taken place. As a result, cultural barriers have arisen that could be broken through only at the psychological cost of regressions, that is, only with extraordinary motivational burdens. German Fascism is an example of a strenuous attempt at a collectively organized regression of consciousness below the thresholds of fundamental scientistic convictions, modern art, and universalistic legal and moral conceptions.

Scientism. The political consequences of the authority enjoyed by the scientific system in developed societies is ambivalent. On the one hand, traditional attitudes of belief cannot withstand the demand for discursive justification established by modern science. On the other hand, short-lived popular syntheses of isolated pieces of information, which have taken the place of global interpretations, secure the authority of science *in abstracto*. The authority of 'science' can thus encompass both the broadly effective critique of arbitrary structures of prejudice and the new esoterics of specialized knowledge and judgment. A scientistic self-affirmation of the sciences can promote a positivistic common consciousness that sustains the public realm. But scientism also sets standards[15] by which it can itself be criticized and convicted of residual dogmatism.[16]

Theories of technocracy and of elites, which assert the necessity of institutionalized civil privatism, are not immune to objections, because they too must claim to be theories.

*Post-auratic art.** The consequences of modern art are less ambivalent. The modern trend has radicalized the autonomy of bourgeois art *vis-à-vis* contexts of employment external to art. This development produces, for the first time, a counterculture, arising from the center of bourgeois society itself and hostile to the possessive-individualistic, achievement- and advantage-oriented lifestyle of the bourgeoisie. Bohemianism – first established in Paris, the capital of the nineteenth century[17] – embodied a critical pretension that had appeared unpolemically in the aura of bourgeois art. The 'alter ego' of the commodity owner – the 'human being', which the bourgeois could at one time encounter in the solitary contemplation of a work of art – thereupon split off from him and confronted him in the artistic avant garde, as a hostile power, at best a seducer. In the artistically beautiful, the bourgeoisie once could experience primarily its own ideals and the redemption, however fictive, of a promise of happiness that was merely suspended in everyday life. But in radicalized art, it soon had to recognize the negation rather than the complement of its social practice. In the aura of the bourgeois work of art – that is, in the cultist enjoyment of the already secularized, museum-ripe shrine – was mirrored a belief in the reality of the beautiful illusion. This belief crumbled along with the aura. The artistic independence of the formalist work of art *vis-à-vis* the art-enjoying public is the form of the new disbelief; and the gap between the avant garde and the bourgeoisie is its confirmation. Under the sign *'l'art pour l'art'*, the autonomism of art is carried to the extreme. The truth thereby comes to light that in bourgeois society art expresses not the promise but

---

* 'Post-auratic art' – a term introduced by Walter Benjamin into critical theory. It is art, especially music, without the 'aura' of ritual, cultic occasion, typical of a live performance. Examples would be radio, television, or recorded music heard by an isolated listener. See M. Jay, *The Dialectical Imagination*, London, 1973, p. 191 [Editor's note].

the irretrievable sacrifice of bourgeois rationalization, the plainly incompatible experiences and not the esoteric fulfillment of withheld, but merely deferred, gratifications.

Modern art is the shell in which the transformation of bourgeois art into the counterculture was prepared. Surrealism marks the historical moment in which modern art destroyed the shell of the no-longer-beautiful illusion in order to pass desublimated over into life. The leveling of the stages of reality between art and life was not, as Benjamin supposed, first brought about by techniques of mass production and mass reception, although it was accelerated by them. Modern art had already shed the aura of classical bourgeois art by making the process of production evident and presenting itself as something that was produced. But art infiltrates the ensemble of use values only when it surrenders its autonomous status. It can just as easily signify the degeneration of art into propagandistic mass art or into commercialized mass culture as, on the other hand, transform itself into a subversive counterculture. No less ambivalent is adherence to formalist art that, on the one hand, resists pressures for assimilation to market-determined needs and attitudes of consumers – and thus resists a false sublation [*Aufhebung*] of art – but that, on the other hand, remains inaccessible to the masses and thus also prevents exoteric preservation of emphatic experiences – in Benjamin's words, secular illuminations. Whether or not Adorno's prediction proves correct *vis-à-vis* that of Benjamin, as long as avant-garde art is not completely deprived of its semantic content and does not share the fate of the more and more powerless religious tradition, it strengthens the divergence between the values offered by the socio-cultural system and those demanded by the political and economic systems.[18]

Universalistic morality. In the moral system, the safety-catch effect that bourgeois ideologies, divested of those components functional for the system, create for the political and economic systems are naturally clearer than those created by the authority of science and the self-dissolution of modern art. During the early development of civilization, the moral order and the legal order were differentiated. In traditional societies, a civic ethic mediatized the particular tribal and familial loyalties. The duties of the citizen competed with family ties. As the domain of validity of normative systems became broader and more abstract with the emergence of a civic ethic, the power of sanction was in part formalized (legalization), in part internalized (internalization). Of course, the moral system and the legal order were still integrated into a unified interpretive framework of world-views that legitimized authority. As soon, however, as traditional societies entered into a process of modernization, growing complexity resulted in control problems that required that the alteration of social norms be speeded up beyond the tempo intrinsic to the nature-like cultural tradition. Thus arose *bourgeois formal law*, which made it possible to release norm-contents from the dogmatism of mere tradition and to determine them intentionally. Positivized legal norms were, on the one hand, uncoupled from the body of privatized moral norms; on the other hand, they needed to be produced (and justified) according to principles. Whereas abstract law is valid only for the area pacified by the power of the state, the morality of bourgeois private persons, which is also raised to the level of general principles, is not limited by the state of nature that persists among states. Since *morality based on principles* [*prinzipielle Moral*] is sanctioned only through the inner authority of conscience, its conflict with the public morality, still tied to the concrete citizen, is embedded in its claim to universality; the conflict is between the cosmopolitanism of the 'human being' and the loyalties of the citizen (which cannot be universalistic as long as international relations are subject to the concrete morality of the more powerful).

If one follows (in the dimensions of universalization and internalization) the developmental logic of global systems of social norms (thus leaving the domain of historical example), resolution of this conflict is *conceivable* only if the dichotomy between in-group and out-group morality disappears, the opposition between morally and legally regulated areas is relativized, and the validity of *all* norms is tied to discursive will-formation. This does not exclude the necessity for compelling norms, since no one can know (today) the degree to which aggressiveness can be curtailed and the voluntary recognition of discursive principles attained. Only at that stage, at present a mere construct, would morality become strictly universal. It would also cease to be 'merely' moral in terms of the distinction made between law and morality. Internalization too would only be complete when the principle of the justification of possible principles (that is, the readiness to engage in discursive clarification of practical questions) was alone internalized, but in other respects the continuous interpretation of needs was given over to communication processes.

Liberal capitalism gave, for the first time, binding force to strictly universalistic value systems, for economic exchange had to be universalistically regulated and the exchange of equivalents provided an effective basic ideology to free the state from the traditionalistic mode of justification. In organized capitalism, the foundation of this bourgeois mode of legitimation crumbled, while at the same time new and increased demands for legitimation arose. However, the moral system can no more simply erase the memory of a collectively attained state of moral consciousness, once practical discourses have been permitted, than the scientific system can retreat behind an attained state of cumulative knowledge or block theoretical progress once theoretical discourses have been institutionalized. If the moral and scientific systems follow inner logics, as I am supposing they do, the evolution of morality, like the evolution of science, is dependent on truth.

I would like to illustrate this strong assertion with respect to the non-contingent *transition* (that is, one for which reasons can be provided) *from bourgeois formal law to political universal morality*. In order to satisfactorily differentiate between these two stages of morality based on principles, I shall refer to the corresponding philosophical systematizations.

I draw the distinction between norm and principle (that is, metanorm, from which norms can be generated) by applying the operation of generalization to itself. Furthermore, universal validity is the only formal point of view from which a principle can stand out from other principles. A morality based on principles is thus a system that allows only general norms (that is, norms without exceptions, without privileges, and without limitations on the domain of validity). *Modern natural law* attempted to develop systems of legal norms meeting these criteria. The generality of the norms guaranteeing equality can be insured through the formal nature of legal norms. Formality means that no concrete obligations (such as those in traditional natural law or in ethics), but only abstract permissions are subject to juridical norms. (Actions may not be commanded, but only left to choice or forbidden.) Therefore, the only norms allowed are those that delimit compatible scopes of action in which the individual can pursue his particular interests privately and autonomously, that is, by the unlimited employment of non-penalized means. These interests are themselves morally neutral. Only the legal system as a whole is morally justified with reference to consequences that maximize welfare or freedom for all citizens. To this extent, ethics remains the foundation of legitimation. This is possible because, by delimiting a domain of legal action, formal law by definition also delimits a complementary domain of moral action.

Universalistic utilitarianism represents a moral system that also regulates this domain, in accordance with the same criteria as natural law. According to universalistic utilitarianism, all strategic actions that maximize the pleasure or advantage of an individual are permitted to the extent that they are compatible with the chances of every other individual to maximize his pleasure or his advantage. Utilitarianism clearly falls below the stage of internalization attained in the conventional ethics of duty. Motives for action remain external to the morally responsible subject. If these motives too are to be included in the domain of moral evaluation, it must be established that the only actions that deserve to be called morally good are those that not only agree with general laws, but are motivated *only* by respect for the law (and not empirically by consideration of the consequences of action). *Formalistic ethics* (Kant) binds the criterion of generality of norms to the further criterion of autonomy, that is, independence from contingent motives.

The limits of formalistic ethics can be seen in the fact that inclinations incompatible with duties must be excluded from the domain of the morally relevant, and they must be suppressed. The interpretations of needs that are current at any given contingent stage of socialization must thereby be accepted as given. They cannot be made in turn the object of a discursive will-formation. Only *communicative ethics* guarantees the generality of admissible norms and the autonomy of acting subjects solely through the discursive redeemability of the validity claims with which norms appear. That is, generality is guaranteed in that the only norms that may claim generality are those on which everyone affected agrees (or would agree) without constraint if they enter into (or were to enter into) a process of discursive will-formation. The question of which sectors should, if necessary, be regulated through compromise or formal norms of action can also be made the subject of discussion. Only communicative ethics is universal (and not, as is formalistic ethics, restricted to a domain of private morality separate from legal norms); only communicative ethics guarantees autonomy (in that it carries on the process of the insertion of drive potentials into a communicative structure of action – that is, the socialization process – 'with will and consciousness').

(*d*) If today there exists no functionally adequate agreement between the normative structures that still have imperative force and the political-economic system, motivation crises could still be avoided by uncoupling the cultural system. By 'uncoupling' I mean a situation in which culture remains an object of private enjoyment or of professional interest, and is even administratively placed under conservation as a kind of free preserve, but is separated from socialization processes. Apart from the fact that substitutes for tradition to fill in for the 'uncoupled' cultural components are not discernible, it can be argued that *fundamental convictions of communicative ethics*, and *experimental complexes of countercultures* in which post-auratic art is incorporated, are today already determining typical socialization processes among several strata, that is, they have achieved motive-forming power. Döbert and Nunner have developed the argument that the 'semantic surplus' of the dominant components of cultural tradition is all the more 'sued for', that is, relevant for behavior, the less we succeed in finding an unobtrusive solution to the problem of the adolescent phase within the framework of conventionalistic norms. K. Kenniston illustrates the meaning of an unconventional outcome of the adolescent crisis by pointing to the reflective attitude toward socially tendered patterns of interpretation which the youth acquires and which allows him, in coming to terms with these cultural interpretations, to work out his definition of identity for himself.

We will need to distinguish more sharply than we have done so far between attitudes and belief systems on the one hand and the cognitive frameworks or developmental levels within which any given attitude or belief is held. William James long ago contrasted the once-born and the twice-born; the once-born are those who unreflectively and 'innocently' accept the convictions of their childhoods; the twice-born are those who may adhere to exactly the same convictions, but who do so in a different way after a protracted period of doubt, criticism, and examination of those beliefs. Viewed as attitudes, the beliefs of the once-born and the twice-born may be identical, but the mind-set, cognitive framework, or developmental level of the once- and twice-born are extremely different. In other words, we need to examine not only the beliefs men hold, but the *way* they hold them — the complexity, richness, and structure of their views of the world. Politically and socially, it may be more important that members of a given subculture possess a relativistic view of truth than that they are conservatives or liberals.[19]

With the help of this distinction, I can express my thesis as follows: the components of the cultural tradition that are today dominant (and dysfunctional in their working) are more likely to be reflected at the level of the personality system, the more frequently the form of development of the adolescent crisis forces a 'second birth' and prevents a conventional outcome of adolescence. For logical reasons, universalistic value systems and countercultural experiential complexes most readily withstand the explicit testing of tradition. That the probability of a conventional form of development of the adolescent crisis is decreasing, can be supported by the following indicators:[20]

- expansion of the educational system is lengthening training periods and making possible for increasing pro-

portions of the population a psycho-social moratorium in early adolescence (from the thirteenth to the sixteenth year) and an extension of this phase (in extreme cases, to the age of 30);
- improved formal schooling of cognitive capacities increases the probability that dissonances between proffered patterns of interpretation and perceived social reality will arise and intensify the problem of identity;
- development of egalitarian family structures and spread of childrearing techniques typical of the middle classes promote processes of socialization that tend to burden youth with adolescent problems;
- loosening of sexual prohibitions made possible by pharmaceutics works itself out (as does the temporary liberation – differentiated according to strata – from directly economic pressures) in such a way that socialization processes free of anxiety, with an expanded scope of experimentation, become more probable for adolescents.

Furthermore, it can be inferred from the presently attained degree of complexity of the role system that in advanced-capitalist societies more and more members have at their disposal basic universalistic qualifications for action within roles. Since a morality based on principle can be credibly offered by tradition only in the form of communicative ethics, which cannot function without conflict in the political-economic system, two outcomes are to be expected from a non-conventional form of development of the adolescent crisis: 1. withdrawal as a reaction to an overloading of personality resources (a behavioral syndrome that Keniston has observed and examined in the 'alienated') and 2. protest as a result of an autonomous ego organization that cannot be stabilized under the given conditions (a behavioral syndrome that Keniston has described in his 'young radicals').[21]

That it makes sense to look among the youth for a potential for critique of the system is also confirmed by an inventory, taken at a pre-theoretical level, of syndromes of behavior critical of legitimation and/or apathetic. On the *activist* side are to be found the student movement, revolts by school children and apprentices, pacifists, women's lib. The *retreatist* side is represented by hippies, Jesus-people, the drug subculture, phenomena of undermotivation in school, etc. This broad spectrum of behavioral potentials cannot be explained by recourse to the trivial psychological assumptions made in economic theories of crisis (deprivation leads to protest).[22]

Notes

1. J. Habermas, *Zur Logik der Sozialwissenschaften*, pp. 290ff.
2. The failure of the 'basic personality approach' in cultural anthropology shows that simple transmission assumptions are incorrect. A plausible model of socialization is contained in the project proposal of Oevermann, Kräppner and Krappmann, 'Elternhaus und Schule', Manuscript, Institut für Bildungsforschung, Berlin.
3. A correspondence between normative and motivational structures is most likely for the ontogenetic levels of moral consciousness. Cf. L. Kohlberg, 'Stage and Sequence: The Cognitive Developmental Approach to Socialization', in D. Goslin (ed.), *Handbook of Socialization Theory and Research*, Chicago, 1969, pp. 397ff.
4. Habermas, 'Natural Law and Revolution', in *Theory and Practice*, Boston, 1973, pp. 82ff.
5. G. A. Almond and S. Verba, *The Civic Culture*, Boston, 1965.
6. On the historical background of this category see C. B. Macpherson, *The Political Theory of Possessive Individualism: Hobbes to Locke*, London and New York, 1962.
7. M. Müller, H. Bredekamp, *et al.*, *Autonomie der Kunst*, Frankfurt, 1972.
8. H. Marcuse, *Counterrevolution and Revolt*, Boston, 1972.
9. D. Käsler (ed.), *Max Weber*, München, 1972; W. Schluchter, *Aspekte bürokratischer Herrschaft*, München, 1972, pp. 236ff.
10. R. Döbert, G. Nunner, *Konflikt- und Rückzugspotentiale*.
11. G. Nunner-Winkler, *Chancengleichheit und individuelle Förderung*, Stuttgart, 1971.
12. D. Hartung, R. Nuthmann, W. C. Winterhager, *Politologen im Beruf*, Stuttgart, 1970; W. Armbruster, H. J. Bodenhöfer, H. J. Hartung, R. Nuthmann, '*Expansion und Innovation*', Manuscript,

Institut für Bildungsforschung, Berlin, 1972.

13. C. Offe, *Leistungsprinzip und industrielle Arbeit*, Frankfurt, 1970.

14. See Part II, Chapter 5.

15. R. Bendix, *Der Glaube an die Wissenschaft*, Konstanz, 1971.

16. J. Mittelstrass, *Das praktische Fundament der Wissenschaft*, Konstanz, 1972.

17. A. Hauser, *The Social History of Art*, 4 vols., New York, 1957.

18. D. Bell, 'The Cultural Contradictions of Capitalism', *Public Interest*, Fall 1970, pp. 16ff.

19. K. Keniston, *Youth and Dissent*, New York, 1971, pp. 387ff.

20. R. Döbert, G. Nunner, *Konflikt- und Rückzugspotentiale*, loc. cit.

21. K. Keniston, *Young Radicals*, New York, 1968.

22. R. Döbert, G. Nunner, *Konflikt- und Rückzugspotentiale*; O. Negt and A. Kluge attempt a theoretically ambitious interpretation of the *experiential* content of the student revolts in *Offentlichkeit und Erfahrung. Zur Organisationsanalyse von bürgerlicher und proletarischer Offentlichkeit*, Frankfurt, 1972.

17. Social conflict, legitimacy and democracy

Seymour M. Lipset

LEGITIMACY AND EFFECTIVENESS

The stability of any given democracy depends not only on economic development but also upon the effectiveness and the legitimacy of its political system. Effectiveness means actual performance, the extent to which the system satisfies the basic functions of government as most of the population and such powerful groups within it as big business or the armed forces see them. Legitimacy involves the capacity of the system to engender and maintain the belief that the existing political institutions are the most appropriate ones for the society. The extent to which contemporary democratic political systems are legitimate depends in large measure upon the ways in which the key issues which have historically divided the society have been resolved.

While effectiveness is primarily instrumental, legitimacy is evaluative. Groups regard a political system as legitimate or illegitimate according to the way in which its values fit with theirs. Important segments of the German Army, civil service and aristocratic classes rejected the Weimar Republic, not because it was ineffective, but because its symbolism and basic values negated their own. Legitimacy, in and of itself, may be associated with many forms of political organization, including oppressive ones. Feudal societies, before the advent of industrialism, undoubtedly enjoyed the basic loyalty of most of their members. Crises of legitimacy are primarily a recent historical phenomenon, following the rise of sharp cleavages among groups which are able, because of mass communication, to organize around different values than those

From S. M. Lipset, *Political Man*, London: Heinemann Educational Books, 1959, pp. 77–95.

previously considered to be the only acceptable ones.

A crisis of legitimacy is a crisis of change. Therefore, its roots must be sought in the character of change in modern society. Crises of legitimacy occur during a transition to a new social structure, if 1. the *status* of major conservative institutions is threatened during the period of structural change; 2. all the major groups in the society do not have access to the political system in the transitional period, or at least as soon as they develop political demands. After a new social structure is established, if the new system is unable to sustain the expectations of major groups (on the grounds of 'effectiveness') for a long enough period to develop legitimacy upon the new basis, a new crisis may develop.

Tocqueville gives a graphic description of the first general type of loss of legitimacy, referring mainly to countries which moved from aristocratic monarchies to democratic republics: '. . . epochs sometimes occur in the life of a nation when the old customs of a people are changed, public morality is destroyed, religious belief shaken, and the spell of tradition broken . . .' The citizens then have 'neither the instinctive patriotism of a monarchy nor the reflecting patriotism of a republic; . . . they have stopped between the two in the midst of confusion and distress'.[1]

If, however, the status of major conservative groups and symbols is not threatened during this transitional period, even though they lose most of their power, democracy seems to be much more secure. And thus we have the absurd fact that ten out of the twelve stable European and English-speaking democracies are monarchies.[2] Great Britain, Sweden, Norway, Denmark, the Netherlands, Belgium, Luxembourg, Australia, Canada and New Zealand are kingdoms, or dominions of a monarch, while the only republics which meet the conditions of stable democratic procedures are the United States and Switzerland, plus Uruguay in Latin America.

The preservation of the monarchy has apparently retained for these nations the loyalty of the aristocratic, traditionalist and clerical sectors of the population which resented increased democratization and equalitarianism. And by accepting the lower strata and not resisting to the point where revolution might be necessary, the conservative orders won or retained

443

the loyalty of the new 'citizens'. In countries where monarchy was overthrown by revolution, and orderly succession was broken, forces aligned with the throne have sometimes continued to refuse legitimacy to republican successors down to the fifth generation or more.

The one constitutional monarchy which became a fascist dictatorship, Italy, was, like the French Republic, considered illegitimate by major groups in the society. The House of Savoy alienated the Catholics by destroying the temporal power of the Popes, and was also not a legitimate successor in the old Kingdom of the Two Sicilies. Catholics were, in fact, forbidden by the church to participate in Italian politics until almost World War I, and the church finally rescinded its position only because of its fear of the Socialists. French Catholics took a similar attitude to the Third Republic during the same period. Both the Italian and French democracies have had to operate for much of their histories without loyal support from important groups in their societies, on both the left and the right. Thus one main source of legitimacy lies in the continuity of important traditional integrative institutions during a transitional period in which new institutions are emerging.

The second general type of loss of legitimacy is related to the ways in which different societies handle the 'entry into politics' crisis – the decision as to when new social groups shall obtain access to the political process. In the nineteenth century these new groups were primarily industrial workers; in the twentieth, colonial elites and peasant peoples. Whenever new groups become politically active (i.e., when the workers first seek access to economic and political power through economic organization and the suffrage, when the *bourgeoisie* demand access to and participation in government, when colonial elites insist on control over their own system), easy access to the *legitimate* political institutions tends to win the loyalty of the new groups to the system, and they in turn can permit the old dominating strata to maintain their own status. In nations like Germany where access was denied for prolonged periods, first to the *bourgeoisie* and later to the workers, and where force was used to restrict access, the lower strata were alienated from the system and adopted extremist ideologies which, in turn, kept the more established groups from accepting the workers' political movement as a legitimate alternative.

Political systems which deny new strata access to power except by revolution also inhibit the growth of legitimacy by introducing millennial hopes into the political arena. Groups which have to push their way into the body politic by force are apt to overexaggerate the possibilities which political participation affords. Consequently, democratic regimes born under such stress not only face the difficulty of being regarded as illegitimate by groups loyal to the *ancien régime* but may also be rejected by those whose millennial hopes are not fulfilled by the change. France, where right-wing clericalists have viewed the Republic as illegitimate and sections of the lower strata have found their expectations far from satisfied, is an example. And today many of the newly independent nations of Asia and Africa face the thorny problem of winning the loyalties of the masses to democratic states which can do little to meet the utopian objectives set by nationalist movements during the period of colonialism and the transitional struggle to independence.

In general, even when the political system is reasonably effective, if at any time the status of major conservative groups is threatened, or if access to politics is denied to emerging groups at crucial periods, the system's legitimacy will remain in question. On the other hand, a breakdown of effectiveness, repeatedly or for a long period, will endanger even a legitimate system's stability.

A major test of legitimacy is the extent to which given nations have developed a common 'secular political culture', mainly national rituals and holidays.[3] The United States has developed a common homogeneous culture in the veneration accorded the Founding Fathers, Abraham Lincoln, Theodore Roosevelt, and their principles. These common elements, to which all American politicians appeal, are not present in all democratic societies. In some European countries, the left and the right have a different set of symbols and different historical heroes. France offers the clearest example of such a nation. Here battles involving the use of different symbols which started in 1789 are, as Herbert Luethy points out, 'still in progress, and the issue is still open; every one of these dates [of major political controversy] still divides left and right, clerical and anti-clerical, progressive and reactionary, in all their historically determined constellations'.[4]

Knowledge concerning the relative degree of legitimacy of a nation's political institutions is of key importance in any attempt to analyse the stability of these institutions when faced with a crisis of effectiveness. The relationship between different degrees of legitimacy and effectiveness in specific political systems may be presented in the form of a fourfold table, with examples of countries characterized by the various possible combinations:

		Effectiveness	
		+	−
Legitimacy	+	A	B
	−	C	D

Societies which fall in box A, which are, that is, high on the scales of both legitimacy and effectiveness, have stable political systems, like the United States, Sweden and Britain.[5] Ineffective and illegitimate regimes, which fall in box D, are by definition unstable and break down, unless they are dictatorships maintaining themselves by force, like the governments of Hungary and eastern Germany today.

The political experiences of different countries in the early 1930s illustrate the effect of other combinations. In the late 1920s, neither the German nor the Austrian republic was held legitimate by large and powerful segments of its population. Nevertheless, both remained reasonably effective.[6] In terms of the table, they fell in box C. When the effectiveness of various governments broke down in the 1930s, those societies which were high on the scale of legitimacy remained democratic, while such countries as Germany, Austria and Spain lost their freedom, and France narrowly escaped a similar fate. Or to put the changes in terms of the table, countries which shifted from A to B remained democratic, while those which shifted from C to D broke down. The military defeat of 1940 underlined French democracy's low position on the scale of legitimacy. It was the sole defeated democracy which furnished large-scale support for a Quisling regime.[7]

Situations like these demonstrate the usefulness of this type of analysis. From a short-range point of view, a highly effective but illegitimate system, such as a well-governed colony, is more unstable than regimes which are relatively low in effectiveness and high in legitimacy. The social stability of a nation like Thailand, despite its periodic *coups d'état*, stands out in sharp contrast to the situation in neighboring former colonial nations. On the other hand, prolonged effectiveness over a number of generations may give legitimacy to a political system. In the modern world, such effectiveness means primarily constant economic development. Those nations which have adapted most successfully to the requirements of an industrial system have the fewest internal political strains, and have either preserved their traditional legitimacy or developed strong new symbols.

The social and economic structure which Latin America inherited from the Iberian peninsula prevented it from following the lead of the former English colonies, and its republics never developed the symbols and aura of legitimacy. In large measure, the survival of the new political democracies of Asia and Africa will depend on their ability to meet the needs of their populations over a prolonged period, which will probably mean their ability to cope with industrialization.

LEGITIMACY AND CONFLICT

Inherent in all democratic systems is the constant threat that the group conflicts which are democracy's lifeblood may solidify to the point where they threaten to disintegrate the society. Hence conditions which serve to moderate the intensity of partisan battle are among the key requisites of democratic government.

Since the existence of a moderate state of conflict is in fact another way of defining a legitimate democracy, it is not surprising that the principal factors determining such an optimum state are closely related to those which produce legitimacy viewed in terms of continuities of symbols and statuses. The character and content of the major cleavages affecting the political stability of a society are largely determined by historical factors which have affected the way in which major issues dividing society have been solved or left unresolved over time.

In modern times, three major issues have emerged in Western nations: first, the place of the church and/or various religions within the nation; second, the admission of the lower strata, particularly the workers, to full political and economic 'citizenship' through universal suffrage and the right to bargain collectively; and third, the continuing struggle over the distribution of the national income.

The significant question here is: Were these issues dealt with one by one, with each more or less solved before the next arose; or did the problems accumulate, so that traditional sources of cleavage mixed with newer ones? Resolving tensions one at a time contributes to a stable political system; carrying over issues from one historical period to another makes for a political atmosphere characterized by bitterness and frustration rather than tolerance and compromise. Men and parties come to differ with each other, not simply on ways of settling current problems, but on fundamental and opposed outlooks. This means that they see the political victory of their opponents as a major moral threat, and the whole system, as a result, lacks effective value-integration.

The place of the church in society was fought through and solved in most of the Protestant nations in the eighteenth and nineteenth centuries. In some, the United States, for example, the church was disestablished and accepted the fact. In others, like Britain, Scandinavia and Switzerland, religion is still state-supported, but the state churches, like constitutional monarchs, have ceased to be major sources of controversy. It remains for the Catholic countries of Europe to provide us with examples of situations in which the historic controversy between clerical and anti-clerical forces has continued to divide men politically down to the present day. In such countries as France, Italy, Spain and Austria, being Catholic has meant being allied with rightist or conservative groups in politics, while being anti-clerical, or a member of a minority religion, has most often meant alliance with the left. In a number of these countries, newer issues have been superimposed on the religious question. For conservative Catholics the fight against socialism has been not simply an economic struggle, or a controversy over social institutions, but a deep-rooted conflict between God and Satan.[8] For many secular intellectuals in contemporary Italy, opposition to the church legitimizes alliance with the Communists. And as long as religious ties reinforce secular political alignments, the chance for compromise and democratic give-and-take are weak.

The 'citizenship' issue has also been resolved in various ways. The United States and Britain gave the workers suffrage in the nineteenth century. In countries like Sweden, which resisted until the first part of the twentieth century, the struggle for citizenship became combined with socialism as a *political* movement, thereby producing a revolutionary socialism. Or, to put it in other terms, where the workers were denied both economic and political rights, their struggle for redistribution of income and status was superimposed on a revolutionary ideology. Where the economic and status struggle developed outside of this context, the ideology with which it was linked tended to be that of gradualist reform. The workers in Prussia, for example, were denied free and equal suffrage until the revolution of 1918, and thereby clung to revolutionary Marxism. In southern Germany, where full citizenship rights were granted in the late nineteenth century, reformist, democratic and non-revolutionary socialism was dominant. However, the national Social Democratic party continued to embrace revolutionary dogmas. These served to give ultra-leftists a voice in party leadership, enabled the Communists to win strength after the military defeat, and, perhaps even more important historically, frightened large sections of the German middle class who feared that a socialist victory would end all their privileges and status.

In France, the workers won the suffrage but were refused basic economic rights until after World War II. Large numbers of French employers refused to recognize French trade-unions and sought to weaken or destroy them after every union victory. The instability of the French unions, and their constant need to preserve militancy in order to survive, made the workers susceptible to the appeals of extremist political groups. Communist domination of the French labor movement can in large part be traced to the tactics of the French business classes.

These examples do not explain why different countries varied in the way they handled basic national cleavages. They should suffice, however, to illustrate the way in which the conditions for stable democratic government are related to the bases of diversity. Where a number of historic cleavages intermix and create the basis for ideological politics, democracy will be unstable and weak, for by definition such politics does not include the concept of tolerance.

Parties with such total ideologies attempt to create what the German-American political scientist Sigmund Neumann has called an 'integrated' environment, in which the lives of the members are encased within ideologically linked activities. These actions are based on the party's assumption that it is important to isolate its followers from the 'falsehoods' expressed by non-believers. Neumann has suggested the need for a basic analytic distinction between parties of representation, which strengthen democracy, and parties of integration, which weaken it.[9] The former are typified by most parties in the English-speaking democracies and Scandinavia, plus most centrist and conservative parties other than religious ones. These parties view their function as primarily one of securing votes around election time. The parties of integration, on the other hand, are concerned with making the world conform to their basic philosophy. They do not see themselves as contestants in a give-and-take game of pressure politics, but as partisans in a mighty struggle between divine or historic truth on one side and fundamental error on the other. Given this conception of the world, it becomes necessary to prevent their followers from being exposed to the cross-pressures flowing from contact with outsiders which will reduce their faith.

The two major nontotalitarian groups which have followed such procedures have been the Catholics and the Socialists. In much of Europe before 1939 the Catholics and Socialists attempted to increase intra-religious or intra-class communications by creating a network of social and economic organizations within which their followers could live their entire lives.

Austria offers perhaps the best example of a situation in which two groups, the Social Catholics and the Social Democrats, dividing over all three historic issues and carrying on most of their social activities in party or church-linked organizations, managed to split the country into two hostile camps.[10] Totalitarian organizations, fascist and Communist alike, expand the integrationist character of political life to the furthest limit possible by defining the world completely in terms of struggle.

Efforts, even by democratic parties, to isolate their social base from cross-pressures clearly undermine stable democracy, which requires shifts from one election to another and the resolving of issues between parties over long periods of time. Isolation may intensify loyalty to a party or church, but it will also prevent the party from reaching new groups. The Austrian situation illustrates the way in which the electoral process is frustrated when most of the electorate is confined within parties of integration. The necessary rules of democratic politics assume that conversion both ways, into and out of a party, is possible and proper, and parties which hope to gain a majority by democratic methods must ultimately give up their integrationist emphasis. As the working class has gained complete citizenship in the political and economic spheres in different countries, the socialist parties of Europe have dropped their integrationist emphasis. The only non-totalitarian parties which now maintain such policies are religious parties like the Catholic parties or the Calvinist Anti-Revolutionary party of Holland. Clearly the Catholic and Dutch Calvinist churches are not 'democratic' in the sphere of religion. They insist there is but one truth, as the Communists and fascists do in politics. Catholics may accept the assumptions of political democracy, but never those of religious tolerance. And where the political conflict between religion and irreligion is viewed as salient by Catholics or other believers in one true church, then a real dilemma exists for the democratic process. Many political issues which might easily be compromised are reinforced by the religious issue and cannot be settled.

Wherever the social structure operates so as to isolate *naturally* individuals or groups with the same political outlook from contact with those who hold different views, the isolated individuals or groups tend to back political extremists. It has been repeatedly noted, for example, that workers in so-called 'isolated' industries – miners, sailors, fishermen, lumbermen, sheepshearers and longshoremen – who live in communities predominately inhabited by others in the same occupation usually give overwhelming support to the more left-wing platforms. Such districts tend to vote Communist or socialist by large majorities, sometimes to the point of having what is essentially a 'one-party' system. The political intolerance of farm-based groups in times of crisis may be another illustration of this same pattern, since farmers, like workers in isolated industries, have a more homogeneous political environment than do those employed in most urban occupations.[11]

These conclusions are confirmed by studies of individual voting behavior which indicate that individuals under cross-pressures – those who belong to groups predisposing them in different directions, or who have friends supporting different parties, or who are regularly exposed to the propaganda of different groups – are less likely to be strongly committed politically.[12]

Multiple and politically inconsistent affiliations, loyalties and stimuli reduce the emotion and aggressiveness involved in political choice. For example, in contemporary Germany, a working-class Catholic, pulled in two directions, will most probably vote Christian-Democratic, but is much more tolerant of the Social Democrats than the average middle-class Catholic.[13] Where a man belongs to a variety of groups that all predispose him toward the same political choice, he is in the situation of the isolated worker and is much less likely to be tolerant of other opinions.

The available evidence suggests that the chances for stable democracy are enhanced to the extent that groups and individuals have a number of crosscutting, politically relevant affiliations. To the degree that a significant proportion of the population is pulled among conflicting forces, its members have an interest in reducing the intensity of political conflict.[14] As Robert Dahl and Talcott Parsons have pointed out, such groups and individuals also have an interest in protecting the rights of political minorities.[15]

A stable democracy requires relatively moderate tension among its contending political forces. And political moderation is facilitated by the system's capacity to resolve key dividing issues before new ones arise. If the issues of religion, citizenship and 'collective bargaining' are allowed to accumulate, they reinforce each other, and the more reinforced and correlated the sources of cleavage, the less likelihood for political tolerance. Similarly, the greater the isolation from heterogeneous political stimuli, the more the background factors 'pile up' in one direction, the greater the chance that the group or individual will have an extremist perspective. These two relationships, one on the level of partisan issues, the other on the level of party support, are joined by the fact that parties reflecting accumulated unresolved issues will further seek to isolate their followers from conflicting stimuli. The best conditions for political cosmopolitanism are again those of economic development – the growth of urbanization, education, communications media, and increased wealth. Most of the obviously isolated occupations – mining, lumbering, agriculture – are precisely those whose relative share of the labor force declines sharply with industrialization.[16]

Thus the factors involved in modernization or economic development are linked to those which establish legitimacy and tolerance. But it should always be remembered that correlations are only statements about relative degrees of congruence, and that another condition for political action is that the correlation never be so clear-cut that men feel they cannot change the direction of affairs by their actions. And this lack of high correlation also means that for analytic purposes the variables should be kept distinct even if they intercorrelate. For example, the analysis of cleavage presented here suggests specific ways in which different electoral and constitutional arrangements may affect the chances for democracy. These are discussed in the following section.

SYSTEMS OF GOVERNMENT

If crosscutting bases of cleavage make a more vital democracy, it follows that, all other factors being constant, two-party systems are better than multi-party systems, that the election of officials on a territorial basis is preferable to proportional representation, and federalism is superior to a unitary state. Of course there have been and are stable democracies with multi-party systems, proportional representation, and a unitary state. In fact, I would argue that such variations in systems of government are much less important than those derived from the basic differences in social structure discussed in the previous sections. Nevertheless, they may contribute to over-all stability or instability.

The argument for the two-party system rests on the assumption that in a complex society parties must necessarily be broad coalitions which do not serve the interests of one major group, and that they must not be parties of integration but must seek to win support among groups which are preponderantly allied to the opposition party. The British Conservative or American Republican parties, for instance, must not basically antagonize the manual workers, since a large part of their votes must come from them. The Democratic and Labour parties are faced with a similar problem *vis-à-vis* the middle classes. Parties which are never oriented toward gaining a majority seek to win the greatest possible electoral support from a limited base – a 'workers' party will accentuate working-class interests, and a party appealing primarily to small businessmen will do the same for its group. For these splinter parties, elections, instead of being occasions for seeking the broadest possible base of support by convincing divergent groups of their common interests, become events in which they stress the cleavages separating their supporters from other segments of the society.

The proposition that proportional representation weakens rather than strengthens democracy rests on an analysis of the differences between multi-party and majority-party situations. If it is true, as suggested above, that the existence of many parties accentuates differences and reduces consensus, then any electoral system which increases the chance for more rather than fewer parties serves democracy badly.

Besides, as the German sociologist Georg Simmel has pointed out, the system of electing members of parliament to represent territorial constituencies rather than groups (as proportional representation encourages), forces the various groups to secure their ends within an electoral framework that involves concern with many interests and the need for compromise.[17]

Federalism increases the opportunity for multiple sources of cleavage by adding regional interests and values to the others which crosscut the social structure. A major exception to this generalization occurs when federalism divides a country across the lines of basic cleavage, e.g. between different ethnic, religious or linguistic areas, as it does in India and Canada. Democracy needs cleavage within linguistic or religious groups, not between them. But where such divisions do not exist, federalism seems to serve democracy well. Besides creating a further source of crosscutting cleavage, it provides the various functions which Tocqueville noted it shared with strong voluntary associations – resistance to centralization of power, the training of new political leaders, and a means of giving the out party a stake in the system as a whole, since both national parties usually continue to control some units of the system.

I might emphasize again that I do not consider these aspects of the political structure essential for democratic systems. If the underlying social conditions facilitate democracy, as they seem to in, say, Sweden, then the combination of many parties, proportional representation, and a unitary state does not seriously weaken it. At most it permits irresponsible minorities to gain a foothold in parliament. On the other hand, in countries like Weimar Germany and France, where a low level of effectiveness and legitimacy weakens the foundations of democracy, constitutional factors encouraging the growth of many parties further reduce the chances that the system will survive.

CONTEMPORARY CHALLENGES:
COMMUNISM AND NATIONALISM

The characteristic pattern of stable Western democracies in the mid-twentieth century is that they are in a 'post-politics' phase – that is, there is relatively little difference between the democratic left and right, the socialists are moderates, and the conservatives accept the welfare state. In large measure this situation reflects the fact that in these countries the workers have won their fight for full citizenship.

Representatives of the lower strata are now part of the governing groups, members of the club. The basic political issue of the industrial revolution, the incorporation of the workers into the legitimate body politic, has been settled.[18] The key domestic issue today is collective bargaining over differences in the division of the total product within the framework of a Keynesian welfare state, and such issues do not require or precipitate extremism on either side. However, even though the working class of the Western democracies is incorporated into the society, it still possesses authoritarian predispositions which, under certain conditions, appear in support of extremist political and religious movements. [. . .]

In most of Latin and Eastern Europe, the struggle for working-class integration into the body politic was not settled before the Communists appeared on the scene, and this fact drastically changed the political game. Communists could not be absorbed in the system in the way that the socialists have been. Communist workers, their parties and trade-unions, cannot possibly be accorded the right of access to actual political power by a democratic society. The Communists' self-image, and more particularly their ties to the Soviet Union, lead them to accept the self-fulfilling prophecy that they cannot secure their ends by democratic means. This belief prevents them from being allowed access, which in turn reinforces the Communist workers' sense of alienation from the government. The more conservative strata in turn are strengthened in their belief that giving increased rights to the workers or their representatives threatens all that is good in life. Thus the presence of Communists precludes an easy prediction that economic development will stabilize democracy in these European countries.

In the newly independent nations of Asia and Negro Africa the situation is somewhat different. In Europe the workers were faced with the problem of winning citizenship from the dominant aristocratic and business strata. In Asia and Africa the long-term presence of colonial rulers has identified conservative ideology and the more well-to-do classes with subservience to colonialism, while leftist ideologies, usually of a Marxist variety, have been identified with nationalism. The trade-unions and workers' parties of Asia and Africa have been a legitimate part of the political process from the beginning of the democratic system. Conceivably such a situation could mean a stable democracy, except for the fact that these political rights predate the development of a stable economy with a large middle class and an industrial society.

The whole system is standing on its head. The left wing in the stable European democracies grew gradually during a fight for more democracy and gave expression to the discontents created by the early stages of industrialization, while the right retained the support of traditionalist elements in the society, until eventually the system came into an easy balance with modifications on both sides. In Asia the left wing is now in power during a period of population explosion and early industrialization, and will have to accept responsibility for all the consequent miseries. And, as in the poorer areas of Europe, the Communists, who capitalize on all these discontents in a completely irresponsible fashion, are currently a major party – the second largest in most Asian states.

Given the existence of poverty-stricken masses, low levels of education, an elongated-pyramid class structure, and the 'premature' triumph of the democratic left, the prognosis for political democracy in Asia and Africa is bleak. The nations with the best prospects – Israel, Japan, Lebanon, the Philippines and Turkey – tend to resemble Europe in one or more major factors: high educational level (all except Turkey), a substantial and growing middle class, the retention of political legitimacy by conservative groups. The others are committed more deeply to a certain tempo of economic development and to national independence, under whatever political form, than they are to the pattern of party politics and free elections which exemplify our model of democracy. It seems likely that in countries which avoid Communist or military dictatorship, political developments will follow the pattern developing in countries such as Ghana, Guinea, Tunisia or Mexico, with an educated minority using a mass movement and leftist slogans to exercise effective control, and holding elections as a gesture toward ultimate democratic objectives and as a means of estimating public opinion rather than as effective instruments for a legitimate turnover in office.[19] With the pressure for rapid industrialization and the immediate solution of chronic problems of poverty and famine, it is unlikely that many of the new governments of Asia and Africa will be able to support an open party system representing basically different class positions and values.[20]

Latin America, economically underdeveloped like Asia, is politically more nearly like Europe in the early nineteenth century. Most Latin-American countries became independent states before the rise of industrialism and Marxist ideologies and so contain strongholds of traditional conservatism. The countryside is often apolitical or traditional, and the leftist movements secure support primarily from the industrial proletariat. Latin-American Communists, for example, have chosen the European Marxist path of organizing urban workers, rather than the 'Yenan way' of Mao, seeking a peasant base.[21] If Latin America is allowed to develop on its own and is able to increase its productivity, there is a good chance that many Latin-American countries will follow in the European direction. Recent developments, including the overthrow of a number of dictatorships, reflect the effects of a growing middle class and increased wealth and education. There is, however, the great danger that these countries may yet follow in the French and Italian direction rather than that of northern Europe, that the Communists will seize the leadership of the workers, and that the middle class will be alienated from democracy. Once a politically active middle class is in existence, the key distinction between 'left' and 'right' political tendencies no longer suffices as a means of differentiation between supporters and opponents of democracy. [. . .]

Notes

1. Alexis de Tocqueville, *Democracy in America*, vol. 1, New York: Alfred A. Knopf, Vintage ed., 1945, pp. 251-2.

2. Walter Lippman in referring to the seemingly greater capacity of the constitutional monarchies than the republics of Europe to 'preserve order with freedom' suggests that this may be because 'in a republic the governing power, being wholly secularized, loses much of its prestige; it is stripped, if one prefers, of all the illusions of intrinsic majesty'. See his *The Public Philosophy*, New York: Mentor Books, 1956, p. 50.

3. See Gabriel Almond, 'Comparative Political Systems', *Journal of Politics*, 18 (1956), pp. 391-409.

4. Herbert Luethy, *The State of France*, London: Secker and Warburg, 1955, p. 29.

5. The race problem in the American South does constitute one basic challenge to the legitimacy of the system, and at one time did cause a breakdown of the national order. This conflict has reduced the commitment of many white southerners to the democratic game down to the present. Great Britain had a comparable problem as long as Catholic Ireland remained part of the United Kingdom. Effective government could not satisfy Ireland. Political practices by both sides in Northern Ireland, Ulster, also illustrate the problem of a regime which is not legitimate to a major segment of its population.

6. For an excellent analysis of the permanent crisis of the Austrian republic which flowed from the fact that it was viewed as an illegitimate regime by the Catholics and conservatives, see Charles Gulick, *Austria from Hapsburg to Hitler*, Berkeley: University of California Press, 1948.

7. The French legitimacy problem is well described by Katherine Munro. 'The Right wing parties never quite forgot the possibility of a counter revolution while the Left wing parties revived the Revolution militant in their Marxism or Communism; each side suspected the other of using the Republic to achieve its own ends and of being legal only so far as it suited it. This suspicion threatened time and time again to make the Republic unworkable, since it led to obstruction in both the political and the economic sphere, and difficulties of government in turn undermined confidence in the regime and its rulers.' Quoted in Charles Micaud,

'French Political Parties: Ideological Myths and Social Realities', in Sigmund Neumann (ed.), *Modern Political Parties*, Chicago: University of Chicago Press, 1956, p. 108.

8. The linkage between democratic instability and Catholicism may also be accounted for by elements inherent in Catholicism as a religious system. Democracy requires a universalistic political belief system in the sense that it accepts various different ideologies as legitimate. And it might be assumed that religious value systems which are more universalistic, in the sense of placing less stress on being the only true church, will be more compatible with democracy than those which assume that they are the only truth. The latter belief, which is held much more strongly by the Catholic than by most other Christian churches, makes it difficult for the religious value system to help legitimate a political system which requires as part of its basic value system the belief that 'good' is served best through conflict among opposing beliefs.

Kingsley Davis has argued that a Catholic state church tends to be irreconcilable with democracy since 'Catholicism attempts to control so many aspects of life, to encourage so much fixity of status and submission to authority, and to remain so independent of secular authority that it invariably clashes with the liberalism, individualism, freedom, mobility and sovereignty of the democratic nation.' See 'Political Ambivalence in Latin America', *Journal of Legal and Political Sociology*, 1 (1943), reprinted in A. N. Christensen, *The Evolution of Latin American Government*, New York: Henry Holt, 1951, p. 240.

9. See Sigmund Neumann, *Die Deutschen Parteien: Wesen und Wandel nach dem Kriege*, Berlin: Junker und Dünnhaupt Verlag, 1932, for exposition of the distinction between parties of integration and parties of representation. Neumann has further distinguished between parties of 'democratic integration' (the Catholic and Social Democratic parties) and those of 'total integration' (fascist and Communist parties) in his more recent chapter, 'Toward a Comparative Study of Political Parties', in the volume which he edited: *Modern Political Parties*, *op. cit.*, pp. 403–5.

10. See Charles Gulick, *op, cit*.

11. This tendency obviously varies with relation to urban communities, type of rural stratification, and so forth. For a discussion of the role of vocational homogeneity and political communication among farmers, see S. M. Lipset, *Agrarian Socialism*, Berkeley: University of California Press, 1950, chapter 10, 'Social Structure and Political Activity'. For evidence on the undemocratic propensities of rural populations see Samuel A. Stouffer, *Communism, Conformity, and Civil Liberties*, New York: Doubleday & Co.,

Inc., 1955, pp. 138–9. National Public Opinion Institute of Japan, Report No. 26, *A Survey Concerning the Protection of Civil Liberties*, Tokyo, 1951, reports that the farmers were the occupational group by far the least concerned with civil liberties. Carl Friedrich, in accounting for the strength of nationalism and Nazism among German farmers, suggests similar factors to the ones discussed here; that 'the rural population is more homogeneous, that it contains a smaller number of outsiders and foreigners, that it has much less contact with foreign countries and peoples, and finally that its mobility is much more limited.' Carl J. Friedrich, 'The Agricultural Basis of Emotional Nationalism', *Public Opinion Quarterly*, 1 (1937), pp. 50–1.

12. Perhaps the first general statement of the consequences of 'cross-pressures' on individual and group behavior may be found in a work written over fifty years ago by Georg Simmel, *Conflict and the Web of Group Affiliations*, Glencoe: The Free Press, 1956, pp. 126–95. It is an interesting example of discontinuity in social research that the concept of cross-pressures was used by Simmel, but had to be independently rediscovered in voting research. For a detailed application of the effect of multiple-group affiliations on the political process in general, see David Truman, *The Governmental Process*, New York: Alfred A. Knopf, 1951.

13. See Juan Linz, *The Social Bases of German Politics* (unpublished PhD thesis, Department of Sociology, Columbia University, 1958).

14. See Bernard Berelson, Paul F. Lazarsfeld and William McPhee, *Voting*, Chicago: University of Chicago Press, 1954, for an exposition of the usefulness of cross-pressure as an explanatory concept.

15. As Dahl puts it, 'If most individuals in the society identify with more than one group, then there is some positive probability that any majority contains individuals who identify for certain purposes with the threatened minority. Members of the threatened minority who strongly prefer their alternative will make their feelings known to those members of the tentative majority who also, at some psychological level, identify with the minority. Some of these sympathizers will shift their support away from the majority alternative and the majority will crumble.' See Robert A. Dahl, *A Preface to Democratic Theory*, Chicago: University of Chicago Press, 1956, pp. 104–5. Parsons suggests that 'pushing the implications of political difference too far activates the solidarities between adherents of the two parties which exist on other, nonpolitical bases so that members of the political majority come to defend those who share other of their interests who differ from

them politically.' See Parsons's essay 'Voting and the Equilibrium of the American Political System', in E. Burdick and A. Brodbeck (eds), *American Voting Behavior*, Glencoe: The Free Press, 1959, p. 93.

16. Colin Clark, *The Conditions of Economic Progress*, New York: Macmillan, 1940.

17. Georg Simmel, *op. cit.*, pp. 191–4. Talcott Parsons has recently made a similar point that one of the mechanisms for preventing a 'progressively deepening rift in the electorate' is the 'involvement of voting with the ramified solidarity structure of the society in such a way, that, though there is a correlation, there is no *exact* correspondence between political polarization and other bases of differentiation.' Talcott Parsons, *op. cit.*, pp. 92–3.

18. T. H. Marshall has analysed the gradual process of incorporation of the working class into the body politic in the nineteenth century, and has seen that process as the achievement of a 'basic human equality, associated with full community membership, which is not inconsistent with a superstructure of economic inequality'. See his brief but brilliant book *Citizenship and Social Class*, London: Cambridge University Press, 1950, p. 77. Even though universal citizenship opens the way for the challenging of remaining social inequalities, it also provides a basis for believing that the process of social change toward equality will remain within the boundaries of allowable conflict in a democratic system.

19. See David Apter, *The Gold Coast in Transition*, Princeton: Princeton University Press, 1955, for a discussion of the evolving political patterns of Ghana. For an interesting brief analysis of the Mexican 'one-party' system see L. V. Padgett, 'Mexico's One-Party System, a Re-evaluation', *American Political Science Review*, 51 (1957), pp. 995–1008.

20. As this chapter was being edited for publication, political crises in several poor and illiterate countries occurred, which underline again the instability of democratic government in underdeveloped areas. The government of Pakistan was overthrown peacefully on 7 October 1958, and the new self-appointed president announced that 'Western-type democracy cannot function here under present conditions. We have only 16 per cent literacy. In America you have 98 per cent.' (Associated Press release, 9 October 1958.) The new government proceeded to abolish parliament and all political parties. Similar crises have occurred, almost simultaneously, in Tunisia, Ghana, and even in Burma, since World War II considered one of the more stable governments in Southeast Asia, under Premier U Nu. Guinea has begun political life as a one-party state.

It is possible that the open emergence of military semi-dictatorships without much of a democratic 'front' may reflect the weakening of democratic symbols in these areas under the impact of Soviet ideology, which equates 'democracy' with rapid, efficient accomplishment of the 'will of the people' by an educated elite, not with particular forms and methods.

21. Robert J. Alexander, *Communism in Latin America*, New Brunswick: Rutgers University Press, 1957.

18. The student movement: crisis and conflict

Alain Touraine

The new conditions and effects of economic growth as well as international tensions and conflicts so completely monopolized attention following World War II that many people gradually came to take for granted that our industrial societies, once past the take-off stage, were no longer subject to great internal social conflicts. Suddenly, student movements broke out almost simultaneously in many countries. Sometimes, they do not reach outside the university; in other cases, they trigger more general political and social crises; in all cases, they hold up to question more than the functioning of a particular institution – they question the fundamental choices and exercise of power in society.

These new movements do not come into being with the clarity that historical and sociological analysis will one day give them. They are formed in a period of rapid social change, and do not, as events, have only one specific meaning. Resistance to change, the breakdown of norms, and institutional crises affect the action of the social movement itself, that is, the struggle by one historical agent against one or several adversaries committed to a parallel and antagonistic effort to gain control of the instruments and effects of social change. We must patiently separate the various elements of each event before inquiring into the nature of its movements, their formation and dynamics.

From A. Touraine, *The Post Industrial Society*, London: Wildwood House, 1971, pp. 86–118.

CRITICISM OF OVER-ALL INTERPRETATIONS

In the face of the French student movement that was both violent and articulate in interpretations of its own action, the analyst is first of all attracted by two opposing tendencies. The first one searches beyond opinions and rationalizations and tries to explain students' unrest by the crisis of the academic system. Isn't it evident that the movement found its principal strength in the university faculties that functioned least well? Many students in the faculties of letters, especially in the field of the human sciences, have only vague professional expectations. In addition, the increase in the number of students has only partially been attended by an increase in the number of diplomas. The university organization was in crisis because a considerable number of students become dropouts and because the diploma and the training that the rest of them receive do not seem to prepare them for professional roles. These observations are supported if we contrast the Universities with the so-called 'great schools'. Students in the classes that are directly preparing for the entrance examinations and, *a fortiori*, students in the professional schools are practically assured both of completing their studies and of finding employment that corresponds to their expectations. For the most part, they remain on the fringe of the movement, using it to modernize their schools rather than participating in its social and political thrust.

This type of explanation quickly reveals its own weaknesses. It is incapable of explaining why and how the movement moved beyond the framework of the university and questioned the whole of society and culture. That this happened in the French experience is evident. Whereas in Germany the phase of the 'critical university' was long and active, there was no direct continuity in France between the criticism of the university, led especially by the Sorbonne liberal arts students around 1964–5, and the crisis of spring 1968. At Nanterre, the phase of the critical university was only an episode that occupied a few days at the end of March and the beginning of April. The determination to emerge from the university, to establish liaison with the militant workers, and to carry on properly political activity quickly took the movement out of the atmosphere in which it began. The population experienced the events of May–June as a general crisis, not as a student revolt.

The second type of analysis tends to identify itself with the consciousness and statements of the involved individuals. The movement then appears to have been carried along by anticapitalist ideology, by the hope for a new society that would be rid not only of the Gaullist regime but of a ruling class which controls society. This type of analysis places great emphasis on the actions of the movement because it is impossible to define the conceptions and program of the students' action. The divergences among the groups are so profound that any attempt to do so is foolish. What common ground is there between the Fédération des Etudiants Révolutionnaires (FER) and the Jeunesses Communistes Révolutionnaires (JCR), or between Daniel Cohn-Bendit and Jacques Sauvageot? For this reason, it is natural to concentrate on the events and the actions of the movement. That it was, like at Berkeley, a free-speech movement is the essential fact to Michel de Certeau. Claude Lefort emphasizes the rejection of limiting programs and constricting organization. The movement is defined by its capacity to transcend its own objectives, as the helpless professors had observed with bewilderment. (What good was it to negotiate or make concessions? What was demanded with passion seemed to lose all interest for the student movement as soon as it was won.) Very early on, Edgar Morin gave the most general formulation of this type of approach. The movement is defined less by its objectives than by the type of community that it creates. Just as, frequently, the principal function of a strike is to create solidarity among the workers rather than to win a salary increase, so also the student commune is its own reason for being. An antisociety is set up in opposition to the dominant social order. Above and beyond the diversity of ideologies, there was practical agreement on new types of human relations, decision-making, and struggle.

At its limit, this analytical approach is reduced to description. Despite appearances, it inevitably comes back to the approach that it opposes. To define a movement by the movement itself necessarily calls for the type of explanation that we first mentioned. A human group found itself locked into a desperately ill-adapted university organization that was frequently experienced as completely meaningless. This group transformed itself into a primary group whose activity has no significance other than to develop the solidarity of the group and its break with the surrounding society. Can one even speak of a social movement, when a group's action is not defined by its contradiction of an adversary and its subsequent effort to control the entire social arena in which their conflict is situated? Is not the university's loss of its role the reason why the students are reduced to purely self-expressive action, which can be extremely effective in terms of disorganizing the established order by rejection and revolt, but which is caught between disastrous alternatives: rejection either leads to marginality or ends by overturning the social order, but it is impotent in the face of the political problems of governing and directing society.

It is certainly not important that such a movement has no future; its lack of political power does not diminish its historical importance. But the image just outlined impoverishes the observable facts just as much as the first type of interpretation to which it is both related and distant.

It is not true that the May Movement was absorbed in self-expression. The spectacular occupation of the Sorbonne, the proliferation of meetings, speeches and posters, and the reign of words fascinate the observer, but they are only one aspect of the May Movement. In France, as elsewhere, the student action was not only self-expressive; it defined its adversaries and struggles. In the United States, the movement at Berkeley and Columbia cannot be separated from the struggle against the Vietnam War and the black revolt; in the socialist countries, the student action was part of the struggle against Stalinist or post-Stalinist techno-bureaucracy; so, almost immediately, the major concern in France was the union of students and workers against the Gaullist regime and capitalist society. The Night of the Barricades led to the general strike and the final great battles took place around the Renault factory at Flins. The struggle constantly moved out of the university faculties and developed in the streets, led by students and young workers who were more and more at one with each other. Beyond all the rhetoric, there developed authentic political action that indeed had no program, strategy or organization, but was deliberately directed against the adversary instead of being turned back on itself to proclaim a student commune. We must recall that the sign of a commune is to create a new power, to make decisions, to appoint and dismiss, to establish laws, government and justice, while the student movement almost never (with unimportant exceptions) set up any authority. There was talk of self-management in the factories and offices but in the university itself self-management was neither proclaimed nor established. The student movement constantly defined itself by its struggle, without giving in to the illusions of establishing an authority as might have been possible in some of the universities.

These two criticisms lead to two conclusions: in the first place, the student movement is a true social movement, that is, an action carried out by particular social groups in order to take over control of social change. Its objectives and meaning are political and must be understood not in terms of the consciousness of the participants nor of the crisis in the university organization, but in terms of the conflicts and contradictions of society and its social and political system. In the second place, the events do not lend themselves to a single type of explanation: anarchy, revolt and revolution are all mixed within the chronological and geographic picture.

We must proceed in two stages: first, we must separate the different meanings of the event that are mixed with each other and which it is vain to want to unify in a single, over-all explanation. Then, we must study the dynamics of the movement, that is, the relations and connections among the various aspects that analysis has distinguished. In this way, our study will be largely historical, transformed and enriched by sociological analysis.

VARIOUS ASPECTS OF THE MOVEMENT

(a) *The university crisis.* The decay of the university is the most visible aspect of the present social crisis. It is also the aspect that is analyzed least well in general terms. The nature and forms of the crisis within the university institution vary very much from one country to another – we will limit ourselves to France. The first thing we notice is the paradox of a university that is in the process of major growth, with the number of students increasing rapidly and buildings being multiplied over a period of ten years, while at the same time its stated objectives and its organization have not been profoundly changed. The old mold was broken under the burden and has not been replaced by a new mold despite a few partial modifications. What explanation is there for this paradox, this growth unaccompanied by development and change in the university system? As strange as it may seem, we do not have analyses and explanations of such an important phenomenon. Let us draw a possible line of analysis.

The renewal of an institutional system seems bound to the conjunction of two opposed forces: the pressure exerted by a new social demand and a powerful capacity for decision-making and organization. An institution, particularly a university, cannot be the direct translation of a movement, but neither is it merely a body of rules and machinery. In France, both during the Napoleonic epoch and in the first decades of the Third Republic, the economic, social and political rise of new social groups or classes was associated with the power of the State that held a *de facto* monopoly over university production. In the present period, on the contrary, there is none of that. The political situation guarantees that there will be no collective rise of the working class. It is true that the university has been opened up to new social groups, but this movement is probably no more important than the opposite movement through which the wealthy classes use the university to give their sons and daughters the means – paid for by the entire nation – to protect themselves against the risks of social decline. The ease of many courses and the rapid expansion of the faculties of letters, which are often less demanding of the students, contribute powerfully to increase the university's role as a social parachute. Democratization is far behind growth.

For its part, the State, while capable of setting up great national plans, does not seek to create the means to actively intervene in economic and social life. It struggles along with its bureaucratic traditions. Despite some not negligible efforts at modernization, the Ministry of National Education is an extraordinarily archaic administration, devoid of modern tools of action. Instead of the establishment of a dynamic liaison between the organizing power of the State and a social thrust, we see close relations set up between professional leaders and the administrative bureaucracy. These partners understand each other easily on the subject of growth, which broadens the labor market and bears witness to the vitality and stability of the social system. They experience the greatest difficulty in questioning themselves and even more in inquiring into the new place of the university in the nation. Policy is reduced to management, carried out by a constant give and take among the leaders of the teachers, the unions and the administrative officials. More than ever, new ideas and accomplishments are relegated to the fringes of the university, particularly to the research bodies.

The crisis of the university is not due to the control of an overly powerful State, but to the actions of a very weak State that is incapable of working out a policy, primarily because it has not been transformed itself by the pressure of new rising social groups. Corporatism and bureaucracy, feeble and often laughable forms of the State's social thrust and its capacity for decision-making, are easily allied in the effort to isolate the university community and thus create the strange situation in which growth is everybody's religion and the maintenance of established rules and interests the common concern.

This decay of the university institution causes more and more violent reactions. The university appears to be a meaningless pole of resistance to social change. On this level of analysis, one cannot yet understand the formation of a social movement. The behavior explained by this analysis would be retreat, indifference, derision and ritualism. Whether one played the game or not, the university would not be taken seriously.

(b) *Rigidity of the institutions.* This agitation might have become a force for social change and thus have led to reforms.

In fact, it did not. Economic growth concentrates attention on consumption, prices, housing, etc. The unions show little interest in university problems which do not yet concern them directly. Access to education seems to them to be a necessary consequence of raising living standards and many wage-earners make preparations to enter their children into educational institutions they respect from a distance, because entrance into them seems to be becoming possible. These social groups are involved in a series of demands that look toward greater participation in the goods of society rather than to a transformation of society. The political independence and secular spirit of many teachers and their organizations have great prestige for the labor union and political forces that concentrate their attacks against the holders of economic and political power. The traditional university involved in its process of growth has almost no enemies on the left. But the students are seen in a bad light by many on that side of things – young unproductive bourgeois, badly organized, intellectual nit-pickers, they awaken more distrust than sympathy. The student movement has no organized ally.

Those who hold political power are simultaneously proud of growth, impotent before the secret games of the bureaucrats and the influential, and deaf to the sounds of the structures cracking up. Neither the most violent labor strikes nor the first waves of the student movement drew their attention. The technocratic world is satisfied with its work and concerned with the most immediate economic problems; it is isolated by the breakup of the old parliamentary forms of representation and the constant concern not to create new forms; it was dominated by the personality of a head of State, de Gaulle, who did not seem ever to have given much attention to the problems of education. For all these reasons, it was incapable of embarking on social transformation of the university. Its bribes in the form of reforms were aimed only at producing an elite of engineers, experts, and researchers needed for economic growth. For it, society caught between the State and the economy did not exist, except as a troublesome burden whose routines must be made to fall into step with the rapid rhythm of economic change.

The agitation born of the decay of the university system

thus led to a clean break, since no institutionalization of social changes and tensions had taken place. This awareness of the break was perhaps more clearly marked among certain teachers than among the students, for the professors had both great facility at making themselves heard and were able to say nothing. All observers have rightly insisted on the rigidity of the university system that hampers its own progressive evolution and fosters the easy spread of discontent and revolt. One of the functions of the present reform is to analyze the university organization, which must both allow initiative and limit explosions.

(c) *Birth of an antitechnocratic social movement.* The university crisis and the rigidity of the political and administrative decision-making system explain the agitation, the revolt and the social disruption. They do not explain the formation of a social movement that, through the university and beyond it, indicted the whole social and political regime. The student movement did not aim at better adaptation to the demands of employment, that is, at the modernization of the university organization. It did not seek to re-establish a decayed order. It simultaneously combated the traditional social function of the university and the education it offered as well as the direction its development was taking. The existence of this movement can be understood only if one grasps the new role of the university in modern societies.

The university and the forces of production. The coming of the mass university signifies first of all that students can no longer find places in those professions that are quite limited and are also for the most part on the margin of the economic system: medicine, law, teaching – the three professions that formerly absorbed the great majority of students. Today, these outlets are bypassed in two ways: first, a growing number of students find no place and do not finish their studies, since they are eliminated by progressive selections, the basis of which is never explained; secondly and more importantly, an increasing number of intellectual activities more and more directly influence the production system. Economic growth no longer relies simply on the accumulation of capital and the utilization of a force of manual labor concentrated in industrial plants. Increasingly, it depends on technical progress, research, management methods, and the capacity to foresee and to organize.

Intellectual techniques, in both the natural and human sciences, have developed far enough that university activity can no longer define itself in terms of the transmission of culture and preparation for the 'social' professions. Consequently, the new role of the university cannot be separated from a more general economic and social transformation. From the moment that knowledge becomes an essential force of production, the organization of teaching and research also becomes a problem of general policy and the choices made in this area can no longer be governed by respect for traditions or by strictly technical demands.

Technocracy and its adversaries. Technocracy does not mean the replacement of political choices by technical choices. Such an idea does not correspond to any type of society and can only suggest a utopia of little importance. No society can reduce ends to means and function without making choices among objectives or, in other words, without the exercise of power. Technocracy is power exercised in the name of the interests of the politico-economic production and decision-making structures, which aim at growth and power and consider society to be only the collection of the social means to be used to achieve growth and to reinforce the ruling structures that control it. On its deepest level, the student movement is antitechnocratic.

Such a movement derives its strength from social forces that are defined by their place within new relations of production and power rather than because they belong to social groups that are either in decline or are relatively far from the centers of decision-making. In the nineteenth century, in a France that was mostly rural, the revolutionary movements were workers movements, because industrial capitalism was the moving force of social and economic change; today, the revolutionary thrust is created in the most modern sectors of economic activity, where the role of knowledge is most important: the advanced industries, centers of research or advanced technology, the universities, information media, etc.

This is not the only current within the university. Growth

also increases the economic system's capacity for integration and upward social mobility. The more or less amateur student, sowing his wild oats while he looks forward without impatience to easy entry into middle-class life, has all but disappeared. For an increasing number, the university is the key to entrance into technical, commercial and civil service officialdom. Many of these students look with favor on any change that will advance them socially. Those groups who were most ready for political action are not in the most professional disciplines but in those where a general intellectual formation and the encounter with acute social problems place the student before the social responsibilities of knowledge, without integrating him into a professional career. In France, as elsewhere, it was mostly students of sociology, philosophy, architecture and urban studies who questioned the social order.

Because their opposition is directed less against the organization and methods of teaching than against the entire social regime, they immediately seek to carry the struggle beyond the university, even to shed their identification as students. This identification seems to them to be a compromise with the society that would like to use them even while they reject it. Student agitation and revolt become a social movement only when transformed into an appeal for a general, rather than a particular, struggle.

The students and the working class. In the United States, Japan, Czechoslovakia and France, the student movement is not defined by the defense of student interests but by an appeal to the social groups oppressed by the economic and political system. In France, the tradition of social struggles, the weak social integration of the working class as indicated by employer paternalism, the weakness of the unions, and the strength of the Communist Party naturally direct student action toward the working class. Just as formerly the program of the labor movement was the alliance of workers and peasants, so now a new movement, based on intellectual workers, proclaims their necessary union with laborers; but this union is not simple. The most visible aspect of the May Movement is that this union was realized more deeply in France than in other places. The methods of social management, unemployment among the young, the stagnation of real salaries, and a governmental policy marked particularly by the weakening of the social security system are elements that help explain the coming together of students and workers which, nevertheless, was only accomplished in the heat that followed the Night of the Barricades, under the banner of common opposition to Gaullist power.

The mixture of students and young workers in the street demonstrations or the bypassing of union organizations in some of the companies during the strike must not conceal the essential truth: the mass of the labor movement did not follow the revolutionary thrust of the militant students. It is easy but arbitrary to say that the working class was betrayed by its political and union leaders. The huge communist union, the CGT, was partially bypassed, indeed, but by workers who wanted a victory in the style of 1936, a spectacular defeat of the power of the employers, but not a revolution. The plants were not opened to the students. Local CGT officials, who had undertaken a modernization of their union activity, were not at all disposed to join in an action that the central authorities had judged to be adventurist.

Union action was not revolutionary, not through the fault of its leaders but because the center of power is no longer located in industry. It is partly located in an international economic system that influences the French economy because of necessary competitiveness; above all, it lies in the complex system of relations between the great economic groups and the State. For a long time, sociology has felt and expressed this changed situation by replacing the concept of the firm with that of the organization. What used to be called a firm is today an organizational system, a whole complex of productive means, a management structure. The conditions of economic growth are less bound than formerly to the risks and profits of the private entrepreneur. Economic progress means training, scientific and technical research, economic information, land management, the formation and mobilization of savings – mechanisms in which political power plays an essential role, either directly or indirectly.

Labor unionism retains important roles: not only the economic defense of wage-earners, but also the struggle against archaic forms of authority and management, even participation in certain aspects of planning. Increasingly, the workers' interests are particular interests. Unionism is a historical reality inseparable from private enterprise. Because this private enterprise is no longer at the heart of decision-making, unionism is no longer at the heart of the movements for social transformation. These remarks indicate the distance that separates labor unionism from the student movement. They do not mean that the new social movement cannot draw strength from industry. Technocratic power is present there also but unionism can no longer be the privileged bearer of the anti-technocratic movement. The workers take part in the struggle only to the degree that they, like others, are placed in a situation of dependent participation in terms of social change. One may think that many worker groups participated actively in the May Movement; this does not mean that the central figure of the present struggles is the working class, defined in terms of its relation to capitalist property.

A revolutionary movement. A social movement is not necessarily revolutionary by nature. It becomes so only if a class struggle comes up against an institutional system that is unable to deal with the state of production and social relations. Such is the case with the May Movement. Its revolutionary nature resulted from the conjunction of the three elements that we have just distinguished: the decay of the university, the inability of the institutional system to deal with the tensions born of change, and the formation of a new social movement.

The conflict between those who hold economic power and the workers who wish to win social control of growth – its directions, means, and results – takes on a revolutionary form only because the new ruling forces are built simultaneously on the older ruling classes and on rigid institutional defenses. This coming together of the new technocracy, the older bourgeoisie, and the monarchical State, worked out under the Gaullist regime, gave the new social conflicts their revolutionary turn. A revolutionary movement is always the rejection of social, cultural and political obstacles that protect the old ruling classes and authority, as well as the struggle against new forms of social domination. It does not break out in stagnant situations but in periods of unbalanced economic and social change. In the French situation, one can even say that the crisis of the institutions was clearer than the formation of a new social movement, for the university was still too archaic for its new role as a production force to be a directly experienced reality.

From this resulted the extreme politicalization of this movement, whose political summit was more solid than its social base. Here, we find traits that are quite traditional in French society where social movements tend more visibly to be revolutionary political forces than movements of social transformation. The struggle against Gaullism was a more tangible reality than the assault on capitalism.

The strength of the student movement – and its weakness, as well as its difficulties in getting organized and maintaining continuity in action – came from its direct attack on the centers of power without burdening itself with the defense of any particular economic interests, or with getting involved in the internal struggles of any highly structured organization.

These observations do not claim to analyze any political alliance that might be possible or to measure the chances of any such alliance among the various groups that oppose those presently in power. They only indicate that today's social movement, of which the students are the principal protagonists, is new and corresponds to a profoundly transformed economic system. There is a great difference between the two kinds of analysis, for the new social movement is still very far from having its own political expression. Some elements of the movement, those most influenced by the Leninist tradition, want to organize a new politics. In May, attempts to move in this direction were cut short and had no effect on political developments. New attempts may be made but it is clear that such a new political organization could have only very limited influence for the immediate future. The movement launched by the students is related to the organized political left in the same way as the worker movement during the Second Republic was related to the Parti Républican. From the point of view of sociological analysis, the novelty of the situation and the social movement is more noteworthy than possible alliances among various elements of the political opposition.

(d) *The cultural revolt.* The combination of all these elements does not explain all the aspects of the movement, particularly the ways in which the militants carried out their participation. In this regard, there has been much discussion of cultural revolt and rejection of the consumer society. Such expressions would seem to cover at least three different realities.

In the first place, one can admit that situations marked by rapid change produce reactions in defense of the lifestyles, mental attitudes, and organizational forms threatened by this change. But if such psychological reactions were produced, it is difficult to discover what collective behavior they caused. In nationalist movements, we often see a turning to the cultural past in order to resist externally determined change. The appeal of the past becomes an indirect instrument of a politics directed toward the construction of an independent future. But this 'nativism' did not show itself in a movement of urban young people who did not belong to any highly organized social and cultural tradition whose integrity might have been threatened.

In the second place, a social movement in the process of formation – one that has not yet found its place in politics and can more easily proclaim a social break than actually introduce changes – is naturally more 'self-expressive' than 'pragmatic'. Words are the weapons of those who do not have the power to create any properly political strategy. The May Movement did not clash directly with a ruling class but with a society in which the power of the new rulers is largely identified with economic development itself. An opposition movement could only respond to the technocratic utopia, according to which economic growth naturally brings about social progress, with a counter-utopia, the image of a communitarian, spontaneous, and egalitarian society. This is how the first anticapitalist movements were formed in the nineteenth century.

Finally and most importantly, the very nature of the social conflicts in our programmed society is different from those in societies during the period of capitalist industrialization. Then, economic power was exercised over labor and a struggle was organized in economic terms against unemployment, low salaries, and all forms of economic exploitation. Today, the workers are not subjected primarily to the law of profits but rather to what is too gently named the exigencies of change. The centers of power and decision-making no longer manipulate people only in their occupational activities but also in their social relations, their styles of consumption, and the organization of their working lives. Opposition can no longer be exclusively economic; it is more diversified because those in power exercise control much more broadly, even though it is often diffused and sometimes is less directly authoritarian.

A society that is oriented toward a model of change, rather than a model of order and hierarchy, is necessarily a society in which the attachment to personal and collective identity is going to be affirmed. This attachment takes many forms, all the way from the desire for self-direction to the direct pressures of individualism, sexuality, and primary groups. The scientific society is also brutal. Resistance to social integration and cultural manipulation explodes with special intensity among the young, who are not yet involved in the network of obligations created by massive organizations and in the pressures to maintain living standards.

The importance of the cultural revolt is that it is both the mark of a utopian and prepolitical movement and a central and lasting phenomenon connected with the nature of the new social constraints.

THE DYNAMICS OF THE MOVEMENT

It is not enough to distinguish the various aspects of the May Movement. We must also inquire how they combine with each other in order to determine what forms the movement may take. If a single meaning were assigned to it, it would only be necessary to ask what its strategy was and how it developed and built up to its climax, triumph, or ruin. The impossibility of following such a course best demonstrates the error of every over-all interpretation.

If we begin from the very open analysis that we have just proposed, the study of the social dynamics of the movement is easily organized around one central question: under what conditions were the reactions to the university crisis transformed into social and political conflict; under what conditions did these reactions, linked with a general cultural revolt, end up creating a relatively isolated atmosphere of rebellion and rejection? Many other combinations of the elements defined above can be envisaged. What is important is not to mechanically construct a typology but rather to grasp the dynamics of a social movement, which, still nascent, can either be transformed into a political force or reduced to a marginal sect.

(a) *The Fusion of May.* The importance of the May Movement in France is that student dissatisfaction, manifested by the November 1967 strike at Nanterre or by the incidents a little earlier at Strasbourg or a little later at Nantes, was rapidly transformed into a social and political movement that affected the whole of French society and awoke echoes in many other countries.

The actions at Nanterre led primarily by Daniel Cohn-Bendit were important because they amalgamated a disorganized but rapidly spreading student agitation movement with ideas of social conflict and cultural revolt embodied in a number of small groups. These had existed for a long time but had not extended their influence very broadly. Some, like the situationists,[1] held positions that deliberately isolated them from the student world, which they treated with disdain. In contrast, the November strike at Nanterre was primarily marked by a desire for university reform and for student participation in the government of the university system. The accomplishment of the 22 March Movement[2] was to move student demands far beyond university reforms and at the same time open up the small ideological groups that, like all sects, were locked in doctrinal disputes, the search for purity, and the taste for abstract programs. Once this first step had been taken and the movement was organized, there was a great risk that it would limit itself to self-affirmation and multiply shock tactics and attacks that would lead to nothing but the provocation of greater and greater resistance within the university itself. At that point, the definitive split took place. This was less the doing of the student movement than of the administrative authorities. Starting from 3 May, the movement was drawn forward both by its own broadened range of activities and the simultaneously repressive and hesitant policy of the authorities.

At the outset, no means of expression and political organization were available to link student dissatisfaction to the activities of the revolutionary groups. The university crisis was too profound for the simply reformist movements to be able to carry on any effective action. This was the case at Nanterre when the joint consultation committee made up of an equal number of teachers and students could take no real action because most of the student delegates were too conservative and the majority of the professors too hesitant. No political party had many militant activists in the university, the Union des Etudiants Communistes (UEC) itself having been very much weakened by the withdrawal of its most vigorous elements. Only open conflict, the challenge laid down by the 22 March Movement, and the repressiveness of the administration and the police made possible the formation of a mass movement and the creation of a social crisis that was soon politicized.

All the aspects of the movement that we have distinguished were then melded and they strengthened each other mutually. The movement did not grow from the bottom upward but from the extremities toward the center. Neither the problems growing out of the university crisis nor the political programs of the revolutionary groups drew the greatest attention during May. Rather, it was the formation of a vast social movement that for the first time brought to light the alliance at various points within society of numerous forces which opposed the orientations and power of society.

(b) *The Winter Crisis.* The May Movement was revolutionary because it united the affirmation of new social and political forces with the struggle against older institutional obstacles. It struggled against the new society by attacking the old regime, particularly its forms of authority and decision-making. These obstacles still partly remain. French society cannot easily get rid of a bureaucratic system which expresses the incapacity of this society to transform its basic social and cultural orientations. Beyond the personnel role of de Gaulle the conservatism of French society will for a long time create permanent tensions. Even before the death of Alexander, the heirs apparent were maneuvering. Other more specific obstacles have been somewhat weakened. The university system, still both bureaucratic and a closed corporation, is today no longer simply a glob of putty. Perhaps even more important is the evolution of business and industry. It is possible that the unsigned Grenelle agreements[3] will have more lasting effects than the agreements signed at Matignon in 1936. Whether one views this as progress or setback, greater progress in the institutionalization of labor conflicts was made within a few months than had been made in the preceding thirty years. It is natural that reaction to this development caused an increase in revolutionary groups opposed to the policies of the great central unions; it does not seem to me possible to say that these unions have been seriously weakened.

In sum, the local institutional problems, in the university or in industry, are absorbed, while a political crisis is still possible and, indeed, preoccupies an increasing number of observers, for the empire that wants to be both authoritarian and liberal has more and more difficulty in finding a workable balance. Under the present semi-presidential regime, such a properly political crisis offers a real opportunity for action only to organized political forces that are capable of forming massive coalitions. Assuredly, a political crisis could open a breach into which student or worker elements could flood to change it into revolutionary crisis. This idea influences various groups but these groups will have less possibility tomorrow than they had during May and June to act in a politically decisive fashion.

Consequently, the student movement, while preparing to act in the hypothesis of a political crisis, is actually closed up within the university and is reduced to affirming itself, instead of being led into a broader field of operation, as happened in May. As a result, it tends to split into two tendencies.

The first, which believes in a serious political crisis, wants to replace the spontaneity of May with a concentration of forces, the elaboration of ideology, and political organization.

This tendency (which did not succeed in making itself felt during May–June) has reappeared with greater strength during the present phase. It is impossible to evaluate its importance since only such a political crisis would give it strength. The diversity of the groups and their lack of clear ideological orientation lead us to conclude that at least for the immediate future this political organization will be able to achieve only very limited successes.

The second tendency is much less organized and systematic. The expectations and motivations that were aroused in the spring remain powerful and seek ways to manifest themselves. Confrontation has been replaced by self-expression. While a meeting during April at Nanterre heightened the collective disposition for action, in November or December the sentiments and reactions expressed without reference to institutions to be fought or changed could only cancel each other out. Extreme groups, whose power does not seem to have grown between spring and autumn, have become more visible, for the simple reason that the movement as a whole is finding it difficult to rise above the most elementary collective behavior. Violence, which with rare exceptions was absent in the university during May, has appeared in a limited way but enough to make the difference from May–June clearly discernible. The political elements of the movement have often tried with lucidity and even with courage to transform this agitation into political action. But such transformation was possible only in two cases: either confrontation would cause the spread and generalization of the struggle and attack political power – which the isolation of the students in the autumn made improbable – or the movement would set itself precise objectives defined in terms of both old and new institutions. Since this solution was ruled out by a movement that was determined to maintain a condition of absolute polarization, whatever political action was undertaken could only fail. The December strike at Nanterre was a failure: the presence of 3000 CRS[4] on the campus caused no important reactions in the other Paris faculties. The movement was so weakened that in January the office of the rector could take measures that it would have found very imprudent a few months earlier. It exercised repression simultaneously in several Paris faculties, and at Nanterre at least had recourse to extremely brutal methods. Certainly, there were protests and strikes; some professors occupied the Sorbonne for a night. These responses were not in vain and probably kept the repression from spreading further. But up to the present there has not been any mass movement and we have seen half the teachers of Nanterre congratulate the dean for having been the first to dare loose his police on his students. Many of these teachers would not have dared to publicly rejoice over this a few months before. There was finally a courageous hunger strike, an unusual form of action, which forced the departure of the guards from Nanterre but was not a movement led by specifically political groups. Both the Nanterre orientation and that of the small groups seem to me to be very much weakened. Does this mean that the exhausted movement is going to disappear? I do not think so but I believe that it will develop in several forms that will be less and less organically connected.

The most visible fact is that a movement that began as the work of sociology students is today led by philosophy professors. Vincennes has taken the place of Nanterre, although there is a group at Nanterre similar to, but less important than, the Vincennes group.[5] The political impotence and lack of organization of the movement are changing it into a movement of intellectuals. Sometimes it is suggested that there be installed into the university itself a revolutionary section in which the definition of knowledge and the means of its transmission would be determined by political commitment. It makes little difference here whether such an attempt seeks to be recognized for what it is or whether it hides under the mantle of the traditional organization; it is even unimportant whether it is a matter of creating a revolutionary university section or only a core of political opposition within the university. The essential fact is that it is a question of opposition action on the part of intellectual groups, which is neither the same as the Nanterre spontaneity nor the spirit of the small ideological groups which had more influence at the Sorbonne. The strength and the 'intellectualization' of the movement is that it means a reduction of opposition and at the same time moves away from social practice and analysis. There is a risk that the idea of revolution will be substituted for the formation of a social movement, and that ideology will take the place of both political action and scientific knowledge.

Other teachers are very far removed from this fusion of political involvement and intellectual activity, and distrust its partisan spirit. They attempt with difficulty and most often as individuals to nourish their scientific work from their intellectual and active participation in the May Movement; for them, criticism of the social discussion is inseparable from more and more demanding scientific research. They do not behave as revolutionaries but, if I may use this tired word, as progressives. While those mentioned first are absolutely opposed to the new institutions, the latter are ready to criticize them, especially from without, to move beyond them rather than ignore them. They fight against repression and conservatism in the university and for the transformation of the political and labor union opposition forces, but they reject anything that might recall, even under a milder form, the brutal opposition between socialist science and bourgeois science.

There is no clear frontier between these two groups: many individuals belong sometimes to one, sometimes to the other. There is, nevertheless, a clear opposition between the two conceptions of intellectual activity; this appears most strongly in the human sciences. There is, in any case, no unity of thought among the teachers who are closest to the May Movement. The SNESUP[6] has as much difficulty in defining a policy acceptable to its left wing as it has in defending itself against the Communists and moderates who have taken over its national office.

On the student side, the divisions are clearer. While the Communists were reorganizing, the leadership of the UNEF[7] came into conflict with the Action Committees. The effort toward political organization clashed with the will for an absolute split. The elements farthest to the left are trapped in self-affirmation which can lead to spectacular actions but does not attract broad support; at the same time, they remain the most inventive and dynamic force in a situation in which the social movement is unable to express itself or exert any real political influence.

In May, both the struggle against authority and the cultural revolt nourished political action; today they tend to pursue their own directions. That is why there remains lively agitation in the secondary schools; a *lycée* is a much more solid and constraining organization than a university faculty. Cultural revolt changes attitudes and expectations, and transforms various segments of the public and cultural expressions ranging from theater to movies, from songs to dance. Many embers remain from the fire of May, as well as a number of smaller or half-hidden fires in various places. The student movement today is deprived of what it had at its inception; it is forced to invent specifically political ideas and objectives under very difficult conditions but its efforts at reflection are today the essential element of the action open to it. The fruitfulness of these efforts will govern the further developments of contestation.

It was quite easy in May to observe the birth of a social movement, the indictment of new forms of power and oppression that are less specifically economic and more social, cultural and political than in the past. In the middle of the winter, the retreat and fragmentation can foster the belief that we are witnessing the end of a crisis, some final rear-guard battles. It is hardly a contradiction to say that we are witnessing the end of a particular historic event, the May Movement, and the appearance of new forms of opposition and contestation that are more underground (sometimes also more marginal), which continue to pose problems and to make fundamental conflicts clear. The present crisis of the movement is due to the fact that it is caught between two opposed orientations.

On one side, it can attack a completely contradictory political system that unites new ruling powers in order to maintain old social and cultural models. I do not say that the May Movement was a movement of social and cultural modernization but that a somewhat vague consciousness of new forces, new problems and new conflicts was activated by its confrontation with a rigid and worm-eaten institutional system.

To the degree that a political crisis still seems possible, it is natural that the movement seeks to accentuate its striking power, its role as the cleaver that broke the political regime, and hopes, one day, to overturn it and to defeat at the same time the economic and social regime. On the other hand, the movement may strengthen itself and make explicit the new social contradictions that account for its revolt and its demands. Until now, the thrust of its opposition has been more 'for others' than 'for itself'. Isn't it necessary to give priority to the analysis of new social problems and to the formation of new forces and new forms of action and to renounce styles of thinking and expression passively taken over from the labor movement of the late nineteenth and early twentieth centuries? The American university movement, because it is more and more related to the movements and problems of today – the black movement, urban disorganization, imperialist wars and interventions – is involved in the creation of social opposition forces that have a much richer future. On the other hand, its capacity for political struggle is much weaker than in France.

It seems impossible for the opposition movement to make a brutal choice for either one of these two ways. An overly clear choice within an ambiguous situation of political uncertainty and social change can lead either to new forms of Blanquism[8] or, just the opposite, to critical action that is more emotional or even more intellectual than politically effective. Are not this complexity and confusion the mark of French society which is quite modern in terms of the social problems of a post-industrial society and quite archaic in terms of the need to attack the inheritances, obstacles and constraints of the traditional systems of authority and decision-making?

This is the point of view from which we must consider the apparent disorganization and internal crisis of a movement which can form neither an organization nor a program but which, by its very contradictions, poses the essential problems of society. One historic moment is over; it was defined by the combination of a crisis of change in French society with the new conflicts of a society in which the structures that govern growth subject to their own interests not only the producer but also the consumer, the member of the massive organizations, the city-dweller and the citizen. The May Movement aggravated the crisis of the State and its institutions but it also unleashed important social changes. The social movement must define itself in terms of its own nature and the nature of its social adversaries as well as of its objectives of over-all transformation, rather than in terms of struggle against models of authority and organization bound to a pre-industrial or bourgeois society, as opposed to modern forms of economic and social power. In May, the struggle against the Gaullist State was a central element of the passage from the student revolt to the general strike. It is possible that tomorrow the on-going movement in the university may not benefit from such a favorable conjunction of forces and may have to discover its own reasons for being, both in theory and in practice. During this phase of incubation, it will live cut off and in isolation, but it will not cease to play its role as revealer of social conflicts and as instrument of the re-organization of the arena in which they are played out.

For the multiple riches of May that have been generously distributed there is now substituted the austerity of winter. Now, one must run the intellectual risk of looking in the apparent disorder and retreat for the broken image of the social movements of tomorrow. It is not a question of waiting for a new May, whose fire was lit on the ridge that separated the old French society from its new forms of activity, organization, and power; in the depths of the new society, tomorrow's history is now being prepared.

Notes

1. A small intellectual group, which seized the leadership of the Student Union of Strasbourg just to prove its weakness. Some of its writings have had a widespread influence.
2. A loose organization created at Nanterre. Its name recalls the first important sit-in in the administration building. Its main leader was Daniel Cohn-Bendit. Anarchists and Trotskyites were the main tendencies among its membership.
3. Nationwide collective agreements prepared under the chairmanship of the prime minister and agreed upon – but not signed – by unions and employers' associations. The Matignon agreements were signed in 1936, and were considered a great victory by the workers; they introduced paid vacations, the 40-hour week, and the

recognition of shop stewards.

4. Compagnies républicaines de sécurité, police force, created after the war to fight communist-led revolutionary strikes and which has played a central role in the repression of public demonstrations since then.

5. The new university of Vincennes was created in 1968 and built in four months. Many leftist professors and students went there.

6. Syndicat nationale de l'enseignement supérieur. One of the two university teachers' unions. Generally controlled by the Communists but whose leadership passed to the leftists just before 1968. The Communists regained its control in 1969.

7. Union Nationale des Etudiants de France, national students' union, controlled by the leftists. It was weakened and disorganized long before 1968, but was a central participation in the May Movement.

8. After Auguste Blanqui (1805–81), prominent revolutionary figure, who advocated violent action at the same time as educational reform. His action was directed more toward the underprivileged than toward the working class.

Further reading

The books listed below are ones which students might read to follow up one or more of the areas in this collection. The list is not intended to be an exhaustive bibliography, but is a guide to further reading in specific topic areas.

SECTION I

P. L. Berger, *Invitation to Sociology: a humanistic perspective*, Harmondsworth: Penguin, 1966.

An excellent introduction, this book is a well-structured, clearly written and lucidly argued invitation to the non-sociologist to take sociology seriously as a humanistic pursuit.

R. Nisbet, *The Sociological Tradition*, London: Heinemann, 1967.

This is a modern classic and discusses the unit ideas of sociology as they developed after the French Revolution of 1789 and the Industrial Revolution. Nisbet points out the deep conservative themes in sociology.

T. Bottomore and R. Nisbet (eds), *A History of Sociological Analysis*, London: Heinemann, 1978.

Contains a series of specially commissioned essays by influential sociologists on the development of sociology. The essays on Marxism; Theories of progress, development and evolution; Social stratification; Power and authority; and Positivism are especially recommended.

A. Giddens, *Capitalism and Modern Social Theory: an analysis of the Writings of Marx, Durkheim and Max Weber*, Cambridge University Press, 1971.

The bulk of the text consists of a highly readable summary of most of the important themes to be found in the work of the three founding fathers of sociology, whilst the last section begins some elements of a comparison.

E. Jones, *Sigmund Freud, Life and Works*, London: The Hogarth Press, 1953–7.

The classic study of Freud in English, and a rewarding read.

Further reading

S. Freud, *Two Short Accounts of Psycho-Analysis*, Harmondsworth: Penguin, 1962.

The first part of this short book consists of five lectures Freud gave in the United States in 1909. Clear and concise statement of some of the basic themes of Freud's work.

P. Rieff, *Freud: the mind of the moralist*, London: Methuen, 1965.

Treats Freud as a *social* theorist, with relevance for culture generally, especially morality, authority and politics, and religion. It is clearly written.

R. Bocock, *Freud and Modern Society: an outline and analysis of Freud's sociology*, London: T. Nelson, 1978.

This discusses Freud's theory from the point of view of sociology, rather than psychology, and ends with a comparison of Fromm and Marcuse.

J. Mitchell, *Psychoanalysis and Feminism*, Harmondsworth: Penguin, 1974.

An important but rather difficult book for newcomers to the area. Well worth reading after some of those mentioned above.

H. Marcuse, *Eros and Civilization*, London: Sphere Books, 1969.

This is Marcuse's classic study of Freud, written in the mid-1950s. The analysis is socio-cultural, rather than concentrating on the individual personality.

S. Lukes, *Durkheim: his life and work*, Harmondsworth: Penguin, 1973.

The standard work on the great French sociologist. A very clear, readable and incisive analysis of all aspects of Durkheim's life and work.

A. Giddens, *Durkheim*, London: Fontana Paperbacks, 1978.

A short overview of Durkheim's major work by an authority in the field. Although it owes a great deal to Lukes's pioneering work, it presents a distinctive viewpoint of its own.

R. Holland, *Self and Social Context*, London: MacMillan, 1977.

Provides useful outlines of many writers in the area of social psychology and role theory, as well as giving the author's own emerging viewpoint on these issues.

A. Brittan, *The Privatised World*, London: Routledge and Kegan Paul, 1978.

L. Taylor, *Deviance and Society*, London: T. Nelson, 1971.

A useful overview of the field as it was understood in the 1970s, when the field really developed as an area of serious sociological concern in Britain.

SECTION II

F. Parkin, *Social Inequality and Political Order*, London: Paladin, 1972.

Well-written discussion of a set of problems difficult in sociology because they are almost intractable in society.

F. Parkin, *Marxism and Class Theory: a bourgeois critique*, London: Tavistock, 1979.

A critical account of classical and neo-Marxist concepts of social class, and current sociological uses of those concepts. Parkin argues that both Marxist and non-Marxist class theories have ignored social differences arising from racial, linguistic, religious and sexual differences.

A. Giddens, *The Class Structure of the Advanced Societies*, London: Hutchinson, 1973.

A well-packed, somewhat dense discussion of class, and an attempt to rethink basic class theory. An important contribution.

J. Foster, *Class Struggle and the Industrial Revolution: early industrial capitalism in three English towns*, London: Weidenfeld and Nicolson, 1977.

A comparative analysis of capitalist development in Oldham, Northampton and South Shields in the late eighteenth and early nineteenth centuries. Foster also traces the complex relationships between economic change, class consciousness and class action.

D. Lane, *The Socialist Industrial State*, London: G. Allen & Unwin, 1976.

This is one of the few serious attempts to develop a sociology of Eastern European societies, including the USSR.

S. Castles and G. Kosack, *Immigrant Workers and Class Structure In Western Europe*, Oxford University Press, 1973.

A detailed analysis of the class position of 'guest-workers' in Europe, concentrating on their role within the capitalist economy, and their problematic relationships with other sections of the working class.

J. Westergaard and H. Resler, *Class in a Capitalist Society: a study of contemporary Britain*, Harmondsworth: Penguin, 1976.

This study uses statistical material from Britain, which is treated as very similar to other capitalist societies, rather than as a *unique* island, found so often in journalistic discussions.

I. Reid, *Social Class Differences in Britain*, London: Open Books, 1977.

More statistics are given here, documenting the effects of class differences. This was the single most accessible, up-to-date source of such data at the time this book went to press.

Further reading

R. Bendix and S. M. Lipset (eds), *Class, Status and Power*, London: Routledge and Kegan Paul, 1967.

Contains a large number of classic writings on class and stratification, inequality and differentiation. Although somewhat dated as a collection of readings, it is an invaluable source-book.

H. Newby, C. Bell, D. Rose, P. Saunders, *Property, Paternalism and Power*, London: Hutchinson, 1978.

A key empirical study of class and status relationships in a rural setting. Concerned with the social structure of capitalist farming in East Anglia, the book deals at length with the role of property in social relations.

SECTION III

T. Shanin, *Peasants and Peasant Societies*, Harmondsworth: Penguin, 1970.

A useful collection of essays on peasants and their social relations throughout the world; includes classic pieces by Marx and Chayanov as well as more modern pieces on peasants in Europe and the Third World.

S. H. Franklin, *The European Peasantry*, London: Methuen, 1969.

Remains the only text to survey the social structural context of peasants in both East and Western Europe. Although the author is a geographer, his work is strongly sociological in tone.

Georges Duby, *Rural Economy and Material Life in the Medieval West*, Edward Arnold, 1968.

A fascinating book about the minutiae of social existence within the feudal society of medieval Europe.

Marc Bloch, *Feudal Society*, London: Routledge and Kegan Paul, 1965.

The standard work, and a starting point for any understanding of the social institutions of feudalism. A brilliant, fascinating and altogether readable book.

R. Nisbet, *Social Change and History*, Oxford University Press, 1969.

A well-written discussion of the large-scale issues involved in social change.

J. Banks, *The Sociology of Social Movements*, London: MacMillan, 1972.

A useful introduction to the study of social movements. Criticizing both Marxist and functionalist explanatory schemas, the author advances some elements of an approach based on the action frame of reference. Contains a good select bibliography.

J. Mitchell, *Woman's Estate*, Harmondsworth: Penguin, 1971.

The classic statement of the Women's Movement in Britain, which still has an influence on social change movements in the area of women and the family.

Barrington Moore, Jr, *Social Origins of Dictatorship and Democracy: lord and peasant in the making of the modern world*, Harmondsworth: Penguin, 1969.

A social historical study of the transition to the modern world in England, France and America and in China, Japan and India. Brilliant, densely packed, comparative analysis.

J. Habermas, *Legitimation Crisis* (translated by T. McCarthy), London: Heinemann, 1976.

A concise, highly theoretical statement by Habermas of his ideas in the area of overlap between sociology and philosophy.

J. Habermas, *Towards a Rational Society* (translated by J. Shapiro), London: Heinemann, 1971.

An easier book in some ways than his others, Habermas here writes about student protest of the 1960s, science and politics. Still worth reading.

R. Miliband, *The State in Capitalist Society*, London: Weidenfeld & Nicolson, 1969.

A fairly easy-to-read, radical statement of a classic problem. Uses English illustrations.

H. Braverman, *Labour and Monopoly Capital*, New York: Monthly Review Press, 1975.

An analysis of the impact of modern technology on work roles in industry and offices.

C. Bell and H. Newby, *Community Studies: an introduction to the sociology of the local community*, London: G. Allen & Unwin, 1971.

A readable and detailed exposition of the sociological pedigree of the concept of 'community'. Contains a lot of interesting material on key community studies.

K. Kumar, *Prophecy and Progress: the sociology of industrial and post-industrial societies*, Harmondsworth: Penguin, 1978.

An analysis of sociological interpretations of the Industrial Revolution serves as a preparation for the author's own discussion of trends within modern industrial societies and his views on the recent and influential development of the field of 'futurology'.

Acknowledgements

For kind permission to reprint published texts in this book, the editors and publishers would like to thank the following:

The American Sociological Association, Washington D.C., for 'The oversocialized conception of man in modern sociology', by Dennis H. Wrong.

Columbia University Press, New York, for 'Postscript 1975' from Dennis H. Wrong, *Skeptical Sociology*.

The Sigmund Freud Copyrights Ltd, the Hogarth Press Ltd, and the Institute of Psycho-Analysis for ' "Civilized" sexual morality and modern nervous illness' and 'Aggression and civilization' from *The Standard Edition of the Complete Psychological Works of Sigmund Freud*, translated and edited by James Strachey; Basic Books Inc., New York, for ' "Civilized" sexual morality and modern nervous illness' from Freud's *Collected Papers*, vol. 2; and W. W. Norton, New York, for 'Aggression and civilization' from S. Freud, *Civilization and its Discontents*.

Beacon Press, Boston, and Penguin Books, Harmondsworth, for 'The hidden trend in psychoanalysis' from Herbert Marcuse, *Eros and Civilization*, copyright © 1955 and 1966 by The Beacon Press; published in Great Britain by Allen Lane, The Penguin Press (1969).

Oxford University Press Inc., New York, for 'Destructive Gemeinschaft' by Richard Sennet, from *Beyond the Crisis*, edited by Norman Birnbaum, copyright © 1977 by Oxford University Press, Inc.

Routledge & Kegan Paul Ltd, London, for 'Sexual stigma: an interactionist account' from K. Plummer, *Problems and Perspectives*; and for 'Working-class criminology' by Jack Young, from *Critical Criminology*, edited by I. Taylor, P. Walton and J. Young.

Lawrence & Wishart Ltd, London, for 'The "political" and the

Acknowledgements

"economic" in Marx's theory of class' by Stuart Hall, from *Class and Class Structure* edited by A. Hunt.

New Left Books, London, for 'Class boundaries in advanced capitalist societies' from Erik Olin Wright, *Class, Crisis and the State*.

The Hutchinson Publishing Group Ltd, London, for 'Some later theories' from Anthony Giddens, *The Class Structure of the Advanced Societies*.

Oxford University Press, Oxford, for 'Immigrant workers and class structure' from Stephen Castles and Godula Kosack, *Immigrant Workers and Class Structure in Western Europe*, copyright © Institute of Race Relations 1973.

The Hutchinson Publishing Group Ltd, London, and Stanford University Press, California, for 'State and society under liberalism and after' from Gianfranco Poggi, *The Development of the Modern State: a Sociological Introduction*, copyright © 1978 by the Board of Trustees of the Leland Stanford Junior University.

Cambridge University Press, Cambridge, for 'The evolution of the family' by J. Goody, from *Household and Family in Past Time*, edited by P. Laslett and R. Wall.

Telos Press Ltd, Washington University, Missouri, for 'Technical intelligence and the capitalist division of labour' by A. Gorz.

Pergamon Press Ltd, Oxford, for 'Urbanism and suburbanism as ways of life' by H. J. Gans, from *Readings in Urban Sociology*, edited by R. L. Pahl.

Heinemann Educational Books Ltd, London, and Beacon Press, Boston, for 'Theorem of motivation crisis' from J. Habermas, *Legitimation Crisis*, copyright © 1975 by The Beacon Press.

Heinemann Educational Books Ltd, London, and Doubleday and Co. Inc., New York, for 'Social conflict, legitimacy and democracy' from S. M. Lipset, *Political Man*.

Wildwood House Ltd, London, and Random House, New York, for 'The student movement: crisis and conflict' from A. Touraine, *The Post Industrial Society*.

Index